Performance-Based Financing Toolkit

Performance-Based Financing Toolkit

György Bèla Fritsche
Robert Soeters
Bruno Meessen

with Cedric Ndizeye,
Caryn Bredenkamp, and
Godelieve van Heteren

THE WORLD BANK
Washington, D.C.

Contents

Maps

Screenshots

Tables

Foreword

Across the developing world, there has been encouraging but uneven progress towards the Millennium Development Goals, a set of international targets that come due in 2015. Even as daunting challenges remain, on health and other critical fronts, our immediate and post-2015 ambitions must be bold, reflecting a fundamental shift towards solutions that make a difference to our real clients—the millions of people in the developing world who still endure extreme poverty and are vulnerable to malnutrition, disease, and premature death.

The Health Results Innovative Trust Fund (HRITF) was set up in 2007 and funded by the governments of Norway and United Kingdom to support countries in the design, implementation, and evaluation of results-based financing programs aimed at accelerating progress towards the Millennium Development goals for women's and children's health. Programs in 31 countries are currently supported by the HRITF. About US$400 million in HRITF grants are co-financing US$1.6 billion in funding from the International Development Association (IDA), the World Bank Group's fund for the poorest countries.

These programs focus on delivering better reproductive, maternal, and child health, using an innovative set of approaches known as "results-based financing." Pioneered in countries such as Cambodia, Rwanda, and Burundi to extremely good effect, several other countries have begun to experiment with this approach, including Zambia, Cameroon, Zimbabwe, and Nigeria. The World Bank Group is committed to advancing such approaches to help ensure that people get the affordable, quality health care necessary to live long, healthy, and productive lives. In September 2013, the World Bank Group—as part of its mission to eliminate extreme poverty and boost shared prosperity—pledged US$700 million in additional financing through the end of 2015 to help developing countries reach the Millennium Development

Goals for women's and children's health and survival. This new pledge will help governments to rapidly scale up successful pilot programs to the national level.

At the front line—that is, at primary health centers and district hospitals—the results-based approach is known in many countries more specifically as "performance-based financing." With funds being paid to these health centers and hospitals directly upon reaching specific measurable and verifiable targets, including the number of children immunized or the number of births taking place at health centers, performance-based financing has been as good as its name, fostering results and injecting new life into run-down health facilities. But the approach isn't just about financing; it also represents fundamental shifts in responsibility, transparency, and accountability. To help increase the focus on tangible results, this toolkit has been produced by practitioners for practitioners and embodies the rich experience of a couple of decades of field testing. While there is no cookie-cutter approach that works everywhere, much can be gained from studying various cases that add more to our understanding of what works and what doesn't, putting the science of service delivery into practice. Delivering services to poor people is a science like any other, and it is important for us to push the frontier of knowledge continually forward.

As this toolkit demonstrates, performance-based strategies have evolved a great deal through testing and modification. There is a huge wave of improvement starting to break across Africa, Asia, and Latin America, enabling poor people to access quality health services and health facilities to motivate their staff and rebuild their dilapidated health infrastructure.

The World Bank Group is helping to shift funding and performance incentives to where the actual work is being carried out. This is growing into a truly transformational exercise, not just because of new funding resources, but also because we are aiming, together with developing country governments, to achieve value for money in health. Universal health coverage is possible if this transformation continues across the developing world.
I hope that you find this toolkit useful.

> Timothy Grant Evans
> Sector Director, Health, Nutrition, and Population
> Human Development Network
> The World Bank
> Washington, DC

Acknowledgments

The authors thank the thousands of health workers who have taught us so much about performance-based financing (PBF) and the members of the performance-based financing community of practice, with whom we often interact and who work so hard at making PBF a journey of improvements and discoveries. Thanks also to the experts who have criticized PBF and whose dialectic has helped us to improve the strategy of PBF approaches. We gratefully acknowledge funding from the Health Results Innovation Trust Fund, which financed this toolkit.

The authors thank the members of the "PBF Expert Advisory Team" who contributed to the review of the toolkit as it was drafted: Nicolas de Borman, Maud Juquois, Christophe Lemiere, Benjamin Loevinsohn, Shun Mabuchi, Ronald Mutasa, Jumana Qamruddin, Sunil Rajkumar, Claude Sekabaraga, Gaston Sorgho, Petra Vergeer, and Monique Vledder. Special thanks to Maud Juquois for translating some key Burundi documents. Also, many thanks to Trina Haque, Hadia Samaha, and Abdo Yazbeck, who were instrumental in moving this product forward.

The authors gratefully acknowledge the internal and external reviewers who spent considerable time reviewing the final product: Nicolas de Borman, Jerry de la Forgia, Jumana Qamruddin, Louis Rusa, and Monique Vledder.

Authors and Contributors

About the Authors

György Bèla Fritsche is a medical doctor specializing in tropical medicine. He received a postgraduate degree in health policy, planning, and financing from the London School of Hygiene and Tropical Medicine. For the past twenty years he has been living and working as a practitioner, public health manager, and advisor in Zambia, Senegal, Afghanistan, Kenya, South Sudan, and Rwanda. For the past ten years he has been closely involved in designing, implementing, and scaling up performance-based financing (PBF) programs in Afghanistan, Rwanda, Burundi, Kyrgyzstan, Nigeria, Djibouti, Lesotho, the Democratic Republic of Congo, and the Republic of Congo. Since 2009 he has worked for the World Bank in Washington, DC as a senior health specialist. He advises colleagues and governments in appropriate design and implementation issues related to results-based financing programs.

Robert Soeters, an independent public health and health-financing specialist, is the director of SINA Health, a consultancy firm that organizes courses, conducts studies, and provides technical support mainly for performance-based health financing programs. He conducted around 200 health-care-related missions since the mid 1980s for such organizations as the World Bank, the Dutch based international NGO Cordaid, the European Union, several bilateral organisations, local governments, and the World Health Organization. He has worked in more than thirty countries, mostly in Africa, Asia, and Eastern Europe. Soeters has a medical degree from the University of Amsterdam, a MPH degree from the Royal Tropical Institute in Amsterdam, and a PhD in public health and health economics from the University of Amsterdam. In 2013, he obtained a Dutch Royal Knighthood for his complete work.

Bruno Meessen holds a master of arts and a PhD in economics (Université Catholique de Louvain, Belgium). He started his international career with Médecins Sans Frontières, where he served six years as an economist, mainly in sub-Saharan Africa and Asia. In 1999, he joined the Institute of Tropical Medicine, Antwerp, Belgium, where he is today a professor of health economics. As a researcher and policy adviser, he played a pioneer role in the design, implementation and evaluation of performance-based financing schemes in Cambodia and Rwanda. His theoretical and empirical works contributed to the worldwide dissemination of the strategy. He is currently the lead facilitator of the performance-based financing community of practice, a group gathering more than 1,000 experts.

About the Contributors

Cedric Ndizeye holds an MD from the Catholic University of Bukavu, Democratic Republic of Congo, and an MPH from the Institute of Tropical Medicine, Antwerp, Belgium. He has been involved in performance-based financing since 2002, when he was the district director of health of Gakoma district in Rwanda, during one of the early PBF pilot schemes in that country. Since then he has worked as a technical advisor for HealthNet-TPO and for Management Sciences for Health as a monitoring and evaluation specialist. He was closely involved in the scaling-up processes for PBF in Rwanda and Burundi, and has provided technical advice on PBF in the Democratic Republic of Congo and Madagascar. He currently works for Management Sciences for Health as the principal technical advisor on performance-based health financing mechanisms.

Caryn Bredenkamp, PhD, specializes in health equity and financial protection, advising and training development professionals and government staff from countries around the world on how to measure equity and design pro-poor health policy. Attracted by the potential of results-based financing to bring health services to the poor, she joined the World Bank's results-based financing team in 2008 and has worked on PBF in the Democratic Republic of Congo and Vietnam, among other countries. Caryn holds a master of arts (economics) from the University of Stellenbosch, Stellenbosch, South Africa, and a PhD in public policy (health economics) from the University of North Carolina–Chapel Hill. She started her working career as a university lecturer in her native South Africa before moving to the World Bank's Washington office to work on Albania and India in 2006. She is now the senior health economist for the Philippines, based in Manila.

Godelieve van Heteren is a physician, senior health systems reform specialist, and director of the Rotterdam Global Health Initiative, a global health innovation coalition, which involves Erasmus University institutes, several international NGOs specializing in health, the City of Rotterdam, and a number of social entrepreneurs. She was trained in Leyden (medical school) and London (postgraduate studies at the Wellcome Institute/UCL). From 1988 to 2002 she was a full-time university lecturer and comparative health systems researcher at Nijmegen University medical school, before entering the Dutch Parliament. As a member of parliament she was spokesperson for health, biotechnology, innovation, and security, and chair of the standing committee on European affairs. In 2008–09 Van Heteren was director of the international development agency Cordaid before moving to her current position. Van Heteren's present chief areas of interest are health policy and reform processes, social sector innovation, transition management and how to build new institutions for the 21st century. She applies these interests to her work as an international PBF consultant and trainer.

Abbreviations

AEDES	European Agency for Development and Health
AFB+	acid-fast bacillus positive
AIDS	acquired immune deficiency syndrome
ANC	antenatal care
ARV	antiretroviral
BCG	Bacillus Calmette–Guérin (vaccine)
BPL	below poverty line
CAAC	Cellule d'Appui a l'Approche Contractuelle
CB	capacity building
CBO	community-based organization
CCT	conditional cash transfer
CHW	community health worker
COD	cash on delivery
COD-Aid	cash on delivery–aid
CORDAID	Catholic Organisation for Relief and Development Aid
COSA	comité de santé (community health committee)
CPA	complementary package of activities
CPVV	Provincial Verification and Validation Committee
CTB	Coopération Technique Belge
DHO	district health office
DHS	Demographic and Health Surveys
DLI	disbursement-linked indicator
DOTS	directly observed therapy for the treatment of tuberculosis

DPT3	diphtheria, pertussis, tetanus
FP	family planning
GRO	grassroots organization
HIS	health information system
HIV	human immunodeficiency virus
HMIS	health management information system
HNI-TPO	Health Net International–Transcultural Psychosocial Organization
ICT	information and communication technology
IT	information technology
ITN	insecticide-treated net
IPTp	intermittent preventive treatment for malaria in pregnancy
IUD	intrauterine device
JSY	Janani Suraksha Yojana
LGA	local government authority
LMIC	lower- and middle-income countries
MDG	Millennium Development Goal
MHIF	Mandatory Health Insurance Fund
MICS	Multiple Indicator Cluster Surveys
MMR	Maternal Mortality Ratio (initial caps)
MoH	ministry of health
MPA	minimum package of activities
NCD	noncommunicable disease
NGO	nongovernmental organization
NSHIP	Nigeria State Health Investment Project
OBA	output-based aid
OCP	oral contraceptive
OECD	Organisation for Economic Co-operation and Development
OPD	outpatient department
PBC	performance-based contracting
PBF	performance-based financing
PBI	performance-based incentives

PEPFAR	U.S. President's Emergency Plan for AIDS Relief
P4P	Pay for Performance
PforR	Program for Results
PHC	primary health care
PHO	provincial health office
PIT	provider-initiated testing for HIV
PMTCT	prevention of mother-to-child transmission of HIV
PRP	Provider Recognition Program
PTB	pulmonary tuberculosis
RBF	results-based financing
SDC	Swiss Agency for Development and Cooperation
SMART	specific, measurable, achievable, realistic, and time-bound
SMOH	state ministry of health
SP	sulfadoxine/pyrimethamine
STD	sexually transmitted disease
TA	technical assistance
TB	tuberculosis
TOT	training of trainers
TT	tetanus toxoid vaccination
TT2	second to the sixth tetanus toxoid vaccination
U-5	Under-5
U5MR	Under-5 Mortality Rate
USAID	United States Agency for International Development
VCT	voluntary counseling and testing for HIV
VVF	vesico-vaginal fistula

Introduction

I.1 The Toolkit

What is performance-based financing (PBF)? Why is this used to finance health services in lower- and lower-middle-income countries? If practitioners want to introduce PBF in their country, how shall they do it?

This toolkit addresses the questions what and why, while focusing on the answer to how it can be done. The toolkit is pervaded by answers to the first question, while explaining the "how to": the process, the planning, the design, and the implementation of PBF schemes. It is written and reviewed by practitioners who have experimented with various methods and who have designed, implemented, witnessed, and evaluated its effects. Methods and approaches in PBF evolve continuously. Even though the toolkit provides guidance based on experience, the experience itself is based on trial and error and constant testing, assessing, and reassessing. And this approach is why the toolkit is not meant as a final product. It attempts to capture the current state of affairs and best practices, while attempting to stay abreast by updating the methods, experiences, and tools used.

Introducing PBF can be a daunting undertaking. For instance, the practitioner will need to complete the following tasks:

- Introduce autonomy
- Introduce revolving drug funds
- Introduce health facility management tools such as the indice tool, the business plan, and individual performance evaluations
- Design and write contracts
- Set fees
- Design quality checklists
- Introduce community collaboration
- Create steering committees at the district and national levels
- Create information technology solutions.

How will the practitioner accomplish all of these tasks? This toolkit provides tools and explanations to help the practitioner do so.

This toolkit is meant to be a one-stop shop for the forms, tools, spreadsheets, contracts, terms of reference, performance frameworks, and so on that have been designed for successful PBF approaches in Asia and Africa.

This toolkit is written by implementers for implementers. It contains lessons learned and experiential knowledge for starting PBF approaches and for scaling up these approaches nationwide. The toolkit contains what we, as implementers, would have liked to know when we first started designing such approaches.

Methods and approaches in PBF continuously evolve. And this evolution is why the toolkit is meant not as a final product but as a product that will be updated regularly. This toolkit is conceived as an organized and structured collection of tools and documents to implement PBF approaches in low- and lower-middle-income countries.

By using this toolkit, countries will be able to implement PBF approaches and to move rapidly in designing and implementing their schemes (box I.1).

BOX I.1

PBF and Universal Health Coverage

As a tool for helping create better, more inclusive, and more accessible health services, PBF is an important component of achieving universal health coverage (WHO 2010). There are three broad areas in which PBF and universal health coverage intercept. These areas are (a) defining the basic and complementary health package and delivering these packages, (b) expanding coverage of health services for the general population and especially for the poorest, and (c) improving access to good-quality health services.

Also, these tools may reduce the barrier to entry for governments and international organizations willing to take on an implementing role in PBF.

This introduction includes a short history of PBF, a discussion of terminology, and a simplified example of what PBF looks like for a health center.

Most chapters contain a mix of conceptual information and practical "how to" guidance. In some chapters, the balance is more on the conceptual information and in others more on the practical information. We have purposefully used this approach so that users can navigate to the chapter of interest directly. The grouping was categorized as first, elements that consider facility-level phenomena, such as services, quality, setting of the fees, equity, and autonomy, and second, a collection of higher-level issues, such as governance and data analysis, as well as technical assistance (figure I.1).

Part 1 (chapters 1–8) deals with facility-level design issues. This part covers topics such as the specific services to purchase, verification and counter-verification mechanisms, verifying and rewarding of quality of services, setting of the unit price, financial risk forecasting, equity, autonomy, payments

FIGURE I.1 The Structure of the Toolkit

Conceptual Issues	• 1. Buying a Quantity of Services • 2. Verification of the Quantity of Services • 3. Measuring and Verifying Quality • 4. Setting the Unit Price and Costing • 5. Addressing Equity
Health Facility-Level Design Issues	• 6. Health Facility Autonomy and Governance • 7. Health Facility Financial Management and the Indice Tool • 8. Performance Frameworks for Health Administration • 9. Investments to Help Start Health Facilities
More Design and Implementation Issues	• 10. Improving Health Facility Management • 11. Governance Issues and Structures • 12. Data Gathering and Dissemination • 13. Data Analysis and Learning
Make It Happen	• 14. PBF Technical Assistance and Training • 15. Designing and Updating a PBF Manual • 16. Pilot Testing PBF • 17. Evaluations of PBF and Frequently Asked Questions

Source: World Bank data.

Note: PBF = performance-based financing.

and financial management, and performance frameworks for the health administration.

Part 2 (chapters 9–16) gives attention to design structures and issues relevant for implementation. This part covers topics such as investment units, health facility management and how to improve it, governance, data capture, data analysis, technical assistance requirements, design of a manual, and pilot testing.

Part 3 (chapter 17) addresses the current evidence on PBF schemes and contrasts the approaches in lower- and middle-income countries and Organisation for Economic Co-operation and Development (OECD) countries. Also, this part contains design tips and a table with frequently asked questions.

At the end of most chapters is a list of documents and tools, which can be accessed through web links (URLs) provided. The entire toolkit, as well as all of the documents and files referenced, can also be accessed at http://www.worldbank.org/health/pbftoolkit.

I.2 A Short History of PBF

Performance-based financing in lower- and middle-income countries can be traced to early experimentation with the introduction of market forces in primary health care. This experiment was in a publicly funded and publicly provided health system, and its purpose was to cofinance primary health care in Zambia's Western Province in the late 1980s and early 1990s (Soeters and Nzala 1994).[1] A further development was spurred in 1999, through Cambodia's contracting of health services experience. In Cambodia, nongovernmental organizations (NGOs) were contracted to provide either health services or management support to government-provided health services (Bhushan, Keller, and Schwartz 2002; Bhushan et al. 2007; Soeters and Griffiths 2003). In Haiti, NGOs were contracted for service delivery (Eichler et al. 2009).

In both Cambodia and Haiti, these contracts were output-based or fixed-price contracts with an element of award fees; this form of performance contracting was called performance-based contracting (PBC) (Loevinsohn 2008). In Afghanistan since 2003, PBC has been introduced as a national strategy for health service delivery (Arur et al. 2009; Loevinsohn and Sayed 2008; Palmer et al. 2006).

Since 2002, PBF has developed in its current form in Rwanda, where actors who had been engaged in Cambodia brought their experience (Meessen et al. 2006; Meessen, Kashala, and Musango 2007; Soeters, Habineza, and Peerenboom 2006). A further boost came through development of similar approaches in the Democratic Republic of Congo (Soeters et al. 2011) and

Burundi from 2006 onward. A small pilot started in Cameroon in 2008 and on Flores, Indonesia, in 2009. In 2009, the Central African Republic began a pilot in one prefecture, which has been expanded to six prefectures (January 2010 onward). Rwanda (in 2006), Burundi (in 2010), and Sierra Leone (in 2011) scaled up PBF approaches to function nationwide.

As of 2013, additional PBF projects and programs have been planned and implemented in a wide range of countries such as Afghanistan, Benin, Burkina Faso, Cameroon, Chad, Djibouti, The Gabon, Gambia, Kenya, the Kyrgyz Republic, Lao People's Democratic Republic, Lesotho, Liberia, Mozambique, Nigeria, Senegal, South Sudan, Tajikistan, Tanzania, Vietnam, Zambia, Zanzibar (Tanzania), and Zimbabwe (see box I.2). More are certain to follow.

PBF approaches are undergoing a dynamic growth in terms of both participating countries and methodological issues (such as design, quality, equity, demand-side interventions, and expansion in the secondary-care level).

BOX I.2
Mayo-Ine Health Center, Nigeria

Mayo-Ine Health Center lies in Fufore district in Adamawa State in northeast Nigeria. One year ago, it was a typical health center in rural Nigeria. Years of neglect had left their mark. The fence was damaged, the roof caving in at places, windows broken, and equipment gone. Medical waste was scattered in the backyard, some of it half burnt. Goats were searching the waste, nibbling on edible bits of carton. The center had no running water. Its latrines were defunct. Essential drugs were out of stock, and vaccines were rarely available. Supervision had been absent from the district for a long time, and staff members were demoralized and on strike.

The population had become accustomed to the situation and rarely used the facility. In December 2011, just four women delivered babies at Mayo-Ine, and, on average, it saw four patients per day. The few patients that came were prescribed expensive treatments with drugs that the health workers had bought and then sold against a hefty markup, thereby making any treatment very expensive. People preferred the local drug vendor who would sell drugs cheaply by the tablet, which fitted their budget better, and consulted with traditional healers.

During 2012, a dramatic change happened. Mayo-Ine Health Center went from 4 deliveries per month to 45 deliveries per month within a 6-month period. It sustained that rate over the rest of the year, and this means that, for its entire subdistrict population, the health center had gone from delivering 10 percent of pregnant women to delivering 100 percent of all expected deliveries in its health facility. Mayo-Ine Health Center has effectively reached universal coverage for institutional deliveries.

So what caused this change? Adamawa State introduced performance-based financing.[a]

a. See http://www.rbfhealth.org/blog/2013/01/30/719/10-100-coverage-institutional-deliveries-nigeria-case-mayo-ine-health-center (accessed March 19, 2013).

MAP I.1 Rapid Expansion of PBF Programs in Africa between 2006 and 2013

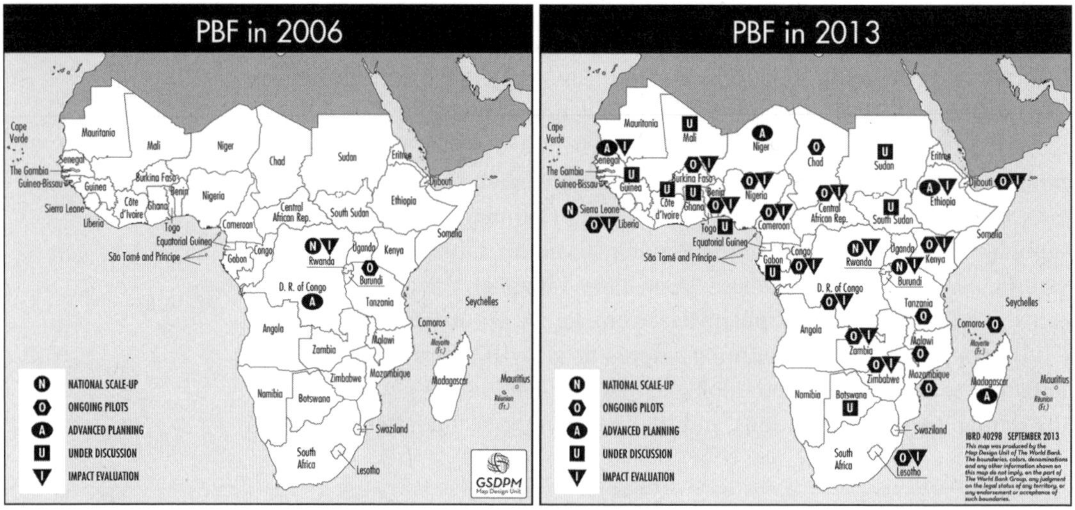

Source: World Bank data.

Note: PBF = performance-based financing.

PBF has expanded rapidly in Africa. Currently (in 2013), there are three countries[2] with nationwide programs and 17 countries[3] with ongoing pilots. Six countries are in the advanced planning stage, and PBF initiatives are being discussed in nine countries. Based on a country's specific context and health sector priorities, the World Bank supports the design, implementation, and evaluation of results-based financing (RBF) programs with financing from the International Development Association and the Health Results Innovation Trust Fund. All the programs are accompanied by rigorous impact evaluations. Map I.1 describes the evolution of PBF in Africa between 2006 and 2013.

I.3 Results-Based Financing: A Profusion of Terms

Many acronyms and abbreviations describe pay-for-performance programs, and this multitude of names can be confusing. Most of the acronyms and abbreviations are synonymous, while some describe a subset of such programs. To create some clarity, Musgrove (2011) has created a useful glossary. Figure I.2, which is drawn from the work of Musgrove, shows some of the various acronyms and abbreviations and some of the different levels. PBF has a unique position in the RBF group. PBF targets health facilities with a fee-for-service (conditional on quality) payment mechanism.

FIGURE I.2 Results-Based Financing: A Profusion of Terms

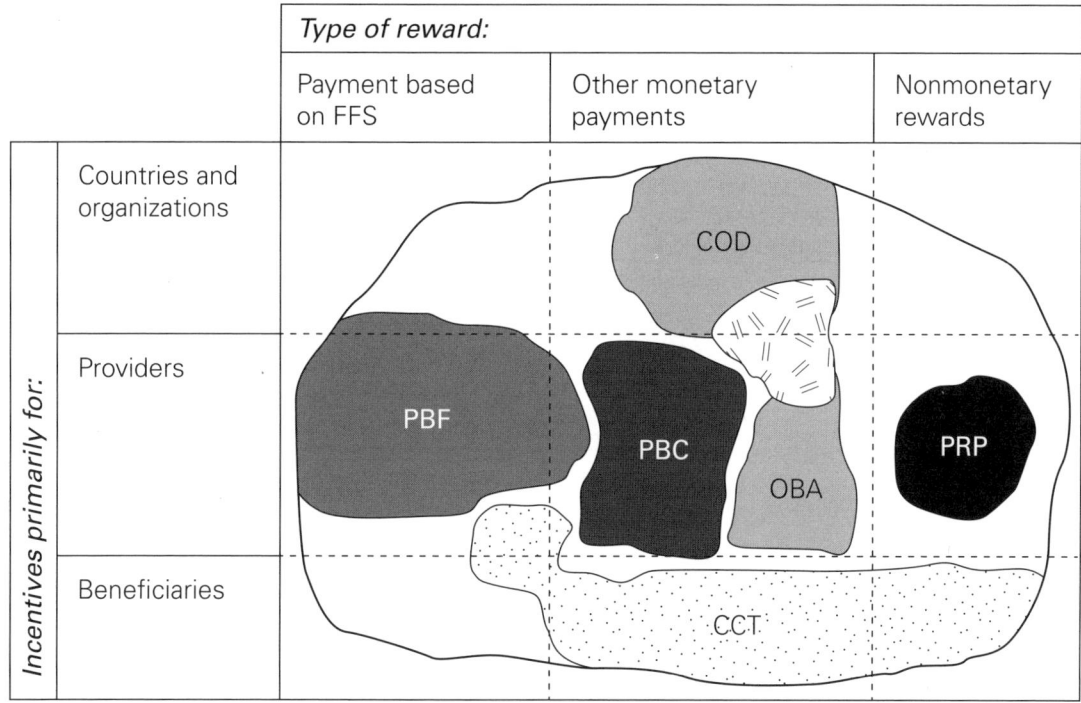

Source: Based on Musgrove 2011.

Note: CCT = conditional cash transfer; COD = cash on delivery; FFS = fee-for-service; OBA = output-based aid; PBC = performance-based contracting; PBF = performance-based financing; PRP = Provider Recognition Program.

In table I.1, the various acronyms and abbreviations are listed with their explanation and with the level on which they are supposed to work. For example, PBF would have incentive schemes at the health facility level, the district level, and the national level.

Increasingly, RBF programs use a combination of RBF approaches. For instance, in the Nigeria State Health Investment Program, the following approaches are mixed:

- COD-Aid (cash on delivery–aid) targeting the states
- DLI (disbursement-linked indicator) approach for the states and the local government authorities
- PBF approach for health facilities and district health administration
- CCT (conditional cash transfer) program targeting mothers and their young children.

PBC and PBF differ mainly in the organization with which they contract. PBC targets NGOs (Loevinsohn 2008; Loevinsohn and Harding

TABLE I.1 RBF and Its Acronyms and Abbreviations

Acronym or abbreviation	Complete spelling	Explanation	Target of incentives
CCT	Conditional cash transfer program (Fiszbein and Schady 2009)	Demand-side incentives include cash rewards to clients on consuming certain social services such as health services or education.	Users of services, targeted geographical areas, and vulnerable groups—frequently mothers
COD-Aid	Cash on delivery–aid (Birdsall and Savedoff 2010)	Payment is for achieving predetermined results.	Governments
DLI	Disbursement-linked indicator	Incentives are linked to certain policy actions or process measures. Terminology is used by the World Bank.	Dependent on design: governments, subnational levels
OBA	Output-based aid[a] (Mumssen, Johannes, and Kumar 2010)	Subsidy payment covers a funding gap, thereby allowing the poor to access basic services	Dependent on design: service provider, client
PBC	Performance-based contracting (Loevinsohn 2008)	Contracting out health services to nongovernment agencies includes many different approaches. PBC can also involve a kind of contracting-in for technical assistance to public health facilities (performance-based management support).	Dependent on design: individual health facility, district, or province level
PBF	Performance-based financing (Basinga et al. 2010; de Walque et al. 2013; Gertler and Vermeersch 2012; Meessen et al. 2006; Meessen, Kashala, and Musango 2007; Meessen, Soucat, and Sekabaraga 2011; Soeters, Habineza, and Peerenboom 2006; Soeters et al. 2011)	Supply-side incentives are predominantly for quantity of services conditional on quality. Experiments are with lowering demand-side barriers by subsidizing providers to apply user fee exemptions for vulnerable populations. Performance frameworks are at multiple levels of the health system. The PBF approach includes introducing management tools for performance enhancement at the facilities. PBF is a form of OBA.	Dependent on design, but a combination at various levels is typical: health facilities, district health teams, provincial health teams, central medical stores, ministries of health, project implementation units, and so on
PBI	Performance-based incentives (Eichler and Levine 2009)	PBI encompasses the entire range of incentive approaches on both the demand and the supply sides. Terminology is frequently used by the USAID and CGD. PBI is synonymous with RBF and P4P	Dependent on design: any level

TABLE I.1 *continued*

Acronym or abbreviation	Complete spelling	Explanation	Target of incentives
PforR	Program-for-Results	PforR is a result-based financing instrument used by the World Bank. It is similar to COD-Aid.	Government
P4P	Pay for performance	P4P encompasses the entire range of incentive approaches on both the demand and the supply sides. Terminology is frequently used by USAID and OECD countries. P4P is synonymous with RBF and PBI.	Dependent on design: any level
PRP	Provider Recognition Program	PRP is a nonmonetary-based program.	Health facility or individual provider
RBF	Results-based financing[b]	RBF encompasses the entire range of incentive approaches on both the demand and the supply sides. It is synonymous with P4P and PBI. Terminology is frequently used by the World Bank.	Dependent on design: any level
Vouchers	Application of output-based aid (Bellows, Bellows, and Warren 2011)	Both demand- and supply-side vouchers are provided. (Vouchers facilitate access to desirable health services by specific groups of clients. Vouchers are also income for providers.)	Health facilities and health providers, individual clients

Source: World Bank data.

Note: CGD = Center for Global Development; OECD = Organisation for Economic Co-operation and Development; RBF = results-based financing; USAID = U.S. Agency for International Development.

a. See http://www.gpoba.org.

b. See http://www.rbfhealth.org/rbfhealth.

2005), whereas PBF involves contracts with individual health facilities, whether public or private (Meessen et al. 2006; Meessen, Kashala, and Musango 2007; Soeters, Habineza, and Peerenboom 2006; Soeters et al. 2011). PBF is done through a "contracting-in" approach: PBF is put onto existing public and private health systems with a significant involvement of nonstate actors.[4]

Using one RBF approach or the other depends on the context (Gorter, Ir, and Meessen 2013). PBC works well in fragile states (for example, Haiti, Cambodia, or Afghanistan), whereas PBF can work in both fragile states and more stable environments.

This toolkit is primarily about PBF in the health sector of lower- and middle-income countries (LMIC). In many countries, this health sector comprises the public and faith-based-organization health facilities. In urban areas, the private for-profit sector is becoming more important, and it is targeted in novel schemes such as the one in Douala, Cameroon.

There are several PBF approaches for health centers and hospitals in LMIC. For health centers, it is very common to use a fee-for-service for the minimum package of services and to pay conditional on the quality of the services. For hospitals, there is a mix of approaches: one uses a fee-for-service approach that is conditional on quality, and the other uses a balanced scorecard that targets quality. The community PBF approach is being piloted.

The PBF approaches addressed in this toolkit have shown impressive results through a rigorous impact evaluation (Basinga et al. 2010; de Walque et al. 2013; Gertler and Vermeersch 2012). The appeal of the PBF approach, notwithstanding the complexity and implementation challenges, is being validated through a nationwide scale-up in Burundi, which was completed in 2010, and through the application of this approach in a growing number of countries.

We are aware of the bewildering array of terms used to denote RBF approaches. For this toolkit, we will be referring to *performance-based financing,* or PBF, when talking about the fee-for-service-conditional-on-quality RBF. The term PBF is used for two reasons. First, this term is used for this type of RBF in Africa, where it originated.[5] Second, RBF designs, which are being introduced in many LMIC, are based on the fee-for-service-conditional-on-quality approaches (Gorter, Ir, and Meessen 2013).

I.4 A Simplified Example of PBF at a Health Facility

A simplified example of PBF is provided in table I.2. The bulleted list with bracketed numbers that follows this paragraph shows how the performance of the health facility is financed and how the health facility chooses to use the financing. In this example, individual health facilities are provided funds based on the quantity and quality of services they produce as independently verified. Each bracketed number refers to a field in table I.2. For example, [1] refers to the number of children the health facility has fully immunized in the past quarter.

1. A health facility fully immunizes 60 children in a quarter.
2. The health facility could earn US$120 (60 × US$2 per child fully immunized).

TABLE I.2 Simplified Example of How Performance-Based Financing Works in a Health Facility

Health facility revenues over the previous period	Number provided	Unit price (US$)	Total earned (US$)
Child fully vaccinated	60 **[1]**	2.00	120.00 **[2]**
Skilled birth attendance	60	18.00 **[3]**	1,080.00
Curative care	1,480	0.50	740.00
Curative care for the vulnerable patient (up to a maximum of 20% of curative consultations)	320	0.80	256.00
[A typical minimum package for a health center would contain 15 to 25 services.]	–	–	–
Subtotal revenues			**2,196.00 [4]**
Remoteness (equity) bonus	+20% **[5]**		439.00
Quality bonus	60% of 25% **[6]**		395.00
Total PBF subsidies			**3,030.00 [7]**
Other revenues (direct payments: out of pocket, insurance, etc.)			970.00
Total revenues			**4,000.00 [8]**
Health facility expenses			
Fixed salaries staff			800.00
Operational costs			350.00
Drugs and consumables			1,000.00
Outreach expenditures			250.00
Repairs to the health facility			300.00
Savings into health facility bank account			250.00
Subtotal expenses			**2,950.00**
Bonuses to staff in the facility = total revenues – subtotal expenses			1,050.00
Total expenses			**4,000.00 [9]**

Source: World Bank data.

3. The health facility could earn US$1,080 for 60 deliveries because each delivery earns US$18. A typical minimum package of PBF services at a health center would contain 15–25 services.
4. This health facility would earn US$2,196 as unadjusted subtotal for the services it produced over the past quarter.
5. The total amount would be adjusted for the remoteness or difficulty of the facility (equity bonus) because urban or peri-urban facilities could earn a disproportionate amount. In the example in table I.2, this particular facility would earn 20 percent more because of the difficulties it faces.
6. The total would also be adjusted by a quality score based on a checklist administered at the facility every quarter. This facility would earn

60 percent of what it would be entitled to because of the quality correction. The quality correction is a maximum of 25 percent of earnings from the past quarter [6]. This facility thus earns 60 percent of the 25 percent for its quality.

7. The funds earned (US$3,030 in this example) are transferred to the bank account of the facility.

8. In this example, the health facility also has some other sources of cash revenue (US$970), and these are added to the PBF earnings.

9. The health facility had US$4,000 in income over the past quarter, and the expenses section illustrates how this could have been used. The income can be used for

   (a) health facility operational costs, such as drugs and consumables, outreach expenses, and health facility maintenance and repair

   (b) performance bonuses for health workers (up to 50 percent) according to defined criteria; this facility decided to spend 26 percent of its total income on performance bonuses (34 percent of its PBF earnings; however, because of other sources of cash income, such funds are managed integrally)

   (c) savings; this health facility is saving not only to buy a motorcycle to facilitate community outreach but also to have a cash buffer.

Notes

1. See http://www.rbfhealth.org/rbfhealth/news/item/347/personal-story-seeking-roots-performance-based-financing-pbf (accessed January 26, 2013).

2. Burundi, Rwanda, and Sierra Leone.

3. Benin, Burkina Faso, Cameroon, the Comoros, the Central African Republic, Chad, the Democratic Republic of Congo, the Republic of Congo, Kenya, Lesotho, Liberia, Malawi, Mozambique, Nigeria, Tanzania, Zambia, and Zimbabwe.

4. "Contracting-out" is also called a service delivery contract, and "contracting-in" is also called a management contract. In Cambodia where this terminology was used, contracting-in was reserved for those interventions whereby NGOs worked with and through the public sector. Contracting-in describes PBF systems best because there are many government–civil society structures with quite a few paid through public funds set up to enhance accountability and transparency.

5. In francophone Africa where the approach gained currency (Burundi, the Democratic Republic of Congo, and Rwanda), it is referred to as *financement basé sur la performance* (FBP), *incentives pour la performance,* or *l'approche contractuelle.*

References

Arur, A., D. Peters, P. Hansen, M. A. Mashkoor, L. C. Steinhardt, and G. Burnham. 2009. "Contracting for Health and Curative Care Use in Afghanistan between 2004 and 2005." *Health Policy and Planning* 25 (2): 135–44.

Basinga, P., P. Gertler, A. Binagwaho, A. Soucat, J. Sturdy, and C. Vermeersch. 2010. "Effect on Maternal and Child Health Services in Rwanda of Payment to Primary Health-Care Providers for Performance: An Impact Evaluation." *The Lancet* 377 (9775): 1421–28.

Bellows, N. M., B. W. Bellows, and C. Warren. 2011. "The Use of Vouchers for Reproductive Health Services in Developing Countries: Systematic Review." *Tropical Medicine and International Health* 16 (1): 84–96.

Bhushan, I., E. Bloom, D. Clingingsmith, R. Hong, E. King, M. Kremer, B. Loevinsohn, and B. Schwartz. 2007. "Contracting for Health: Evidence from Cambodia." Weatherhead School of Management, Case Western Reserve University, Cleveland, OH. http://faculty.weatherhead.case.edu/clingingsmith/cambodia 13JUN07.pdf.

Bhushan, I., S. Keller, and B. Schwartz. 2002. "Achieving the Twin Objectives of Efficiency and Equity: Contracting Health Services in Cambodia." ERD Policy Brief No. 6, Asian Development Bank, Manila.

Birdsall, N., and W. Savedoff, eds. 2010. Cash on Delivery, *A New Approach to Foreign Aid*. Washington, DC: Center for Global Development.

de Walque, D., P. J. Gertler, S. Bautista-Arredondo, A. Kwan, C. Vermeersch, J. de Dieu Bizimana, A. Bingawaho, and J. Condo. 2013. "Using Provider Performance Incentives to Increase HIV Testing and Counseling Services in Rwanda." Policy Research Working Paper 6364, World Bank, Washington, DC.

Eichler, R., P. Auxila, U. Antoine, and B. Desmangles. 2009. "Haiti: Going to Scale with a Performance Incentive Model." In *Performance Incentives for Global Health: Potential and Pitfalls,* edited by R. Eichler and R. Levine, 165–88. Washington, DC: Center for Global Development.

Eichler, R., and R. Levine, eds. 2009. *Performance Incentives for Global Health: Potential and Pitfalls*. Washington, DC: Center for Global Development.

Fiszbein, A., and N. Schady. 2009. "Conditional Cash Transfers: Reducing Present and Future Poverty." Policy Research Report, World Bank, Washington, DC.

Gertler, P., and C. Vermeersch. 2012. "Using Performance Incentives to Improve Health Outcomes." Policy Research Working Paper WPS6100, World Bank, Washington, DC.

Gorter, A. C., P. Ir, and B. Meessen. 2013. "Evidence Review: Results-Based Financing of Maternal and Neonatal Health Care in Low- and Lower-Middle-Income Countries." Study, Deutsche Gesellschaft für Internationale Zusammenarbeit (GIZ), Eschborn, Germany.

Loevinsohn, B. 2008. *Performance-Based Contracting for Health Services in Developing Countries: A Toolkit*. Health, Nutrition, and Population Series. Washington, DC: World Bank.

Loevinsohn, B., and A. Harding. 2005. "Buying Results? Contracting for Health Service Delivery in Developing Countries." *The Lancet* 366 (9486): 676–81.

Loevinsohn, B., and G. D. Sayed. 2008. "Lessons from the Health Sector in Afghanistan: How Progress Can Be Made in Challenging Circumstances." *Journal of the American Medical Association* 300 (6): 724–26.

Meessen, B., J. P. Kashala, and L. Musango. 2007. "Output-based Payment to Boost Staff Productivity in Public Health Centres: Contracting in Kabutare District, Rwanda." *Bulletin of the World Health Organization* 85 (2): 108–15.

Meessen, B., L. Musango, J. P. Kashala, and J. Lemlin. 2006. "Reviewing Institutions of Rural Health Centres: The Performance Initiative in Butare, Rwanda." *Tropical Medicine and International Health* 11 (8): 1303–17.

Meessen, B., A. Soucat, and C. Sekabaraga. 2011. "Performance-Based Financing: Just a Donor Fad or a Catalyst Towards Comprehensive Health-Care Reform?" *Bulletin of the World Health Organization* 89 (2): 153–56.

Mumssen, Y., L. Johannes, and G. Kumar. 2010. *Output-Based Aid: Lessons Learned and Best Practices.* Washington, DC: World Bank.

Musgrove, P. 2011. "Financial and Other Rewards for Good Performance or Results: A Guided Tour of Concepts and Terms and a Short Glossary." World Bank, Washington, DC. http://www.rbfhealth.org/system/files/RBF%20glossary%20long%20revised.pdf.

Palmer, N., L. Strong, A. Wali, and E. Sondorp. 2006. "Contracting Out Health Services in Fragile States." *British Medical Journal* 332 (7543): 718–21.

Soeters, R., and F. Griffiths. 2003. "Improving Government Health Services through Contract Management: A Case from Cambodia." *Health Policy and Planning* 18 (1): 74–83.

Soeters, R., C. Habineza, and P. B. Peerenboom. 2006. "Performance-Based Financing and Changing the District Health System: Experience from Rwanda." *Bulletin of the World Health Organization* 84 (11): 884–89.

Soeters, R., and S. Nzala. 1994. "Primary Health Care Trading Companies for Sustainable Development." *World Health Forum* 15 (1): 51–55.

Soeters, R., P. B. Peerenboom, P. Mushagalusa, and C. Kimanuka. 2011. "Performance-Based Financing Experiment Improved Health Care in the Democratic Republic of Congo." *Health Affairs* 30 (8): 1518–27.

WHO (World Health Organization). 2010. *World Health Report: Health Systems Financing—The Path to Universal Coverage.* Geneva: WHO.

PART 1

HEALTH FACILITY–LEVEL DESIGN ISSUES

CHAPTER 1

Buying a Quantity of Services

MAIN MESSAGES

→ When buying a quantity of services in PBF, give priority to those services that have inadequate coverage but have a strong public health effect.

→ Purchasing such services sends important signals to health workers about strategic choices.

→ Some services are easier to purchase than others because of the ease with which they can be measured.

→ PBF practitioners agree to a large extent on what services should be purchased.

→ One can address pressure from lobbies to add more services by insisting that those advocates find the additional resources to pay for the services.

COVERED IN THIS CHAPTER

1.1 How to buy a quantity of services in PBF: Four points to consider

1.2 How to handle important design issues in purchasing services: Which services are easy to purchase and which are not, and what services are commonly purchased?

1.1 How to Buy a Quantity of Services in PBF: Four Points to Consider

It is sensible to pay for a particular quantity or volume of services. In high-income countries, this practice has been common for many years and is referred to as a fee-for-service. When you buy health services, consider these four points:

- *Buy services that are cost-effective.* There is little point in buying services that are ineffective or inefficient. Beginning with the *World Development Report 1993: Investing in Health* (World Bank 1993), consensus has been emerging on which services or interventions provide good value for money. For example, child immunization, vitamin A supplementation, and skilled birth attendance are widely seen as effective and costing relatively little per life saved. Although some controversies remain over which services are the most cost-effective, the opinions of those implementing performance-based financing (PBF) in real-world situations appear to converge: there is a growing consensus about which services to buy (see table 1.3 later in this chapter).

- *Be cautious in selecting services because your choices send an important signal to health workers about priorities.* Governments or other purchasers often accord high priority to particular services. This prioritization is an essential part of a good health sector strategy. When everything is a priority, nothing takes precedence! Thus, selecting a particular service does not mean that other services are without value. Instead, it means that in a given situation, some services will take precedence over others in terms of effort and resources. For example, in an epidemic of human immuno-deficiency virus (HIV) concentrated in high-risk groups, one will select services concentrated among those populations that are most at risk. Voluntary counseling and testing for HIV (VCT) services among the general population may be considered less of a priority than an increase in postnatal care in high-risk circles.

- *Be strategic in purchasing: Do not pay for volume if volume is not the problem.* Where the coverage of specific services is low, PBF can help to increase coverage. Where coverage of specific services is high, or where services are overproduced, paying for volume of services is not sensible. For example, if the level of skilled birth attendance is already 94 percent and has been for a few years, paying for volumes of skilled deliveries is inefficient. In such circumstances, it would be more strategic to emphasize quality of care. This situation is not a theoretical concern. In the Kyrgyz Republic, for example, nearly 100 percent of deliveries take place in hospitals. Thus, the government decided to focus on paying for improvements in the quality of care (see chapter 3).

• *Be aware that preventive services really lag: Such services are often underprovided and should be stimulated.* In many countries, preventive and health promotion services are supposed to be "free of charge at the point of delivery." In practice, this wording means that they are financed through input financing, like drugs or medical consumables. Frequently, preventive services are underused by clients and underprovided by health workers. PBF has proven to be an effective way to subsidize such services and to increase health workers' attention in providing them.[1] This approach can result in a rapid increase in coverage of such highly effective but badly appreciated interventions.

1.2 How to Handle Important Design Issues in Purchasing Services

Purchase Services Rather Than a Change in Indicators

Purchasing Health Outcomes Is Challenging

It is challenging to purchase a decrease in indicators such as the Maternal Mortality Ratio (MMR) or the Under-5 Mortality Rate (U5MR). Although an important goal of all health systems is to reduce maternal or child deaths, use of such indicators in PBF is usually not realistic for a number of reasons: (a) measurement, especially at the level of a catchment area of a health facility, is very difficult; (b) the time between the delivery of a service and any visible effect at population level is so long that it interferes with providing any incentives to health workers or managers; and (c) any changes in those indicators are difficult to ascribe to specific actions of individual health workers because the indicators can be influenced by factors beyond the workers' control. Although purchasing health outcomes is difficult, it is not impossible, and there may be situations where it can be tried. For example, one may be able to pay for nutritional outcomes, tuberculosis (TB) cures, or repair of cataracts.

Purchasing Changes in Coverage Rates Does Not Appear to Work Well

Some implementers have tried to purchase a change in output indicators such as immunization coverage rates, but they have encountered many practical problems. First, the catchment population size of a health facility is frequently imprecise and quite changeable (with either increasing or decreasing numbers of people counted). This imprecision makes the calculation of coverage rates inaccurate. Second, a better-performing clinic may attract clients from additional adjacent catchment areas, thereby blurring any calculations of the true coverage rate. Such movements could, in fact, result in a coverage rate above 100 percent. This situation would make the purchaser's job more challenging. It could also anger providers who might not think they are adequately compensated for their efforts. For several cases that illustrate those complications, see boxes 1.1–1.3. Third, purchasing a change in coverage rates could penalize providers who performed well at baseline and thus

---

BOX 1.1

Paying for Performance in Senegal

In Senegal, the Ministry of Health launched its pay-for-performance pilot in April 2012. Three districts have been selected (Darou Mousty, Kaffrine, and Kolda). So far, 16 health facilities have signed a PBF contract. These facilities (and their health workers) are rewarded in proportion to their achievements related to nine quantitative indicators (mostly related to child and maternal health) and to a quality of care checklist. The pilot has also been an opportunity to identify several limitations in the existing design:

1. The portion of PBF bonuses allocated to staff is very small (less than 10 percent of their salaries), in comparison to what is observed in other PBF experiences (that is, 40 percent in Rwanda and Benin). This portion is too low for adequately incentivizing health workers to achieve all PBF objectives.

2. Contrary to other PBF experiences, the Senegal pilot rewards the achievement of targets/thresholds (that is, coverage based) and not the production of services. Although this choice is theoretically very attractive, its implementation is notoriously difficult (especially at the beginning of a PBF program). Indeed, it requires that detailed baseline data be available for all services (and for all health facilities). Health workers also find this approach more difficult to understand.

3. The verification of reported achievements is done by a corporate audit firm, whose costs are tremendously high. This verification can be done by a nongovernmental organization (NGO) or a research center at a much lower cost.

4. There are no incentives for subsidizing health care demand from households.

would find it more difficult to further increase coverage. This change of rates could also interfere with any additional efforts to reach the poorest or most marginalized populations. This so-called step-function approach, as opposed to constant incremental rewards, can also discourage providers because it offers strong incentives close to the threshold for the reward and disincentives far above or below a threshold (Miller and Babiarz 2013).

Purchasing from the First Service versus Purchasing from Baseline Performance

To date, PBF schemes have purchased from the first service—from the first immunization or the first outpatient visit—and at the same value for each subsequent service provided. That approach has been sensible: it is simple to calculate, and baseline performance is frequently unknown. The routine reporting systems often perform poorly and are not verified routinely or rigorously. As PBF evolves and can begin to rely on more robust baselines, it becomes possible to use other approaches that emphasize improvements from an agreed baseline.

Purchase Both Quantity and Quality of Services

In many settings worldwide, the quantity of health services provided is still far below optimal. Thus, PBF schemes are typically interested in increasing the quantity of services through a unit fee for each service delivered. However, there is a legitimate concern that just paying for the volume of services will encourage providers to cut corners on the quality of care. Ensuring that the quality of care is not compromised and is substantially improved is a major challenge in PBF. The way to address quality of care is discussed in chapter 3.

Ensure Compatibility between Services and the Routine Information System

When learning which services to buy under PBF, you should ensure that the definitions are compatible with the routine data collection forms in the health management information systems (HMISs). This is often not the case. For example, in many PBF schemes, "new family planning acceptor" is mentioned as a service that is purchased. Usually, this refers to "modern methods" of family planning (such as injections of Depo-Provera, oral contraceptives, intrauterine devices, and implants). By contrast, the HMIS may track all methods, including traditional ones (for example, rhythm method) that are not used for PBF because they are difficult to verify objectively.

Primary data collection tools, such as HMIS registers, may need to be adapted for PBF. Often, additional information is required to be able to track the patient. For instance, one may insert a column in the register that records the name of the head of the household, village, street address (if available), a household number (if available), or a mobile phone number. This information is needed for carrying out verification. (See table 1.1 for an example of

TABLE 1.1 Example of Column Headers Needed for a Curative Care Register

Nr	Date	Last name	First name	Name of head of household	Village	House number	Mobile phone number	Other

Source: World Bank data.

Note: Nr = number.

the kind of information required. The necessity of improving record keeping is addressed in more detail in chapter 2.)

Be SMART in Selecting PBF Services

When choosing which services to purchase under PBF, you will find a number of practical considerations that can make the process challenging. Some SMART (specific, measurable, attributable, realistic/relevant, time bound) criteria that usually apply in such purchasing are listed. After explaining these criteria, we provide specific examples of services that have been purchased under different PBF schemes and describe how they performed in the real world.

- *Specific:* Any PBF service should have a clear operational definition that is easy to understand. For example, buying "antenatal care" is not sufficiently defined. Is it the first antenatal visit that is meant or the fourth visit that will be purchased? What is the minimum content for a service to be considered a real antenatal visit?

Tip—Be careful about age groups: Paying for "consultations among children under 5 may be programmatically important but poses verification nightmares in actual settings. Providers find this service easy to manipulate by including older children, whose exact age can be difficult to verify.

- *Measurable:* To be viable, a PBF service needs to be easily measurable (see box 1.4). In practice, this means the following:
  - → The date of an individual service can be easily extracted from a standardized register or patient file. This allows independent verification of whether the service was actually delivered and when.
  - → The number of services provided can be easily counted from the register or patient files (counting is easier than calculating rates or ratios).
  - → Individual patients can be tracked so that a surveyor can verify: (a) whether the patient exists; (b) whether the patient received the service and when; and (c) whether the patient was satisfied with the service provided.
- *Attributable:* The service needs to be within the control of the provider to actually deliver. For example, tubal ligation or caesarean section would obviously not be an appropriate service to purchase from a health center. However, you need to be careful to avoid furnishing providers with an excuse for not delivering services. Health centers have many ways to strengthen service delivery (see box 1.5).

BOX 1.4

How to Measure Whether Services Are PBF-SMART

For a PBF system to be SMART, it must be measurable. One must be able to trace a consumer/client in the community, question the client whether he or she received the specific service, and then receive a reliable answer from the client. If the answer is no, you can almost be sure your indicator is not SMART.

Multiple issues can arise. This tracing may be done by modestly trained community members, without any medical background. Measurability breaks down if the registers cannot be used to verify the clients' identity or, while the client is being interviewed, the content of the service provided cannot be detailed.

Examples of inadequate registers are the "tick-lists." Here clients and patients are merely indicated by tick marks in a register. No identifying information is provided (see table B1.4.1). In some places, this type of register is still typical when monitoring growth for children under 5 years old, or recording vaccinations by some outreach programs.

Using such "tick-lists" limits the ability to find and trace any client in the community, which is the basis of well-performing PBF systems!

TABLE B1.4.1 Example of a "Tick List":
An Inadequate Register

DPT1	√ √ √ √ √ √√ √ √√ √ √√ √
DPT2	√ √ √√ √ √√ √ √
DPT3	√ √ √√ √

Source: World Bank data.

Note: DPT = diphtheria, pertussis, and tetanus (vaccination).

BOX 1.5

What Health Workers Can Do to Influence the Quantity of Services

Sometimes health workers complain that they have little influence over the number of patients they see. They blame this on lack of demand for services, poor or difficult transportation to the health facility, or a run-down physical infrastructure with a shortage of supplies.

There are indeed some services that are challenging to promote. For instance, because of cultural barriers, it is often difficult to convince a pregnant woman to have a first antenatal clinical visit before the fourth month. Nonetheless, health workers can exercise their influence on the quantity of services they provide using some of the following actions: (a) changing a clinic's opening hours, (b) organizing outreach campaigns, (c) mobilizing community health workers and traditional birth attendants, (d) improving quality of care, (e) adding additional staff members (through its increased revenue and autonomy on financial management), (f) improving staff members' motivation (through passing on bonus revenues in an equitable and transparent manner), (g) treating all patients present (instead of closing the door at noon), and (h) reinforcing staff members' technical knowledge (mastery of protocols is demand-driven rather than imposed from higher management). For advanced strategies, see chapter 10.

- *Realistic/Relevant:*
  - → A realistic PBF service is already collected through the routine HMIS, the service has its routine registers, and its definition poses no problems with staff or with verifiers.
  - → Overburdening the verifiers with many services or services with difficult composite indicators that need routine checking through multiple files and registers will push such verifiers to cut corners. It is very important to keep in mind the workload of many verifiers. Be realistic with the choice of services and the time requirements involved in controlling the outputs. Field testing PBF tools such as registers is advisable. This testing would include assessing the levels of effort by controllers and interobserver and intraobserver variability.
- *Time bound:* PBF payments should be made with regular intervals. Generally, the longer the period between an action and the payment for that action, the less effective is the reward. A typical payment cycle is once per quarter, so the service you purchase needs to fit within that time frame.

Consider the Practical Experience with Specific Services in Existing PBF Schemes

Table 1.2 lists a series of PBF services that have been used at the health center/community level and provides direct comments about how well these services have worked in the field. Table 1.3 contains such PBF services for the first-level referral hospital.

TABLE 1.2 Examples of PBF Services for the Health Center/Community Level and Their Implementation Experience

No.	PBF service: Minimum package of activities	Rating	Comments on implementation
1	New outpatient consultation	Very good	Easy to implement. Paying a subsidy for each curative care visit opens the door for regulating the quality of that consultation. The purchaser can negotiate the out of pocket expense downward. It also facilitates subsidizing of free health care.
13	Institutional delivery	Very good	Easy to implement. Paying a sufficient fee will enable the facility to pay traditional birth attendants and community health workers a fee to bring women to deliver in a facility. In addition, it will enable the facility to wave formal or informal fees and to purchase gifts for the mother: the so-called welcome baby packages. For more details on how this is done, see chapter 10, table 10.3, of this toolkit for advanced strategies.

(table continues on next page)

TABLE 1.2 *(continued)*

No.	PBF service: Minimum package of activities	Rating	Comments on implementation
15	Any emergency referral and patient arrival at hospital	Good	Relatively easy to measure but requires a standardized referral and counter-referral slip. The availability of the counter-referral slip at the health center is the basis for payment. The slip offers proof that the patient has arrived at the hospital and has been attended to. The approach is frequently combined with paying for referrals received at the hospital level. However, fraud can occur with referral and counter-referral slips.
5	First antenatal care visit	Good	Easy to implement and easy to verify. However, it does not help encourage women to visit the clinic early in the pregnancy.
3	New outpatient consultation for a child less than 5 years old	Average	Hard to avoid fraud because of older children being included. However, it can be important if many children are dying of easily treated diseases such as diarrhea or pneumonia.
4	New outpatient consultation for a poor person	Average	Difficult to set rules and to enforce and easy to game. Subsidizing care for the poorest is desirable. If there are user charges, then these can be financed through this reimbursement category. Frequently, the purchaser relies on partial cross-subsidization. The approach is made operational by limiting the number to, for instance, 20 percent of all consultations. Strong community involvement is a prerequisite.
2	New outpatient consultation with a malaria diagnosis	Poor	Easy to game and impossible to verify. Payment will lead to many cases categorized as malaria, especially when the malaria diagnosis pays out more money than the "normal consultation." It can lead to unnecessary overprescription of expensive antimalarial drugs.
35	Vesico-vaginal fistula (VVF) referral	Poor	Although treating VVF is desirable, it makes sense to pay for this referral only if there is a good supply of accessible surgical services for VVF. It could also be a challenge to verify this service.
Never tried	Maternal Mortality Ratio (MMR)	Impossible	Fortunately, MMR as an indicator is a rare occurrence. Expensive surveys would need to be undertaken, which will lead to very wide confidence intervals. Results would not be available on time to pay providers regularly. Paying considerable money for fewer deaths would lead to gaming through manipulation of reports.

Source: World Bank data.

Note: "No." refers to the number of a service in a long list of services available as a linked file in this chapter. PBF = performance-based financing.

TABLE 1.3 List of PBF Services Commonly Used at the First Referral Hospital Level

No.	PBF service	Rating	Comments on implementation
1	New outpatient consultation by a medical doctor	Very good	Easy to document and easy to verify. This is an incentive for referred cases to be seen by a doctor, instead of by lesser-qualified medical staff.
4	Minor surgery	Very good	Easy to document and easy to verify.
7	Complicated delivery	Good	Easy to document and more difficult to verify. If the fee for an assisted delivery is much higher than that for a normal delivery, misclassification might easily occur.
8	Cesarean section (C-section)	Good	Easy to document and easy to verify. If the fee for a C-section is very high, then too many C-sections may occur. However, in many areas, not nearly enough C-sections are performed. It would be desirable to indicate a range or an upper limit for such C-sections.
10	Inpatient day for a poor person	Average	Difficult to set rules and difficult to enforce. However, subsidizing care for the poorest is necessary. If user charges occur, then these are financed through this reimbursement category. Frequently, the purchaser relies on partial cross-subsidization. This approach is made operational by limiting the number to, for instance, 20 percent of all inpatient days.
3	Counter-referral slip arrival at the health center	Average	Difficult to verify. This system needs signed proof by the hospital that the health center has received the counter-referral slip written by the medical doctor. It is meant to reinforce the referral pathways between different levels of care.
17	Documented death	Poor	Sometimes, national programs attempt to investigate maternal deaths. This is a very uncommon service to procure. However, it might be a strategy to counterbalance underreporting of such deaths.

Source: World Bank data.

Note: "No." refers to the number of a service in a long list of services available as a linked file in this chapter. PBF = performance-based financing.

Table 1.2 lists examples of health center indicator/services that range from "very good," PBF SMART, to "impossible." Each service has a clear definition (an example of such definitions can be found in the links to files in this chapter, under the "service protocol reference guides"), although it can vary slightly, depending on the particular country context. For compiling such a list for all PBF services, you need very good primary data collection tools, such as registers and individual patient cards (see chapter 2). A longer list with services is available in the links to files in this chapter. The numbers in tables 1.2 and 1.3 refer to the numbers in this longer file.

On What Services Do Existing PBF Schemes Focus?

Although there are many specific contextual factors to consider in purchasing PBF services, a fair degree of convergence exists in the various PBF schemes that have been developed recently (see table 1.4). This amount at least suggests that different people confronting different situations still agree about what makes sense. The 20 most commonly purchased services from 16 different PBF schemes are listed in order of frequency in table 1.4. The complete table, which also includes some less frequently used services, is available in the links to files in this chapter.

TABLE 1.4 Top 20 Services Purchased at Health Centers in 16 PBF Projects

No.	Minimum package of activity—PBF service	Percent
1	New outpatient consultation	100
2	New or existing user of modern family planning method	100
3	Institutional delivery	100
4	Second to the fourth antenatal care visit	93.8
5	Fully vaccinated child	87.5
6	Tetanus vaccination numbers 2 to 5 for a pregnant woman	81.3
7	Any emergency referral and patient arrival at hospital	75.0
8	A mother-child pair treated with ARVs/PMTCT	62.5
9	First antenatal care visit	56.3
10	New AFB+ PTB case	56.3
11	AFB+ PTB case cured	56.3
12	Admission/inpatient day	50.0
13	IUD insertion/Norplant	50.0
14	VCT	50.0
15	Postnatal care visit	43.8
16	Second dose of sulfadoxine/pyrimethamine (IPTp)	43.8
17	Growth monitoring visit for child 11–59 months old	43.8
18	STD treated	43.8
19	Woman tested in PMTCT	43.8
20	Mosquito net distribution	37.5
	Average number of services across 16 PBF projects = 20 (range 9–31)	

Source: World Bank data.

Note: "No." refers to the number of a service in a long list of services available as a linked file in this chapter. AFB+ = acid-fast bacillus positive; ARV = antiretroviral; IPTp = intermittent preventive treatment for malaria in pregnancy; IUD = intrauterine device; PMTCT = preventing mother-to-child transmission; PTB = pulmonary tuberculosis; STD = sexually transmitted disease; VCT = voluntary counseling and testing for HIV; PBT = performance-based financing.

1.3 How to Select Services: The Process in Practice

General Issues

When you are about to select which services to purchase, the following questions should come to mind: (a) Which types of services are required? (b) How is the service package balanced in terms of which conditions or diseases are included? and (c) How many services should there be and what weight can you give to each service?

In some cases, you might only need to propose a balanced PBF package that has worked well in a similar environment to your own. With minor modifications, such a package might be readily accepted. In other instances, however, you will have to enter into painstaking negotiations over what type of services to include or omit. This can be a time-consuming process, which—if not managed well—could lead to stakeholders' anger with each other.

> **"You do not like the services I'm proposing; therefore, you do not like me?"**

In yet other settings, high-level persons may insist that certain services be included for political reasons (for instance, in the case of Rwanda when vesico-vaginal fistulas were included). These choices may be not so SMART, but in the face of huge political pressure, technical arguments may not always win. You could find yourself confronted by supporters of a vertical disease program, who are pushing for a disproportionate share of "their indicators" to be included in the PBF packages.

As a result, and because of time pressures, discussion might get bogged down and people might turn to a compromise package that resembles a "wildebeest constructed by a committee" (in an African myth, the wildebeest was the last creature that God created on earth from the remains of other animals). Therefore, considerable diplomatic skills may be needed to arrive at the most appropriate set of services to buy (see box 1.6). In the following paragraphs, we will discuss how to assess numbers and to weigh the importance of services.

How Many Services Should One Buy?

How many PBF services should one buy? The following guidance is based on practical knowledge accumulated by PBF implementers. This knowledge is rapidly developing. In 16 PBF projects, the average is 20 services (with

Learning from Experience

Managing policy processes in an inclusive manner can be difficult when dealing with a large number of stakeholders, such as in Rwanda in 2005–06. The intention was to keep the number of PBF services at the health-center level manageable (the system started with 30 services, and 14 of these were HIV related). Every encounter between policy actors seemingly led to a "creep" in the number of services. This was partly due to the lack of knowledge related to purchasing HIV services by partner agencies. One year later, after a review of the system, much more experienced policy actors decided to reduce the number of PBF services to 24 (14

services as a minimal package and 10 HIV-related services), cutting many services that were found to be either not practical or too difficult to verify objectively. Also, the actors had realized that each service had a transaction cost and that any attempt to control a large number of services led to skimping on the verification processes. The reason for the large number of services in a country with an HIV prevalence of 3 percent was that as a PEPFAR (U.S. President's Emergency Plan for AIDS Relief) focus-country, Rwanda had many HIV program implementing partners and considerable money to pay for HIV services.

packages ranging from 9 to 31 services). See also table 1.3 in the links to files in this chapter.

Always keep in mind the following points. First, mind the *balance*: a balanced service package is necessary and represents what should be provided in a reasonable manner. What you do not buy could be in danger of being offered less. Although there is no evidence of this, it would be wise to consider this possibility. Thus, opt for broad categories:

- "New curative consultation" captures all new outpatient consultations for any curative condition.
- "Fully vaccinated children" captures all obligatory childhood vaccinations before the age of 1 year.
- "ANC 2–4" captures all recommended antenatal care (ANC) consultations during a pregnancy, and it suggests that the first one has occurred.
- "New and re-visit for a modern FP method" captures all family planning (FP) visits for modern methods (any new visit for a modern method and any re-visit for a three-month supply of additional oral contraceptives or a new injection).

Second, mind the *context*: context-specific problems and challenges are crucial for implementing any package of services. What services are underprovided?

Third, mind the *budget*: much depends on your output budget (see chapter 4). With a larger output budget, you can offer higher fees and expand your service package. You also have a trade-off between more services and higher fees per service.

Fourth, mind the *transaction costs* (time and money costs) of verifying and counterverifying the services you select (see chapter 2). Each service takes a certain time to verify in the health facility registers. Verification can become more efficient, but an excessive number of services will make the work of verifiers more difficult.

In general, a package of between 15 and 25 services at each level (health center and hospital) is reasonable, although some experts advise increasing this to as many as 30 services. But as shown, much depends on the context, budget, and transaction costs. See also table 1.4, which illustrates the practice in various PBF projects.

Use the Modified Delphi Technique for Selecting PBF Services and Attributing Relative Weight

Resource allocation decisions are one of the great challenges in health care. Rational and transparent methods are needed to assist decision makers who often must consider multiple variables at the same time (Baltussen and Niessen 2006).

To select PBF services and allocate weight to each service, one can use a modified Delphi technique. The Delphi method is a consensus-building tool that was originally developed after World War II to forecast the impact of technology on warfare. The method has evolved and is currently being used with group decision-making processes, especially those in which certain groups tend to dominate. The method helps avoid the phenomenon of group thinking, which is so often the case when many political influences are present, time is short, and the stakes are high. Group thinking occurs in situations in which members of a group try to avoid conflict and attempt to build consensus to such a degree that rational thinking and clear option appraisal suffer.

The modified Delphi technique has been used in forecasting the impact of new technologies. It has aided multistakeholder approaches in participative policy making in developing countries, has assisted in policy making with interactive web-based tools (e-democracy),[2] and has helped in program evaluation (Wilson et al. 2010). PBF implementers can use this modified Delphi technique to establish a list of indicators in a fair and conscientious manner.

Normally, the modified Delphi technique can be applied during a one-day workshop. If, however, you combine this service selection process with the weighing of services and a financial risk forecasting tool to determine draft fees, you will need about **two days** for the entire exercise.

Exercise: The Modified Delphi Technique in Nine Steps

The modified Delphi technique has been used in several African countries (see box 1.7). The materials required are as follows:

- Introductory Microsoft PowerPoint file
- Microsoft Excel file of long list of services/indicators and template for calculating scores
- Basic costing tool example (see links to files in this chapter).

The Nine Steps to Apply the Modified Delphi Technique

Step 1. Create a panel of experts who are mandated to decide on the PBF indicators. Before the workshop, think about and then discuss with decision makers the composition of the panel. In countries with PBF experience, the rule is to compose the panel with PBF experts only. This approach is preferred because many discussions tend to have elements of desirability such as "this is an important service/indicator," but such services are difficult to obtain through PBF techniques (measurement problems). Panel members with PBF experience understand such constraints better than those who do not have such experience. In any case, the panel should consist of public health specialists who have broad interest areas and know the local context. A panel should have about 7–9 experts.

BOX 1.7
Using the Modified Delphi Technique

The modified Delphi technique has been tested extensively in Rwanda. In February 2006, it was used in a workshop designing the national performance-based financing (PBF) model (Rusa and Fritsche 2007) and later in determining which indicators/services should be included in the HIV services package. During the second half of 2007, the technique was used in consensus building for allocating weights to the various components of the Rwanda PBF-quantified quality checklist. From Rwanda, the use of the modified Delphi technique has spread. In September 2009, it was used in designing the basic and complementary PBF service packages for the national PBF model in Burundi, and in June 2010, it was applied during a national workshop in Benin to compose the list of PBF services to be included in the basic service package.

Step 2. Organize a workshop. Introduce the method in the plenary session and choose a workshop facilitator. The facilitator needs to have experience in applying this method and be perceived as neutral.

Step 3. Make use of existing PBF services (perhaps from a nearby country or from a pilot in the same country) to construct your long list. You could create a list of about 40 services and use a list of PBF services that have been successfully used in other contexts. Print sufficient copies of this long list (see the Microsoft Excel file in the links to files in this chapter).

Step 4. Limit the number of services the panel can choose. Always set the targeted number of services below your ideal number. For instance, if you think that your basic package ought to have about 18 services, tell the panel they must choose 15 services. This gives you some flexibility during negotiations.

Step 5. Each panel member must mark each service on the long list as "1," "2," or "3." The score "1" denotes the highest agreement with the service, score "3" is the lowest agreement, and score "2" is an intermediate score. This is an individual process. Ask panel members to limit the number of "1s" to the maximum number of services available (for instance, 15). In countries with large HIV programs, discuss beforehand how many HIV services should be contained in such a package (for instance, 3–4 out of 15) because it is important to balance the service package (see table 1.5). In table 1.5, an expert thought that services 1, 4, and 5 needed to be included in the package, while service 2 ought not to be included, and service 3 was a possibility.

Step 6. The facilitator enters all scored sheets in the spreadsheet (see Delphi.xlsx in the links to files in this chapter) and presents the findings to

TABLE 1.5 **Example of PBF Service Scores**

No.	PBF service	Score from expert A
1	New outpatient consultation	1
2	New outpatient consultation with a malaria diagnosis	3
3	New outpatient consultation for a child less than 5 years old	2
4	New outpatient consultation for an indigent	1
5	First antenatal care visit	1
	Other	

Source: World Bank data.

Note: "No." refers to the number of a service; PBF = performance-based financing.

the expert panel. See table 1.6 for an example of a hypothetical result for four services.

The mean and standard deviation are calculated for you. You can then perform a "sort" (Menu:Home:Sort & Filter:Sort A to Z), and the lowest figure is sorted first (the most desirable service). The result is shown in table 1.7.

As shown, there is agreement on services 1, 3, and 4. Service 2 scored 2.42857, meaning there is more opposition to it than support, and service 2 also scored lowest. When you fill in the entire sheet, it is best to use 2 as a cut-off point. All scores between 1 and 2 have more support than those scores between 2 and 3. The standard deviation says something about the level of disagreement between the experts. Service 2 has the highest standard deviation.

The goal is to engage in a plenary session in a technical assessment of the results of this first-round Delphi exercise. The cut-off point for the package is the number of services agreed on at the onset, for example, 15. Frequently, it is appropriate to remove the HIV services and discuss these at a later stage

TABLE 1.6 Example of MPA Service Scores

No.	MPA service	A	B	C	D	E	F	G	Mean	Standard deviation
1	New outpatient consultation	1	1	1	1	1	1	1	1	0
2	New outpatient consultation with a malaria diagnosis	3	1	2	3	3	3	3	2.42857	0.78680
3	New outpatient consultation for a child less than 5 years old	2	2	1	1	1	1	2	1.42857	0.53452
4	New outpatient consultation for an indigent	1	2	2	1	3	2	1	1.71429	0.75593

Source: World Bank data.

Note: "No." refers to the number of a service; MPA = minimum package of activities.

TABLE 1.7 Example of Sorted Scores of MPA Services

No.	MPA service	A	B	C	D	E	F	G	Mean	Standard deviation
1	New outpatient consultation	1	1	1	1	1	1	1	1	0
3	New outpatient consultation for a child less than 5 years old	2	2	1	1	1	1	2	1.42857	0.53452
4	New outpatient consultation for an indigent	1	2	2	1	3	2	1	1.71429	0.75593
2	New outpatient consultation with a malaria diagnosis	3	1	2	3	3	3	3	2.42857	0.78680

Source: World Bank data.

Note: "No." refers to the number of a service; MPA = minimum package of activities.

(typically, experts tend to choose many more HIV services than the 3–4 that have been agreed to at the outset). Such HIV services can then also be proposed with vertical donors who might be interested in buying into the scheme.

Important questions to address in the plenary discussion are the following:

- Is the package balanced?
- How many services are there with a score between 1 and 2?
- Are there any duplicate services or services that are implied or subsumed in others?
- Are there any technical reasons to remove or add services (importance, cost-effectiveness, and so forth)?
- Are we in agreement?

Step 7. If after these discussions the panel still disagrees on the number of services to include in the package (even after extending the package to, for instance, the 18 that the facilitator had in mind), a second round of Delphi can be done, by repeating steps 5–7. Full consensus is normally reached by round three. But frequently, one round of Delphi suffices to get consensus (see box 1.8).

Step 8. Determine the weights for the individual services. The weights are used for the costing of the PBF services. The weight reflects the relative value, importance, and desirability of a service as compared to other services. More information on how the weights are used for costing the PBF services is provided in chapter 4. The same modified Delphi technique as used above can be used to determine the weights of PBF services:

a. Print copies of the sheet titled "weighting_MPA_Round1," after copying the list of retained services. Print one or two copies per expert.
b. List the service "new outpatient consultation" as the first service (assuming that this service is retained, which is almost always the case), and give it an index of, for instance, 100. It is helpful to pitch this index value at about US$0.30 to US$0.40 worth of local currency units. The specifics on costing are addressed in chapter 4.
c. Let the experts weight each service as compared to this base index. Then repeat steps 5–7. Table 1.8 provides an example of this approach. Relative to the base index of 100, various experts attach different weights to each chosen service. An average weight/index follows. The standard deviation illustrates the level of agreement between the experts. A plenary discussion can lead to a final index for which a column is created ("plenary"). For instance, in this imaginary example, the first round of Delphi led to a suggestion that a delivery is valued at 10 times the base index,

BOX 1.8

Use of the Modified Delphi Technique in PBF Processes: A Drill Down in Rwanda

The government of Rwanda had decided to scale up PBF in 2006 (Government of Rwanda 2005). Three PBF pilot programs were functioning, covering an estimated 40 percent of the public and faith-based organization health delivery network by December 2005 (Rusa et al. 2009). There was one in the former Cyangugu province (Soeters, Habineza, and Peerenboom 2006), a second in Butare province (Meessen et al. 2006), and a third in central Rwanda (Kantengwa et al. 2010; Rusa et al. 2009).

This would be the first scaling-up of PBF in a low-income country setting. The problem for the Government of Rwanda was that the proponents of the three PBF approaches each had their own strong views about the proper PBF approach. Views and opinions diverged from the appropriate institutional set-up (who contracts whom and whether there should be contracting at all), the role of the Ministry of Health (a concurrent decentralization during 2005–06 put the power in the hands of the Ministry of Local Administration, leading to initial role confusion), and what indicators/services to purchase and how many to the type and frequency of monitoring activities, to the role of quality (or whether quality ought to be measured separately from the quantity by different entities) to the issue of separation of functions to the issue of community client surveys, business plans, and so on.

During a three-day workshop in February 2006, two consensus-building techniques were applied: first, a modified Delphi technique to determine the goals and attributes of a national

PBF approach for health centers; and second, the "six thinking hats" to get agreement on some areas, such as the quality measure and the institution that had to do the quality verification (de Bono 1985). The first technique was more or less successful in defining the separation of functions and the role of the various institutions related to these functions. The second technique failed. One powerful member knew the latter technique and blocked it, thereby preventing full consensus on some of the details of the national PBF model for health centers, even after a fourth day of negotiations. The Ministry of Health managed to take the lead in these processes in June 2007, and eventual consensus emerged.

For the Delphi technique, a panel of experts was created. Each expert was asked to individually list up to five goals that such a national PBF approach would need to achieve. These were mapped (similar goals were grouped), and a long list of goals was thus created. This long list was printed and given to each of the experts, for their score. Two rounds of Delphi technique led to an agreement on the goals of a new PBF approach (see the links to files in this chapter).

After this exercise, the expert panel was asked individually to list up to five attributes for each of the three areas of (a) the monitoring and verification system, (b) the regulator function, and (c) the indicators. These attributes were then used to create a long list, which was then sorted according to these areas. Two rounds of Delphi technique were applied, and the expert panel agreed on the results.

TABLE 1.8 Example of Weighted Scores of MPA Services

No.	MPA service	Base index	A	B	C	D	E	F	G	Average index	Plenary	Standard deviation
1	New outpatient consultation	100	100	100	100	100	100	100	100	100		0.00
2	First antenatal care visit		50	20	200	50	75	25	50	67		61.3
3	2–5 tetanus vaccination		25	25	50	35	100	50	75	51		27.6
4	Second dose of sulfadoxine/ pyrimethamine		50	75	25	150	50	75	25	64		42.9
5	Institutional delivery		500	1,000	750	2,000	1,500	500	750	1,000		559
6	Women tested in PMTCT		200	250	300	250	500	600	150	321		165.4
7	VCT for couples		250	200	500	150	250	350	200	271		118.5
8	New AFB+ PTB case		8,000	5,000	1,500	5,000	2,500	2,500	2,000	3,786		2,324.8
9	Other											

Source: World Bank data.

Note: "No." refers to the number of a service. AFB+ = acid-fast bacillus positive; PMTCT = preventing mother-to-child transmission; PTB = pulmonary tuberculosis; VCT = voluntary counseling and testing for HIV; MPA = minimum package of activities.

whereas diagnosis of a new case of pulmonary tuberculosis would carry a weight of 37 times the base index.

d. Once you have arrived at a consensus, input such weights in the basic costing tool (see chapter 4).

Step 9. Input the weights into the basic costing tool (an example from Nigeria is provided in the links to files in this chapter):

a. Prepare the costing tool by inputting the basic coverage data, the population size, the available budget, and the assumptions related to the coverage rate increases under the PBF scheme.

b. You can use this draft costing tool in the second day of the workshop (allowing for time to set up the costing tool in the late afternoon of the first day) to finalize the weights to gain agreement on the unit subsidies and underlying assumptions.

c. Frequently, public health specialists are surprised to see their resource allocation decisions translated into budget figures

d. Talk the expert panel through this approach, and allow them to take ownership of it. This approach ensures that after the second day of the workshop, you will have created momentum to take the work forward.

1.4 How to Handle Additional Requests for Inclusion of Services

How to Handle Additional Requests for Inclusion

As serious PBF implementer, be proactive in talking to potential donors about contributing components to the PBF package. For instance, services for HIV, tuberculosis, and sexually transmitted disease compose a package of 6–7 services and could be funded by the Global Fund, the GAVI Alliance, or USAID/PEPFAR (U.S. Agency for International Development/U.S. President's Emergency Plan for AIDS Relief). The information technology that drives PBF databases can handle various fund holders at the same time (see chapter 12). In addition, more donor involvement will lead to greater financial sustainability and can promote better donor coordination.

In seeking donations, keep in mind the balance needed in the service package. This balance is important because PBF packages can become skewed by an excessive focus on HIV or other vertical programs, especially when donors bring money to the table.

The package of PBF services should be reviewed once a year. If you are not getting the results you want (too little of some, too much of others), you can change unit fees (for strategic purchasing, see chapter 4). Sometimes, you may want to stop purchasing one service or add another. But beware of services inflation when expanding the number of services, and keep a meaningful package with important unit subsidies offered to providers. Inflating the number of services while keeping the same budget will dilute other services. A package with too many services (more than 25–30) will run the risk of too high transaction costs (verification and counterverification).

Thus, you may have to make tough resource allocation decisions. The Delphi tool will help you in making these difficult choices.

What Happens to Nonincentivized Services and How Should They Be Handled?

Paying for some services and not for others can lead to the neglect of nonincentivized services. Thus, for PBF, it is advisable (a) to use broad service categories, (b) to choose between 15–30 services, and (c) to choose a balanced package that reflects the health priorities of the local community.

It is also important to continue monitoring the type of services received and the quantity of those services (see chapters 4 and 13).

Note that in many contexts, a package of 15–30 services is much more than what local facilities have produced before. In any case, this is an area for future research.

1.5 Links to Files and Tools

The following toolkit files can be accessed through this web link: http://www.worldbank.org/health/pbftoolkit/chapter01.

- Delphi.xlsx: Microsoft Excel spreadsheet for use with the modified Delphi technique for PBF service selection
- Delphi.pptx: Microsoft PowerPoint file, which can be adapted as an introduction to the Delphi method
- Basic_Costing_Tool_Nigeria.xlsx: sample basic costing tool, which can be adapted to the local context (see also chapter 4)
- Link to files containing the indicators or services, including their unit fees or weights:
  - Three Rwandese PBF pilots (2002–06)
  - DRC South Kivu PBF pilot (2005 to present)
  - Burundi PBF pilot (2006–09)
  - Rwandese national PBF models for health centers and hospitals (2006 to present)
  - Central African Republic PBF pilot (2008 to present)
  - Indonesia Flores PBF pilot (2008 to present)
  - Zambia Katete PBF pilot (2009 to present)
  - Burundi National PBF model (2010 to present)
  - Benin PBF pilot (2011 to present)
  - Cameroon PBF pilot (2011 to present)
  - Chad PBF pilot (2011 to present)
  - Nigeria PBF pilot (2011 to present)
  - Zimbabwe PBF pilot (2011 to present)
  - Afghanistan PBF pilot (2012 to present)
  - Republic of Congo PBF pilot (2012 to present)
  - Burkina Faso PBF pilot (2013 to present)
- Tables 1.2 and 1.3, extended versions
- Table 1.4, extended version.

Notes

1. PBF targets health facilities, not health workers. However, it directs the attention of the managers and health workers to desired services.
2. http://en.wikipedia.org/wiki/Delphi_method (accessed December 18, 2013).

References

Baltussen, R., and L. Niessen. 2006. "Priority Setting of Health Interventions: The Need for Multi-criteria Decision Analysis." *Cost Effectiveness and Resource Allocation* 4: 14. doi:10.1186/1478-7547-4-14.

de Bono, E. 1985. *Six Thinking Hats.* New York and Boston: Little, Brown.

Eichler, R., P. Auxila, and J. Pollock. 2001. "Promoting Preventive Health Care: Paying for Performance in Haiti." In *Contracting for Services: Output Based Aid and its Applications,* edited by P. J. Brook and S. Smith, 65–72. Washingotn, DC: World Bank.

Government of Rwanda. 2005. *Health Sector Strategic Plan 2005–2009.* Kigali: Government of Rwanda.

Kantengwa, K., L. De Naeyer, C. Ndizeye, A. Uwayitu, J. Pollock, and M. Bryant. 2010. "PBF in Rwanda: What Happened after the BTC-Experience?" *Tropical Medicine and International Health* 15 (1): 148–49.

Meessen, B., L. Musango, J. P. Kashala, and J. Lemlin. 2006. "Reviewing Institutions of Rural Health Centres: The Performance Initiative in Butare, Rwanda." *Tropical Medicine and International Health* 11 (8): 1303–17.

Miller, G., and K. S. Babiarz. 2013. "Pay-for-Performance Incentives in Low- and Middle-Income Country Health Programs." NBER Working Paper 18932, National Bureau of Economic Research, Cambridge, MA.

Rusa, L., and G. Fritsche. 2007. "Rwanda: Performance-Based Financing in Health." In *Emerging Good Practice in Managing for Development Results: Sourcebook,* 2nd ed., 105–16. Washington, DC: World Bank.

Rusa, L., W. Janssen, S. van Bastelaere, D. Porignon, J. de Dieu Ngirabega, and W. Vandenbulcke. 2009. "Performance-Based Financing for Better Quality of Services in Rwandan Health Centres: 3-Year Experience." *Tropical Medicine and International Health* 14 (7): 830–37.

Rusa, L., M. Schneidman, G. Fritsche, and L. Musango. 2009. "Rwanda: Performance-Based Financing in the Public Sector." In *Performance Incentives for Global Health: Potentials and Pitfalls,* edited by R. Eichler, R. Levine, and Performance-Based Incentives Working Group, 189–214. Washington, DC: Center for Global Development.

Soeters, R., C. Habineza, and P. B. Peerenboom. 2006. "Performance-Based Financing and Changing the District Health System: Experience from Rwanda." *Bulletin of the World Health Organization* 84 (11): 884–89.

Wilson, D., J. Koziol-McLain, N. Garrett, and P. Sharma. 2010. "A Hospital-Based Child Protection Programme Evaluation Instrument: A Modified Delphi Study." *International Journal for Quality in Health Care* 22 (4): 283–93.

World Bank. 1993. "World Development Report 1993: Investing in Health." Oxford University Press , New York.

——. 2011. "Aide Memoire: Technical Assistance Mission for Performance-Based Contracting, May 2–13, 2011, Monrovia, Liberia." World Bank, Washington, DC.

CHAPTER 2

Verification of the Quantity of Services

MAIN MESSAGES

→ Verification is a cornerstone of PBF.

→ PBF verification makes use of systematic data audits in health facility registers and client tracing in the community.

→ Before starting PBF, put in place a set of primary data collection tools for verification (registers and patient cards) with information through which one can trace the patient (address and telephone number).

→ Verification should be independently carried out: separation of functions is key, with a clear demarcation between purchasing, fund holding, provision, and regulation and community voice.

COVERED IN THIS CHAPTER

2.1 Introduction: Verification Is a Cornerstone of PBF

Verification is the cornerstone of any performance-based financing (PBF) system. It is the key element of a PBF program that ensures that the services submitted for payment have been provided and have been delivered at good quality. For verification of the quantities of PBF services and their proper delivery, a set of primary data collection tools (registers and patient cards) should be in place at each health facility. For PBF verification to function properly, important prerequisites are the correct layout of registers; the availability of appropriate expertise in health facilities and with purchasers; and a solid separation of functions among purchasers, verifiers, and providers. This chapter deals with the various quantity verification mechanisms, while chapter 3 treats the quality measures.

2.2 PBF Verification Systems

PBF verification systems must be rigorous. Evidence on what works best is gradually emerging. PBF verification mechanisms are dense and multilayered and involve different institutions. For a number of reasons, PBF quantity and quality verification have been split:

- They each involve different methodologies: quantity verification is much more akin to an audit, whereas quality verification entails more technical feedback.
- They both constitute a considerable workload: combining the two verification procedures could easily lead to an excessive amount of work, which could jeopardize careful procedures. PBF quality checklists are substantial and quite long, and they often involve multiple visits to a health facility over a certain period of time. Not taking this workload into account could lead to verifiers cutting corners.[1]
- The split between quantity and quality verification adds to governance and transparency. It allocates different verification tasks to different institutions, and the use of local agencies serves as an additional element in the desired separation of functions.

Most of the time, the purchasing agency[2] carries out *PBF quantity verification*. The agency uses systems to ensure that the services that have been recorded and claimed for payment have actually been received by the clients. The agency also coordinates clients' feedback on these services.

PBF quality verification is usually delegated to the regulator, most frequently the district health team. The district health department is under a performance contract to carry out this function regularly and correctly. Such engagement of the local authorities in the verification process adds to their supervisory roles and strengthens the health system rather than creating a parallel setup.

2.3 Ex Ante and Ex Post Verification of Quantity of Services

Two types of mechanisms exist for quantity verification: those that are carried out before any PBF payment is made (ex ante verification) and those that are undertaken after payment is made (ex post verification). The latter are community client satisfaction surveys and other forms of counterverification.

Verification can be labor intensive. © G. B. Fritsche.

Ex Ante Quantity Verification

Ex ante verification is concerned with recounting the claimed monthly performance in the primary data collection registers. This exercise ensures that all PBF services are registered correctly, completely, and legibly in the various registers and guarantees that the quantities of services claimed have been documented in a rigorous enough manner. In this way, the ex ante verification also prepares the ground for the later, ex post verification: it ensures that this later verification will not pose any difficulty, by controlling the proper entry of addresses and mobile phone numbers of clients, and so on. It also stimulates discipline at the health facility level to have all client-related data, including a serial number, accurately recorded in a continuous numbering from January 1 through December 31 of each year.

For the various ex ante verification tasks, the purchasing agency employs verifiers who visit health facilities on a monthly basis. Verifiers have a specific profile. They often have a medical degree and have experience working in the local health system. In addition, they have been trained in PBF, have trainers' skills, and are familiar with the various strategies that have been used successfully to boost productivity and quality in various PBF systems (see the sample terms of reference for a verifier in the links to files in this chapter). In most health districts, one full-time equivalent verification officer per seven or eight health facilities works well, especially because verifiers also operate as coaches and capacity builders. To assist verifiers in these roles, they can use the *service protocol reference guide,* a helpful tool that lists each PBF service with an elaborate definition and demonstrates the specific primary and secondary data collection instruments (registers and individual patient cards).

Given the stringency of the PBF verification requirements, the PBF verification system generally does *not* rely on existing routine data collection systems for its primary data. In nearly every conventional health management information system (HMIS), for instance, client address details—essential for PBF counterverification—are insufficiently documented (see chapter 12). In fact, PBF verification can be seen as the equivalent of a systematic data-quality audit on all data elements. This is an intensive and time-consuming process. As a consequence, the types of services that are purchased through PBF are limited to 20–30 for both the health center/community level and the first-level referral hospital.

For the ex ante verification, each health facility prepares a monthly provisional PBF invoice. In principle, the verification process follows this monthly schedule, but in practice, it can also be done once every two or three months, depending on local circumstances such as travel distances and the general accessibility of the terrain. When starting PBF, one is advised to adhere as much as possible to a monthly verification cycle to correct quickly any start-up problems that may occur with the new registers and such other PBF instruments as the business plan and the indice tool. Intense coaching is often necessary during this start-up phase.

After the ex ante verification has been completed, and data have been consolidated with the quality score (see chapter 3) and validated in the district PBF steering committee, health facilities can be paid for their performance. Most commonly, PBF payments occur on a quarterly basis. At the health facility level, the management tools—such as the indice tool (see chapter 7) and the individual performance evaluation tool (see chapter 10)—assist in converting the quarterly payment to monthly performance bonuses for staff. Health staff should be paid at acceptable intervals.

Ex Post Quantity Verification

Ex post verification refers to any verification that is undertaken *after* the PBF payment has been made. Ex post quantity verification aims to ascertain whether the services paid for have been received by real, as opposed to phantom, clients. In addition, it tries to gauge the level of client satisfaction with the services rendered. This particular type of ex post verification is therefore frequently termed a *community client satisfaction survey*. Ex post verifications send two signals. On the one hand, they signal to providers that there is a strong chance that one will be caught if one cheats (by claiming phantom patients).[3] On the other hand, providers, clients, and communities are shown that in PBF, there is a serious desire to elicit feedback on the perceived quality of health service provision.

Details on the community client satisfaction surveys discussed below are drawn from Soeters (2013).

To carry out one of the main forms of ex post quantity verification—the community client satisfaction survey—the purchaser selects a local grassroots or nongovernmental organization (NGO) for each health center that holds a principal PBF contract. Although there is a strong preference for organizations with objectives linked to health, reproductive rights, or the fight against poverty, the organization could also be, for example, a local soccer club. The local organization must have been registered with the appropriate government authority for at least two years, must be known by the local authorities, and must carry a good reputation. It should have no close ties with the health facility concerned. Members of such organizations with a suitable profile are selected as interviewers and are trained to carry out the survey. They should be literate and understand the local languages. They should be available for about six days every three months to conduct the interviews. They should be capable and willing to reach households within two hours travelling distance by foot or by their own means of transport (by bicycle, for example). In addition, they should have the social skills to fulfill their tasks in a friendly manner and with commitment, discipline, honesty, and integrity. At least one woman should be available to audit family planning activities, and she should be trained to counsel sensitive issues confidentially.

The purchasing agency performs the random sampling in the health facility registers and then passes on the identifying information (name and address) to the interviewers while retaining information related to the service provision, such as the exact date and type of service received. The interviewers' work is performance based: they are paid a fee for each fully completed questionnaire. The lump-sum payments vary by context and are usually between US$5 and US$8 for each fully completed questionnaire.

2.4 Operational Challenges

The Challenge of Finding the Correct Sample Sizes

Implementers of PBF often become entangled in debates over the sample size that is necessary for community client satisfaction surveys. If one wished only to yield statistical analyses and relevance, such community client satisfaction surveys could quickly become a very expensive and time-consuming affair. In practice, one must make a trade-off among statistical validity, costs, and the desired effects on the provider such as discouraging gaming) (see box 2.1).

BOX 2.1

Sample Techniques for PBF Community Client Satisfaction Surveys

What sampling techniques have been used for the PBF community client satisfaction surveys? A few examples from practice are as follows:

1. *The Cordaid experience:* Most Cordaid–PBF projects take a random sample of 60–80 households per health center catchment area each quarter. Community-based organizations (CBOs) are selected in each of the catchment areas and are coached by a community verification officer of the contracting/verification agency. The CBO must be known by local authorities, must have a good reputation, and preferably should have been in existence for at least two years. The CBO should not have a close relationship with the designated health facility. The selection criteria for the interviewers may include the following[a]:

   - Ability to read, write, and understand local languages, with the knowledge of other main languages being an added advantage
   - Availability for about six days every three months to conduct the interviews
   - Capability and willingness to reach households within two hours travelling distance by foot or by their own means of transport (for example, by bike)
   - Skills to fulfill the tasks in a friendly atmosphere, with commitment, discipline, honesty, and integrity
   - At least one woman should be available for auditing family planning activities. She should be trained in counseling sensitive issues and maintaining confidentiality
   - Payment of US$8 may be given per interview for which standard questionnaires are used. The CBOs transfer the informa-

tion to the contracting and verification agency, which in turn will use the information to provide feedback to the health facilities. It may also influence the contract renewal discussions.

2. *The Rwandese national health center community client satisfaction surveys:*
   - Early method (2007–10): After PBF was scaled up for health centers in 2006, a protocol for community client satisfaction surveys was tested and implemented in 2007. Each quarter, 15 of 500 health centers were randomly selected. The protocols selected health facilities randomly and targeted the previous three months (or six months, depending on the interval) of production. They would sample six or seven services of the service package of about 25 (in principle, also randomly) and then select 15 clients randomly from the selected register (using the register as the sampling matrix), using a defined sampling interval (total production over the defined period/15) and a randomly chosen first number to start the sampling. The ex post verification verified, among other issues, whether the ex ante registration had been done correctly.
   - Later method (2011 to present): The early sampling method was revised during 2011. Because of the small sample size (only 15 patients per service and equivalent by service regardless of the average monthly "production"), the confidence intervals for indicator "% of patients identified in the community" were considered very wide (and only slightly

meaningful when aggregated by health center). It was quite likely that in a case of fraud whereby one person in the health center is added at the end of the day or at the end of the week, extra patients would be missed. Quality assurance sampling methodology was applied to generate appropriate new sample sizes and decision rules. As a consequence, the new sampling methodology involves a random selection of 15 health centers. Of the 25 PBF package services, three or four are randomly selected. For each of these services, 70 client-provider contacts are randomly selected from the primary registers. If fewer than 64 contacts are retrieved, the batch is rejected. Only when 64 or more patients for each service are traced—and have acknowledged use of the service concerned on a particular day—is the site classified as "good." With this method, there is a 6.0 percent chance of classifying an honest site as fraudulent and an 8.4 percent chance of classifying a fraudulent site as honest.[b,c]

3. *The Burundi counterverification mechanism (2010 to present):* The Burundi system consists of both a decentralized community client satisfaction survey performed by the provincial public purchaser (Provincial Verification and Validation Committee, or CPVV) and an ex post counterverification performed quarterly by an external agent. This third-party agent draws random samples of performance assessments at all levels of the health system (central technical support unit; provincial health department; and district health department and health facilities). For the health facilities, it samples 4 of 17 districts. In each district, it samples 25 percent of the health centers (the district hospital is automatically included). The actual production over the preceding three months is assessed and triangulated with the production as certified by the CPVV. In each health center, the third-party agent samples six PBF services. Over the preceding six months' production, it samples 10 client-provider contacts. The third-party agent selects and recruits members from a suitable local grassroots organization, trains them, and has the clients traced in the communities.[d]

a. They should not be members of the health committee of the health facility nor providers at the same health facility, because sometimes the same people working at a health facility are active in different local associations.

b. There are many reasons for not being able to trace patients. For instance, there may be women who, for reasons of confidentiality when using family planning services, give the incorrect name or address because their husbands may not know that they are using birth control. Likewise, patients may be seasonal workers, patients from neighboring counties, people who migrate to work on their pastures, and so on, and thus the results from the community-based organizations must be analyzed in depth to identify the real reasons for lack of traceability before concluding that fraud has occurred.

c. A report detailing this method is available through the links to files in this chapter: "Report of Audit on: Quantity Verification and Client Satisfaction, Quality Counter Verification and Performance-Based Financing System and Procedures, period February–March 2011," L. de Naeyer, J. B. Habaguhirwa, and C. Ndizeye.

d. A report detailing this method is available through the links to files in this chapter: "Synthese Globale de la Contre Verification du FBP au Burundi (2011–2012)," Republique du Burundi, Ministere de la Sante Publique et de la lutte contre le SIDA.

Selecting the sample size for ex post quantity verification in PBF is therefore firmly connected to an assessment of the other accountability mechanisms already in place in the country and district, such as the state of contracts, verification mechanisms, and transparency and governance procedures. All such accountability mechanisms should be part and parcel of any well-designed and well-implemented PBF scheme. In fact, they can significantly decrease the chances of fraud and thereby reduce the necessity to carry out extremely expensive ex post surveys.

After the clients for the surveys have been selected, they are contacted. In urban areas, verifiers can use mobile phone numbers, which are systematically requested upon registration of clients in health facilities. In rural areas, clients' mobile phone numbers, household numbers, or exact household address (village and name of the head of the household) are used. The increasing coverage of mobile phones in low-income countries/lower- and middle-income countries can decrease survey costs considerably. At this point, the local NGOs or grassroots organizations are approached and can start their work.

The Importance of Reliable Registers: Registers as the Cornerstone of PBF

Proper ex post verification clearly depends to a large extent on registers into which detailed client contacts with the health facility have been entered. Only when such PBF registers are in order can a random selection of clients be drawn for ex post verification.

Registers and their linked individual client cards are the cornerstone of PBF systems. When setting up a PBF system, implementers should give special care to ensure that primary and secondary data collection tools are available and up to standards. One should start with a thorough analysis of the existing HMIS. One nearly always finds severe deficiencies in the routine data collection systems. Clinics tend to be overburdened with a plethora of routine data collection instruments and special control registers for every imaginable vertical disease program. Reporting upward is, at best, incomplete and, at worst, totally absent. Consolidated data rarely make it back to the health facility, let alone undergo analysis at the source of production.

Through its specific financial incentives, PBF radically changes the rules of registration and data collection. When data are not completely and legibly registered, health facilities are simply not paid. Through specific PBF instruments, such as the quantitative quality checklist at the health facility level, management of the routine data collection mechanisms is rewarded, including the self-analysis of trends over time. At the district level, the district health management team is also under a performance framework (see chapter 8) that rewards both data collection and data analysis (that is, collecting and analyzing data from health facilities, reporting upward to government and back to the health facilities, and performing capacity building of health facility staff related to specific topics encountered during technical data analysis).

For use in registers in the PBF systems, see the sample column headers for the MPA (minimum package of activities) and the CPA (complementary package of activities) in the links to files in this chapter.

Specific Importance of the Separation of Functions in PBF Verification

PBF uses high-powered incentives. Verification and validation of performance are linked to significant amounts of money. It is therefore vital that PBF verification be carried out by qualified persons with a high degree of integrity who have been recruited using a merit-based selection process. They should be paid well by the purchasing agency. It is also evident that the purchasing agent should be as independent as possible from the provider to carry out its purchasing and verification functions with integrity.

In general, PBF has introduced the principle of separation of functions to improve transparency and governance for PBF (for its full description, see chapter 11). To decrease conflicts of interest, the functions of fund holder, purchaser, provider, regulator, and communities should be separated as much as possible.

Separation of functions is also known as *segregation of duties,* a term used by businesses, accountants, and experts in information technology development. The purpose of segregation of duties is to avoid having one person or agency be responsible for carrying out various sensitive tasks; such tasks should be split among various persons, agencies, and institutions.

One of the main issues often encountered when setting up public PBF systems—and when dealing directly with the government (as a fund holder)—is the separation of functions among the provider, the purchaser, and the verifier. "Why should we spend so much money on this independent purchasing?" is a frequently heard complaint.[4] The answer is plain: it is difficult (and unwise) to perform PBF without this most basic degree of separation of functions. Nonseparation of functions is the most frequent PBF design error. Figure 2.1 represents a segregation of duties in the verification, authorization, recordkeeping, and reconciliation processes for PBF (for governance issues, see also chapter 11).

FIGURE 2.1 Separation of Functions

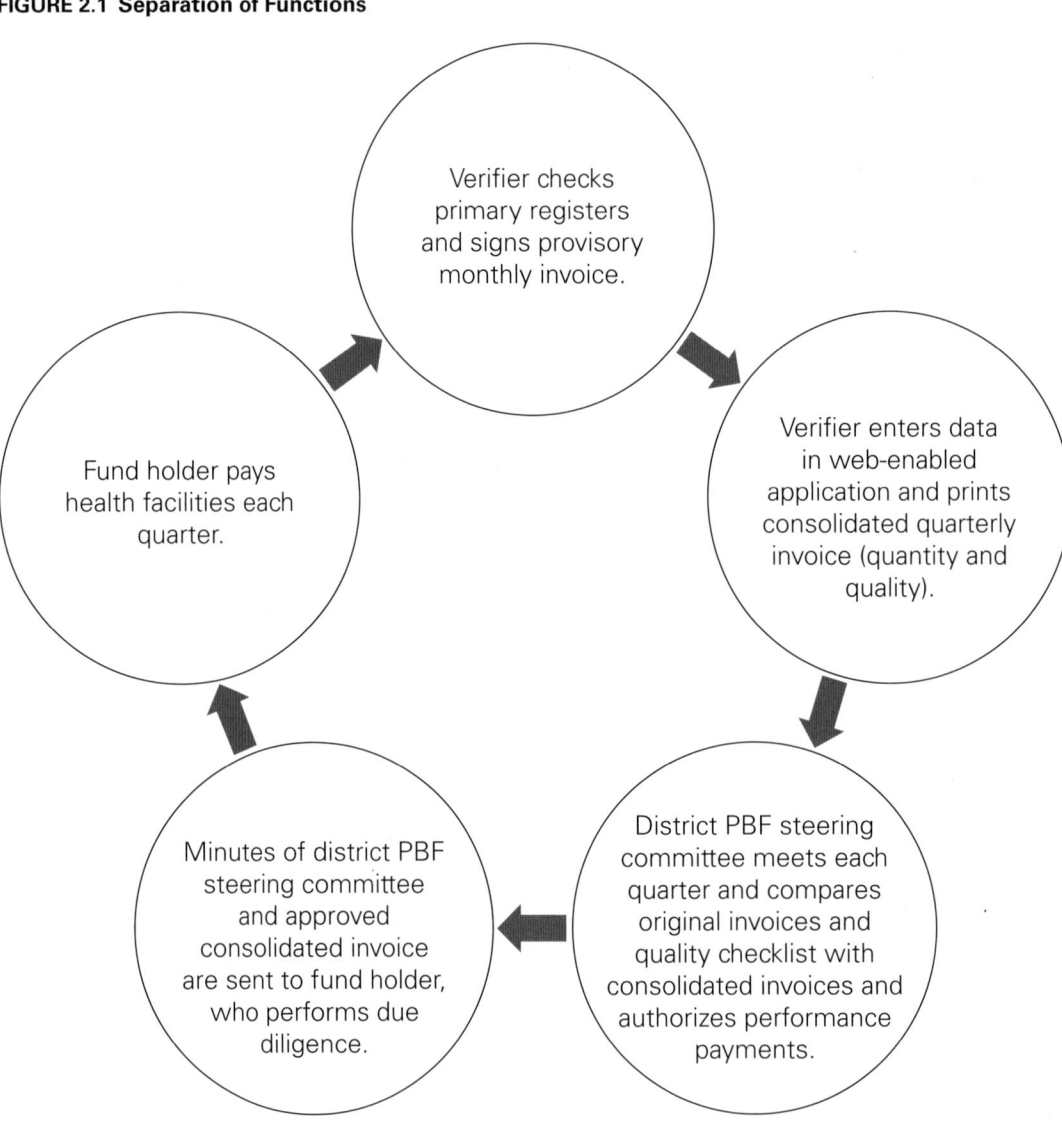

Source: World Bank data.

2.5 Transitional Issues: Rigorous Implementation

PBF changes the rules of strategy. When PBF systems are correctly designed and implemented, health workers and their managers are quite devoted to making things work and moving toward getting results. In most countries, health workers are trained with a mission: to provide good health services to their population. Frequently, however, they find their work frustrating because they have no means to influence the quantity or the quality of their work and output. They are underpaid, they fight against many adverse conditions, and often they cannot devote all their time to servicing the public good. Well-designed PBF systems offer such health workers and their managers the opportunity to do what they were originally trained to do and to offer higher-quality services to the patients in their area.

It is important to recall that while relying on health workers' internal motivation, PBF also introduces high-powered incentives. The system should be protected. Allowing even a few health workers and managers to get away with wholesale fraud would discourage the majority that are working hard to get results. Therefore, it is crucial to state unambiguously the rules of the system and to follow those rules.

First and foremost, it is important to explain the new rules of the system. Continuous support during the early stages of introducing PBF—when people are still grappling with understanding the new system—is vital (for details on technical assistance, see chapter 14). One must learn to work with newly acquired autonomy, to work toward results, to manage resources and staff, and to respond to the new reporting requirements. These responsibilities all pose a variety of challenges. Many mistakes can easily be found in new PBF systems, mistakes often simply a result of lack of understanding of the system. Therefore, good technical support and coaching are no luxury.

In more mature systems, the focus can be switched to ensuring that there are disincentives for cheating the system and for fraud. Such focus demands the implementing of verification and counterverification mechanisms as designed and the taking of swift action when there are irregularities (box 2.2).

The message should be loud and clear: cheating is not permitted. If you cheat, you will be caught. When you are caught, you will likely lose your job (for instance, as the person in charge of the health center). At the same time, it will be made known publicly that you have cheated. Your health center will be pressured to repay the money that has been earned dishonestly, and your district management team will be pressured to act on the basis of the irrefutable evidence that you have cheated. In short, implement PBF systems rigorously. Abide by the rules. Take action when fraud has been detected.

BOX 2.2

Verification and Counterverification Challenges

Balancing the need to be seen as authoritative and trustworthy while being accountable for obvious cases of fraud is not easy, as shown in the following examples:

- In Rwanda, during the scale-up of PBF 2006–08, technical partners strongly advised the Ministry of Health to include counterverification measures in its PBF designs. Early evidence from pilot projects had demonstrated the need to do so. Community client satisfaction surveys were introduced in December 2008, after the first such survey showed an acceptable—and low—5 percent of services that could not be traced in the community. The ministry had been afraid that a larger percentage of clients would be untraceable, thereby undermining the approach.

- In Rwanda, unannounced visits to hospitals by a third party led to very different measures for the quality checklists as obtained by the official peer-evaluation visits. Clearly, the peers were too close to each other to remain objective in their scoring.

- In Burundi, a third party that had contracted to validate the verifications at all levels of the PBF systems found considerable differences in the quality assessments in health centers and hospitals as measured and reported by the health administration and by the peers. This finding led to stricter rules and penalties.

- In Burundi, to improve the routine data reporting, the provincial verification committee introduced a system of financial penalties for health facilities that wrongly reported their performance.

2.6 Links to Files and Tools

The following toolkit files can be accessed through this web link: http://www.worldbank.org/health/pbftoolkit/chapter02.

- Sample PBF monthly provisory invoice
- Sample service protocol reference guides for the minimum package of activities and the complementary package of activities
- Sample reports on the Rwandese and Burundi community client satisfaction surveys (in French and English)
- Sample column headers for the MPA and the CPA
- Sample terms of reference for a verifier
- Sample terms of reference for a counterverification agent—Burundi
- Annual PBF reports 2010 and 2011—Burundi

Notes

1. If there is a suspicion of cheating, it is important to cross-check among services, such as tracing some sampled clients from the reception to the consultation to the pharmacy via the lab to learn if the patient exists.

2. It is also called the contract management and verification agency, because in many quasi-public purchasing arrangements, the government (central or local) is the purchaser but uses an agency to manage the contracts and to verify performance. In addition, the fund holding is separated in such instances from this purchasing agency, leaving the agency with the core essential tasks of negotiating and managing the contracts (on behalf of the government) and verifying performance.

3. Phantom claims are also a common occurrence in Organisation for Economic Co-operation and Development health systems; in the United States, it has been estimated that up to 10 percent of all Medicare expenditure is based on insurance fraud. In 2010, of an estimated US$528 billion in Medicare spending, an estimated US$47.9 billion was improper payments. The total U.S. health expenditure for 2010 was estimated at US$2.6 trillion. The Federal Bureau of Investigation estimates that for 2010, about 3 percent of total health expenditure was due to insurance fraud.

4. Up to 30 percent of the PBF budget is spent for the purchasing, verification, counterverification, and coaching functions. The actual amounts depend on the PBF budget and the context (gross domestic product, geographical factors, and so on).

Reference

Soeters, R., ed. 2013. *PBF in Action: Theory and Instruments—Course Guide, Performance-Based Financing.* The Hague: Cordaid-SINA. http://www.sina -health.com/?page_id=585 (accessed April 23, 2013).

Measuring and Verifying Quality

MAIN MESSAGES

→ PBF purchases services conditional on the quality of those services: providers who offer services with improved quality are paid more for those services.

→ PBF uses quantifiable quality checklists, and it measures and rewards specific components of quality. The checklist is context specific and can contain structural, process, and sometimes content-of-care measures.

→ Update PBF quality checklists regularly to incorporate lessons learned and set the quality standards progressively higher.

COVERED IN THIS CHAPTER?

3.1 Introduction

In performance-based financing (PBF), quality assessments tend to provoke heated debates. In many low-income countries, merely increasing the volume of desirable public health services is of great importance. But a larger volume of services should not be created at the expense of good quality. Good quality is a prerequisite for providing greater effectiveness of services.

Therefore, PBF purchases services *conditional* on the quality of those services. PBF provides the incremental funding necessary to increase both the volume *and* the quality of services at the same time. This form of strategic purchasing is one of PBF's hallmarks and sets PBF schemes apart from many other provider payment mechanisms.

Traditionally, many health systems analyzed quality in a fragmented manner—with little analysis, for example, by the district health teams. Vertical programs with their own quality schemes complicated matters and only added to the fragmentation (Soeters 2012).

PBF postulates that quality cannot be improved if managers close to the field do not have certain powers to manage:

- Health facility managers should have the autonomy and financial power to influence quality more directly. They should, for example, be able to recruit additional skilled staff if necessary, to buy new equipment and furniture, or to rehabilitate their health facility infrastructure when things fall apart.
- Health facility managers should have the instruments and skills to apply individual performance contracts to their health staff and thereby influence the staff's behavior.

In PBF, health facilities are reviewed regularly and are held to various standards:

- Local health authorities and peer review group members from other hospitals regularly review health facilities to monitor quality. To do so, they have at their disposal SMART (specific, measurable, achievable, realistic, and time bound), nationally agreed-upon composite quality indicators.
- When local health authorities and peer reviewers are conducting regular quality reviews on local health facilities, they work systematically and make use of the composite indicators lists. One composite indicator may contain several elements, all of which must be satisfied to earn the quality points attached to that particular indicator. The weight of an indicator may vary between 1 and 5 points, depending on its importance. For ex-

ample, to meet the composite indicator "cold chain fridge assured," health facilities must fulfill the following criteria to obtain a point: (a) a thermometer is available, and regular control temperature is maintained; (b) a refrigerator is present, and temperature form is available and is completed twice a day, including the visit day; (c) temperature remains between 2 and 8 degrees Celsius (°C) in register sheet; (d) supervisor verifies functionality of thermometer; (e) temperature is between 2 and 8°C also according to thermometer; and (f) temperature tag has not changed color.

- Based on the quality score, both positive and negative incentives can be mobilized to reward good quality and to discourage poor performance.
- The regulator and purchaser should not accept a below-standard quality score of health facilities. The regulator should be able to close health facilities in the event their performance constitutes a health risk for the population.
- Purchasing agencies can give health facilities advance payments of their subsidies to speed up quality improvements. Investment units (for example, US$1,000 for health centers and US$5,000 for hospitals in local currency) may also be made available against the infrastructure or the equipment business plan. This money is released when the health facility has achieved progress in its improvements, which is normally verified by an engineer. This demand-driven investment approach seems to be more efficient than centralized planning (Soeters 2012).

Quality assurance has thus become a fundamental part of performance contracting. In PBF, you can find heightened attention for quality in both demand- and supply-side decisions. The idea can be rephrased in economic terms. Increases in quality increase the quantity demanded. An increase in the quality also increases the cost of provision and that, in turn, decreases the quantity supplied. Thus, a new market equilibrium will occur with a new equilibrium price (Barnum and Kutzin 1993; Barnum, Kutzin, and Saxenian 1995).

To measure and reward quality, PBF uses a quantified quality checklist. Clearly, however, quality is multidimensional and context specific. PBF acknowledges that some quality dimensions can be easily measured and rewarded, while others cannot. This discrepancy poses some restrictions on rewarding quality of care through PBF. That is why, in practice, PBF goes hand in hand with other strategies to improve quality, such as quality assurance, formative supervision, and continuous education.

PBF provides incentives for quality capacity strengthening at the district level (health authorities; see chapter 8), and at the same time, it measures the quality performance at the health center or hospital level (providers). This interplay often prompts specific requests for capacity building by the health workers, as a recent Rwandese PBF impact evaluation has documented well (Basinga et al. 2010).

3.2 Diversification of Quality Stimulation: The Carrot-and-Carrot versus the Carrot-and-Stick Approach and Their Distinct Effects

Quality at All Levels

PBF operates through performance frameworks. Performance frameworks are sets of individually weighted, objectively verifiable criteria that add up to 100 percent of the desired performance. They typically include a set of process measures and target different levels of the health system. Performance frameworks are found at the following levels:

- Health center
- First-level referral hospital
- District administration
- District PBF steering committee
- Semiautonomous public purchaser
- Surveyors from the grassroots organizations carrying out the community client satisfaction surveys
- Community health worker cooperatives
- Central-level technical support unit coordinating and steering the PBF effort
- Institution responsible for paying for performance
- Sectors other than health (schools, and so on).

This chapter deals with the performance frameworks for the health center and the first-level referral hospital. Other performance frameworks (for example, for the administration) are discussed in chapter 8.

Frameworks for Health Center and First-Level Hospital: Carrot-and-Carrot and Carrot-and-Stick Methods

For the health center, two slightly different performance frameworks are used. Both can be framed as fee-for-service provider payments, conditional on quality. They are called the carrot-and-carrot and the carrot-and-stick methods. The carrot-and-carrot method consists of purchasing

PBF services and adding a bonus (for example, up to 25 percent) for the quality performance. The carrot-and-stick method entails purchasing PBF services but detracting money in case of bad quality performance. When using a carrot-and-stick method, one can inflate the carrots a bit, thereby assuming a certain effect on the quality factor.

Behavioral science teaches that human beings are relatively more sensitive to the fear of losing money than to being offered the prospect of earning more. So theoretically, the carrot-and-stick approach should be the more powerful approach (Mehrotra, Sorbrero, and Damberg 2010; Thaler and Sunstein 2009). In practice, however, different choices are being made. Afghanistan, Benin, Rwanda, and Zambia use the carrot-and-stick method,[1] whereas Burundi, Cameroon, Chad, the Central African Republic, the Democratic Republic of Congo, the Kyrgyz Republic, Nigeria, and Zimbabwe have opted for a carrot-and-carrot approach. Equally, nongovernmental organization (NGO) PBF fund holders also seem to prefer the carrot-and-carrot method, as was the case in the following:

- Rwanda PBF pilot (2002–05)
- Burundi PBF pilot (2006–10)
- Central African Republic PBF pilot (2008 to present)
- Cameroon PBF pilot (2009 to present)
- Democratic Republic of Congo, South Kivu PBF Pilot (2006 to present)
- Flores, Indonesia PBF pilot (2008–11).

Whatever the exact effect, a remarkable feature of both performance frameworks is that they manage two actions at once: (a) to increase the quantity of health services and (b) to increase the quality of those services (Basinga et al. 2011).

Choosing Carrot and Carrot or Carrot and Stick

The main reasons for choosing one or the other method—apart from philosophical considerations and local preferences—are the level of deprivation of health facilities and the availability of alternative sources of cash income. A carrot-and-carrot method (quality as a bonus rather than as a risk) enables health facility managers to better forecast their income—income that in some situations derives predominantly from PBF. A carrot-and-carrot method is therefore advisable in settings in which alternative sources of cash income are limited. Such can be the case in environments with free or selective free health care and in settings in which cash subsidies from the central level are lacking, especially when this setting is aggravated by poor infrastructure, a lack of procedures, and the absence of equipment. In more mature systems—especially those with multiple sources of cash income—one can turn to a carrot-and-stick system.

Differing Effect: Different Scenarios with Carrot and Carrot versus Carrot and Stick

The two PBF approaches, carrot and carrot and the carrot and stick, have a different effect on the earnings of health facilities. They send different signals to the provider. The following example may show how the quality calculus works in practice. Let's start with the formulae for the two approaches, assuming both approaches use the same output budget.

Under the carrot-and-carrot approach, one counts

total payment to health facility = [total quantity payments due]
+ [total quantity payments due * quality score * X%]   (3.1)

where X% is 25%.

Under the carrot-and-stick approach, one calculates

total payment to health facility = [total quantity payments due]
* [quality score %].   (3.2)

In both cases, the quality score can range from 0 percent to 100 percent. Different results occur under a carrot-and-carrot regime when compared with a carrot-and-stick method.

The quality will rarely be 100 percent. If one assumes that under the carrot-and-stick approach the average quality will be 60 percent, then one may inflate unit fees accordingly if working with the same output budget. For the carrot-and-carrot approach, a cut-off point for quality is frequently applied below which a quality bonus is not paid. In the current example, this cut-off point is set at 60 percent.

To show the different effects, three scenarios are demonstrated: Scenario A, in which the total quality scores are 100 percent (tables 3.1 and 3.2); Scenario B, in which the total quality score is 0 percent (tables 3.3 and 3.4); and Scenario C, in which the quality score is 59 percent (tables 3.5 and 3.6). Tables 3.1–3.6 explain what differences may ensue between the carrot-and-carrot and carrot-and-stick approaches. Table 3.7 compares the approaches.

Scenario A: High Quality (100 percent)

Tables 3.1 and 3.2 show the two approaches for Scenario A with the quality scores totaling 100 percent.

TABLE 3.1 Scenario A: The Carrot-and-Carrot Approach

Health facility revenues over the previous period	Number provided	Unit price (US$)	Total earned (US$)
Child fully vaccinated	60	2.00	120.00
Skilled birth attendance	60	18.00	1,080.00
Curative care	1,480	0.50	740.00
Curative care for the vulnerable patient (up to a maximum of 20% of curative consultations)	320	0.80	256.00
Subtotal revenues			**2,196.00**
Remoteness (equity) bonus	+20%		439.00
Quality bonus	100% of 25%		594.00
Total PBF subsidies			**3,184.00**
Other revenues (direct payments: out of pocket, insurance, etc.)			970.00
Total revenues			**4,154.00**
Health facility expenses			
Fixed salaries of staff			800.00
Operational costs			350.00
Drugs and consumables			1,000.00
Outreach expenditures			250.00
Repairs to the health facility			300.00
Savings into health facility bank account			250.00
Subtotal expenses			**2,950.00**
Staff bonuses = total revenues − subtotal of expenses			1,204.00
Total expenses			**4,154.00**

Source: World Bank data.

TABLE 3.2 Scenario A: The Carrot-and-Stick Approach with Unit Prices Inflated, Assuming an Average of 60 Percent Quality[a]

Health facility revenues over the previous period	Number provided	Unit price (US$)	Total earned (US$)
Child fully vaccinated	60	3.33	200.00
Skilled birth attendance	60	30.00	1,800.00
Curative care	1,480	0.83	1,228.00
Curative care for the vulnerable patient (up to a maximum of 20% of curative consultations)	320	1.33	425.00
Subtotal revenues			**3,653.00**
Remoteness (equity) bonus	+20%		731.00
Quality stick	100%		
Total PBF subsidies (4,384.00*100% = 4,384.00)			**4,384.00**
Other revenues (direct payments: out of pocket, insurance, etc.)			970.00
Total revenues			**5,354.00**
Health facility expenses			
Fixed salaries of staff			800.00
Operational costs			350.00
Drugs and consumables			1,000.00
Outreach expenditures			250.00
Repairs to the health facility			300.00
Savings into health facility bank account			250.00
Subtotal expenses			**2,950.00**
Staff bonuses = total revenues – subtotal of expenses			2,404.00
Total expenses			**5,354.00**

Source: World Bank data.

a. In this particular method, the prices are inflated as the quality measure affects the earnings. A higher price can therefore be offered while staying within the budget.

Scenario B: Very Low Quality (0 percent)

A quality of 0 percent is a purely fictitious situation. However, depending on the context, a quality as low as 20 percent sometimes appears in practice (see tables 3.3 and 3.4). Most of the time, health facilities in such a state also have a very low volume of services. The two aspects—quantity and quality—tend to go hand in hand.

TABLE 3.3 Scenario B: The Carrot-and-Carrot Approach

Health facility revenues over the previous period	Number provided	Unit price (US$)	Total earned (US$)
Child fully vaccinated	60	2.00	120.00
Skilled birth attendance	60	18.00	1,080.00
Curative care	1,480	0.50	740.00
Curative care for the vulnerable patient (up to a maximum of 20% of curative consultations)	320	0.80	256.00
Subtotal revenues			**2,196.00**
Remoteness (equity) bonus	+20%		439.00
Quality bonus	0%		0.00
Total PBF subsidies			**2,635.00**
Other revenues (direct payments: out of pocket, insurance, etc.)			970.00
Total revenues			**3,605.00**
Health facility expenses			
Fixed salaries of staff			800.00
Operational costs			350.00
Drugs and consumables			1,000.00
Outreach expenditures			250.00
Repairs to the health facility			300.00
Savings into health facility bank account			250.00
Subtotal expenses			**2,950.00**
Staff bonuses = total revenues − subtotal of expenses			655.00
Total expenses			**3,605.00**

Source: World Bank data.

TABLE 3.4 Scenario B: The Carrot-and-Stick Approach

Health facility revenues over the previous period	Number provided	Unit price (US$)	Total earned (US$)
Child fully vaccinated	60	3.33	200.00
Skilled birth attendance	60	30.00	1,800.00
Curative care	1,480	0.83	1,228.00
Curative care for the vulnerable patient (up to a maximum of 20% of curative consultations)	320	1.33	425.00
Subtotal revenues			**3,653.00**
Remoteness (equity) bonus	+20%		731.00
Quality stick	0%		0.00
Total PBF subsidies (earnings * 0 = 0)			**0.00**
Other revenues (direct payments: out of pocket, insurance, etc.)			970.00
Total revenues			**970.00**
Health facility expenses			
Fixed salaries of staff			800.00
Operational costs			0.00
Drugs and consumables			170.00
Outreach expenditures			0.00
Repairs to the health facility			0.00
Savings into health facility bank account			0.00
Subtotal expenses			**970.00**
Staff bonuses = total revenues – subtotal of expenses			0.00
Total expenses			**970.00**

Source: World Bank data.

Scenario C: Average Quality (of 59 percent)

In Scenario C, tables 3.5 and 3.6 use a quality score of 59 percent to show differences that may occur between the carrot-and-carrot and the carrot-and-stick approaches. Table 3.7 compares the three scenarios.

TABLE 3.5 Scenario C: The Carrot-and-Carrot Approach with 60 Percent Cut-off Point for Paying Bonus

Health facility revenues over the previous period	Number provided	Unit price (US$)	Total earned (US$)
Child fully vaccinated	60	2.00	120.00
Skilled birth attendance	60	18.00	1,080.00
Curative care	1,480	0.50	740.00
Curative care for the vulnerable patient (up to a maximum of 20% of curative consultations)	320	0.80	256.00
Subtotal revenues			**2,196.00**
Remoteness (equity) bonus	+20%		439.00
Quality bonus	<60% = 0%		0.00
Total PBF subsidies			**2,635.00**
Other revenues (direct payments: out of pocket, insurance, etc.)			970.00
Total revenues			**3,605.00**
Health facility expenses			
Fixed salaries of staff			800.00
Operational costs			350.00
Drugs and consumables			1,000.00
Outreach expenditures			250.00
Repairs to the health facility			300.00
Savings into health facility bank account			250.00
Subtotal expenses			**2,950.00**
Staff bonuses = total revenues − subtotal of expenses			655.00
Total expenses			**3,605.00**

Source: World Bank data.

TABLE 3.6 Scenario C: The Carrot-and-Stick Approach

Health facility revenues over the previous period	Number provided	Unit price (US$)	Total earned (US$)
Child fully vaccinated	60	3.33	200.00
Skilled birth attendance	60	30.00	1,800.00
Curative care	1,480	0.83	1,228.00
Curative care for the vulnerable patient (up to a maximum of 20% of curative consultations)	320	1.33	425.00
Subtotal revenues			**3,653.00**
Remoteness (equity) bonus	+20%		731.00
Quality stick	59%		
Total PBF subsidies (4,384 * 59% = 2,587)			**2,587.00**
Other revenues (direct payments: out of pocket, insurance, etc.)			970.00
Total revenues			**3,557.00**
Health facility expenses			
Fixed salaries of staff			800.00
Operational costs			350.00
Drugs and consumables			1,000.00
Outreach expenditures			250.00
Repairs to the health facility			300.00
Savings into health facility bank account			250.00
Subtotal expenses			**2,950.00**
Staff bonuses = total revenues − subtotal of expenses			607.00
Total expenses			**3,557.00**

Source: World Bank data.

TABLE 3.7 Comparison of Scenarios A, B, and C

Scenario	Quality (%)	Carrot-and-carrot approach, provider earnings (US$)	Carrot-and-stick approach, provider earnings (US$)	Conclusion
Scenario A	100	4,154.00	5,354.00	Under higher quality, higher earnings for providers under a carrot-and-stick regime
Scenario B	0	3,605.00	970.00	Under 0 (very low) quality, higher earnings under a carrot-and-carrot regime and very low earnings under a carrot-and-stick regime
Scenario C	59	3,605.00	3,557.00	In situations of average quality, about equal earnings under both regimes

Source: World Bank data.

Conclusions and Implications

Three main conclusions can be drawn from those practical scenarios:

- In situations of very high quality, the carrot-and-stick method leads to more money for the best-performing health facilities.
- When quality levels are very low, the carrot-and-carrot method better protects basic health facilities' income while penalizing low-quality, low-volume health facilities.
- When the quality level is average, both methods lead to similar income levels.

The findings have important implications:

- When cash sources of income are diversified and PBF is just one of several sources of cash income in a given health facility, the carrot-and-stick method might be preferable. PBF will leverage all other sources of cash income, too, and direct them to maximizing quantity and quality of services. Such situations become more quality driven.
- When the only cash stems from PBF income, the carrot-and-carrot method might be preferable. It will protect the basic income of the facility (by paying for the volume of services) and, at the same time, provide the additional resources to increase quantity and to fight low quality of services. Such situations are more quantity driven.

3.3 Quality Tools: How Quality Is Paid for through PBF

Tools Travel

PBF has distinct quality tools for the performance measures related to the minimum or basic package of health services in health centers, on the one hand, and for the complementary package of health services for first-level referral hospitals on the other. The tools for the health centers have their origin in the NGO fund holder PBF approaches (see Soeters 2012). The quality tools for the hospital can be traced to the quantified quality checklists used by the Belgian Technical Cooperation PBF pilot in Rwanda (Rusa et al. 2009). In the incremental development of those tools, several phases of change can be distinguished. Tools appear to travel.

- The Kyrgyz rayon hospital's quantified quality checklist and balanced scorecard found its origin in the Rwandese district hospital checklist that included peer evaluation.

- The Benin health center quality checklist drew inspiration from the Burundi health center quality tools.
- The Burundi health center and hospital quality checklists drew their inspiration from the Rwandese quality checklists.
- The Nigerian quality assessment tools are based on eclectic sources (NGO fund holder PBF approach and Rwandese and Burundi tools) adapted to the local context (box 3.1).

BOX 3.1

Nigerian Quantified Quality Checklist

The Nigerian quantified quality checklist for health centers is used in the states of Adamawa, Nasarawa, and Ondo. It contains 15 services among which 249 points are allocated for 162 mostly composite indicators. Each indicator is weighted individually for a certain number of points. The summary scores are in table B3.1.1.

The Nigerian checklist has been sculpted to reflect priority issues relevant to quality of care at the health center level in Nigeria. There is a large emphasis on management of essential drugs, minimal stock levels, and rational prescribing. A few examples of these indicators are shown in tables B3.1.2–B3.1.4.

TABLE B3.1.1 Nigerian Quantified Quality Checklist

No	Service	Points	Weight %
1	General Management	11	4.4
2	Business Plan	9	3.6
3	Finance	10	4.0
4	Indigent Committee	7	2.8
5	Hygiene	25	10.0
6	OPD	34	13.7
7	Family Planning	22	8.8
8	Laboratory	10	4.0
9	Inpatient Wards	10	4.0
10	Essential Drugs Management	20	8.0
11	Tracer Drugs	30	12.0
12	Maternity	21	8.4
13	EPI	18	7.2
14	ANC	12	4.8
15	HIV/TB	249	100.0

Source: See the links to files in this chapter.

Note: "No" refers to the number of a service. ANC = antenatal care; EPI = expanded program on immunization; HIV = human immunodeficiency virus; OPD = outpatient department; TB = tuberculosis.

TABLE B3.1.2 Example from the Outpatient Department Section, Nigerian Quantified Quality Checklist

6.16	Proportion of outpatient visits treated with antibiotics <30%		
6.16.1	See last 100 cases in register, check diagnosis and calculate the rate (< 30 cases).	4	0

Source: See the links to files in this chapter.

TABLE B3.1.3 Example from the Essential Drugs Management Section, Nigerian Quantified Quality Checklist

10.3	Main pharmacy store delivers drugs to health facility departments according to requisition		
10.3.1	Supervisor verifies whether quantity requisitioned equals quantity served.		
10.3.2	Drugs to clients are uniquely dispensed through prescriptions. Prescriptions are stored and accessible.	10	0
10.3.3	Drugs and medical consumables prescribed are all in generic form.		

Source: See the links to files in this chapter.

TABLE B3.1.4 Example from the Tracer Drugs Section, Nigerian Quantified Quality Checklist

11	Tracer Drugs (min. stock = Monthly Av. Consumption/2) [max 30 points]	Available YES > MAC/2	Available NO < MAC/2
11.1	Paracetamol 500 mg tab	1	0

Source: See the links to files in this chapter.

Tools Evolve

Initially, there were considerable disagreements between health reform actors on how "quality" should be made operational. During the PBF scaling-up processes in Rwanda and Burundi, the fiercest disagreements revolved around the quality measures. Although the quantified quality checklist was pioneered in 2002, using it for a positive effect on PBF payments long remained a novelty in many places. The checklist's evidence base, therefore, is still being built.

Despite this slow evolution, the applicability and appropriateness of checklists is being demonstrated by the mounting successful uses across many low-income and low-middle-income countries. The nationwide application of the tool in Rwanda from 2006 onward led to significant positive results on quality documented in a rigorous impact evaluation. This finding has helped the quantified quality checklist become an element of great importance in PBF design (Basinga et al. 2010; 2011). Similarly, clients have recognized increases in structural quality of care, thus significantly influencing demand (Acharya and Cleland 2000). Rewarding poor country hospitals for adhering to treatment protocols decreased morbidity and mortality in Guinea-Bissau (Biai et al. 2007).

Thus, PBF quantified quality checklists are not static instruments. They evolve. They originated in compilations of routine supervisory forms used in low-income district health systems. Various elements of the forms were gradually made to conform to SMART quality indicators and became objectively verifiable. They evolved by incorporating standard supervisory forms, for example, in the expanded program on immunization or family planning or in the maternal and child health services. They were made quantifiable, meaning that the variables could be counted in a nonarbitrary manner (possibly with 0 or 1). In addition, variables received a weight, which quantified the relative (subjective) importance from one set of variables to another. Basic checklists were tested in practice for years, and valuable feedback was incorporated from end users.

In Rwanda, during the final quarter of each year, a special working group (drawn from technicians from the extended team and mandated by the latter; see chapter 14) incorporates feedback from end users and observations made by the technical teams in the field. Then, in the first quarter of every following year, a slightly modified checklist is introduced. Generally, this modification leads to a brief drop of the quality results across the country. Then, while people adjust to the new conditions, results increase over the course of the year, and the cycle begins again. Quality performance can constantly be improved. The flexibility of the tool is considerable: it can include any important treatment protocol, norms, and standards as they become available. However, rewarding quality through quantified checklists has its limitations. Checklists measure certain dimensions of quality quite reliably, such as inputs and accreditation. Other dimensions, however, cannot be captured easily, because of nonverifiability, lack of time, or financial constraints. To foster quality in the system, the PBF tool should be complemented by other strategies.

3.4 Design Tips for the Quantified Quality Checklist

When choosing a checklist for your country, select one of the examples provided in section 3.5, and use it as the starting point of a consultative process.

Choosing Measures for the Quantified Quality List

The type of measures that you include in the list depends on local circumstances, such as the following:

- What is the size of the health facility, the number and type of professional staff members, and the number of services?
- What is the level of sophistication of the service delivery network? Consider the following types of protocols already in use:
  - → In Benin, for instance, the Burundi quality checklist was adapted to the Benin context. That checklist was less complex than the Rwandese checklist.
  - → In Zambia, a modified and much simplified version of the Rwandese checklist was adapted to local realities.
- Is the health facility run down? If so, the primary focus should be on physical infrastructure—water, electricity, latrines, and hygiene and equipment measures. The importance of improving basic elements can be flagged through the weighing mechanism. Later on, more sophisticated measures can be added.

Nine Points to Consider

Consider the following nine points when choosing a checklist:

- Always keep in mind the end users of the quality checklists. They are district or hospital supervisors. Use appropriate, accessible language, and format the list for them. If designed well, the checklist will be quite educational.
- Ensure that the criteria are objectively verifiable. The checklist will generate a single composite quality score that will be used to determine the performance rewards. Ensure that when a counterverification takes place (that is, the verification of the verified results), the repeated score will be more or less the same as the original (see box 3.2).
- Remember that some clinically desirable quality variables may be quite useless as objectively verifiable PBF indicators; they are non-PBF SMART. The verification methodology in PBF limits itself to the types of indicators or services that one can purchase effectively, efficiently, and credibly.
- Do not oversimplify the checklist or make it too easy. Health staff members can appreciate being held to standards. You do not need to hold them to all standards at once, but at least make them accountable for those that matter the most.
- Remember that one of the systemic effects of the quantified quality checklists is a significantly increased exposure time between members of

Important Message

Because the primary verification of quality is done through the district health administration (in the case of health center quality assessments) or peer evaluators (in the case of hospital quality assessments), there is an incomplete separation of functions (see chapter 11). Experience shows that when there are no counterverification measures, the results might become less reliable as time progresses. A credible counterverification, which leads to visible action in case of discrepancies between the ex ante and the ex post verifications, is important (figure B3.2.1).

FIGURE B3.2.1 Difference between Ex Ante and Ex Post Verification of the Quality in Burundi District Hospitals during 2011

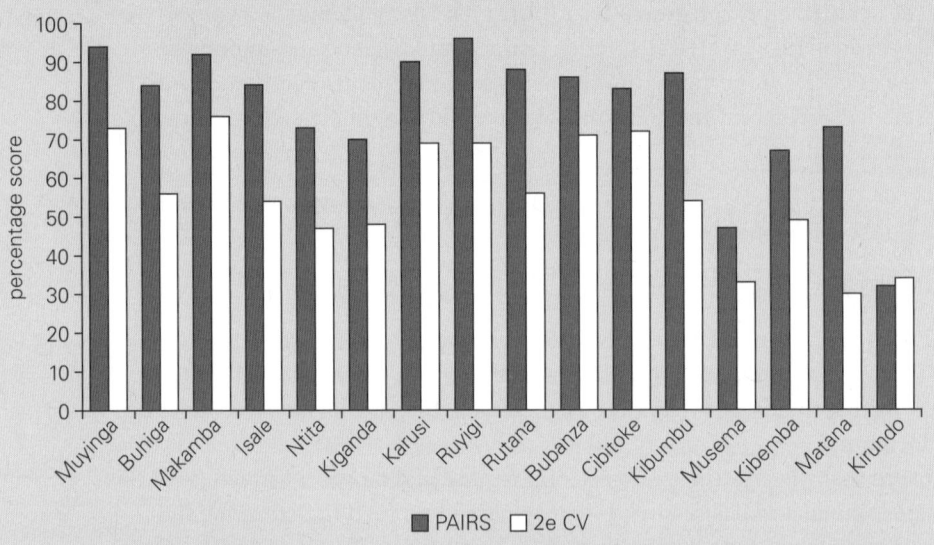

Source: Burundi, Ministry of Health 2011.

Note: "PAIRS" refers to the evaluation done by the peers (ex ante verification). "2e CV" refers to the counterverification done by a third party (ex post verification). The x-axis has the names of the hospitals, and the y-axis is the percentage score from the quantified quality checklist.

the health staff and their supervisors. Configure the checklists to promote this as quality time. Because supervisors are under a performance framework that links a large share of their performance earnings to the correct and timely execution of the quality assessment function, they will take this work seriously. In turn, frontline health staff members frequently report they are pleased with increased exposure time, which provides them better feedback on their work (Kalk, Paul, and Grabosch 2010).

- Use the modified Delphi technique (see chapter 1), for finalizing the design of the quality checklist. The technique will make designing the checklist much easier, and it will maximize transparency in the decision-making process for allocating the general weights to the various components and subcomponents.
- Test the checklist to document interobserver and intraobserver reliability.
- Pilot the checklist in a limited number of facilities to fine-tune it.
- Update the checklists regularly (for example, once a year), and involve the end users (technical assistants, district health staff members, and heads of facilities).

Counterverification Is Necessary

Paying a considerable reward for quality performance has far-reaching implications. You will need to take into account separation of functions (see chapters 2 and 11). In reporting quality performances, you are wise to secure some counterverification mechanisms. Lessons from the field make it clear that if you do not counterverify reported quality performance, the reports easily become unreliable. To counterverify, use random elements of randomly selected checklists.

3.5 Differing Contexts: Different Examples of Quality Checklists

The following quantified quality checklists are provided as examples. They can be accessed in the web links to files in this chapter (see section 3.6). A multitude of performance measures exists, each with its own rationale. Here we present a short description of the various contexts in which the tools were designed and implemented.

- NGO fund holder PBF approach for health centers
- Rwandese health center PBF approach
- Rwandese district hospital PBF approach
- Burundi health center PBF approach
- Burundi district hospital PBF approach
- Zambian health center PBF approach
- Kyrgyz Republic rayon hospital PBF approach.

To understand an individual quality tool in detail, study its operations manuals and talk extensively to the implementers (see chapters 14 and 15).

NGO Fund Holder Health Center

The NGO fund holder PBF approach is a common form of the private purchaser PBF approach (see chapter 11).

- This quality tool is used in the NGO fund holder PBF approach at the level of the health center and minimum package of health services.
- The quality tool is contracted on a performance basis to the regulatory authority. Depending on the context, the regulatory authority can be the first-level referral hospital or the district health management team. In principle, the regulatory authority must be a ministry of health (MoH) organization.
- The correct and timely execution of the quarterly checklist in all the health centers of a district health system is the main determinant of the performance payment to the MoH organization.
- The NGO fund holder PBF approach uses a carrot-and-carrot method. Each quarter, up to 25 percent of the total earnings of the past quarter can be earned as an extra bonus if the quality measure is 100 percent. This quality measure is typically weighted 50 percent for the result of the quarterly quality checklist and 50 percent for results based on a patient satisfaction index obtained through community client surveys.

The tool shows the 15 components of the quality questionnaire used in the Cordaid PBF pilot. See the links to files in this chapter.

Rwandese Health Center

The Rwandese health center's quarterly quality checklist was constructed in early 2006 from the tool originally used in the NGO fund holder PBF approach. The checklist has since been amended annually (changes for 2008–11). In the links to files in this chapter, the 2008–11 versions are provided. The 2008 version is the last version that was substantially edited. After 2008, it underwent only minor changes.

The Rwandese health center PBF model uses a carrot-and-stick method. Each quarter, a quality score is applied to the earnings of the previous quarter. The earnings are discounted by the score. This method has a strong and documented effect on the performance gap, the gap between what providers know is best practice and what they actually do (Gertler and Vermeersch 2012). Similarly, it affects the quality as measured through instruments at the health center level (Basinga et al. 2011). See the links to files in this chapter.

Ship To:

VINDY-BXC-Store - 22314329y-1
35 SW 12th Avenue, Ste 102
22314329-Y
Dania Beach, FL 33004

Buyer PO #: 22314329y-1

Order ID: 113-4707114-0244254

Thank you for buying from EMS Media on Amazon Marketplace.

Shipping Address:	Order Date:	Thu, Mar 19, 2026
VINDY-BXC-Store	Shipping Service:	Standard
35 SW 12th Avenue, Ste 102	Buyer Name:	RB
22314329-Y	Seller Name:	EMS Media
Dania Beach, FL 33004		

Quantity	Product Details
1	**Performance-Based Financing Toolkit [Paperback] [2014] Fritsche, György Bèla; Soeters, Robert; Meessen, Bruno** **SKU:** S58-Q7K-QRE-DK1 **ASIN:** 1464801282 **Condition:** Used - Very Good **Order Item ID:** 156153879347521 **Condition note:** S58. New, but with sticker on cover.

Returning your item:

Go to "Your Account" on Amazon.com, click "Your Orders" and then click the "seller profile" link for this order to get information about the return and refund policies that apply.

Visit https://www.amazon.com/returns to print a return shipping label. Please have your order ID ready.

Thanks for buying on Amazon Marketplace. To provide feedback for the seller please visit www.amazon.com/feedback. To contact the seller, go to Your Orders in Your Account. Click the seller's name under the appropriate product. Then, in the "Further Information" section, click "Contact the Seller."

Rwandese District Hospital

The Rwandese district hospital PBF approach was developed in July 2006 from a mix of previous experiences of the Rwanda PBF pilot projects. It drew on the Belgian Technical Cooperation tool, which was used earlier in hospital evaluations, and modified the tool. The Rwandese approach used the peer evaluation concept that had been piloted by the NGO fund holder PBF approach (Rwanda and Ministry of Health 2006). The Rwandese approach became well documented.

The two characteristic aspects of this particular PBF approach are (a) the weighting and financing and (b) the peer evaluation concept.

Weighting

In the 2008/09 tool, the weighting amounted to allocating 20 percent to administration, 25 percent to supervision, and 55 percent to clinical activities. All available funds (Rwandese government, U.S. government, German Organisation for Technical Cooperation, and so on) for the purchase of hospital performance in Rwanda were virtually pooled. An allocation mechanism was set up for each district hospital subject to various criteria. Subsequently, fund holders were identified and a hospital performance purchaser that would agree to pay the performance invoice was identified for each hospital. The fund holder would transfer the performance earnings based on the invoice directly into the health facility's bank account.

In this way, an internal market for the purchasing of hospital performance was created. Over the years, entry to and exit from this market have been smoothly coordinated by the central PBF technical support unit. The government has remained the largest purchaser of hospital performance. As was the case with the health center PBF internal market in Rwanda, agencies collaborating with the U.S. government were able to purchase performance on this internal market. This internal market has had tremendous implications for system strengthening, demonstrating how off-budget bilateral funding can be used for such purposes.

Performance budgets could represent up to 30 percent of the cash earnings of a hospital. Hence, they were a significant source of new and additional revenues. Through integrated and autonomous management of resources, PBF contributed to the significant variable earnings of hospital staff. It also allowed hospitals to boost their number of doctors from one to two on average before the reforms (2005) to six to seven per hospital a few years thereafter. Doctors were drawn away not only from Rwanda's capital city, Kigali, but also from labor markets in neighboring countries.

For the 20 percent weighting for administration, the total "staff" weight of staff members present in each hospital was added. (The staff weight is usually based on a certain weight given to a staff category as compared to a base weight).[2]

With regard to supervision staff, the number of health centers that a hospital supervised was taken as the allocation factor. In Rwanda, the supervisors of the health centers tend to be located in the district hospitals, and thus, a supervision "output budget" was allocated to each hospital. This forged an important link between the verification mechanism for the quality performance of the health centers and those at the hospital level. The hospital is paid on a performance basis for the correct and timely execution of supervising the health centers. The performance frameworks of the health center and the hospital are thus linked. This has turned out to be a very effective—and cost-effective—way of implementing PBF. It exemplifies how PBF works as scaled up. A host of other measures related to the supportive function of the hospital toward the lower echelons of the health care system are also incentivized. Those include capacity building activities and the analysis and feedback of health management information system data.

For assessment of clinical activities, 17 clinical services were chosen. The total annual production of those services for the entire country was assessed and a weighting was applied. Matching this assessment with the available budget led to a unit value for each clinical service or activity.

In addition, there was a perceived need to "let the money follow the activity." Therefore, volume-driven performance measures were used for part of the quantified quality checklist.

For each indicator in each category, a certain number of composite criteria were defined that would yield a certain number of performance points, frequently on an all-or-nothing basis. For supervision and administration, the total number of points was fixed, although each hospital had its specific point value (because of differing global prospective performance budgets).

For the clinical activities portion, the volume of activities would drive the number of points to be earned. Yet here too, the points were conditioned on a long list of composite criteria on an all-or-nothing basis. In short, the earnings for the clinical activities were driven by a mix of quantity and quality of services. Earnings could not be increased by boosting only the volume because the composite quality criteria had such a large effect on the performance earnings.

This Rwandese district hospital method is a carrot-and-stick method. (For further explanations, see the Rwandese district hospital PBF manual in the links to files in this chapter.)

Peer Evaluation Concept

Peer evaluation was scaled up after an initial pilot phase. In short, each quarter, three core staff members from three hospitals reviewed a fourth hospital during a peer evaluation session. The core staff normally consisted of the medical director or deputy medical director, the chief nurse or deputy chief nurse, and the administrator or the senior accountant. The peer evaluations were coordinated by the central PBF technical support unit and were made operational by the extended-team mechanism (see chapter 14). Each quarter, a representative from the central MoH and a donor technical agent joined the peer evaluations as an observer.

Participation in peer evaluations (with the composite criteria of "completeness" and "timeliness" on an all-or-nothing basis) was assessed in the performance evaluations of each hospital that participated in the evaluation and weighted. Participation turned out to be 100 percent. The peer evaluation teams tend to consist of about 10–14 peers and observers. They take half a day once every quarter to evaluate one hospital. Normally, the group splits into three subgroups and works in parallel to assess performance measures. They reconvene toward the end of the evaluation and provide feedback in a plenary session to the hospital management and staff on the findings and performance results.

As part of the performance measuring, the hospital staff does an auto-evaluation and follows the same checklist. For this performance measure, the score they find would have to be within a certain range of the score that their peers noted.

Electronic forms were designed with Microsoft InfoPath, a software program that converted into a summary invoice to be sent to the fund holder. Because of the large amount of data (the Rwandese checklist contained about 350 different data elements), effective data analysis remained a major challenge. In addition, the criteria tended to change incrementally each year. A data collection platform developed for such purposes needed the flexibility to integrate such changes smoothly. Therefore, after 2009, the data compilation and analysis program was changed to Microsoft Excel.

The philosophy of the peer evaluation and checklist approaches is based on the understanding that for a hospital to provide good quality care, its microsystems must be fully operational. Systems such as management, hazardous waste disposal, hygiene, maintenance of equipment, and adherence to treatment protocols must be in place. External and internal drug and medical consumable management, quality assurance mechanisms, data analysis, internal capacity building, and "learning by teaching" are also essential and must be functioning for the hospital to provide good quality care.

The Rwandese peer evaluation mechanism includes aspects of accreditation and total quality management or continuous quality improvement mechanisms. It rewards process rather than results. It rewards the presence of a quality assurance team that assesses its own department's performance; sets its own priorities; and follows up on its own identified priorities, rather than outcomes, such as lower mortality rates. The Rwandese peer review philosophy is that medical professionals and managers are responsible for—and are rewarded for—introducing reviewing mechanisms and that the successes or failures of a system are a professional responsibility.

Interestingly, the peer reviews often boost coordination and communication within departments and between departments and management. This is in line with current cutting-edge thinking on quality assurance processes in health care, the vital importance of communication among staff members, and interdepartmental coordination (Gawande 2010; Klopper-Kes et al. 2011; Wauben et al. 2011).

In sum, after a few years of undertaking peer review evaluations, one can observe the following:

- By and large, peer evaluation is perceived as useful by the end users.
- Peer reviews have stimulated significant positive changes in hospital performance in relatively short periods of time.
- At the hospital level, the quantified quality checklist must be changed annually as is done for the health center checklist. This will keep the evaluations dynamic.
- During performance of independent counterevaluations, significant discrepancies have been observed sometimes between the reported and the counterverified results. In conclusion, even with the use of relatively open and transparent verification methods such as a peer evaluation mechanism, biases and active conflicts of interest can arise.

On the basis of this experience, introduce counterverification mechanisms at the outset, stipulate sanctions against fraud clearly in the purchase contracts, and point out these strategies in the various trainings. Another possibility is to use unannounced evaluations instead of planned and programmed ones. See the links to files in this chapter.

Burundi Health Center

The Burundi health center quality checklist is based on the NGO fund holder PBF approach. A mandated task force modified the checklist. Correct and timely execution of the quality assessment is included in the performance framework of the provincial and district health offices. The web-enabled database captures the subelements of the quality checklists and will therefore provide comprehensive comparative data on the various quality features.

The Burundi PBF system is a carrot-and-carrot system. The quality checklist is applied each quarter in each Burundi health center and constitutes 60 percent of the value of the quality bonus (the second carrot). Forty percent of the value of the quality bonus is determined by the quantified results of patient perceptions obtained through the community client surveys. The maximum quality bonus is 25 percent of the earnings over the PBF quantity earnings of the preceding three months. The Benin PBF quality checklist is based on the Burundi health center quality checklist. As Benin began its PBF approach in 2011, it chose the Burundi checklist because that checklist seemed less sophisticated than the Rwandese checklist. Benin will be applying a carrot-and-stick method. For the Burundi health center PBF approach, see the links to files in this chapter.

Burundi District Hospital

The Burundi district hospital quality checklist is based in part on the health center quality checklist and in part on elements drawn from the Rwandese district hospital quality checklist. It is applied through a peer review mechanism, and a third-party counterverification is built into this program (as for all performance frameworks throughout the entire PBF system in Burundi). The quality checklist works through a carrot-and-carrot method. The maximum quality bonus is 25 percent over the PBF quantity earnings of the three preceding months (Burundi and Ministry of Health 2010). See the links to files in this chapter.

Zambian Health Center

The Zambian health center quality checklist has been created from the Rwandese health center quality checklist. However, it has been modified and simplified extensively. The Zambian health center, on average, has a lower number of qualified staff members compared to the Rwandese health center. The checklist was field tested in the Katete district PBF before the pilot project began.

The Zambian quality checklist works through a carrot-and-stick method; the earnings from the preceding three months are discounted by the quality score obtained. The timely and correct application of this checklist has been contracted on a performance basis to the district hospital.

The Zambian PBF design, a contracting-in PBF approach, was rolled out as a pilot through a significant part of the Zambian districts in 2012. A rigorous impact evaluation has been planned. See the links to files in this chapter.

Kyrgyz Republic Rayon Hospital

The Kyrgyz Republic first-level referral hospital (rayon hospital) PBF approach is based on the Rwandese district hospital PBF approach (box 3.3). Criteria have been adapted to fit the Kyrgyz Republic context.

The Kyrgyz Republic faces problems of relatively high maternal and infant mortality figures. The country has an elaborate service delivery network and a fairly well-established public health system with good coverage of basic essential services. Vaccination coverage is nearing 100 percent, and all deliveries take place at the first-level referral hospital or at higher

---

BOX 3.3

Total Quality Management and Quality Assurance Indicators for the Kyrgyz Republic PBF Approach

Table B3.3.1 provides some examples of the indicators used in the Kyrgyz Republic PBF approach.

Table B3.3.1 Examples of Total Quality Management and Quality Assurance Indicators, Balanced Scorecard for Kyrgyz Republic Rayon Hospitals

20	4.2	Departmental Quality Assurance Groups [80]			
		Composite: The following criteria should be met: the QA group exist in <u>each of the four</u> departments (Gyn/Obs, Ped/Internal, Surgery, Infectious Diseases) and the monthly minutes contain:	Yes	No	Score
		[Decision Rule]: all or nothing for 3 reports for each of the four department (12 valid reports in total): if *n* department QA group fails then (4-*n*/4) score			
4.2.1		Description of the activities that were implemented in the previous month to achieve quality improvements			
4.2.2		Evaluation of the quality improvements			
4.2.3		Conclusions, decisions, and recommendations for quality improvements			
4.2.4		Written proof of transmission to the hospital QA committee of the conclusions, decisions, and instructions related to quality improvements			

Source: See the links to files at the end of this chapter.

Note: GYN/OBS = Gynecology and Obstetrics; Ped = Pediatric; QA = quality assurance.

---

levels of the echelon. Stakeholders agree that the relatively high maternal and infant mortality rates are due to low quality of care in the hospitals. These hospitals suffer from a lack of maintenance, poor access to blood, and a paucity of modern protocols and procedures. Informal payments are common in post–Soviet Union health systems (Aarva et al. 2009), and in the Kyrgyz Republic, about 50 percent of clients are estimated to make informal payments to staff and for drugs (Kyrgyz Republic and Ministry of Health 2008, 31).

The PBF was scheduled to be field tested in one district and then rolled out through a significant part of the delivery network in 2013. A rigorous impact evaluation is planned. It will use responses by civil society for a basis for capacity building and for transparency purposes. It will also use the peer evaluation mechanism.

In addition, the Kyrgyz Republic hospitals have a fair degree of autonomy. About one-third of their cash revenues are driven by volume (payment by the Mandatory Health Insurance Fund [MHIF] based on the number of treated cases and adjusted for the diagnosis-related group type and certain other variables). The PBF payments will be added to this payment mechanism through a carrot-and-carrot method. The MHIF quality department staff will also be closely involved in the peer evaluation mechanisms. See the links to files in this chapter.

3.6 Links to Files and Tools

The following toolkit files can be accessed through this web link: http://www.worldbank.org/health/pbftoolkit/chapter03.

- Quantified quality checklists of the following
  - Rwandese district hospital PBF approach (2008, 2010)
  - Rwandese health center PBF approach (2008, 2009, 2010, 2011)
  - Burundi district hospital PBF approach (2010, 2011)
  - Burundi health center PBF approach (2010, 2011)
  - NGO fund holder PBF approach for health centers (2011)
  - Nigerian district hospital PBF approach (2011)
  - Nigerian health center PBF approach (2011)
  - Kyrgyz Republic rayon hospital PBF approach (2012)
  - Zambian health center PBF approach (2012).
- Rwandese district hospital PBF manual (2009).

Notes

1. Zambia will be transitioning to a carrot-and-carrot approach.
2. Allocating budget based on historic staffing patterns or number of beds is fraught with problems. However, Rwanda already had significant decentralizing of human resource policy. Thus, the health facilities had been made much more autonomous, and about one-half of all staff members were contract workers who were paid from the hospital's revenues. This initial staff benchmarking, based on 2007 staffing data for the 2008 PBF tool, was kept constant afterward, and managers could not influence their future expense budgets by increasing the numbers of their staff.

References

Aarva, P., I. Ilchenko, P. Gorobets, and A. Rogacheva. 2009. "Formal and Informal Payments in Health Care Facilities in Two Russian Cities, Tyumen and Lipetsk." *Health Policy and Planning* 24 (5): 395–405.

Acharya, L. B., and J. Cleland. 2000. "Maternal and Child Health Services in Rural Nepal: Does Access or Quality Matter More?" *Health Policy and Planning* 15 (2): 223–29.

Barnum, H., and J. Kutzin, eds. 1993. *Public Hospitals in Developing Countries: Resource Use, Cost, Financing.* Baltimore: Johns Hopkins University Press.

Barnum, H., J. Kutzin, and H. Saxenian. 1995. "Incentives and Provider Payment Methods." *International Journal of Health Planning and Management* 10 (1): 23–45.

Basinga, P., P. Gertler, A. Binagwaho, A. Soucat, J. Sturdy, and C. Vermeersch. 2010. "Paying Primary Health Care Centers for Performance in Rwanda." Policy Research Working Paper 5190, World Bank, Washington, DC.

Basinga, P., P. Gertler, A. Binagwaho, A. Soucat, J. Sturdy, and C. Vermeersch. 2011. "Effect on Maternal and Child Health Services in Rwanda of Payment to Primary Health-Care Providers for Performance: An Impact Evaluation." *The Lancet* 377 (9775): 1421–28.

Biai, S., A. Rodrigues, M. Gomes, I. Ribeiro, M. Sodemann, F. Alves, and P. Aaby. 2007. "Reduced In-Hospital Mortality after Improved Management of Children under 5 Years Admitted to Hospital with Malaria: Randomised Trial." *British Medical Journal* 335 (7625): 862–65.

Burundi, Ministry of Health. 2010. *Manuel des Procédures pour la mise en œuvre du financement basée sur la performance au Burundi.* Bujumbura: Ministry of Health.

———. 2011. *Synthèse Globale de la Contre Verification du FBP au Burundi (2011–2012).* Bujumbura: Ministry of Health.

Gawande, A. 2010. *The Checklist Manifesto: How to Get Things Right.* New York: Metropolitan Books Henry Holt.

Gertler, P., and C. Vermeersch. 2012. "Using Performance Incentives to Improve Health Outcomes." Policy Research Working Paper WPS6100, World Bank, Washington, DC.

Kalk, A., F. A. Paul, and E. Grabosch. 2010. "'Paying for Performance' in Rwanda: Does It Pay Off?" *Tropical Medicine and International Health* 15 (2): 182–90.

Klopper-Kes, A. H. J., N. Meerdink, C. P. M. Wilderom, and W. V. H. Harten. 2011. "Effective Cooperation Influencing Performance: A Study in Dutch Hospitals." *International Journal for Quality in Health Care* 23 (1): 94–99.

Kyrgyz Republic, Ministry of Health. 2008. "Mid-term Review Report: Manas Taalimi Health Sector Strategy." Ministry of Health, Bishkek. http://www.un.org .kg/en/publications/article/5-Publications/3483-mid-term-review -report-manas-taalimi-health-sector-strategy (accessed April 23, 2013).

Mehrotra, A., M. Sorbrero, and C. Damberg. 2010. "Using the Lessons of Behavioral Economics to Design More Effective Pay-for-Performance Programs." *American Journal of Managed Care* 16 (7): 497–503.

Rusa, L., W. Janssen, S. van Bastelaere, D. Porignon, J. de Dieu Ngirabega, and W. Vandenbulcke. 2009. "Performance-Based Financing for Better Quality of Services in Rwandan Health Centres: 3-Year Experience." *Tropical Medicine and International Health* 14 (7): 830–37.

Rwanda, Ministry of Health. 2006. Proceedings of a two-day workshop to create a national PBF model for district hospitals, Kigali, January.

Soeters, R. ed. 2012. *PBF in Action: Theory and Instruments—PBF Course Guide.* 4th ed. The Hague: Cordaid-SINA.

Thaler, R. H., and C. R. Sunstein. 2009. *Nudge: Improving Decisions About Health, Wealth, and Happiness.* New York: Penguin Books.

Wauben, L. S. G. L., C. M. Dekker-van Doorn, J. D. van Wijngaarden, R. H. Goossens, R. Huijsman, J. Klein, and J. F. Lange. 2011. "Discrepant Perceptions of Communication, Teamwork, and Situation Awareness among Surgical Team Members." *International Journal for Quality in Health Care* 23 (2): 159–66.

CHAPTER 4

Setting the Unit Price and Costing

MAIN MESSAGES

→ PBF uses strategic purchasing. The goal is to realize the greatest amount of benefit while effectively managing the costs. In PBF, the purchaser determines from whom to purchase services and for how much. The government determines which services are available to purchase and sets the quality standards.

→ For PBF to succeed, specific health reforms, such as increasing decision rights on financial and human resources, the ability to make a profit, the possibility to pay performance bonuses, and a general strengthening of management, are very important.

→ Using a solid output budget is crucial; more is better than less.

→ Fees are negotiable; the purchaser is able and allowed to renegotiate set fees regularly.

→ PBF uses fee-for-service conditional on quality; this provider-payment mechanism is open at the microlevel and closed at the macrolevel.

4.1 Introduction

How do you cost performance-based financing (PBF) and set fees so that you do not go over your budget? That is the pivotal question around which this chapter revolves. This chapter focuses on the necessary preconditions for a successful PBF intervention, discusses the importance of balancing health facility revenues and expenses, and explains the necessary output budget. The financial effect of quality will also be examined, because it is linked to the total quantity earnings of a health facility. Once the minimum and complementary package of services has been determined, the unit fees can be calculated. A practical example will illustrate the costing methodology.

PBF's fee-for-service provider payment method leads to an increased desire for services. This puts pressure on available budgets. The chapter will, therefore, conclude with a discussion about how to handle these pressures and engage in strategic purchasing.

4.2 Costing Background: PBF as a Health Reform Approach

In PBF, we look at "the forest" before "the trees." In analyzing PBF, consider the whole set of systemic interventions and system reengineering that together generate particular effects (the forest), before the individual incentives or the provider payment mechanism (the trees). As many have emphasized, system thinking is really necessary to understand PBF (de Savigny and Adam 2009; Meessen, Soucat, and Sekabaraga 2011; von Bertalanffy 1969), especially when related to costing.

Performance-based financing is a health reform approach that introduces a specific kind of provider payment—fee-for-service conditional on quality. This approach rewards health facilities for the quantity and quality of health services provided. However, this particular provider payment mechanism is only one dimension of PBF. The whole approach is far more comprehensive and works with multiple performance frameworks at all levels in the health system—from the community client survey groups to the central technical unit in government that steers the implementation and coordination of all efforts. This comprehensive approach entails the following:

- Increasing health facility autonomy
- Stimulating integrated management of funds at the health-facility level
- Promoting autonomous human-resources management and efficient procurement of drugs and medical consumables
- Aiming for strategic purchasing of essential services and continuously increasing the standards for quality performance (see section 4.6 in this chapter).
- Fostering management by results and also providing the incremental funding needed to carry out these results (increasing service volume and quality of services)
- Introducing new forms of governance and accountability by involving community members and civil society in health facility boards and in district PBF steering committees, and by publishing quantity and quality performance of health facilities; gathering formal feedback on client satisfaction and informing public officials and health facilities on these perceptions are vital elements of a PBF system
- Strengthening the stewardship function of government by creating capacity for data analysis at all levels of the health system and providing assistance
- Ensuring that the data on cost-effectiveness of health packages and the quantity and quality results assist policy makers in their allocation decisions.

The health systemic changes necessary to make PBF successful can be fundamental and challenging. In reality, many reforms are initiated by working from experience, responding to pressures on the ground, and then discussing the enabling environments for PBF. Often PBF starts with a pilot program. A successful PBF pilot program in designated districts or provinces accumulates data needed to promote the necessary changes for the system at large. Frontline health workers, managers, and district health officials of successful PBF pilot programs are often the most fervent proponents. They become the real PBF advocates and champions and turn PBF into an opportunity that is difficult for decision makers to refuse.

4.3 The Importance of Balancing Health Facility Revenues and Expenses

In low-income countries, public health facilities, especially in the basic echelons of the system, rarely manage cash. Or if they do, such as fees for consultations or specific procedures, health facilities have to submit such revenues to a higher-level administrative agency. For example, drug revolving funds based on the Bamako Initiative have generated revenues that could be managed at the health-facility level. But in most of those cases, the facility's decision rights on these resources were put in the hands of higher-level administrators who had to sign off on virtually all of the expenses.

PBF starts from the assumption that there is a financing gap at the health-facilities level. This financing gap is not always immediately visible. But there is a plethora of signs and symptoms hinting at its existence. They range from staff absenteeism, double practice, moonlighting, drug shortages, drug pilfering, irrational prescribing, and polypharmacy (frequently linked to alternative-income-generating activities) to lack of hygiene, poor facility maintenance, low volume of services in general, and low quality of care.

PBF systems attempt to address these problems by tackling the financing gap. In essence, PBF intervention is defined as *injecting performance-based cash into the facility while increasing local decision rights on all financial and productive resources, and also strengthening local accountability and oversight mechanisms*. In addition, enhanced formative supervision and intense monitoring for quantity and quality results have become integral aspects of PBF. The main tools in PBF are, therefore, related to cash.

The key management support and coaching instruments are tools related to managing cash income and expenditure (indice tool, see chapter 6); strategies to increase quantity and quality of services (business plan, see chapter 10); and individual staff performance assessments (see chapter 10). Regular and rigorous external performance assessments of both the quantity and the quality of services follow, as does pay for staff performance.

In a PBF health facility, the combined amount of cash revenue from all different sources needs to be sufficient to keep increasing both quantity and quality of health services. Through PBF, health workers become stakeholders in their own health facilities and social entrepreneurs—they work on behalf of public health goals, yet have a stake in the financial viability of their institution. If revenues are too low compared to expenditures, new sources of revenue should be found or expenses should be reduced. When aiming to achieve activities of higher quality standards, the health facility requires more revenue. A balance between revenues and expenses is needed.

Another concern in trying to balance revenues and expenses arises if health facilities are forced to provide free or nominal health services when sufficient third-party payments are not available to compensate for lost revenues. The total health facility revenues should be able to provide quality and equitable health services and to pay staff members remuneration sufficient to cover their basic needs (see also public choice theory and Maslow's pyramid of needs [Maslow 1943]). This leads to two practical dictums: (a) staff members must be offered an incentive package compelling enough for them to stay; and (b) any provider obligation dictated by politics, such as free health care, must be compensated to be sustainable.

4.4 The Necessary Budget

For a PBF output budget to be effective, the calculations must address the financing gap. An output budget inaccurately configured may lead to insufficient effects and major disappointments.

One needs an accurate approximation of how much output budget is necessary to plug the financing gap. For that, the earnings of the health facility must be considered. They include all cash for the recurrent and investment costs necessary for the facility to function. In addition, an estimate of how many additional resources would be needed for variable bonuses used to bring the take home salary of health workers to acceptable levels is also needed. Containing the health worker earnings gap is key: the approximate amount to be paid through performance results to health workers must be found. This earnings gap notion is a vague concept. It might be helpful in the early design stages to commission studies to learn how much health workers actually earn from additional sources of income. Find out how much income would be necessary for health workers to sustain themselves in their specific locations.

The take-home salary of health workers is fundamental to the budget. The bonuses gained through PBF are the variable element of their remuneration.[1] The bonus percentage variable is very dependent on location. Getting this element approximately correct is of paramount importance. The following are a few examples:

- In Ghana, health workers earn fair salaries. The expert panel that was composed to propose a certain variable PBF bonus clearly took this situation into account. The panel's advice was to use a modest 15–20 percent of variable income as compared to take-home earnings, while relatively more was planned as allocations to nonbonus recurrent budgets.

- In Rwanda, the size of the PBF bonuses represented 60–100 percent of the base salary of health workers, and in Burundi, 100–200 percent.
- In other locations, such as the Kyrgyz Republic, the bonus is influenced by perceptions of the amount the health system could afford to continue paying.[2] In such cases, two scenarios may arise. On one hand, if staff bonuses decrease in response to perceived sustainability issues, the effect of the PBF intervention could also potentially decrease. This would in turn decrease the sustainability of the intervention by another routing because fewer effects of PBF would be documented, which could negatively influence decision makers and development partners. On the other hand, if interventions have shown significant effects—and explicit links between performance budget and causal pathways for performance are made—this may lead to existing funds being reprogrammed into the performance-based budget and, consequently, enhance sustainability. Substantive performance budgets, backed by causal pathways, could indeed enhance sustainability. It is important to keep such considerations in mind.

Of course, the output budget is not solely for the payment of the variable bonus of staff workers. In the majority of PBF systems, about 50 percent of PBF earnings are commonly used for the staff performance payments while the remainder goes to nonsalary recurrent costs. It all depends on the location and existing financing arrangements. Moreover, financial data have to be assessed from an integrated, systemic point of view. For instance, a rigid civil service with a flawed allocation of human resources may need multiple reforms (see box 4.1) to make PBF function as designed. There are no fixed guidelines on the appropriate size of an output budget. However, a useful rule of thumb in low-income countries is an overall output budget of US$3 per capita per year. Nevertheless, although subsidies for curative care services are part and parcel of PBF approaches, the US$3 per capita per year assumes that the larger part of curative care is paid from personal funds or through a third party in addition to PBF.[3] In middle-income countries or countries with significant infrastructural challenges, a much higher-output budget may be necessary.[4] In practice, the system appears to work if from this amount, about two-thirds is set aside for the health center or community level and one-third for the first-level referral hospital (Fritsche and Vergeer 2010; Soeters, Habineza, and Peerenboom 2006; Soeters et al. 2011).

Decentralizing Human Resource Management to Health Facilities: The Case of Rwanda

In 2005, the Ministry of Health in Rwanda concluded that the central administration of government health facilities and health workers was inefficient. But at the same time, the government did not want to privatize government health facilities. In 2008, management of government health facilities was made autonomous whereby staff recruitment and salary payments became the responsibility of the health facility management. Staff positions were tied to health facilities, and only the highest level of nursing staff (A0) was allocated by central levels. Management of all other human resources was given to the districts. About half of all health facility staff members were contract workers, and a ministerial instruction defined the new rules, whereby health facility staff had to be paid according to the same rules and entitlements, independent from the funding source and independent from status as a civil servant or not. Staff who desired a transfer to another facility would have to apply for this position and could do so only when a position was available in the other facility. The district would also have to vet the transfer.

The government pays only a fixed lump-sum subsidy to each health facility. In general, the subsidy covers the basic salaries of government health staff. But the salaries of contracted health workers and the individual bonus payments to health facility managers come from the variable subsidy payments (through PBF), income from the community-based health insurance reimbursements, and cost-recovery revenues. This policy has had significant effects on human resources for health facilities in a very short period of time. By 2008, qualified staff in rural areas had increased by 90 percent as compared to 2005. The number of doctors increased by 151 percent, and the number of nurses increased by 32 percent. District hospitals on average had 8 medical doctors and 30 nurses by 2008. The numbers of doctors and nurses working for the civil service in the rural areas increased much faster as compared to the capital. Although the number of doctors in the capital increased from 24 to 27, the number of doctors in rural areas increased from 153 to 285 during the same period. And although the number of nurses in the capital decreased from 283 to 254, the number of nurses in the rural areas increased from 3,481 to 4,543 during the same period.

Source: Additional inputs from Dr. Claude Sekabaraga, former Director of Policy and Planning, Rwanda, Ministry of Health.

4.5 Setting of Unit Fees to Stay within Budget

A key feature of PBF design is setting the unit fees for the quantity of services. Keeping expenses within the allocated output budget is an operational priority. In section 4.6, we provide a tested example of how to set unit fees. In section 4.7, we discuss the issue of how to engage in strategic purchasing and remain within the allocated budget.

Important General Characteristics of PBF Output Budgets and Unit Fees

The following are important general characteristics of PBF output budgets:

- A PBF output budget typically covers 3–4 years.
- The fee-for-service PBF provider payment mechanism is open at the microlevel. This means that within the parameters of the purchase contract and the agreed fees, facilities are paid for each contracted service. There is no cap. If facilities produce more services, they are paid for those services.
- The fee-for-service PBF provider payment mechanism is closed at the macrolevel. This means that the output budget for all PBF payments—combined over a given period—is a given.
- PBF output budgets are set at an average per capita basis.
- Within this average, certain regions can be allocated a higher per capita sum because of agreed-upon equity considerations, and other regions can be allocated a lower sum per capita.
- PBF fee setting results in an average agreed-upon set of fees for services. Within regions, certain facilities can be offered a higher set of unit fees, because of rural hardship considerations, while other less disadvantaged regions can be offered a lesser set of unit fees.
- Fees can be changed if necessary. Usually, PBF purchase contracts are written for one year with the specification that fees can be renegotiated quarterly.

PBF as Leverage

The relationship between PBF unit fees and the cost of services is frequently misunderstood. In fact, the actual cost of health services that are provided in health facilities has little to do with a PBF unit fee. PBF works through leveraging. PBF leverages all existing productive assets at a health facility: human resources, buildings, land, equipment, donated drugs and medical consumables, and income (if any exists). In this sense, PBF unit fees are frequently referred to as *unit subsidies,* because they are leverage instruments.

PBF increases the amount of cash available at the health facility, while promoting increased autonomy in the use of all available cash resources. PBF increases the cash revenue of the health facilities that springs from an incremental increase in the supply of these subsidized services. Soon after PBF is implemented, it increases substantially the volume of services provided (see box 4.2 for a simplified example). It also increases the quality of

BOX 4.2

Unit Fee Calculations

A simplified calculation of three services (consultations, deliveries, and family planning [FP]) illustrates the unit fee calculations. Assume that a health center serves a population of 5,000 people. The average public health budget is about US$3 (local currency) per capita per year, which costs the government about US$15,000 per year for this health center. Before PBF, activity levels are about 100 patients per month (0.24 consultations per person per year), with about four infant deliveries each month (23 percent of expected) and four visits by women for family planning each month (4 percent of expected). A few more services are provided for a total of 108 services per month for this facility.

Over a period of time, PBF would inject, on average, about US$2 per capita per year in additional performance-based public financing into this system. The total public financing would be, on average, about US$5 per capita per year, or US$25,000. PBF would raise curative care to 1.5 consultations per person per year, deliveries to 65 percent, and FP to 25 percent over a period of two years. This would be, on average, 625 consultations per month, 13 deliveries per month, and 93 visits for FP services per month. More services could be offered, but just three services are the focus in this example. In total, 713 services are now provided per month. In the pre-PBF case, the average cost is US$15,000/(108*12) = US$11.60 per service. In the PBF case, the average cost is US$25,000/(713*12) = US$2.93 per service. In addition to the increase in volume, the quality also increased from a baseline of 17 percent to an average of 65 percent two years later. This means that every service output was achieved with an increase in quality as well. This result is referred to as *value for money* (OECD 2010).

those services. In the mid- to long-term period, PBF increases the average cost of services as health facilities increase their investment in human resources, infrastructure, and equipment to respond to the challenging quantitative and qualitative performance measures.

This increase in volume of services is a desired effect. PBF subsidies target essential health services that were undersupplied and had a low coverage. Therefore, in the purchasing of services, it is essential to know what to pursue in the interest of public health. Each PBF service should have baselines and targets. For example, in a given location, if on average 4.8 percent of the population is pregnant, at an aggregate level, this leads to a given number of pregnancies each year and to a desirable number of women who could deliver in a health facility that provides good-quality obstetric care. The absolute goal for safe deliveries is 100 percent. In the PBF costing tool (see section 4.6), an assumption could then be built that the share of women delivering in a health facility would have to increase from a low of 16 percent to a target of 65 percent over a three-year period.

Currently, coverage baselines are often compiled from existing data sources such as Demographic and Health Surveys and Multiple Indicator Cluster Surveys. In an ideal world, a specific health needs assessment would have to provide more accurate baselines for a given target population. In well-designed PBF pilot projects, such health needs assessments are carried out and provide accurate information for the purchaser as to the effect of its project. Although the primary intention of such household surveys is to obtain baseline data and to validate the coverage increases suggested by the purchased services, the surveys also function as a rich source of data for additional use as a time series of before-and-after data (Soeters and Kimanuka 2005; Soeters, Musango, and Meessen 2005; Soeters et al. 2011).

In short, setting a baseline and a set of coverage targets for each service and feeding these data into a model allow the purchaser to determine fees and forecast the financial risk related to the fee-for-service provider payment mechanism (see box 4.2). See the links to files in this chapter for various examples of costing for PBF. They include unit fee costing for Rwanda, Burundi, and Nigeria.

4.6 A Tested Example of Costing the Minimum Package of Health Services

Two cases are used to illustrate PBF costing and financial-risk forecasting. The first example, given in this section, displays the basic concepts. The second example, available through the links to files in this chapter (Basic Costing Tool, Explanation of Basic Costing Tool), introduces the *basic costing tool* used by PBF designers to cost out its program. The second example includes costing of overheads related to administration, coaching, verification, and counterverification. The second example will be especially useful to program officers who design a PBF program and to donors who consider financing PBF schemes. The first example draws on the case of Nigeria. The Microsoft Excel file (Nigeria_Costing_Example1.xlsx) is available in the links to files in this chapter.

Nigerian Costing Example

This costing is based on the fee setting and financial-risk forecasting that was used in a PBF pilot project in three districts across three Nigerian states. The main assumptions are stated in the worksheet titled "Key_assumptions," which is available in the Microsoft Excel file. The main assumptions include the following:

- In 2011, the population was 385,242.
- The annual population growth rate is estimated at 3.2 percent.
- There is US$1.80 per capita per year available for the minimum package of activities.
- There is US$0.90 per capita per year available for the complementary package of activities.
- The average quality over 2012 is assumed to reach 60 percent.
- The quality bonus is 25 percent (if 50 percent or higher quality).
- A carrot-and-carrot PBF mechanism is being applied: the amount of money set aside for the quality bonus has been adjusted downward to account for the average quality effect.
- The U.S. dollar (US)–Naira (₦) exchange rate is US$1.00 to ₦157.00.
- The intervention runs for three years.

Prior to starting any costing exercise, you will have determined the following:

- Step 1. The services that you want to purchase (see chapter 1)
- Step 2. The relative weights for your services (see chapter 1)

For this example, steps 1 and 2 have already been determined. Here, only the subsequent steps are discussed:

- Step 3. Determine the number of services to buy each month based on saturated coverage.
- Step 4. Assess the baseline coverage of each service.
- Step 5. Determine the amount of coverage you want to achieve for each service.
- Step 6. Parcel out service coverage increases between baseline and end line.
- Step 7. Set the index fee, and adjust the indices to consume the available budget.
- Step 8. Review the budget allocation across services.

Step 3. Determine the Number of Services to Buy Each Month Based on Saturated Coverage

- Open the second worksheet, titled "ControlPanel_MPA."
- In column B, the minimum package of activities (MPA) is listed. These are services at the health center and community levels.
- In column F, monthly targets are listed (see table 4.1).
- For each of the services in column B, a monthly target is provided in column F. These targets are location specific. In Nigeria, for instance, it is assumed that each inhabitant would have to visit a health facility on average once per

year for curative care. Therefore, the expected target coverage, if 100 percent is reached in 2011 (column G), will yield 32,104 new outpatients (each month's population/12 or 385,242/12 = 32,104 new outpatients). In table 4.1, such targets are provided for each of the 21 services.

- Columns G, H, I, and J contain the actual services per month for 2011, 2012, 2013, and 2014, respectively, when there is full coverage (maximum numbers).

TABLE 4.1 Example of Services and Their Saturated Monthly Targets for the MPA

No.	Indicator/Service MPA	Monthly_Target	Explanation
1	New outpatient consultation	pop/12	A fairly common assumption for Sub-Saharan Africa is a target of one new curative care consultation per inhabitant per year. Set this according to your baseline. In Nigeria, the baselines are very low.
2	New outpatient consultation by an indigent patient	pop/12 * 20%	A maximum of 20% of all new curative consultations will be subsidized using a higher rate (and waiving out-of-pocket payments for this category).
3	Minor surgery	pop/12 * 5%	5% of the population would need some form of minor surgery each year.
4	Arrival of referred patient at the cottage hospital	pop/12 * 1%	1% of the curative care consultations would lead to a referral to a higher level. PBF purchases the proof of the arrival of that referral to the hospital (counter-referral note).
5	Completely vaccinated child	pop/12 * 4.3%	4.3% of this population is children under one year old.
6	Growth monitoring visit for child	pop/12 * 17.1% * 4	17.1% of this population is children ages 11–59 months. PBF purchases a maximum of four "standard visits" per child. (Officially, the guidelines are that such children ought to be seen once per month. PBF purchases one visit each quarter.)
7	2–5 doses of tetanus vaccination of pregnant women	pop/12 * 4.8%	4.8% of this population is pregnant women.
8	Postnatal consultation	pop/12 * 4.8%	4.8% of this population has delivered a child.
9	First ANC visit before 4 months of pregnancy	pop/12 * 4.8%	4.8% of this population needs a first ANC visit at fourth month of pregnancy.
10	ANC standard visit (2–4)	pop/12 * 4.8% * 3	4.8% of this population would need a second, third, and fourth "standard" ("according to protocol") ANC visit. Individual women might come more frequently, but only the standard visits are purchased.
11	Provision of second dose of SP to a pregnant woman	pop/12 * 4.8%	4.8% of this population would need two doses of SP according to protocol; only the second dose is purchased.

Performance-Based Financing Toolkit

TABLE 4.1 *(continued)*

No.	Indicator/Service MPA	Monthly_Target	Explanation
12	Normal delivery	pop/12 * 4.8% * 80%	4.8% of this population would need to deliver in a health facility: 80% does so at the health-center level (10% at the hospital as normal delivery, and 10% at the hospital as a complicated delivery).
13	FP: total of new and existing users of modern FP methods	pop * 22.5%/12 * 25% * 4 * 90%	22.5% of this population is women of reproductive age (16–49 years); the unmet need in this population is 25%; modern family planning methods are purchased (IUD; injection Depo-Provera); during each FP visit, a three-month supply/coverage is provided; 90% will collect this at the health-center level and 10% at the hospital level. So "three-month coverage" is purchased.
14	FP: implants and IUDs	pop * 22.5%/12 * 8% * 90%	22.5% of this population is women of reproductive age (16–49 years); the assumption is that 8% of women would seek an implant or IUD, of which 90% will be offered at the health-center level and 10% at the hospital level.
15	VCT/PMTCT/PIT test	pop/12 * 5%	7% of the population will be tested each year; 5% will be tested at the health-center level.
16	PMTCT: HIV+ mothers and children treated according to protocol	pop/12 * 4.8% * 5% * 90%	5% of all pregnant women are HIV+ (in this population; the exact target will vary between states), and the prevailing protocol is purchased; 90% will receive this at the health-center level and 10% at the hospital level.
17	STD treatment	pop * 5%/12 * 70%	5% of this population is assumed to need treatment for STDs each year, of which 70% is provided at the health-center level.
18	New AFB+ PTB patient	pop/100,000 * 151 * 60%/12	PTB incidence is 151/100,000; 60% is assumed to be diagnosed at the health-center level.
19	PTB patient: completed treatment and cured	pop/100,000 * 151 * 60%/12	100% cure rate is the target, assuming that 60% of new PTB patients are followed through the health-center and community levels.
20	ITN distribution	pop/3/12/4.6 * 2	Each household would need at least two nets (national target); the average household is 4.6 persons; one net lasts three years on average.
21	New family's use of a latrine	pop/3/12/4.6	Each household would need one latrine; average household size is 4.6 persons; one latrine lasts three years.

Source: World Bank data.

Note: AFB+ = acid-fast bacillus positive; ANC = antenatal care; FP = family planning; HIV = human immunodeficiency virus; ITN = insecticide-treated net; IUD = intrauterine device; MPA = minimum package of activities; No. = number; pop = population; PIT = provider-initiated testing for HIV; PMTCT = prevention of mother-to-child transmission of HIV; PBF = performance-based financing; PTB = pulmonary tuberculosis; SP = sulfadoxine/pyrimethamine; STD = sexually transmitted disease; VCT = voluntary counseling and testing for HIV.

Step 4. Assess the Baseline Coverage of Each Service

- Baseline coverages for these services are in column K of the second worksheet, titled "ControlPanel_MPA."
- The coverages are expressed in percentage coverages (see table 4.2).
- For PBF, the entire population in a given geographic area is covered; that is, in an entire district or entire province, rather than in just the coverage area of a health facility.
- In many instances, a baseline has not been established. Ideally, a needs assessment in the target area is necessary (through a household survey); this was not done.
- The model will yield certain productivity as the project starts. This productivity will be the de facto baseline. The model will have to be adapted on the basis of these early figures.

TABLE 4.2 Example of Baseline Coverage of Each Service in 2011

No.	Indicator/Service MPA	Baseline_11	Explanation
1	New outpatient consultation	20.0%	There are an estimated 0.20 consultations per person per year in Nigeria. In the target districts, based on field observations, this is probably about 0.10–0.20 consultations. There is extremely low utilization of public health services.
2	New outpatient consultation by an indigent patient	n/a	On average, 22.5% of Nigeria is indigent (fifth quintile). According to the DHS, there are large variations among the states. However, it is assumed that health facility in-charges will categorize up to 20% in this category. The actual utilization by this category of current services (probably very low) is unknown.
3	Minor surgery	10.0%	It is assumed that 5% of the population would receive some form of minor surgery once per year. For the 35 contracted facilities, this equals about 45 such interventions per facility each month. Assume that 10% of this is currently achieved.
4	Arrival of referred patient at the cottage hospital	10.0%	Of those that are currently being seen and need referral, assume that 50% are actually referred.
5	Completely vaccinated child	19.2%	DHS
6	Growth monitoring visit for child	10.0%	No baseline is available. The amount is an assumption.
7	2–5 doses of tetanus vaccination of pregnant women	45.0%	DHS
8	Postnatal consultation	38.0%	DHS

TABLE 4.2 *(continued)*

No.	Indicator/Service MPA	Baseline_11	Explanation
9	First ANC visit before 4 months of pregnancy	16.0%	DHS (amount seems high)
10	ANC standard visit (2–4)	45.0%	DHS
11	Provision of second dose of SP to a pregnant woman	12.0%	DHS
12	Normal delivery	16.0%	DHS
13	FP: total of new and existing users of modern FP methods	25%	DHS population baseline measure is 9.7%. If unmet need would be satisfied, then 35% would be covered; this is 9.7/35 * 90% = 25%.
14	FP: implants and IUDs	5.0%	The amount is an assumption. (IUD use in rural areas is 0.4%, and implants were not measurable.)
15	VCT/PMTCT/PIT test	n.a.	n.a.
16	PMTCT: HIV+ mothers and children treated according to protocol	n.a.	n.a.
17	STD treatment	n.a.	n.a.
18	New AFB+ PTB patient	n.a.	n.a.
19	PTB: patient completed treatment and cured	n.a.	n.a.
20	ITN distribution	25.0%	Recent survey data (DHS 2008 is 17%)
21	New family's use of a latrine	24.6%	DHS

Source: World Bank data.

Note: AFB+ = acid-fast bacillus positive; ANC = antenatal care; DHS = Demographic and Health Surveys; FP = family planning; HIV = human immunodeficiency virus; ITN = insecticide-treated net; IUD = intrauterine device; MPA = minimum package of activities; No. = number; n.a. = not applicable; n/a = not available; PIT = provider-initiated testing for HIV; PMTCT = prevention of mother-to-child transmission of HIV; PTB = pulmonary tuberculosis; SP = sulfadoxine/pyrimethamine; STD = sexually transmitted disease; VCT = voluntary counseling and testing for HIV.

Step 5. Determine the Amount of Coverage You Want to Achieve for Each Service

- Targets are set for 2012, 2013, and 2014 (see table 4.3).
- For the indigent population, their allocation is set at a maximum of 20 percent of actual new outpatient consultations.
- Field observations confirm that the current utilization levels are extremely low.
- Some targets are set at (much) less than 100 percent. The assumption here is that 100 percent target achievement cannot be reached over the next three years.

TABLE 4.3 Example of Targets Set for 2012, 2013, and 2014

No.	Indicator/Service MPA	Baseline_11	Target_12	Target_13	Target_14
1	New outpatient consultation	20.0%	40%	60%	80%
2	New outpatient consultation by an indigent patient	n.a.	n.a.	n.a.	n.a.
3	Minor surgery	10.0%	20%	35%	50%
4	Arrival of referred patient at the cottage hospital	10.0%	20%	30%	40%
5	Completely vaccinated child	19.2%	35%	50%	55%
6	Growth monitoring visit for child	10.0%	20%	40%	60%
7	2–5 doses of tetanus vaccination of pregnant women	45.0%	55%	65%	75%
8	Postnatal consultation	38.0%	55%	65%	75%
9	First ANC visit before 4 months of pregnancy	16.0%	20%	30%	40%
10	ANC standard visit (2–4)	45.0%	55%	65%	75%
11	Provision of second dose of SP to a pregnant woman	12.0%	20%	65%	75%
12	Normal delivery	16.0%	25%	45%	65%
13	FP: total of new and existing users of modern FP methods	25%	35%	50%	65%
14	FP: implants and IUDs	5.0%	15%	25%	45%
15	VCT/PMTCT/PIT test	n.a.	50%	75%	100%
16	PMTCT: HIV+ mothers and children treated according to protocol	n.a.	50%	75%	100%
17	STD treatment	n.a.	10%	25%	40%
18	New AFB+ PTB patient	n.a.	50%	75%	100%
19	PTB patient: completed treatment and cured	n.a.	40%	70%	95%
20	ITN distribution	25.0%	40%	60%	80%
21	New family's use of a latrine	24.6%	30%	40%	50%

Source: World Bank data.

Note: AFB+ = acid-fast bacillus positive; ANC = antenatal care; FP = family planning; HIV = human immunodeficiency virus; ITN = insecticide-treated net; IUD = intrauterine device; MPA = minimum package of activities; No. = number; n.a. = not applicable; PIT = provider-initiated testing for HIV; PMTCT = prevention of mother-to-child transmission of HIV; PTB = pulmonary tuberculosis; SP = sulfadoxine/pyrimethamine; STD = sexually transmitted disease; VCT = voluntary counseling and testing for HIV.

Step 6. Parcel Out Service Coverage Increases between Baseline and End Line

- Most (but not all) PBF services—if they take off well—typically follow a curve that shows a rapid increase in the beginning and levels off later (see figures 4.1 and 4.2).
- Some services take off earlier than others.

- The model is driven by hundreds of assumptions.
- Parcel out the coverage increases for each quarter between the annual targets (see table 4.4).

FIGURE 4.1 Typical Target Curve for Number of PBF Services

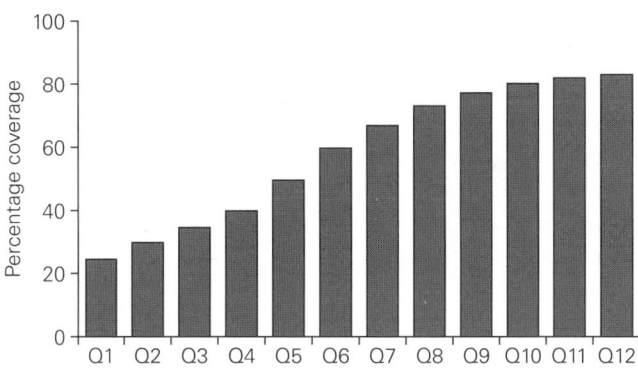

Source: World Bank data.

Note: PBF = performance-based financing; Q = quarter.

FIGURE 4.2 With a Set Fee, Disbursements Begin Low, Experience a Rapid Expansion, and Reach a Plateau, Lesotho PBF

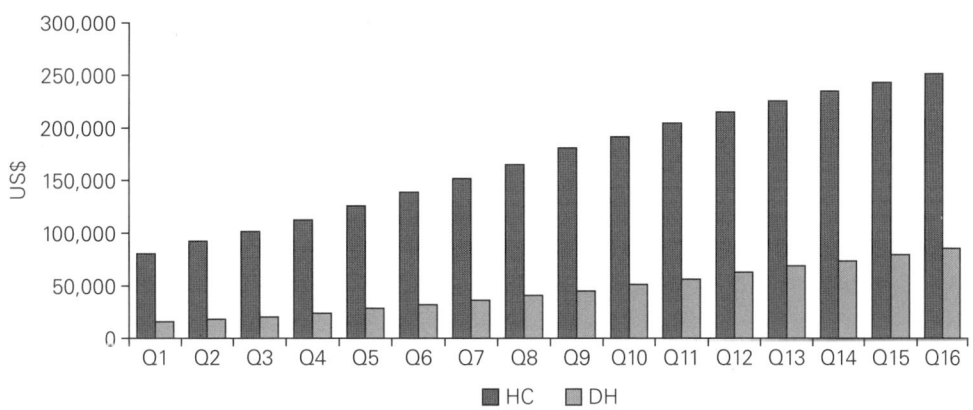

Source: World Bank data.

Note: DH = district hospital; HC = health center; PBF = performance-based financing.

TABLE 4.4 Example of Coverage Increases

No.	Indicator/ Service MPA	Baseline_11	Target_12	1Q12	2Q12	3Q12	4Q12	Target_13	1Q13	2Q13	3Q13	4Q13	Target_14
1	New outpatient consultation	20.0%	40%	25%	30%	35%	40%	60%	45%	50%	55%	60%	80%
2	New outpatient consultation by an indigent patient	—											
3	Minor surgery	10.0%	20%	12%	15%	17%	20%	35%	24%	28%	32%	35%	50%
4	Arrival of referred patient at the cottage hospital	10.0%	20%	13%	15%	18%	20%	30%	23%	25%	28%	30%	40%
5	Completely vaccinated child	19.2%	35%	23%	25%	30%	35%	50%	40%	43%	45%	50%	55%
6	Growth monitoring visit for child	10.0%	20%	12%	15%	17%	20%	40%	25%	30%	35%	40%	60%
7	2–5 дозеs of tetanus vaccination of pregnant women	45.0%	55%	47%	50%	52%	55%	65%	57%	60%	62%	65%	75%
8	Postnatal consultation	38.0%	55%	40%	45%	50%	55%	65%	57%	60%	62%	65%	75%
9	First ANC visit before 4 months of pregnancy	16.0%	20%	17%	18%	19%	20%	30%	22%	25%	27%	30%	40%
10	ANC standard visit (2–4)	45.0%	55%	47%	50%	52%	55%	65%	57%	60%	62%	65%	75%
11	Provision of second dose of SP to a pregnant woman	12.0%	20%	13%	15%	18%	20%	65%	30%	40%	50%	65%	75%
12	Normal delivery	16.0%	25%	18%	20%	30%	35%	45%	40%	45%	50%	55%	65%
13	FP: total of new and existing users of modern FP methods	25.0%	35%	27%	30%	35%	40%	50%	45%	50%	55%	60%	65%
14	FP: implants and IUDs	5.0%	15%	7%	10%	13%	15%	25%	17%	20%	23%	25%	45%
15	VCT/PMTCT/ PIT test	—	50%	20%	30%	40%	50%	75%	60%	65%	70%	75%	100%

TABLE 4.4 *(continued)*

No.	Indicator/ Service MPA	Baseline_11	Target_12	1Q12	2Q12	3Q12	4Q12	Target_13	1Q13	2Q13	3Q13	4Q13	Target_14
16	PMTCT: HIV+ mothers and children treated according to protocol	—	50%	20%	30%	40%	50%	75%	60%	65%	70%	75%	100%
17	STD treatment	—	10%	3%	5%	7%	10%	25%	15%	20%	23%	25%	40%
18	New AFB+ PTB patient	—	50%	20%	30%	40%	50%	75%	60%	65%	70%	75%	100%
19	PTB patient: completed treatment and cured	—	40%	20%	30%	35%	40%	70%	50%	60%	65%	70%	95%
20	ITN distribution	25.0%	40%	30%	32%	35%	40%	60%	45%	50%	55%	60%	80%
21	New family's use of a latrine	24.6%	30%			28%	30%	40%	32%	34%	37%	40%	50%

Source: World Bank data.

Note: In the spreadsheet, the percentage coverage is related to actual quantities drawn from the targets for each service in the population. — = not available; AFB+ = acid-fast bacillus positive; ANC = antenatal care; DHS = Demographic and Health Survey; FP = family planning; HIV = human immunodeficiency virus; ITN = insecticide-treated net; IUD = intrauterine device; MPA = minimum package of activities; No. = number; PIT = provider-initiated testing for HIV; PMTCT = prevention of mother-to-child transmission of HIV; PTB = pulmonary tuberculosis; SP = sulfadoxine/pyrimethamine; STD = sexually transmitted disease; VCT = voluntary counseling and testing for HIV.

Step 7. Set the Index Fee, and Adjust the Indices to Consume the Available Budget

- The first fee set is the index fee in the cell in column D, row 2 (that is, cell D2) of the second worksheet, titled "ControlPanel_MPA".[5]
- Because all other fees are linked to the indices in column C, the other fees automatically populate column D.
- Titrate the index fee while observing cell AA24, which draws from the "Key_assumptions" worksheet that represents the three-year budget available for purchasing MPA services: adjust this index fee until the expenditure forecast matches available budget.
- Frequently, indices are adjusted, because the actual fee for a service might seem too high or too low. This exercise is subjective and is best carried out in a plenary session with public health experts. This process is described in the modified Delphi technique in chapter 1 of this toolkit.
- Services 2 and 21 are void for the first six months. The plan is to start the purchase of these services only after six months.
- The example shows, based on hundreds of assumptions, the initial fees that could be used (see table 4.5).

TABLE 4.5 Setting the Index Fee to Consume the Available Budget

No.	Indicator/Service MPA	Index	Fee (US$)
1	New outpatient consultation	1.0	0.40
2	New outpatient consultation by an indigent patient	3.0	1.20
3	Minor surgery	3.0	1.20
4	Arrival of referred patient at the cottage hospital	8.0	3.20
5	Completely vaccinated child	5.0	2.00
6	Growth monitoring visit for child	0.3	0.12
7	2–5 doses of tetanus vaccination of pregnant women	1.0	0.40
8	Postnatal consultation	3.0	1.20
9	First ANC visit before 4 months of pregnancy	5.0	2.00
10	ANC standard visit (2–4)	2.0	0.80
11	Provision of second dose of SP to a pregnant woman	3.0	1.20
12	Normal delivery	25.0	10.00
13	FP: total of new and existing users of modern FP methods	8.0	3.20
14	FP: implants and IUDs	15.0	6.00
15	VCT/PMTCT/PIT test	2.0	0.80
16	PMTCT: HIV+ mothers and children treated according to protocol	40.0	16.00
17	STD treatment	15.0	6.00
18	New AFB+ PTB patient	50.0	20.00
19	PTB patient: completed treatment and cured	100.0	40.00
20	ITN distribution	3.0	1.20
21	New family's use of a latrine	15.0	6.00

Source: World Bank data.

Note: AFB+ = acid-fast bacillus positive; ANC = antenatal care; DHS = Demographic and Health Survey; FP = family planning; HIV = human immunodeficiency virus; ITN = insecticide-treated net; IUD = intrauterine device; MPA = minimum package of activities; No. = number; PIT = provider-initiated testing for HIV; PMTCT = prevention of mother-to-child transmission of HIV; PTB = pulmonary tuberculosis; SP = sulfadoxine/pyrimethamine; STD = sexually transmitted disease; VCT = voluntary counseling and testing for HIV.

Step 8. Review the Budget Allocation Across Services

- Open the third worksheet, titled "MPA."
- This worksheet draws from data in the second worksheet, titled "ControlPanel_MPA."
- The maximum subsidy for the "new curative consultation for an indigent" category is set at 20 percent of the forecasted "new curative consultation" category.
- It converts the percentage coverages and numeric data into financial information. For each quarter, based on assumed quarterly coverage for each service and the fee chosen, what would be the maximum quarterly disbursement if this target could be reached?

- Scroll to column AN, where the actual budget for each service is shown. Column AO shows the corresponding percentage of the total budget. It is worthwhile to check whether the budgets allocated make sense.
- As shown in the worksheet, about 52.4 percent goes to maternal health and 13.9 percent to child health (see table 4.6).

TABLE 4.6 Budget Per Service and Percentage of Total Budget Available Per Service

Budget Total (US$)	% Budget	Indicator/Service MPA	No.
$260,638	14.86%	New outpatient consultation	1
$150,419	8.58%	New outpatient consultation by an indigent patient	2
$21,627	1.23%	Minor surgery	3
$10,426	0.59%	Arrival of referred patient at the cottage hospital	4
$43,936	2.50%	Completely vaccinated child	5
$35,418	2.02%	Growth monitoring visit for child	6
$14,470	0.82%	2–5 doses of tetanus vaccination of pregnant women	7
$42,610	2.43%	Postnatal consultation	8
$31,935	1.82%	First ANC visit before 4 months of pregnancy	9
$77,779	4.43%	ANC standard visit (2–4)	10
$32,025	1.83%	Provision of second dose of SP to a pregnant woman	11
$223,900	12.77%	Normal delivery	12
$319,062	18.19%	FP: total of new and existing users of modern FP methods	13
$28,256	1.61%	FP: implants and IUDs	14
$32,310	1.84%	VCT/PMTCT/PIT test	15
$25,008	1.43%	PMTCT: HIV+ mothers and children treated according to protocol	16
$74,914	4.27%	STD treatment	17
$14,637	0.83%	New AFB+ PTB patient	18
$27,036	1.54%	PTB patient: completed treatment and cured	19
$114,531	6.53%	ITN distribution	20
$173,062	9.87%	New family's use of a latrine	21
$1,753,997	100.00%		
$1,768,261	52.36%	Maternal health	
	13.90%	Child health	

Source: World Bank data.

Note: AFB+ = acid-fast bacillus positive; ANC = antenatal care; DHS = Demographic and Health Survey; FP = family planning; HIV = human immunodeficiency virus; ITN = insecticide-treated net; IUD = intrauterine device; MPA = minimum package of activities; No. = number; PIT = provider-initiated testing for HIV; PMTCT = prevention of mother-to-child transmission of HIV; PTB = pulmonary tuberculosis; SP = sulfadoxine/pyrimethamine; STD = sexually transmitted disease; VCT = voluntary counseling and testing for HIV.

The remaining worksheets apply the same methodology to the complementary package of activities (CPA). The fees and the quarterly budget forecasts have been set in a web-enabled application, which will allow you to follow the service quantity, service quality, and budget disbursements. See chapter 12 for more details.

In the forecasting of financial risk, calculations should be checked by at least one other person. Because of the many formulas, it is easy to make mistakes.

4.7 Strategic Purchasing

With all these instruments in place, you can now embark on strategic purchasing with PBF and actively determine what is bought, from whom, and for how much (Preker et al. 2007; WHO 2000). Strategic purchasing is vital but not easy. It is riddled with complications, even in developed countries' health systems, as was well documented some years ago for European health reform experiences by Figueras, Robinson, and Jakubowski (2005).

Beginning in 2002, nongovernmental organizations (NGOs) engaged in piloting PBF have embarked on strategic purchasing. The small scale of the initial pilot projects allowed the purchasing agency managers to control the fees through Microsoft Excel spreadsheets. Scaled-up PBF systems, however, such as in Rwanda and Burundi, necessitated other instruments. In Rwanda, PBF management reverted to information technology solutions that allowed national-level purchasing (beginning in 2007). In Burundi, a second-generation application of this same technology enabled regional-level purchasing (beginning in 2010).

These web-enabled applications provide comprehensive information on unit fees and disbursements in combination with quantity and quality results, which allows the PBF purchaser to actively manage fees and results while remaining within a given output budget. They provide safeguards against overspending. They allow the purchaser to follow disbursements real-time, change fees, and issue amendments. High-volume services, such as curative care, are levers that—with only minor adjustments—can influence disbursements rapidly (see box 4.3). The unit fees and quarterly disbursement forecasts, extracted from Microsoft Excel models, such as the one discussed in section 4.6, are entered in this web-enabled application.

Through a dashboard of line graphs and bar charts, accurate information on the progress of PBF services can be obtained. Such information is essential for monitoring of potential moral conflicts from the provider side, such as providers focusing only on easily achievable services to the detriment of

BOX 4.3

The Difference between Purchasing of Curative Care and Strategic Purchasing Using PBF That Targets Preventive Care

There is a difference between purchasing of curative care conditions and strategic purchasing using PBF approaches. PBF, in principle, mostly targets preventive services. Such preventive services have a certain maximum well-defined target in the population. For instance, in a certain population, there could be 4.5 percent who are children under one year of age to target with vaccinations or 4.8 percent who are pregnant women to convince to deliver in a health facility. Although one can be confronted with unexpectedly high expenditures if purchasing curative care conditions (and especially so when using a cost-reimbursement method), such is not the case with financing preventive services using PBF. When a purchaser finances preventive services, there is a certain maximum that can be bought in the population, and knowing this maximum enables the purchaser to better forecast its risk. Excessive use of preventive services resulting from fee-for-service payment to providers has never been documented (Xingzhu and O'Dougherty 2004; see Davis et al. 1990).

other services that may be equally important from a public health perspective. The use of a business plan (see chapter 10), in which explicit strategies are related to each of the PBF services, in combination with strategic purchasing—the ability to set fees for each facility and to issue quarterly amendments—enables the purchaser to act on such eventualities.

The various institutional arrangements for purchasing are covered in chapter 11 of this toolkit, and the information technology solution that enables strategic purchasing is discussed further in chapter 12.

4.8 Links to Files and Tools

The following toolkit files can be accessed through this web link: http://www.worldbank.org/health/pbftoolkit/chapter04.

- Basic Costing Tool (exercise file for Example 2)
- Burundi MPA and CPA costing
- Explanation of Basic Costing Tool
- Nigeria_Costing_Example1.xlsx (exercise file)
- Nigerian MPA and CPA costing
- Rwandese HIV costing
- Rwandese MPA costing.

Notes

1. In autonomously managed health facilities with various sources of income, the variable performance bonus paid to health workers might originate from the overall profit from the health facility, which is composed not only of PBF funds. In addition, and also important, the PBF earnings are used for nonbonus expenses.

2. This perception is the reason that in PBF, fees should be negotiated by the health facilities to pay for the entire bill. Centrally set fees that do not help bridge this gap cannot assist the facility in closing the earnings gap.

3. An area of increasing interest is the issue of how to allocate this PBF budget. In most systems, this consists of a mix of free services or waivers for specific categories of clients (for which the provider is reimbursed through PBF).

4. In the Nigerian example in section 4.5, a per capita output budget of US$2.70 was used. Nigeria is a lower-middle-income country, and this amount might be insufficient. However, because of low preexisting investment at the frontlines, this new PBF money represents a significant additional investment. In addition, the Nigerian public health system has a host of systemic problems, such as a faltering central supply of drugs and severe misallocation of human resources. The idea is to see what US$2.70 per capita per year in additional PBF money will do in conjunction with significant other reforms (management strengthening program, coaching, and so on) and to alter the system as needed.

5. The "new outpatient consultation" service is chosen as the base index value for the ability to compare relative effort of any other activity relative to this common service.

References

Davis, K., R. Bialek, M. Parkinson, J. Smith, and C. Velozzi. 1990. "Reimbursement for Preventive Services: Can We Construct an Equitable System?" *Journal of General International Medicine* 5 (suppl 5): S93–98.

de Savigny, D., and T. Adam, eds. 2009. *Systems Thinking for Health Systems Strengthening.* Geneva: World Health Organization.

Figueras, J., R. Robinson, and E. Jakubowski, eds. 2005. *Purchasing to Improve Health Systems Performance.* European Observatory on Health Systems and Policies Series. New York: World Health Organization on behalf of European Observatory on Health Systems and Policies.

Fritsche, G., and P. Vergeer. 2010. "Performance-Based Financing Drill Down." Paper presented at a World Bank workshop, "Results-Based Financing," Washington, DC.

Maslow, A. H. 1943. "A Theory of Human Motivation." *Psychological Review* 50: 370–96.

Meessen, B., A. Soucat, and C. Sekabaraga. 2011. "Performance-Based Financing: Just a Donor Fad or a Catalyst towards Comprehensive Health Care Reform?" *Bulletin of the World Health Organization* 89 (2): 153–56.

OECD (Organisation for Economic Co-operation and Development). 2010. *Value for Money in Health Spending.* OECD Health Policy Studies. Paris: OECD.

Preker, A. L. Xingzhu, E. Velenyi, and E. Baria, eds. 2007. *Public Ends Private Means: Strategic Purchasing of Health Services.* Washington, DC: World Bank.

Soeters, R., C. Habineza, and P. B. Peerenboom. 2006. "Performance-Based Financing and Changing the District Health System: Experience from Rwanda." *Bulletin of the World Health Organization* 84 (11): 884–89.

Soeters, R., and C. Kimanuka. 2005. "Enquete menage d'evaluation, du programme d'appui aux soins de sante de base dans la province de Cyangugu" [Household survey of the program to support basic health care in the province of Cyangugu, Rwanda].

Soeters, R., L. Musango, and B. Meessen. 2005. "Comparison of Two Output Based Schemes in Butare and Cyangugu Provinces with Two Control Provinces in Rwanda." Report, Global Partnership on Output-Based Aid, Washington, DC, and Ministry of Health, Rwanda, Kigali.

Soeters, R., P. B. Peerenboom, P. Mushagalusa, and C. Kimanuka. 2011. "Performance-Based Financing Experiment Improved Health Care in the Democratic Republic of Congo." *Health Affairs* 30 (8): 1518–27.

von Bertalanffy, L. 1969. *General System Theory: Foundations, Development, Applications.* New York: George Braziller.

WHO (World Health Organization). 2000. *The World Health Report 2000: Health Systems—Improving Performance.* Geneva: WHO.

Xingzhu, L., and S. O'Dougherty. 2004. "Purchasing Priority Public Health Services." HNP Discussion Paper. Washington, DC, World Bank.

CHAPTER 5

Addressing Equity

MAIN MESSAGES

→ Health care use by poor people lags those who are better off. Poor people risk being more deeply impoverished by the cost of seeking care.

→ PBF provides incentives to health workers to increase the quantity and quality of services and focuses on improving equity in health care use.

→ The likelihood of achieving this potential is greatly enhanced if PBF design includes explicit pro-poor features, such as targeting resources at poor areas, pro-poor user fee policies, incentives for community health workers, and complementary demand-side incentives.

→ PBF program managers must regularly monitor and evaluate the effect of the PBF program on equity. This approach requires knowledge of the necessary analytical techniques for equity analysis and collection of the appropriate data.

COVERED IN THIS CHAPTER

5.1 Introduction: Why worry about equity?
5.2 PBF: An innovative approach to enhancing equity
5.3 How to make PBF schemes more pro-poor
5.4 Measuring and monitoring equity in PBF

5.1 Introduction: Why Worry About Equity?

It is a well-known fact that the health status and health care use of the poor tend to lag that of those who are better off. This difference can occur because of distance (many poor people live far from the health services that they need, especially in rural areas), affordability (often the costs of health services and quality food are too expensive for them), lack of information (the poor tend to be less knowledgeable about appropriate health-promoting practices), inadequate access to other services that are good for health (such as clean water, good sanitation, and safe housing), and lack of empowerment (they lack the voice needed to make social services work for them).

The differences between the health care use of the rich and the poor can be very great indeed, including for many of the maternal and child health services frequently targeted by performance-based financing (PBF). For example, data from the latest Demographic and Health Surveys (DHS) indicate that the difference in the average use of antenatal care (four or more visits) and skilled birth attendance among the poorest and richest 20 percent of households in Sub-Saharan Africa can differ by a factor of up to 8 (see figure 5.1).

FIGURE 5.1 Percentage of Use of Antenatal Care and Skilled Birth Attendance by Poorest and Richest Quintiles

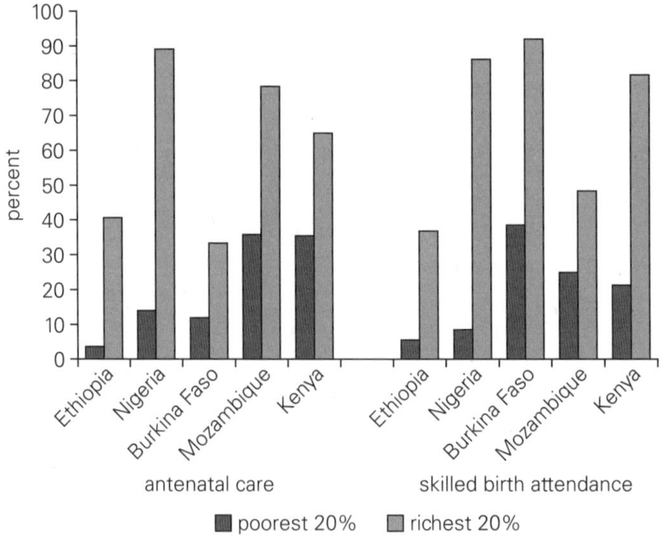

Sources: World Bank based on data from Ethiopia Demographic and Health Survey (DHS) 2005, Nigeria DHS 2008, Burkina Faso DHS 2006, Mozambique DHS 2003, and Kenya DHS 2008/09.

The relationship between poverty and illness is two directional: not only are the poor more likely to fall ill and less likely to seek health care, but falling ill and seeking care are also a major cause of poverty. This is partly due to the costs associated with seeking health care, including spending on consultations, diagnostic tests, medicine, and informal payments. The 2010 World Health Report found that every year about 150 million people incur "catastrophic" health expenditures and 100 million are pushed below the poverty line as a result of these types of health expenditures (WHO 2010). In addition, the transportation costs associated with seeking care can be expensive. Finally, there is the loss of household income when a breadwinner falls ill and stops working. In some cases, other household members may also have to stop working to care for the sick person, sell assets to cover medical expenses, borrow at high interest rates, or become indebted to the community.

Consequently, it is no surprise that improving equity and financial protection are often explicitly stated as health system goals or yardsticks of system performance (Roberts et al. 2004; WHO 2010; World Bank 2007). Good health systems attempt to improve the health status of the whole population, but especially the health status of the poor among whom ill health and poor access to health care tend to be concentrated, and to protect households from the potentially catastrophic effects of out-of-pocket payments for health care.

Traditionally, governments have implemented a variety of policies and programs to reach the goals of reducing inequalities in health outcomes and health care use and of enhancing financial protection (see the case studies included in Gwatkin, Yazbeck, and Wagstaff 2005, as well as Yazbeck 2009). Generally, these include mechanisms that help overcome the financial, geographic, social, and psychological barriers to accessing care and help reduce the out-of-pocket costs of treatment. Examples fall into the following broad categories:

- Reducing the direct cost of care at the point of service, for example, through reducing or abolishing user fees for the poor, expanding health insurance to the poor (including the coverage, depth, and breadth thereof), and reducing copayments
- Reducing the indirect costs of accessing care such as travel costs, child care, and time away from the job, for example, through building more facilities closer to the poor, using mobile outreach for hard-to-reach locations, providing vouchers to offset travel costs, and offering conditional cash transfers
- Overcoming social and psychological barriers to accessing care, for example, through targeted health promotion and community outreach

- Increasing the efficiency of care to reduce the total amount of care that people use, for example, by limiting "irrational drug prescribing," strengthening the referral system, and improving the quality of care provided (especially at the lower levels)
- Strengthening the overall regulation and structure of both public and private health care markets.

5.2 PBF: An Innovative Approach to Enhancing Equity

PBF is a new, innovative strategy for reaching the poor. By supplying financial incentives to providers to improve the quantity and quality of a set of targeted services and by monitoring that they do so, PBF shows excellent potential to increase the service use and health status of the poor.

PBF works in the following ways:

- *PBF and equity in service use.* When health workers are paid only on a salary basis (as is the case in many countries), there is very little financial motivation to see additional patients, unless these patients offer to pay an additional under-the-table (informal) payment or are seen in the health worker's private practice (so-called "moonlighting").[1] Even in countries where the poor are exempt from user fees, this provider payment structure tends to bias service delivery in favor of the better-off patients who can more easily afford to make additional payments for care. In contrast, when a salary-based payment mechanism is complemented by a PBF payment mechanism, health workers have a financial incentive to see the most patients possible, regardless of a patient's ability to pay.
- *PBF and financial protection.* By encouraging the use of care, and especially the preventive care included in the typical PBF package, PBF increases the likelihood that patients will seek care before their illness progresses to the point at which the costs of seeking care (and the financial consequences of illness) are likely to be higher. Moreover, because PBF also offers incentives to providers to improve the quality of the care that they give, the effectiveness of treatment will likely improve, reducing the probability that patients return for additional care related to that illness episode, and thus reducing the total burden of out-of-pocket health expenditures.

Clearly, PBF has excellent potential to improve health equity and enhance financial protection. As with any health care reform, however, there is no guarantee. There have also been very few rigorous studies of the effects of supply-side PBF (as defined in this toolkit) on the poor. The potential of

PBF to enhance equity and financial protection is crucially dependent on the behavioral response of the provider/worker/facility to the PBF incentives. This, in turn, will depend on the broader institutional environment (for example, degree of autonomy of the provider over fees and staffing) and incentive structures (salary, informal payments, user fees, moonlighting opportunities, and working conditions). Consequently, those who design, manage, and evaluate PBF schemes should carefully consider the building blocks of their PBF; formulate hypotheses as to the likely effects on equity, given the institutional environment and incentive structure facing health workers (as well as the constraints facing patients); and reflect on how the PBF scheme can be modified to increase the likelihood that the program reaches the poor. As Gwatkin (2010, 1) warns:

> Many plausible approaches are available for directing benefits toward the poor. . . . Even when such approaches are applied, however, predicting the equity impact of any given [results-based financing (RBF)] strategy in any particular setting remains more of an art than a science; and only after the fact, through careful monitoring, is it possible to assess an RBF project's equity consequences with reasonable certainty.

In this chapter, we explore different approaches that can be used to help ensure that PBF schemes realize their potential of reaching the poor.

5.3 How to Make PBF Schemes More Pro-Poor

In its relatively short history, PBF has proven to be a very versatile approach that can be modified in different ways to make it more pro-poor. This section describes specific design elements of PBF that can be used to increase the extent to which PBF resources reach providers in destitute areas, services reach the poor, and any potential costs to the poor are mitigated. In practice, this often involves complementing PBF schemes with some of the more traditional (frequently demand-side) mechanisms described above.

Table 5.1 summarizes the various PBF design elements that are considered in this section, the expected effect on equity goals, and some country examples.

The country examples used for each of these design elements are currently being, or have been, implemented within the context of PBF schemes. However, excellent examples of how to design and implement some of these elements, such as user fee exemption, in-kind demand-side incentives, vouchers schemes, and conditional cash transfer programs, can also be found outside of PBF schemes and have a longer history of implementation.

TABLE 5.1 PBF Design Elements and Their Anticipated Effect on Equity

Design element	Effect on equity and financial protection	Examples
Choose services that are underused by the poor	Increased use of selected services by the poor	All PBF that focuses on Millennium Development Goals 1, 4, 5, and 6.
Pay providers more for reaching a poor person than a nonpoor person	Increased use by the poor more than by the nonpoor	Benin, Burkina Faso, Cameroon, Lesotho, Liberia
Pay providers more for services delivered in poor areas	Increased use by people in poor areas more than by people in nonpoor areas; more resources pushed to poor areas	Burundi; South Kivu, Congo, Dem. Rep.; Djibouti; Lesotho; Nigeria; Zimbabwe
Include an equity indicator or target as an item in the balanced scorecard	Increased use by the poor more than by the nonpoor	Afghanistan, Argentina
Subsidize user fees	Reduced out-of-pocket costs, thus enhancing financial protection and increasing use	Most PBF programs; Cambodia is a well-known example
Incentivize community health workers	Overcoming information and social barriers for the poor	India, Rwanda community PBF
Add complementary demand-side incentives	Overcoming financial barriers (such as transportation costs and related expenses)	In-kind incentives: Rwanda community PBF Vouchers: Bangladesh; Bolivia; Cambodia; Kenya; Pakistan; Uganda; Yemen, Rep. Conditional cash transfers: Congo, Dem. Rep.; Nigeria

Source: World bank data.

Note: PBF = performance-based financing.

Well-designed PBF programs often bundle together many of these approaches in an integrated fashion. A well-designed PBF program might combine all of the following interventions known to assist the poor:

a. *Choose services that are underused by the poor.* Focus on a package of carefully selected services at community, health center, and hospital levels.

b. *Pay more for reaching a poor person.* Provide a higher fee for treating a poor person for curative care, and for a select group of other PBF services.

c. *Subsidize user fees.* Almost all PBF programs have a subsidy for curative care that enables providers to lower their user charges and enables the purchaser to negotiate a lower rate for user charges.

d. *Incentivize community health workers.* Many PBF schemes that operate at the health-center level incentivize community health workers to reach more of their target population. They can, for instance, pay rewards to community health workers and traditional birth attendants who bring women to deliver in health centers.

e. *Add complementary demand-side incentives.* Some PBF programs experiment with conditional in-kind incentive programs, such as providing a piece of cloth or an umbrella to mothers when they deliver in a health facility. Other programs may pay a cash reward.

Choose Services That Are Underused by the Poor

As noted in the introduction, there are large inequalities in the use of many types of services and a gap between the need for services and service coverage. The extent of these inequalities varies by service type with the rich-poor gap in service use being much greater for certain services than for others. Where resources are scarce and only a limited range of services can be included in the PBF scheme, PBF program architects should consider targeting those services that are the most underused by the poor.

In general, services related to maternal health (such as skilled birth attendance, antenatal care use, and bed-net use while pregnant) tend to be among those most inequitably distributed. Also, in general, if PBF schemes are focused on the Millennium Development Goals (MDGs), they will tend to be pro-poor because most of the illnesses and health conditions encapsulated by the MDGs are concentrated among the poor. One exception is human immunodeficiency virus (HIV), which, in most developing countries, is concentrated among the better-off population. Also, although noncommunicable diseases (NCDs) are an emerging health problem and constitute a growing share of the overall disease burden even in the lowest-income countries, NCDs for the most part are still concentrated among the relatively wealthy rather than the relatively poor. As PBF programs increasingly expand in Asia and Southeast Asia (for example, the Kyrgyz Republic, the Lao People's Democratic Republic, Tajikistan, Vietnam, and other countries), there will be more experimentation with purchasing services related to NCDs.

Inequalities in service delivery will be largely location specific because the barriers to accessing services may vary from one country to another and, within countries, from one region to another. Consequently, program architects should inform themselves about the patterns of inequalities in health care use in the countries in which they will be working. Good sources of information on country-specific inequalities in health service use include the World Bank's Health Equity and Financial Protection country datasheets, the World Bank's HealthStats database, and the MEASURE DHS Statcompiler (see the list of recommended resources at the end of this chapter).

A list of services used in PBF programs can be accessed through the linked files of chapter 1 (see section 1.5).

Pay More for Reaching a Poor Person Than a Nonpoor Person

A very direct way to encourage health workers to make an extra effort to reach the poor is to pay more for a service provided to a poor person than for one provided to a nonpoor person. In practice, this requires differentiating the PBF fee schedule according to the poverty status of the client/patient.

A good example is a PBF pilot in Benin. Of the 18 PBF services, the financial reward associated with two services—antenatal care and institutional delivery—doubles when the beneficiary is poor. Identification of poor and nonpoor women is possible by means of a "poverty certificate" (which, in half the districts, has been replaced by a biometric card). These certificates have been issued to beneficiaries of a health equity fund (put in place several years ago) after a process of community-based identification of needy individuals.

Another example is an urban PBF program in Douala, Cameroon. The program systematically pays more for a poor person than for a wealthier client. Three of the 25 services (curative care, inpatient days, and minor surgery) offered at the community/health center level have a premium fee for the poor.

The most difficult implementation challenge is to identify who is poor and who is not. Three main methods are commonly used to identify the poor for the purposes of inclusion into social programs:

- With *means testing*, a program official directly assesses whether someone should be considered poor based on direct verification of income. This approach can be very accurate, but also typically requires high levels of literacy and is administratively demanding.
- *Proxy means testing* involves constructing a score for each household based on a small number of easily observable characteristics or assets. This approach is easily verifiable, but it also requires reasonably high administrative capacity.
- *Community targeting* typically involves having a community leader or group decide who in the community should be considered poor (for the purposes of a program). This approach, which might be the most feasible one for small-scale PBF programs, takes into consideration local knowledge of individual circumstances, allows for local definition of need, and transfers the costs of identifying beneficiaries from the program to the community. However, local personnel may have other incentives,

besides accurately identifying program beneficiaries, which could continue or exacerbate patterns of social exclusion. Refer to Coady, Grosh, and Hoddinott (2004) for a more detailed discussion of these methods, their strengths and weaknesses, and examples of application to the health sector.

Even this brief discussion indicates that identifying the poor can be difficult and entail large administrative costs that will need to be balanced against the gains. Consequently, if individual targeting (paying more for reaching the poor) is going to be implemented within PBF, it should be used where an existing social program has already identified the poor and issued identification cards marking them as beneficiaries, as in the case of Benin. If not, then the PBF scheme will have to establish its own targeting mechanism. Using existing targeting arrangements not only will reduce costs and complexity, but because the identification of individuals is the outcome of a separate third-party process, they also will minimize stigma and mitigate additional political risks.

There is extensive experience in targeting the poor through health equity funds, for instance in Cambodia (Annear 2010). In Cambodian Health Equity Fund programs, both preidentification and postidentification work well, but preidentification is the most effective and most cost-effective targeting method. In many PBF pilot programs, health facility managers have discretion in categorizing a share (for example, 10–20 percent) of the curative care patients in the "poor" category (Soeters 2012). This approach is akin to the postidentification targeting of the Cambodian Health Equity Fund schemes. More operational research is needed to determine how this can best be implemented.

Pay More for Services Delivered in Poor Areas—Equity Bonuses, Remoteness Bonuses, and Isolation Bonuses

This strategy for reaching the poor involves adjusting the payment schedule so that providers in poor areas are paid higher amounts for each service delivered than providers in wealthier areas. This additional payment can be termed a remoteness bonus (for example, in Zimbabwe), an isolation bonus (for example, in parts of the Democratic Republic of Congo), or an equity bonus (for example, in Burundi). These bonuses are a form of geographic targeting—a way to push more resources to underfunded facilities in remote, and typically poor, areas where health outcomes tend to be worse. This method increases the overall funding envelope for certain geographical areas that are known to be disadvantaged. This approach allows scarce resources to be used more efficiently and also avoids the need to design difficult and administratively expensive interventions that assess who is poor and who is nonpoor.

The fundamental idea behind this approach is to enable destitute facilities to have relatively more resources for paying the higher cost of providing quality services to their population. Attracting and retaining good health care workers and paying for the higher cost of transportation are some of the reasons behind this approach.

A good example is the PBF scheme in Burundi (see box 5.1), where total PBF payments to facilities are a combination of two types of payments: (a) interprovincial equity bonuses for disadvantaged provinces (the province's poverty score is one of the indicators) and (b) intraprovincial equity bonuses for disadvantaged health facilities (the number of poor people in the catchment area and the characteristics of the health facility are two of the indicators).

In the Democratic Republic of Congo—in separate PBF schemes in South Kivu, Bas Congo, Kasai Oriental, Kasai Occidental, Province Oriental, North Kivu, and Bandundu provinces—health facilities in far-flung areas can earn a bonus up to 20 percent larger than those in urban facilities (Bredenkamp 2009).

The first step in targeting PBF resources to poor areas is to decide at which level bonuses will be differentiated. Equity bonuses can vary across administrative subdivisions (such as states, provinces, or districts) or, as is more commonly the case in PBF, at the level of the catchment areas of providers (such as hospitals or health centers). In general, the smaller the geographic area at which the bonus is differentiated, the more specific and accurate will be the targeting of resources.

The second step is to determine which (health) areas are poor and which are not. There is extensive international experience with different approaches to geographic targeting[2] (see, for example, the excellent compilation of Coady, Grosh, and Hoddinott 2004, 62–69). The simplest form of geographic targeting involves the use of a single, easily available indicator that is strongly related to the objectives of the program:

- For example, the Honduran cash transfer program (Family Allowance Program, Programa de Asignación Familiar, or PRAF) used child nutritional status to target resources.
- Targeting can also be based principally on the judgment of program officials familiar with the field conditions of facilities that serve poor areas. Unfortunately, this approach is also less transparent, less formal, and more subjective.

BOX 5.1

Burundi: A Multipronged Approach to Equity in Financing and Use

In April 2010, the pilot PBF scheme in Burundi was scaled up to the national level. In 2006, to improve *equity in use* and enhance *financial protection*, a free health care policy was introduced, effectively eliminating all user fees for select vulnerable groups at the point of service. This selective free health care policy faced some implementation challenges, including reimbursing providers in a timely manner and containing costs. Consequently, these funds were merged with the new national PBF scheme.

In addition, the Burundi PBF sought to improve *equity in financing* across provinces. In the Burundi PBF approach, the PBF subsidy is moderated by two types of equity bonuses: (a) interprovincial equity bonuses for disadvantaged provinces and (b) intraprovincial equity bonuses for disadvantaged health facilities.

The size of the interprovincial equity bonus depends on four indicators: the province's poverty score, the isolation of the province, the population of the province, and the number of health facilities in the province. Based on these indicators, provinces are classified into five different categories.

The size of the intraprovincial equity bonus, applied at the facility level, depends on six indicators: the population to be covered by each health facility; needs in terms of medical staff; needs in terms of small equipment; distance from the District Health Office; geographic isolation; and the *number of indigents supported by a health facility*. Based on these indi-

cators, facilities are classified into five different categories.

The overall fee-for-service amount for each service type is a function of the base fee, the province's score on the interprovincial equity bonus, and the individual score on the interprovincial equity bonus. Combining these incentives, facilities can earn up to 40 percent over the base fee based on the interprovincial equity score and an additional 40 percent over the base fee based on the intraprovincial score such that the worst-scoring facilities in the worst-scoring provinces are eligible for a fee-for-service rate that is 80 percent higher than that of the best-scoring facilities in the best-scoring provinces.

The main motivation behind the equity bonuses in Burundi was to enhance equity in financing and mitigate the risk (under PBF) that the better-equipped facilities will be better able to take advantage of the PBF incentives, and thus attract even more funding, while the less successful ones will continue to be relatively disadvantaged. At the time of writing, program managers report that the interprovincial equity bonus is being implemented without difficulty, and reduction of inequity in financing across the provinces is occurring. The intraprovincial equity bonus is being applied in some hospitals, but with great difficulty, and it is not yet being applied at the health center level because of lack of funding. Consequently, at the time of writing, all health centers were still in the category with the base rate (tied to the specific province).

- A more sophisticated version of geographical targeting uses statistical techniques (usually principal component analysis) to calculate a summary poverty indicator for different areas based on many different indicators associated with poverty and usually based on data obtained from household surveys and sometimes administrative data (such as the area's literacy rates, housing conditions, access to services, and so on). This approach was used in the initial geographic targeting stage for the PROGRESA (Programa de Educación, Salud y Alimentación, or Education, Health, and Nutrition Program of Mexico, now called Oportunidades) conditional cash transfer program in Mexico.

The third step is to determine how many resources should be given to different areas. In some cases, the gradation is slight, so that on a per capita basis the poorest facility may receive only 10 percent more per capita than the richest. In other cases, the gradation is quite sharp with the poorest areas receiving several times as much as the richest. Factors to consider in making this decision include the available resource envelope, variation in poverty rates and health status, and, most importantly, political and social preferences.

Pay Explicitly for Equity in the Balanced Scorecard

One option is to pay directly for facilities' or districts' performance on equity by including an equity score as a line item in the balanced score card. In some RBF programs, such as in Plan Nacer in Argentina,[3] or the Afghanistan RBF program, an equity measure is included. However, in the vast majority of PBF programs that directly contract with health facilities and regularly pay them, including such a measure is very difficult.

The approach is best illustrated by an example. In Afghanistan, the balanced score card (see figure 5.2) includes among other items: (a) an outpatient concentration index and (b) a patient satisfaction concentration index. A concentration index measures the degree of inequality with a positive value indicating that health service use and patient satisfaction are pro-rich and a negative value indicating that health service use and patient satisfaction are pro-poor. The larger the value of the concentration index, the more pro-rich (if positive) or pro-poor (if negative) the distribution is. Those facilities that reach their targets with respect to equalizing service delivery across rich and poor groups and that reach their targets for relative patient satisfaction of the poor and the rich receive the bonuses associated with these line items.

An alternative to using the concentration index as the equity measure (because its meaning can sometimes be difficult to communicate to policy makers) would have been for the Afghanistan program manager to use simpler measures to capture equity in service use. For example, instead of using the concentration index, the program manager could have used a measure of the ratio of the use of the rich to the use of the poor. Another alternative

FIGURE 5.2 Afghanistan Health Sector Balanced Scorecard, Provincial Results, 2004–06

		Benchmarks		Badakhshan		
		Lower	Upper	2004	2005	2006
	A. Patients & Community					
1	Overall Patient Satisfaction	66.4	90.9	86.4	94.2	86.8
2	Patient Perception of Quality Index	66.2	83.9	77.6	82.9	77.5
3	Written Shura-e-sehie activities in community	18.1	66.5	35.6	8.4	73.4
	B. Staff					
4	Health Worker Satisfaction Index	56.1	67.9	63.5	64.8	70.6
5	Salary payments current	52.4	92.0	54.9	83.0	75.2
	C. Capacity for Service Provision					
6	Equipment Functionality Index*	61.3	90.0	69.6	49.5	73.3
7	Drug Availability Index	53.3	81.8	52.9	81.5	74.0
8	Family Planning Availability Index	43.4	80.3	54.2	65.5	80.2
9	Laboratory Functionality Index (Hospitals & CHCs)	5.6	31.7	31.7	32.3	38.2
10	Staffing Index — Meeting minimum staff guidelines	10.1	54.0	38.0	37.2	66.3
11	Provider Knowledge Score	44.8	62.3	48.6	67.3	61.8
12	Staff received training in last year	30.1	56.3	68.9	87.3	53.7
13	HMIS Use Index	49.6	80.7	60.9	27.6	72.0
14	Clinical Guidelines Index	22.5	51.0	18.3	40.2	48.1
15	Infrastructure Index	49.3	63.2	63.2	35.5	38.9
16	Patient Record Index	56.1	92.5	51.5	51.4	66.4
17	Facilities having TB register	8.3	26.6	32.5	38.1	46.3
	D. Service Provision					
18	Patient History and Physical Exam Index	55.1	83.5	54.2	67.7	72.6
19	Patient Counseling Index	23.3	48.9	23.3	31.1	35.0
20	Proper sharps disposal	34.1	85.0	64.4	34.4	75.6
21	Average new outpatient visit per month (BHC > 750 visits)	6.7	57.1	27.3	26.7	23.1
22	Time spent with patient (> 9 minutes)	3.5	31.2	21.0	12.0	23.1
23	BPHS facilities providing antenatal care	28.9	82.8	28.9	35.8	90.6
24	Delivery care according to BPHS	10.5	39.3	38.0	20.5	31.5
	E. Financial Systems					
25	Facilities with user fee guidelines	80.3	100.0	94.8	84.4	70.7
26	Facilities with exemptions for poor patients	64.4	100.0	68.5	70.9	100.0
	F. Overall Vision					
27	Females as % of new outpatients	46.5	59.7	46.9	52.4	54.6
28	Outpatient Visit Concentration Index	48.0	52.7	48.9	49.0	49.8
29	Patient Satisfaction Concentration Index	49.0	50.9	50.9	50.0	50.0
	Composite Scores					
30	**Upper Benchmarks Achieved**	10.3	30.8	17.2	17.2	24.1
31	**Lower Benchmarks Achieved**	75.9	89.7	86.2	82.8	93.1
	Mean scores across indicators 1 through 29	48.8	56.5	50.9	51.1	61.4

KEY

Score Above Upper Benchmark	
Score Between Lower & Upper Benchmark	
Score Below Lower Benchmark	

*Benchmark set at 90%, though top quintile from 2004 was 74.1

Source: Afghanistan Ministry of Public Health, Johns Hopkins University, and IIHMR (Indian Institute of Health Management Research) 2006.

Note: BHC = Basic Health Center; BPHS = Basic Package of Health Services; CHC = Comprehensive Health Center; HMIS = health management information system; TB = tuberculosis.

would have been to simply set targets for use by the poor and vulnerable. In the Plan Nacer program in Argentina, one of the 10 tracer indicators on the basis of which financing is transferred from the central Ministry of Health to the provincial ministries relates to the inclusion of indigenous populations (World Bank 2009).

Note that paying directly for equity in this manner still requires that facilities are able to easily collect information on the socioeconomic status of those who use services. Even using a rich-poor ratio requires identifying the poor and the nonpoor, which, in turn, requires that the poor have a poverty card or other form of identification.

Subsidize User Fees

Subsidizing user fees—possibly even fully so that the patient pays no formal charges to the provider—would remove one of the major barriers to accessing health care and one of the major sources of destitution. Consequently, the removal or reduction of user fees is an important strategy for reaching the poor and can be implemented within a PBF scheme. Such a removal ought to go hand-in-hand with compensation to the provider of the income lost through this user fee removal, because a poorly planned or implemented user fee abolishment program leads to poor results in general (Hercot et al. 2011; Meessen, Gilson, and Tibouti 2011; Meesen et al. 2011; Orem et al. 2011). A reduction of user fees can be adopted in varying degrees of intensity: subsidizing fees across the board for all categories of patients; subsidizing fees only for particular categories of patients, such as pregnant women and children under six; or subsidizing fees only for the poor and vulnerable.

Fees for essential services such as deliveries can be quite high for vulnerable groups (Perkins et al. 2009) with the result that the effect of financing such fees through PBF can be quite dramatic. This is illustrated by a personal story from Burundi (see box 5.2).

However, the removal of user fees can also have a number of adverse consequences. First, it can deprive facilities of an important source of revenue that is often needed for operating costs or for supplementing meager staff salaries. Second, it can lead to moral hazard and excess demand for services, overburdening staff and compromising quality. Third, when user fees are eliminated only for the poor (as is often the case), there is a risk of discrimination by providers that have greater (financial) incentives to serve the nonpoor than the poor. Fourth, there is also the risk that the facility, in an effort to replace revenues, will simply start to charge informal (under-the-table) payments with little or no net benefit for the patient.

Selective Free Health Care Is Financed through PBF in Burundi: A Personal Story from a Batwa Woman

Madame Esperance Kamurenzi tells of her great joy to be treated for free.

(Excerpt from an interview conducted with vulnerable groups of Batwa[a] in Mukoni, Muyinga Province)

My name is Esperance Kamurenzi. I am a Mutwakazi. I am 28 years old. With my first husband, I had five children, but all died! Now I'm with another man, and we have two children only!

During the crisis, I lived in refugee camps. Yes, it's where I lived with other Batwa. In refugee camps, life was very hard: I did not go to the health center: ISHWI DA![b] = Never, ever did I attend the hospital! I've never been to see a doctor. Always I was afraid to go to the hospital without money. ISHWI DA! I could not go. The others would make fun of me!

I always gave birth at home. I did not even know what prenatal care was. I never brought my children for immunization. ISHWI DA! I also think that's why my kids are dead [she seems to cry]! My husband also did not go to see the doctor! We all stayed at home. We were very unhappy!

Today things have changed. First, I live in a beautiful house here in Mukoni! The state gave us these beautiful houses covered with sheets. I no longer have the desire to always seek permanent straw to cover the house. It is very good [she smiles].

One day, I was walking around selling my pots and I stopped to listen to the radio. It said that pregnant women are not going to pay anything for consultation or childbirth. I asked if the Batwa were also involved. I then spoke to my husband. We danced. All night we danced. Even that one came to sensitize us to go to the health center.[c] He told us that now the question of money is no longer an obstacle.

Today, I'm going to prenatal and for consultation and they cannot ask me anything. No time I was asked for money. I had a caesarean section every time. Nurses welcomed me very well. They do not treat me that I'm Mutwa. No, they do not hate me. After regaining some energy, I hear their voices tell me, SPE,[d] get up and go home. Things went well! And I take my child. And we go home. Without paying anything! We are very happy. I extend my sincere thanks. Eh! MUNTUWE[e] I say this to the doctors: Esperance said, thank you! God even said thank you.

Source: MSPLS 2012.

a. Batwa are an indigenous pygmy population in Burundi.
b. Strong expression to express an emphatic "No!"
c. She points at the person who has accompanied us to visit her.
d. Elliptical word used to call her name ("Esperance" or "Hope").
e. A term used to shout at someone, to catch his or her attention.

When user fee removal is implemented within the context of PBF, some of these adverse consequences can be sharply mitigated, especially the first concern (revenue loss) and fourth concern (informal payments). In fact, where providers have the autonomy to determine the user fees charged by their facilities, the reduction of formal user fees is often a rational revenue-maximizing response by providers to the introduction of PBF: to increase the demand for their services, facilities might choose to lower their fees so that they receive a larger overall PBF subsidy (Soeters 2012). Those who wish to complement the introduction of PBF with user fee subsidies should educate providers that there is an opportunity for both large revenue gains and better access for more patients.

Health equity funds are a very particular type of PBF scheme that includes the exemption of user fees for the poor (see Annear 2010 for a literature review). In East Asia, health equity funds have been in place in Cambodia since 2000, and to a lesser extent also in Lao PDR and Vietnam. In Africa, they have been used in Benin. At the core of making exemptions effective is separation of the responsibility for assessment of exemption eligibility (nongovernmental organizations [NGOs] or the state) from the provision of care (health facilities) and the compensation of providers for lost fee revenue (the fund). Providers offer care to poor patients free of charge, but are reimbursed for service provision on a fee-for-service basis by the health equity fund. This model can easily be adopted by other existing PBF schemes.

There are two final considerations on subsidizing user fees within the context of PBF. First, note that because user fees are only a part of the total cost of accessing care, subsidizing user fees may not be sufficient to induce the desired level of care-seeking behavior, especially among poor households. Each health care visit is also associated with other significant financial costs, including travel costs and various opportunity costs. Second, note that in health systems with the third-party (state to provider) fee-for-service reimbursement mechanism that characterizes PBF schemes, user fees (from patients) counter supplier-induced demand (that is, where providers supply more services than patients need out of financial interest). Although removing user fees within the context of a PBF scheme could potentially enhance equity, it could also deter efficiency.

Add Conditional Financial In-Kind Incentives for Community Health Workers

Incentivizing community health workers is an important way to overcome the social, psychological, and informational barriers that the poor may face in accessing care.

When community health workers are formally or informally integrated into PBF programs, they are paid a fee or remunerated in-kind for bringing certain clients to health facilities or providing services directly to clients in the community itself. One example of a formal arrangement is the incentives paid to community health workers (accredited social health activists, or ASHAs) in India's Janani Suraksha Yojana (JSY) program for bringing women and children to government health centers for institutional deliveries, postnatal visits, and BCG (Bacillus Calmette–Guérin) vaccinations, as well as incentives to private sector providers for emergency caesarean-section deliveries (see, for example, Dagur, Senauer, and Switlock-Prose 2010). Another example is the incentives paid by the NGO BRAC to community health workers for supervision of directly observed treatment, that is, short course directly observed therapy for the treatment of tuberculosis (DOTS) in tuberculosis patients in Bangladesh. The community health worker must supervise the treatment on a daily basis and is paid when the patient successfully completes DOTS.

Apart from these formal arrangements, providers involved in PBF schemes have been known to devise informal incentive-based arrangements with community health workers to encourage them to bring clients to the health facility. Such arrangements are much more common than the formal ones. Providers do this because they recognize that by paying a community health worker a small sum for identifying a pregnant woman, for example, and bringing her to the health facility, the facility-based workers may gain additional remuneration for the antenatal care visits and delivery-related services that will be used by this woman. Appropriate training can help make facility-based workers aware of the possibility and feasibility of implementing an informal arrangement such as this.

Add Demand-Side Financial or In-Kind Incentives for Patients

Many demand-side incentives are in the form of cash transfers, dependent on use of a particular service. They are designed to offset the financial and opportunity costs of accessing care. An example is the demand-side financial incentives paid to a pregnant woman for delivering in an accredited government health institution as part of the India JSY program in which they are complementary to the supply-side payments to the community health workers discussed above. From an equity perspective, the program makes a special effort to reach the poor and overcome the barriers they may face in accessing care because the amount of cash provided varies by the profile of the state (good-performing and worst-performing facilities), the urban-rural location of the facility, and the woman's status of living "below poverty line" (BPL). Pregnant women also receive transportation vouchers.

Vouchers are a special type of financial incentive that is provided to households to obtain free or highly subsidized health services, such as treatment of tuberculosis or sexually transmitted infections. Vouchers for safe motherhood services are fairly common. They are used in many countries in

Africa, Asia, and Latin America, although mainly at a small scale and often with the support of NGOs (Bellows and Hamilton 2009; Bellows, Bellows, and Warren 2011; Bellows et al. 2013; Obare et al. 2013). The health facility retains these vouchers and is paid by the government or a private organization on the basis of the number of services provided. As with the pure conditional cash payments, because these incentives address both financial barriers and informational barriers, by generating awareness of the importance of a service, they are expected to disproportionately benefit the poor.

Smaller in-kind incentives tend to focus on making the consultation or patient-provider interaction more comfortable. They have been most commonly used to promote use of reproductive health services, but they can be used for other types of services, too. For example, in Katete district in Zambia some facilities prepare "welcome baby packages," including, for example, soap, napkins, second-hand baby clothes, and so on for women who deliver in facilities. In Rwanda, a formal national in-kind transfer program is now linked to the national PBF system. Women are offered a package of gifts if they consume certain services (such as antenatal care, skilled delivery, and postnatal care). This nationwide scale-up was built on the experience of pilot schemes from 2002 to 2005 when individual health facilities successfully attracted clients by offering mothers "welcome baby packages."

Interestingly, although these conditional in-kind incentive programs could easily exist in the absence of PBF, PBF has often facilitated their implementation by creating a better administrative infrastructure. Through the increased autonomy introduced into facilities by PBF, as well as opening of facility bank accounts (often for the first time) by PBF, government is able to transfer cash to the facility bank accounts and facilities are then able to procure these goods on the local market using their own purchase committee (rather than using a centralized supply chain). Consequently, this is an excellent example of the complementary and synergistic effects of supply-side PBF and demand-side incentive programs for reaching the poor. The PBF scheme creates the supply-side preconditions (that is, autonomy, bank accounts, and the ability to respond to increased demand) for the implementation of a demand-side incentive scheme that, in turn, contributes to the same service objectives as the PBF.

5.4 Measuring and Monitoring Equity in PBF

The effects of PBF on equity have not yet been well documented in the published literature. This is in large part due to the more general paucity of rigorous studies of PBF in developing countries. As the number of rigorous studies of PBF expands, program managers, principal investigators, and data analysts will have the opportunity to contribute to the evidence base on the effects of PBF on equity. Doing so will require (a) that impact evaluations and other studies collect the data necessary for the measurement of the effects of PBF on equity and (b) that the PBF community is equipped with the analytical tools needed to measure equity.

In the following sections, we provide a synopsis of items to consider when measuring and monitoring the effects of PBF on equity. However, note that many of the steps provided will require the help of people with specialized experience if they are to be done properly.

Applying the Correct Analytical Techniques

In measuring and monitoring PBF's effect on equity, one is likely to be concerned with three main types of questions.

Have Inequalities in Health Care Use and Health Status (Illness) Improved?

This question can be answered using a few different techniques. First, health outcomes can be disaggregated by quintile to show how health outcomes vary across wealth groups. Most commonly, outcomes are disaggregated by quintile (from the poorest 20 percent of the population to the wealthiest 20 percent of the population) or by deciles (into tenths). The results are presented in a table or in a bar graph like that in figure 5.3, panel a. Although the results of this analysis are very easy to interpret with one period of data, comparing multiple bar graphs over multiple time periods (which one would want to do to assess the effect of PBF on equity) is more difficult to do accurately.

A second technique can provide a summary measure of inequality. In this technique, the relationship between the top quintile and the bottom quintile can be expressed as a ratio to obtain a summary measure of inequality (for example, 88 percent in the richest quintile divided by 64 percent in the poorest quintile gives a ratio of 1.4 in the case of figure 5.3).

A third technique, also a summary measure of inequality, is the concentration index. This has one major advantage over the quintile ratio measure, namely, that it takes into account inequalities across the entire income distribution, rather than only the gap between the top quintile and the bottom quintile. The concentration index can range between –1 and +1. A negative value means that the indicator takes a higher value among the poor, while a positive index means that the indicator takes a higher value among the better-off population. The larger the index in absolute size, the more

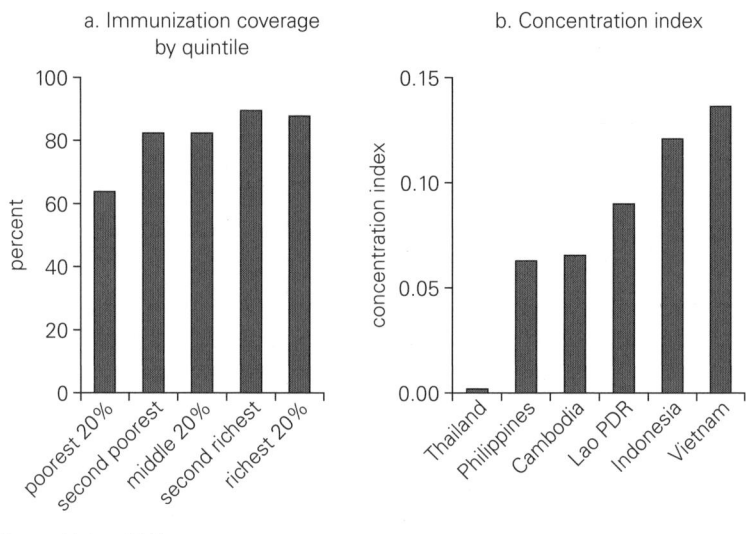

FIGURE 5.3 Immunization Coverage in the Philippines, Quintile Analysis and Concentration Index

a. Immunization coverage by quintile

b. Concentration index

Source: Various DHS surveys.

inequality there is (see figure 5.3, panel b). For example, if in the future the concentration index for immunization coverage in the Philippines falls from the 0.062 shown in the figure to 0.04, then although immunization coverage remains concentrated among the better-off population in both years, it will have become less pro-rich.

Is Financial Protection Improving So That Households Are Being Protected from the Risks of Large Out-of-Pocket Health Expenditures?

The first technique used to answer this question considers whether out-of-pocket spending on health is "catastrophic." Catastrophic payments are defined as health care payments in excess of a predetermined percentage (for example, 10 percent, 20 percent, 25 percent, and 40 percent) of the patient's total household or nonfood spending. The *incidence* of catastrophic payments is the percentage of households that incur health care payments in excess of that predetermined percentage. The *severity* of catastrophic payments is the average amount by which households exceed the predetermined threshold.

The second technique used to answer this question considers whether out-of-pocket spending on health is "impoverishing." If out-of-pocket health spending is large enough to push a household from being above the poverty line before the health expenditure to being below the poverty line after the health expenditure, then the expenditure is classified as impoverishing. The *incidence* of catastrophic payments is the percentage of households that incur health care payments that push them below the poverty line.

Is Government Spending on Health Becoming More or Less Pro-Poor?

After a few years of implementation of PBF, especially if PBF has made a special effort to reach the poor, policy makers may want to know whether government spending on health is becoming more pro-poor. Whether this is the case depends on two factors: first, how pro-poor the use of government health care services is; and second, the amount of money flowing to the government-subsidized services that are used by the poor. PBF will potentially have an effect on both of these pathways. The technique used to assess the net effect of these two factors is called benefit-incidence analysis. It answers the question whether, and by how much, government health expenditure disproportionately benefits the poor.

Applying these techniques will require knowledge of the methods and access to the software used to implement these techniques. Fortunately, many resources are available to provide assistance. To learn more about these techniques and the way to implement them using the free ADePT software, visit the ADePT Resource Center at http://www.worldbank.org/povertyandhealth to download software, manuals, training courses, and teaching materials. For an excellent resource to learn more about how to implement these techniques in STATA, see O'Donnell et al. (2008).

Collecting the Right Data

Only rarely can administrative data—data from the health information system (HIS)—be used to apply the techniques needed to assess equity. One limitation is that most HISs do not contain information on who is poor and who is not.[4] A second, more important limitation is that the HIS only captures data on those people who actually use health services and not on the population as a whole. Consequently, the HIS cannot tell us how PBF has improved equity in health care use or financial protection across the entire population. Therefore, for effective measuring and monitoring of equity, data from household surveys are needed. Obtaining the data involves selecting a representative sample of households or individuals from the population of the intervention area and administering a questionnaire to gather information on various characteristics of the household (such as income, location, and assets) and of individuals within that household (such as age, sex, education, illness, health care use, and health expenditure).

To measure equity in health care use and health status, one needs data on living standards (information on a household's economic well-being or socioeconomic status that enables one to construct a continuous variable that ranks households from poorest to richest, such as data on assets, consumption, or expenditure), household size, illness variables, and health care use variables (information on the services that are targeted by PBF, for example, antenatal care, skilled birth attendance, and immunization). The DHS provides a good model both for the construction of an asset index (as a measure of living standards) and for a method to measure the preventive care and maternal and child health–related services that are typically targeted by PBF.

To measure financial protection, one needs data on household consumption or expenditure (assets are not sufficient), household size, and out-of-pocket health expenditure. The household survey instrument contained in the World Bank's RBF Impact Evaluation Toolkit is a good model for the collection of data on consumption and on health expenditure.[5]

To conduct benefit-incidence analysis, one needs data on living standards (consumption, expenditure, or assets), data on use of health care, and, crucially, information on government health care expenditure on health facilities of different types. Data on government health expenditure can be obtained from National Health Accounts reports or directly from ministries of health.

Using Equity Analysis to Inform Policy

The objective of equity analysis is to inform policy—policy that is directly related to PBF and policy that is complementary to PBF. Knowing how to conduct equity analysis and collecting the data needed to do so is just the first step. It is essential that the results are used to monitor the effects of PBF programs over time and to provide input into the way PBF programs are designed and implemented. While any PBF program that improves average health care use should be considered a success, making a difference for the poorest population is an even more important concern. If the PBF program does not achieve this, then its design and implementation arrangements should be carefully examined to determine where changes could be made. Introducing some of the design elements discussed in this chapter would be a good first step.

Recommended Resources

Section 1

For easily accessible statistical data on inequalities in health care use by country and region, see the following:

Health Equity and Financial Protection Country Datasheets, World Bank, Washington, DC, http://www.worldbank.org/povertyandhealth: country-specific factsheets on equity in health outcomes and service use, including data by quintile, and financial protection.

HealthStats (database), World Bank, Washington, DC, http://datatopics .worldbank.org/hnp: select health indicators, including quintile data.

MEASURE DHS STATcompiler, ICF International, Calverton, MD, http:// www.statcompiler.com: customizable country table on health outcomes, including by quintile and region, based on demographic and health surveys.

For case studies of health care interventions that were designed to reduce inequalities and enhance financial protection, see the following:

Gwatkin, D., A. Yazbeck, and A. Wagstaff, eds. 2005. *Reaching the Poor with Health, Nutrition, and Population Services: What Works, What Doesn't, and Why*. Washington, DC: World Bank.

Yazbeck, A. 2009. *Attacking Inequality in the Health Sector: A Synthesis of Evidence and Tools*. Washington, DC: World Bank.

Section 3

For theoretical and practical information on targeting health services at poor areas and poor people, see the following:

Coady, D., M. Grosh, and J. Hoddinott. 2004. *Targeting of Transfers in Developing Countries: Review of Experience and Lessons*. Washington, DC: World Bank.

For examples of how PBF can be designed to be more pro-poor:

See the references cited in each part of section 3.

Join the online conversations of the PBF and Equity Working group at http:// www.healthfinancingafrica.org/join-our-cops.html: click "Results Based Financing," click "sign in," and then click "sign up."

Section 4

For more information on how to measure and monitor equity, see or visit the following:

Health Equity and Financial Protection, World Bank, Washington, DC, http://www.worldbank.org/povertyandhealth: ADePT Training Resource Center, including ADePT software, ADePT Health Manual, and online training materials.

Impact Evaluation Toolkit. World Bank, Washington, DC, http://go.world bank.org/IT69C5OGL0: information on implementation of surveys and a model survey instrument that includes the variables needed to measure equity.

MEASURE DHS, World Bank, Washington, DC, http://www.measuredhs .com: Demographic and Health Surveys (DHS) instruments as examples of good survey instruments for measuring living standards and access to care.

O'Donnell, O., E. van Doorslaer, A. Wagstaff, and M. Lindelow. 2008. *Analyzing Health Equity Using Household Survey Data. A Guide to Techniques and Their Implementation*. Washington, DC: World Bank (for guidance on statistical techniques and STATA do-files).

Notes

1. We are not suggesting that health workers are motivated only by money; we know that they feel a strong moral obligation to serve all patients. We simply mean that beyond health workers' moral motivation to serve their clients, the salary system provides fairly little additional *financial* motivation to provide services compared to other remuneration schemes.
2. The process of distinguishing between rich and poor areas is also sometimes referred to as poverty mapping.
3. A new nationwide follow-up program is called Plan Sumar.
4. There are some exceptions. In systems where poor households are identified by a poverty card (such as India's BPL card) or a different type of health insurance card (such as that in Indonesia's Jamkesmas program), it would be possible to collect information on who is poor by using the health information system.
5. Visit http://www.worldbank.org/health/impactevaluationtoolkit.

References

Afghanistan Ministry of Public Health, Johns Hopkins University, and IIHMR (Indian Institute of Health Management Research). 2006. *Afghanistan Health Sector Balanced Score Card National and Provincial Results: Round Three 2006*. Kabul: Afghanistan Ministry of Public Health, Johns Hopkins University, and IIHMR.

Annear, P. 2010. "A Comprehensive Review of the Literature on Health Equity Funds in Cambodia 2001–2010 and Annotated Bibliography." Health Policy and Health Finance Knowledge Hub Working Paper No. 9, Nossel Institute for Global Health, University of Melbourne, Melbourne.

Bellows, N. M., B. W. Bellows, and C. Warren. 2011. "The Use of Vouchers for Reproductive Health Services in Developing Countries: Systematic Review." *Tropical Medicine and International Health* 16(1): 84–96.

Bellows, B., and M. Hamilton. 2009. "Vouchers for Health: Increasing Use of Facility-Based STI and Safe Motherhood Services in Uganda." Maternal and Child Health P4P Case Study, Health Systems 20/20, Abt Associates Inc., Bethesda, MD.

Bellows, B., C. Kyobutungi, M. K. Mutua, C. Warren, and A. Ezeh. 2013. "Increase in Facility-Based Deliveries Associated with a Maternal Health Voucher Programme in Informal Settlements in Nairobi, Kenya." *Health Policy and Planning* 28(2): 134–42.

Bredenkamp, C. 2009. "The Puzzle of Isolation Bonuses for Health Workers." RBF Technical Brief, World Bank, September. http://www.rbfhealth.org/rbfhealth /library/doc/214/puzzle-isolation-bonuses-health-workers.

Coady, D., M. Grosh, and J. Hoddinott. 2004. *Targeting of Transfers in Developing Countries: Review of Experience and Lessons.* Washington, DC: World Bank.

Dagur, V., K. Senauer, and K. Switlock-Prose. 2010. "Paying for Performance: The Janani Suraksha Yojana Program in India." P4P Case Study, Health Systems 20/20, Abt Associates Inc., Bethesda, MD. http://www.healthsystems2020.org/content /resource/detail/2609/.

Gwatkin, D. R. 2010. "Ensuring that the Poor Share Fully in the Benefits of Results-Based Financing Programs in Health." RBF Working Paper, World Bank, Washington, DC. http://www.rbfhealth.org/system/files/RBF_Tech_Equity_03.pdf.

Gwatkin, D., A. Yazbeck, and A. Wagstaff, eds. 2005. *Reaching the Poor with Health, Nutrition, and Population Services: What Works, What Doesn't, and Why.* Washington, DC: World Bank.

Hercot, D., B. Meessen, V. Ridde, and L. Gilson. 2011. "Removing User Fees for Health Services in Low-Income Countries: A Multi-Country Review Framework for Assessing the Process of Policy Change." *Health Policy and Planning* 26 (suppl 2): ii5–15.

Meessen, B., L. Gilson, and A. Tibouti. 2011. "User Fee Removal in Low-Income Countries: Sharing Knowledge to Support Managed Implementation." *Health Policy and Planning* 26 (suppl 2): ii1–4.

Meessen, B., D. Hercot, M. Noirhomme, V. Ridde, A. Tibouti, C. K. Tashobya, and L. Gilson. 2011. "Removing User Fees in the Health Sector. A Review of Policy Processes in Six Sub-Saharan African Countries." *Health Policy and Planning* 26 (suppl 2): ii6–29.

MSPLS (Ministere de la sante publique et de la lutte contre le SIDA). 2012. *Rapport annuel de mise en oeuvre du financement basé sur la performance au Burundi.* Bujumbura: MSPLS.

Obare, F., C. Warrren, R. Njuki, T. Abuya, J. Sunday, I. Askew, and B. Bellows. 2013. "Community-Level Impact of the Reproductive Health Vouchers Programme on Service Use in Kenya." *Health Policy and Planning* 28 (2): 165–75.

O'Donnell, O., E. van Doorslaer, A. Wagstaff, and M. Lindelow. 2008. *Analyzing Health Equity Using Household Survey Data: A Guide to Techniques and Their Implementation*. Washington, DC: World Bank.

Orem, J. N., F. Mugisha, C. Kirunga, J. Macq, and B. Criel. 2011. "Abolition of User Fees: The Uganda Paradox." *Health Policy and Planning* 26 (suppl 2): ii41–51.

Perkins, M., E. Brazier, E. Themmen, B. Bassane, D. Diallo, A. Mutunga, T. Mwakajonga, and O. Ngobola. 2009. "Out-of-Pocket Costs for Facility-Based Maternity Care in Three African Countries." *Health Policy and Planning* 24 (4): 289–300.

Roberts, M. J., W. Hsiao, P. Berman, and M. Reich. 2004. *Getting Health Reform Right: A Guide to Improving Performance and Equity*. New York: Oxford University Press.

Soeters, R., ed. 2012. *PBF in Action: Theory and Instruments, Performance-Based Financing Course Guide*. The Hague: Cordaid.

WHO (World Health Organization). 2010. *World Health Report: Health Systems Financing—The Path to Universal Coverage*. Geneva: WHO.

World Bank. 2007. *Healthy Development: The World Bank Strategy for Health, Nutrition, and Population Results*. Washington, DC: World Bank.

———. 2009. "Argentina: Provincial Maternal and Child Health Insurance: A Results-Based Financing Project at Work." En Breve 150, World Bank, Washington, DC.

Yazbeck, A. 2009. *Attacking Inequality in the Health Sector: A Synthesis of Evidence and Tools*. Washington, DC: World Bank.

CHAPTER 6

Health Facility Autonomy and Governance

MAIN MESSAGES

→ Increasing health facility autonomy is vital for successful PBF.
→ Introducing PBF and health facility autonomy resembles creating a cooperative in which health workers become stakeholders.
→ PBF encourages health workers to act as social entrepreneurs.
→ Autonomy demands accountability and good governance structures.

COVERED IN THIS CHAPTER

6.1 Introduction: The importance of health facility autonomy
6.2 Main elements of health facility autonomy
6.3 Enhancing autonomy: Improving results
6.4 Autonomy demands accountability
6.5 Fee setting and drug revolving funds

6.1 Introduction: The Importance of Health Facility Autonomy

Performance-based financing (PBF) for health services is premised on a substantial degree of health facility autonomy. For a PBF program to be successful, health facilities need to be given considerable flexibility. They need sufficient funds and the freedom to manage resources in order to increase the quantity and quality of health services.

Health facilities should have ample freedom for autonomous human resource management, hiring, and firing; procurement of supplies in a competitive and well-regulated market; and autonomous management of assets both fixed and liquid. Health facilities should have the right to decide how to improve the quantity and quality of their services. As the agencies that provide the services, they have intimate knowledge of how these services can best be produced. In an ideal scenario, health facility managers are very familiar with the living conditions of the population in the area and know important details about population dispersion, location of villages, and travel distances. They attend regular population gatherings, in churches, schools, and other places. They are aware of who the traditional leaders are and what local health customs exist. They know what buildings, staffing, and equipment are required. Guided by this knowledge, health facilities should be allowed to manage their activities and function according to a solid business plan, with a sharp assessment of available resources and a keen eye on quality improvements.

Unfortunately, in most challenged or dysfunctional health systems, the realities are very different from this ideal situation. In poor countries, health facilities face a wide array of problems. In general, government health facilities are managed through central planning and input financing of salaries and commodities. Frequently, they do not manage any money themselves. Or if they do, they are forced to operate under restraints, such as having to pass on their income to a higher-level administrative system or having to obtain a distant administrator's approval of the expense. A well-functioning central command, control, and planning system could work if it operated as designed. In reality, this is rarely the case. Health staff members are told what to do and how to behave, but are not provided with the inputs necessary to carry out their work.

In such circumstances, the term "health facility autonomy" may even stir anxiety and fear. In many districts, asking how health facilities could actually be considered "autonomous" is a reasonable question. The broad set of existing rules and regulations that pertain to the handling of cash, the management of cash income, or human resources forms a clear obstacle and blocks any sense of developing health facility autonomy. Some staff members and workers' unions themselves may even resist autonomy in such situations out of fear of the unpredictable effects such changes could bring to staff employment and wages.

Nonetheless, PBF deems moving in the direction of health facility autonomy vital for sustainable improvements. The concrete results of PBF in several more autonomous settings may validate the case. Over the past decades, PBF has flourished in rather heterogeneous environments. It has taken off in South Kivu, the Democratic Republic of Congo, where government is virtually absent, salaries of health workers are not being paid, and health facilities are surviving through the user fees obtained from the population. PBF has boomed in Rwanda, where government reigns with a strong hand. PBF has succeeded in environments such as in Burundi, where the government is recovering from conflict and trying to rebuild its authority. From the do-it-yourself attitude in the Democratic Republic of Congo to the strong governance of Rwanda or the initially weak governance structures of Burundi,[1] one common variable stands out in all these settings. That variable explains in part why, in these three very different contexts, PBF is still making strides. That variable is health facility autonomy.

6.2 Main Elements of Health Facility Autonomy

The elements that need to be introduced to facilitate autonomous management of a health facility are listed in table 6.1. The table may be a useful aid in discussing autonomy with government counterparts.

6.3 Enhancing Autonomy: Improving Results

The Path

Expanding health facility autonomy does not happen overnight. To change established ways of operating and overcome traditions of central command and control is hard work. The process of hiring and firing staff members cannot be changed immediately, nor can rigid or dysfunctional central medical procurement and supply systems be changed without considerable effort. And neither can the perception that "health staff cannot manage cash" be easily discarded. At the outset, resistance can be considerable. However, each of the transformations mentioned is necessary for PBF to work, and the various processes leading to change are, therefore, worth studying in depth.

TABLE 6.1 Elements of Health Facility Autonomy

Decision ability	Reasons
Use cash income.	Cash income can spring from various sources, such as user fees (drug revolving funds), performance-based payments, and other sources. Cash is necessary for carrying out activities in the business plans, implementing advanced strategies, procuring drugs and medical equipment, carrying out minor repairs, and paying performance bonuses to staff.
Procure inputs locally (rather than from central supply management).	Drugs and medical consumables should be procured from certified distributors, which can include, but are not restricted to, the central medical stores. Such an arrangement in conjunction with the quarterly quality checks will ensure efficient use of resources, because they are procured with the health facility income and less waste. A waste of money would lead to lower performance bonuses for staff. Efficient stock management will yield benefits both in performance scores and in increased cash. Other inputs like cleaning materials, minor repairs, and equipment can be equally procured in an efficient manner. Products that are bought using health facility income will be managed carefully.
Open and operate a designated bank account.	A bank account is necessary to manage cash income.
Hire, fire, and discipline facility-recruited staff.[a]	As operations expand, income can be used to recruit additional staff members if necessary. This staff can best be managed by the health facility.
Organize clinic operations and outreach activities.	Management should handle hours of operation for the clinic, including opening time. The days on which specific activities are carried out and the frequency and target of outreach activities are best determined by local management, which has clear insights into local constraints. For example, although there may be central guidelines on the frequency for carrying out family planning clinics (once or twice per week) or antenatal care clinics (once or twice per week), health facility management should be allowed to adapt these guidelines to maximize quantity and quality production.
Develop and negotiate business plans.	In conjunction with its health facility committee, the health facility management is best positioned to negotiate with the purchaser on the business plans.
Apply the indice tool.	The indice tool assists the health facility management in handling all cash income and expenses in a comprehensive manner and manages individual staff performance and bonuses. This process promotes transparency.

Source: World Bank data.

a. Autonomous human resource management of all staff members would be ideal.

PBF practice indicates that these contentious issues should be tackled early in the discussions with your PBF counterparts.

Implementers may be aided by the fact that many of the necessary transformations can be linked to broader, ongoing social or administrative reforms. For example, the policies of hiring and firing may be connected to general civil service protocol. If a country decides to embark on civil service reforms (which was the case in Rwanda), this may facilitate the introduction of PBF health facility autonomy in staff recruitment as well (see box 6.1). Another example is a case in which health facility autonomy requires the existence of health facility bank accounts; this transformation is sometimes demanded in a country for reasons other than PBF as well.

In Rwanda, for instance, the government decided to decentralize human resource management to the district level and tied available civil servant positions to specific health facilities. In addition, it continued to invest—predominantly through available bilateral funding—into improving the performance of its central medical stores, which work through a "pull" system and a Bamako-type drug revolving fund. This approach met PBF requirements. In Rwanda, about half of the health workers are contract workers who are employed directly by the health facility. In Burundi, this figure is about 10–30 percent. Such developments can be catalyzed further, when PBF quantity and quality of health services increase and income, in turn, rises. This may encourage health facility managers to find the most efficient staffing patterns, fueling further powers of staffing management.

Step by Step

Table 6.2 provides a simplified illustration of different situations used to enhance autonomy and results they are likely to produce. Going step by step from situations 1 to 5, one can see the progression from less autonomy to

TABLE 6.2 Enhancing Autonomy and Improving Results Step by Step

	Situation	Level of health facility autonomy and expected results
1	Tell the facility what to do and how to do it. Do not supply the drugs and equipment to do it.	Severely compromised autonomy and limited results
2	Tell the facility what to do and how to do it. Supply the drugs and equipment to do it.	Compromised autonomy and limited results
3	Tell the facility what to do, but not how to do it. Provide a budget to do it.	Increased autonomy and improved results
4	Tell the facility what to do, but not how to do it. Pay the facility on the basis of outputs and quality, but do not let the staff share in profits.	Enhanced autonomy and improved results
5	Tell the facility what to do, but not how to do it. Pay the facility on the basis of outputs and quality, and let the staff share in the profits.	Enhanced autonomy and enhanced results

Source: World Bank data.

Note: This typology is meant for illustration only and does not necessarily reflect reality, which is much more complex. It is a simplification of various existing situations.

more autonomy. In situation 5, in which health staff members are told what to do, guided by the services and the quality norms, much discretion is given for how to go about achieving the objectives. In this situation, health staff members can participate. They are made stakeholders in their own health facility and can earn significant performance-related bonus payments. This approach is quite the opposite of situation 1. In situation 5, health staff members are provided the cash necessary to deliver services and to improve quality, and they earn more money by working harder and by delivering more good-quality results. In situation 5, health staff members are made autonomous and responsible for their own results. Situation 5 approaches PBF.

6.4 Autonomy Demands Accountability

Greater autonomy requires accountability. PBF makes use of a whole range of instruments to ensure accountability: dealing with funds locally, at health facility level; regulating the income; dispensing staff bonuses; and ensuring that the cash entering the health facilities is spent in a transparent fashion.

Tools that help manage total health facility income in an integral manner, while allocating performance bonuses to individual health workers as a share of the income, are the indice tool (see chapter 7) and the individual performance evaluation (see chapter 10).

The Stimulus of Staff Bonuses

Staff bonuses are derived from the income of the health facility. Health facility income is obtained from user fees, health insurance, PBF, and eventual other sources. Bonus payments are, therefore, not only derived from PBF payments but also result from the holistic management of total health facility income.

In most environments of enhanced autonomy and increased responsibility for results, frequently there are certain spending rules related to bonus payments. Often, a cap is determined, setting a maximum amount that can be spent on bonus payments. For instance, 40–60 percent of the income of a health facility can be spent on staff bonuses and salaries.

The How and Why of Health Facility Committees

Enhanced autonomy with regards to the use of public funds requires oversight, which necessitates the creation of a health facility committee. Apart from the standard financial management tools used for accounting purposes, such as the income and expense registers and the quarterly income and expense statement that are auditable through the regular bureaucratic oversight mechanisms, public oversight is achieved through creating a health facility management committee (see box 6.2).

BOX 6.2
Community Participation and Voice Mechanisms in Burundi

What is the role of the community in managing its health services? In Burundi, qualitative research on the role of community health committees (comités de santé, or COSAs) and community-based organizations (CBOs) was carried out. In general, COSAs in health facilities that were under PBF schemes functioned better than those that were not under PBF schemes; these COSAs were involved in developing business plans, and community members were paid a sitting allowance as opposed to COSAs in non-PBF facilities. However, overall, the COSAs' role was focused on supporting the health staff and not on representing the population. The role of the CBOs in PBF facilities was more promising: they were contracted by the nongovernmental organizations to verify whether patients had actually received services and to learn the patients' opinions on those services. More analysis and experimentation is needed to learn how to develop better accountability mechanisms (Falisco et al. 2012)

Although fairly new, the experience with such health facility committees for PBF is promising, and increased experimentation is necessary to learn more about the ways in which these committees can become more effective in strengthening the community voice (Falisse et al. 2012).

The exact size and composition of such a committee varies according to location, but a few suggestions are as follows: (a) it should be small, and (b) it should have one or two members from the health facility participate but without voting rights.

In many primary health care systems, various health facility committees, also named "neighborhood committees" or "ward development committees," exist. However, in nearly all cases, their membership is too large to be transplanted into the desired format, which requires a much smaller membership. A good approach is to create a subcommittee from such a larger preexisting committee containing the essential persons (chair, treasurer, and others).

The chair of the health facility committee cosigns the purchase contract conjointly with the official in charge of the health facility. One member of this health facility committee (its chair, or treasurer) could countersign checks. The functioning of the health facility committee is assessed each quarter using the quantified quality checklist.

Frequently, health facility committee members asked to be paid. This is not advisable; if they are paid, they will lose their impartial nature. Minor expenses such as a sitting allowance or a travel per diem and food and drinks during the meetings can help compensate members for their time.

6.5 Fee Setting and Drug Revolving Funds

PBF uses public funds to subsidize services. PBF is concerned with bringing cash to health facilities. Whether the health facility raises cash through other sources (for example, user fees or drug fees for a drug revolving fund) is a decision for the health facility and its community. Community members, seated in the health facility management committee (the governing board), will form the interface between the community and the health facility and assist in setting such fees. Leveraging all other sources of cash (for instance, from user fees or drug revolving funds) and managing these holistically is an explicit aim of PBF. Public funds will be better managed (and targeted), as will all other sources of cash income.

PBF payments tend to focus predominantly on preventive services. It is best to focus a large part of the PBF financing on services that are typically undersupplied by providers or underused by their patients. Of course, PBF funds also target curative care, which allows the purchaser to command quality related to content of care, such as rational prescribing of drugs and adherence to treatment protocols. Curative services are generally in high demand. Subsidizing curative care is a good strategy to lower financial barriers to access to services. However, the ability to offer subsidies depends on the budget available. Very poor countries rarely have sufficient public funds to pay for both curative and preventive care in any sustainable manner while also maintaining good quality and improving coverage.

A good strategy is to introduce a drug revolving fund and to explain to health staff members the relationship between lowering of the financial cost to their patients (rational prescribing and limited mark-ups) and increased usage of services with the ability to increase total earnings by limiting missed opportunities (for vaccinations, antenatal care services, and family planning services). Such a strategy supports financial sustainability (multiple sources of cash financing, that is, not just from public funding) and opens the door to the introduction of risk-pooling arrangements (as a result of the cost signal for curative services).

Note

1. The nationwide successful scaling up of PBF in Burundi has created a case study in how to introduce good governance in a fragile state.

Reference

Falisse, J.-B., B. Meessen, J. Ndayishimiye, and M. Bossuyt. 2012. "Community Participation and Voice Mechanisms under Performance-Based Financing Schemes in Burundi." *Tropical Medicine and International Health* 17 (5): 674–82.

CHAPTER 7

Health Facility Financial Management and the Indice Tool

> **Lack of money is the root of all evil.**
> —George Bernard Shaw

MAIN MESSAGES

→ Cash income of health facilities can be from different sources, including PBF. The indice tool helps the in-charge person of the health facility to manage holistically all sources of cash income and expenses and to allocate a performance-based share of the profits to each health worker.

→ PBF makes health workers shareholders in the financial health of their health facility.

→ Individual health-worker effort is rewarded each month. If you work harder, you receive a higher performance bonus. If you work less, then you receive a lower performance bonus.

7.1 Introduction

Cash income of health facilities can originate from different sources, including performance-based financing (PBF). In PBF, building capacity to handle this cash at the facility level in an integrated and accountable manner is crucial. The indice tool helps the in-charge person of the health facility to manage all sources of cash income and expenses and to allocate a performance-based share of the profits to each health worker.

Linking results to money requires good accountability structures to be in place:

- Produce good-quality results data to confirm if the intended results have been achieved.
- Introduce accountability mechanisms for the governance of the public funds, which in turn promotes civil society and community involvement.
- Use budget disbursement as a proxy indicator for total performance, which can lead to good benchmarking of providers.

7.2 General Sources of Cash Income of a Health Facility

PBF is premised on cash being handled by health facilities. Possible sources of cash income for a health facility are (a) out-of-pocket payments; (b) fixed cash support from government or aid agencies, for instance, to pay for basic salaries or operational expenses; (c) income from health insurance payments; and (d) payments of PBF subsidies or cash from other sources. The exact mix of cash income sources depends largely on context.

Especially in the PBF design phase, determine what existing cash sources are available and how much each of those sources contributes to the total income of a health facility. The possible scenarios range from cases in which no formal cash income reaches the facility to those in which the sources of income are well diversified. Ideally, a health facility should have a well-diversified income spectrum, to which PBF would be additional income. PBF is supposed to leverage all productive resources: land, buildings, equipment, medical supplies, and human resources, as well as all cash income.

The indice tool was developed for transparent management of cash income. This tool helps manage all sources of cash income in an integral fashion.

7.3 Verification of the Amounts

For PBF cash payments to be transferred to the health facility level for the delivery of quality services, the amounts due are verified at different levels (see box 7.1):

- The amounts are verified at the health facility level by the management and the health center committee, who scrutinize the invoice before approving it (see the sample health facility invoice in the links to files in this chapter).
- The amounts are verified monthly at the health facility level by the purchaser's verifier, who verifies the quantity performance in the registers and approves the monthly invoice (see chapter 2).
- The amounts are verified quarterly at the level of district or provincial PBF steering committee meetings in which the quantity and quality performance is validated and the consolidated district invoice is approved.
- The amounts are verified at the level of the purchaser, who executes a due diligence of procedures (steering committee meeting minutes, signed and validated district invoices) for the production of a consolidated payment order and its submission to the fund holder (see the sample consolidated quarterly invoice in the links to files in this chapter).
- The amounts are verified at the level of the fund holder, who transfers the funds to the health facilities.

BOX 7.1
Decentralized Decision Making on PBF Results in Nigeria

In the Nigeria State Health Investment Project (NSHIP) decisions on the amounts to be paid are made at a decentralized level (figure B7.1.1). The local government authority (LGA)—the district level—has a newly constituted body called the LGA Results-Based Financing (RBF) Steering Committee. At this decentralized level, the results of the quantity performance (the amounts

(box continues on next page)

---

to be paid based on the volume of services) and the quality performance (the quality score determined quarterly for each health facility) are scrutinized. By use of a web-enabled application, a consolidated quarterly invoice is created for each district RBF steering committee. In the district steering committee meetings, the proof of actual performance (the original monthly invoices and the results of the quarterly quality evaluations) is compared against the district invoices printed from the database. The steering committees are the governing boards for PBF. They include the local government authority, the state ministry of health, the purchaser (the state primary health care development agency), and civil society representatives.

In these decentralized meetings, performance is ratified. Higher levels (the purchaser and the fund holder) carry out due diligence only on procedures.

FIGURE B7.1.1 NSHIP PBF Administrative Model

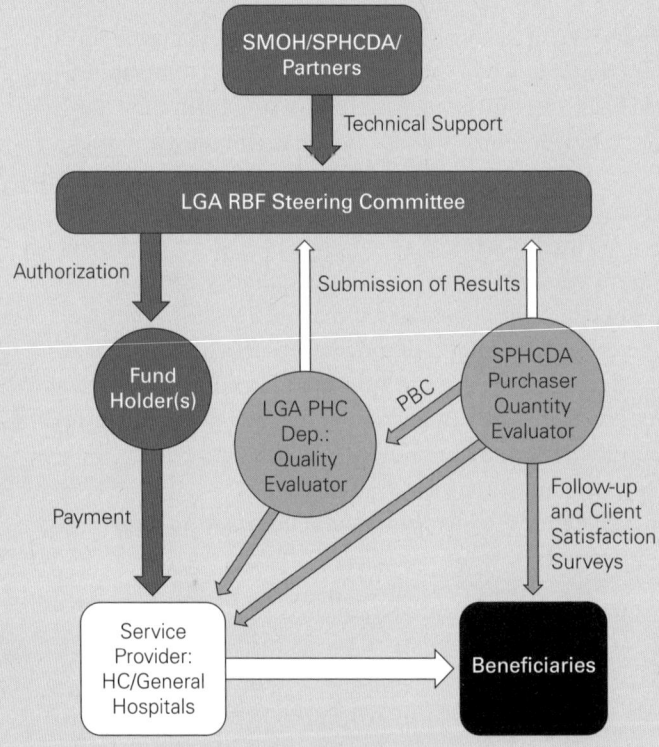

Source: World Bank data.

Note: HC = health center; LGA = local government authority; NSHIP = Nigeria State Health Investment Project; PBC = performance-based contracting; PHC = primary health care; PBF = performance-based financing; RBF = results-based financing; SMOH = state ministry of health; SPHCDA = state primary health care development agency.

7.4 The Processing of Payments to Health Facilities

Once the parties agree on performance payments, the money should be transferred directly from the fund holder to the health facility's bank account. There should be as little delay as possible in paying for performance. However, in practice, paying for actual performance through the public financial management structures can still be tedious and time consuming, as is illustrated in box 7.2.

In each PBF scheme, some details on payment to health facilities need to be formulated, such as the following:

- The initial performance payment
- The frequency of payment
- Lack of banking facilities
- Accounting for the money.

BOX 7.2

Payment for Performance in Burundi

In the Burundi PBF system, a quasi-public purchaser approach, payment for performance can take between 43 and 50 working days. The various fund holders (about 10 in total in the country) have different payment cycles. The cycle that takes most time—that is 50 days—belongs to the public fund holder, which currently pays about 70 percent of all the PBF expenses in Burundi. For the public fund holder, the various steps in the payment cycle are (a) creation of the invoice for the previous month by the health facility (5 days); (b) verification at the source of the monthly invoice by the provincial purchaser (14 days); (c) data validation by the provincial purchaser (1 day); (d) synthesis, compilation, due diligence, and transmission of payment order to the General Resources Directorate

(5 days); (e) due diligence by the General Resources Directorate and transfer of payment request to the Ministry of Finance (3 days); and (f) payment by the ministry to health facilities (21 days). Payment for quantity production is monthly. Each quarter, the third month's production is combined with the additional quality bonus based on the quality obtained. However, even though the procedures seem long, the previous system for reimbursing providers for selective free health care services (for pregnant women and children under five years of age) often took up to six months. The processing time changed after scaling up PBF in April 2010. Currently, the Burundi PBF system combines funding for PBF with funds available for selective free health care.

The Initial Performance Payment

Health staff may have a long wait for the first performance payment. Consider this issue when scaling up PBF. Staff members may have heightened expectations: they have worked hard to make a difference, yet must wait two months after the end of the first quarter to receive their first payment (up to five months into the program). This initial delay in rewards can create resentment. Two ways of dealing with this delay are (a) to introduce quality improvement units and to finance the business plan (see chapter 9) and (b) to allow a lump-sum payment by the end of the second month into the next quarter of the PBF program (for the previous quarter's performance). A lump sum will demonstrate to the staff that PBF is a reality, and it can help kick-start the quarterly payment cycle (because the payment for the first quarter will arrive in month five).

The Frequency of Payment

Payment is best made once a quarter. Although payment could be monthly, as in Burundi it is probably easier for the system to pay once per quarter. The indice tool not only helps the health facility manager distribute performance bonuses quarterly (by dividing the bonus portion over three months), but also assists in the financial planning.

Lack of Banking Facilities

Some health facilities have no access to formal banking services. An absence of formal banks can be an obstacle for PBF, and creative thinking is often needed to find a solution, as illustrated in box 7.3.

Accounting for the Money

Accounting for the money is part and parcel of PBF practice. For the funds they handle, health facilities use income and expense registers to document their daily cash flows. The quarterly income-expense statement, which is part of the PBF indice tool (see section 7.5) and the business plan (see chapter 10), is used by the health facility management committee, the purchasing agency, and the district health management. Health facility staff members are involved closely in deciding how much to spend on what. Their management regularly informs them about their individual performance evaluations and performance bonus payments. Health facility staff members are also closely consulted when an investment must be made that would require

Getting Money to Facilities

In South Kivu province, the Democratic Republic of Congo, Cordaid, a Dutch nongovernmental organization, has been managing a multisectoral PBF project since 2007. In this far-away region, health facilities could not open an account at a formal bank. The only bank branches were in the province's capital, Bukavu. Cordaid decided to use agricultural cooperatives and microcredit lenders. Although those institutions are not banks, they are registered and legitimate entities. Shabunda did not have even an agricultural cooperative, which meant that Cordaid initially had to use cash in an unsafe area. As a solution to this problem, the start-up costs of a cooperative were financed (which amounted to less than US$20,000). Today, Shabunda has a bank that traders and the purchasing agent use. With these arrangements, there have been no problems transferring money from the purchasing agent to the health facilities.

In Chad, a World Bank–funded project employs a performance-purchasing agency, the European Agency for Development and Health (AEDES) to carry out the purchasing function on behalf of the government. Chad has very low banking coverage. PBF is implemented in eight remote districts. For security reasons, AEDES was not willing to transport cash from a bank to the 120 contracted facilities. Initially, AEDES thought this lack of transportation would pose a major obstacle. In reality, there were many more options on the ground than the agency had accounted for. Money transfer agencies, microcredit institutions, and church-based payment systems were willing to step in. Ultimately, almost half the contracted facilities opened a bank account at an *express union*—a local money transfer agency that was ready to open a separate account for each facility. The other half of the facilities used the services of a microcredit agency (such as caisses d'épargne et de retraite de Koumra, PARCEC, Moissala, and CECI Lai). Five health facilities (mostly hospitals) opted to open an account in an official bank.

forfeiting part or whole of their performance bonuses. Making staff members of a health facility stakeholders in the financial health of their facility involves intense teamwork and a large degree of financial transparency and shared decision making. Health facilities can be subject to routine financial audits by the public administration.

7.5 The Indice Tool

The indice tool is a financial management tool that helps the manager (a) manage all cash income and expenses of the facility in a holistic and integrated manner; (b) provide a summary snapshot on the income and expense statements of the health facility and, therefore, is also a budget planning tool; and (c) allocate performance bonuses to individual health workers in a transparent manner.

The indice tool exists in a paper form and in a Microsoft Excel form (see box 7.4). In this section, the paper form is presented. For guidance on using the Microsoft Excel form, see the document explaining its functionality in the links to files in this chapter. The Microsoft Excel form is typically used in larger facilities that have access to electricity and computers. The paper form is mostly used in smaller facilities such as health centers.

The Paper-Based Indice Tool

The indice tool exists in many variants. The example used here is from Nigeria (see the links to files in this chapter). The Nigerian tool contains four sections:

a. Revenues and expenses for the past quarter: statement of quarterly financial activities
b. Revenues and expenses for the past month and proposed monthly revenues and expenses for the next quarter
c. Budget for performance bonuses; point value and monthly performance bonus
d. Individual indice value and bonus.

Revenues and Expenses for the Past Quarter: Statement of Quarterly Financial Activities

This first part of the indice tool lists the cash income that the health facility has received and specifies the source of this cash over the previous quarter. It also itemizes the health facility expenditures in various categories over the same quarter, and it gives the bank balance. Table 7.1 is an example of the tool.

BOX 7.4

The Three Health Facility PBF Tools

The indice tool forms part of the three PBF health facility tools: (a) the business plan, (b) the indice tool, and (c) the individual monthly health worker performance evaluation. These tools would best be presented together in chapter 10, titled "Improving Health Facility Management." However, because of the nature of the indice tool, it is discussed in this chapter.

TABLE 7.1 Example of Quarterly Financial Activities
Naira

	Statement of quarterly financial activities			Quarter/year	
N_R	**Revenue categories**	**Revenues**	**N_E**	**Expense categories**	**Expenses**
1	Cost recovery (user charges)	242,550	9	Salaries	0
2	Cost recovery (prepayment schemes)	0	10	Performance bonuses	140,000
3	Salaries from government and other sources	0	11	Drugs and medical consumables	195,000
4	PBF subsidies from fund holders	427,980	12	Subsidies for subcontracts	0
5	Contributions from other sources	0	13	Cleaning and office costs	50,000
6	Other	0	14	Transport costs	46,200
7	Cash in hand	55,525	15	Social marketing	24,855
8	Bank balance at the beginning of the quarter	45,000	16	Infrastructure rehabilitation	150,000
	Total revenue	771,055	17	Equipment and furniture	150,000
			18	Other	15,000
			19	Amount put into reserve (cash at hand plus bank balance at the end of the quarter)	0
				Total expenses	771,055
				Balance (total revenue – total expenses)	0

Source: World Bank data.

Note: N_E = number of expense; N_R = number of revenue; PBF = performance-based financing.

In this example, a total of ₦771,055 came in as income (revenue), and ₦771,055 was spent (expenditure) over the past quarter. This income-expense statement also figures in the quantified quality checklist tool (see chapter 3) under the finance section.

The following observations can be made:

- The health facility received ₦427,980 for PBF payments over the previous quarter. (These payments actually represent the performance of the quarter preceding the previous quarter, because PBF payments are received only once per quarter and the payments take about two months to be processed). Besides PBF, the cash income in this example stemmed from out-of-pocket payments. Various other income categories in this example did not yield income, such as cash subsidies from the government and other sources.

- Income from salaries is 0, because salaries were paid directly to the health workers and were not counted in this income-expense statement. If part or all of salaries would be paid in cash to the facility management, for instance, if human resources management were decentralized to the facilities, then the cash income for the salaries would be put under that particular income category on the indice sheet.
- On the expenditure side, only ₦140,000 was used for performance bonuses in this example. In Nigeria, the PBF system could allow up to 50 percent of the PBF income, that is, ₦213,990 (₦427,980/2), to be spent on performance bonuses. However, for some reason, the facility management in this example decided to invest more in infrastructure rehabilitation (₦150,000) and the acquisition of equipment and furniture (₦150,000).
- The facility's income from out-of-pocket payments was ₦242,550, while spending on drugs and medical consumables was ₦195,000. The facility is probably operating a Bamako-type drug revolving fund. The health facility staff would have been trained and would be coached systematically in understanding the link between rational prescribing of generic drugs (lower costs to the clients) and increased use (decreased financial barriers to access to services) and increased income through PBF (targeting of predominantly preventive services).
- The "social marketing" category reflects expenses for outreach activities (vaccinations; bed nets; latrine construction; information, education, and communication campaigns; and so on).
- In the "subsidies for subcontracts" category, the facility can pay any contractor. In this Nigerian example scheme, the main PBF contract holder is allowed to subcontract certain services to other health providers (either public or private), and it would then claim their production on its monthly invoice. The facility in this example, however, has not yet started subcontracting
- In this particular Nigerian PBF project, the quarterly income-expense statements, which are collected through the quarterly quality checklists, are entered in the web-enabled application. They will be used for summary and comparative analyses.

Revenues and Expenses for the Past Month and Proposed Monthly Revenues and Expenses for the Next Quarter

In the second section of the indice tool, one can fill out the planned income and expenses for the next quarter. The section contains two tables: the first for the income and the second for the expenses. The facility knows the quantity production of the previous three months (the monthly quantity invoices of those months would have been completed), and it can calculate the linked income. Therefore, by knowing its quality score, the health facility can fairly accurately predict its income for the next quarter through PBF. In addition, the facility can use this tool for its financial planning. In table 7.2, fictitious figures have been introduced as projected income.

With regard to the revenue side, note the following:

- The past month's revenue is taken as an indication of a certain trend. Seasonal influences are accounted for. The income can be higher in rainy seasons than in dry seasons because of the higher volume of patients accessing services for malaria- and diarrhea-related conditions.
- For PBF subsidies, one-third of the total PBF income of the previous quarter is taken (the amount allocated for performance bonus payments for that particular month). Bonuses are paid once a month, and the revenue from PBF is paid once a quarter.
- The facility expects to receive ₦600,000 from PBF based on the past quarter's performance.
- The facility has budgeted ₦100,000 to be set aside as reserve.

Table 7.3 shows the expense side.
With regard to the expense side, note the following:

- No salaries are paid. In this particular health facility, there are only public servants and they receive their salaries directly.
- The facility has budgeted ₦300,000 for performance bonuses that represent 50 percent of the projected income from PBF, which is the limit

TABLE 7.2 Example of Past and Projected Income
Naira

Revenues	Past monthly revenues	Proposed revenues next quarter
Cost recovery (user charges)	80,850	350,000
Cost recovery (prepayment schemes)	0	0
Salaries from government and other sources	0	0
PBF subsidies from fund holder	142,660	600,000
Contribution from other sources	0	0
Other	0	0
Cash in hand	55,525	xxxxxx
Bank balance at the end of the quarter	45,000	100,000
Total	324,035	1,050,000

Source: World Bank data.

Note: PBF = performance-based financing.

TABLE 7.3 Example of Past and Projected Expenses
Naira

Expenses	Past monthly expenses	Proposed expenses next quarter
Salaries	0	0
Performance bonuses	47,000	300,000
Drugs and medical consumables	100,000	300,000
Subsidies for subcontracts	0	0
Cleaning and office costs	35,000	60,000
Transport costs	30,000	65,000
Social marketing	17,000	50,000
Infrastructure rehabilitation	100,000	50,000
Equipment and furniture	75,000	100,000
Other	15,000	25,000
Amount put into reserve	0	100,000
Total	419,000	1,050,000

Source: World Bank data.

according to this specific Nigerian PBF scheme. The facility management can decide to spend less than 50 percent on performance bonuses—as it had in the previous quarter—but not more than 50 percent.
- The projected income is equal to the projected expense.

Budget for Performance Bonuses; Point Value and Monthly Performance Bonuses

In the third section of this indice tool (see table 7.4), the manager must fill in the following information:

- In the first row, the budget for performance bonuses for the next quarter is entered (this was ₦600,000). This component is called (**a**).
- In the second row, the number of indice points for all available staff for the past quarter is entered. This component is called (**b**).
- In the third row, the point value (**pv**) for the coming quarter is calculated as (**a**)/(**b**). In this example, (**pv**) = ₦454. The point value is expressed in the local currency.
- In the fourth row, the maximum monthly point value (**pm**) is provided: (**pv**)/3 = ₦151. This calculation means that for each month in the following quarter, a point is worth ₦151. So, if a nurse or midwife works well and is assessed at 100 percent on his or her individual performance

evaluation, then he or she is entitled to receive 90 (indice nurse) * 151 (**pm**) = ₦13,590 performance bonus for that month. (See chapter 10 for a discussion of the individual performance evaluations.) If that nurse or midwife would have scored 50 percent on the individual monthly performance evaluations, then he or she would have received 90 * 50% * 151 = ₦6,795.

- This method, therefore, not only allows spreading of the once-quarterly PBF payment to the facility over three months but also allows targeting of a performance-based share of that allocated performance bonus budget to an individual health worker.

Assume that the facility staff in this example had 1,320 points. As shown in table 7.5, each health staff category has a certain indice value. The facility's in-charge person has a value of 100 points, indicating a more essential staff member, whereas a cleaner has a value of 10 points, indicating a less essential staff member. The total number of points for all staff members who were present during the past quarter (the numbers can fluctuate) is 1,320 points. The individual indice values mean that from whatever amount, a share of 100/1,320 will accrue to the facility's in-charge person and a share of 10/1,320 will accrue to a cleaner or security guard. These indices can be adapted according to the local situation. In table 7.5, there is a very large number of security guards and cleaners (20). Giving them a lower indice value allows more of the performance bonus points to be passed on to the more essential staff.

TABLE 7.4 Example of Budget for Employee Performance Bonuses

Budget component	Naira or points	Naira (₦) or points
Budget for performance bonuses for next quarter (**a**)	600,000	₦
Number of points for all staff for the past quarter (**b**)	1,320	points
Point value (**pv**) coming quarter = (**a**)/(**b**)	454	₦
Maximum point value per month (**pm**) = (**pv**)/3	151	₦
Individual monthly performance bonus = (% of individual performance score (**p**)) * (individual indice value (**i**)) * (**pm**)		₦

Source: World Bank data.

Note: pv = point value; pm = per month; p = % of individual performance score, i – individual indice value.

TABLE 7.5 Example of Employee Indice Value

No.	Category of worker	Indice value for Samina HC	Samina HC staff no	Points
1	In-charge person	100	1	100
2	Community health officer	80	2	160
3	Nurses and midwives	90	3	270
4	Community health extension worker	60	4	240
5	Technician	60	3	180
6	Junior community health extension worker	25	2	50
7	Ward aides and attendants	20	6	120
8	Security guards and cleaners	10	20	200
			Total	**1,320**

Source: World Bank data.

Note: HC = health center; No. = number.

Individual Indice Value and Bonus

The individual indice value is recorded in the motivation contract that each health worker signs with the health facility committee (see chapter 10). In the Nigerian PBF system, the rules are as follows:

- The indice tool uses (a) the maximum point value for each staff member from his or her motivation contract (see chapter 11), (b) the individual performance evaluation for each staff member (see chapter 10), and (c) the point value for the following quarter obtained from the budget for employee performance bonuses (see table 7.4, row 3).
- Each month of the following quarter, staff members are assessed using the individual performance evaluation (see chapter 10). The score is recorded in a specific register.
- Indice scores are discussed within the facility management team and presented to the health facility committee.
- Each month before the middle of the following month and after vetting by the health facility committee, staff members receive their variable performance bonus.
- Staff members who are not employed at the facility during the month in which the bonus is paid (for example, if they have left the facility and are no longer employed) are not entitled to a performance bonus payment.
- Unspent bonus money is automatically placed in the reserve fund.

- The facility management, in close collaboration with the facility health committee, reserves the right to invest in the facility infrastructure or equipment instead of paying the performance bonuses. Such a decision should be endorsed by the majority of the staff.

The indice tool ends with a list of all staff members and includes their indice values and individual monthly performance evaluations (see table 7.6).

TABLE 7.6 Consolidated Indice Values and Performance Evaluations of Employees

No	Family name, first name	Indice (i)	Monthly_ Point_Value (pm)	%_Perform_ Eval (p)	Gross_Bonus (pb) = (i)*(p)*(pm)	Taxes (t)	Net_Bonus (pb) – (t)
1							
2							
3							
4							
5							
6							
7							
8							
9							
10							
11							
12							
13							
14							
15							
16							
17							
18							
19							
20							
21							
	Total (b)						

Source: World Bank data.

Note: i = individual indice value; No = number; p = % of individual performance score; pb = performance bonus; pm = point value per month; t = tax.

7.6 Links to Files and Tools

The following toolkit files can be accessed through this web link: http://www.worldbank.org/health/pbftoolkit/chapter07.

- Sample health facility monthly invoice
- Sample district PBF steering committee quarterly invoice
- Nigerian indice tool
- Microsoft Excel–based indice tool
- Document explaining the functionality of the Microsoft Excel–based indice tool.

CHAPTER 8

Performance Frameworks for Health Administration: Incentivizing Regulatory Tasks

MAIN MESSAGES

→ PBF administrators should work with performance frameworks.

→ Performance frameworks focus on core functions that are under the health administration's control and are important for reaching PBF results at the health facility level: furnishing regular supportive supervision, applying the quality checklist quarterly, organizing capacity building on select topics, maintaining the vaccine supply facility, ensuring hygiene in other sectors such as hotels and markets, ensuring a well-functioning pharmaceutical sector, and functioning as the secretariat of the district PBF steering committee.

→ The financial rewards attached to the performance framework should be high enough to cover individual performance payment and recurrent cost elements.

8.1 Introduction: The Reason for PBF Performance Frameworks for Health Administration

Performance frameworks for the health administration are a vital ingredient of performance-based financing (PBF). They facilitate the health administration's regulatory engagement in PBF. Performance frameworks focus on core functions that are under the health administration's control—such as supportive supervision, the quality checklist, and the secretariat for the PBF district steering committee—and are key in reaching PBF results at the health facility level. It is crucial that the financial rewards attached to the performance framework are high enough to cover individual performance pay and recurrent cost elements.

This chapter deals with the background to these performance frameworks. It discusses how they should be designed and how much money should be used. The content of an average performance framework is illustrated. Through the links to files in this chapter, you can access specific examples from Burundi, Nigeria, Rwanda, and Zambia.

8.2 Performance Frameworks for Health Administration: How They Work

Purchasing agencies use performance frameworks to assess the level of performance of administrative entities. Administrative entities at the district, regional, or central level can be paid performance-based rewards if they carry out certain tasks well.[1] Performance frameworks are set out in a contract (for contracts, see chapter 11) with money attached to results.

In early PBF pilots in Rwanda (2002–05), performance frameworks were used to engage district health departments. The departments were paid according to the level of achievement of certain preagreed functions like supportive supervision, training, coordination activities, and, in some cases, the application of a quantified quality checklist.

This system was disrupted in the move from a private purchaser approach (nongovernmental organization [NGO] or bilateral agency PBF pilot with the purchaser also holding the funds) to a public purchaser approach in which funds were managed through the Ministry of Finance. The concept of paying health administration staff members a financial reward for activities they were supposed to perform in the first place met with fierce opposition.

Under the new regime, the pay-for-performance schemes of many health facilities ran into trouble. The administrative units tasked with executing the quantity verification and applying the quality checklist did not do their part. They were late or did not carry out their tasks sufficiently. Health facilities did not receive any money and began to rebel. Ultimately, the solution was found in pay-for-performance methods applied inside the public administrative system (see box 8.1).

8.3 What Performance Frameworks Include and Who Assesses Them

PBF performance frameworks measure and reward objectively verifiable actions related to system-strengthening tasks. The district health administration is well positioned to carry out such systemic tasks, which include the following:

- Application of the quality checklist to health centers (see chapter 3)
- Functions in the pharmaceutical sector and district pharmacy stores
- Hygiene checks at different levels such as households, hotels, bars, markets, and garbage disposal by urban authorities
- General coordination and capacity building
- Management of the secretariat for the district PBF steering committee
- Formative supervision or coaching related to the business plan; the indice tool
- Coordination of the vaccine supply facility.

A generic example of a performance framework is provided in table 8.1. This example can be adapted to fit specific needs. The example illustrates that as a PBF designer, one should take care to work with objectively verifiable performance measures. Specify which supporting documents are required, and articulate any subcriteria very clearly. For each indicator, a weight must be established. The weights can be adapted depending on the emphasis to be given to a certain activity and its performance requirements. By using clear

BOX 8.1
The Need for Performance Frameworks: Learning the Hard Way

In Rwanda in 2006, the scaled-up PBF model used a public purchaser approach. Purchase contracts were signed by the district mayors—on behalf of the Ministry of Health—and the health facilities. The decentralized district administration, which officially fell under the Ministry of Local Administration, was allocated the task of performing the monthly quantity verification for PBF. The district hospital, which reported to the Ministry of Health, was allocated the task of carrying out the quantified quality checklist once per quarter for each contracted facility. In addition, district hospitals had to participate in peer evaluations that assessed each other's quality performance. A district-level steering committee was supposed to meet once per quarter to validate the results and follow up on reported performance.

Initially, nothing ran smoothly. The local administration staff members had to be put in cars organized by the supporting NGOs and brought to the health facilities to carry out the monthly verifications. They claimed to not have transportation or fuel. The hospital staff was reluctant to carry out the quality checklists and performed poorly, inflating results to cover such inadequacy. Peer evaluation of hospitals was not carried out in a timely manner.

In the course of time, several solutions were found. For hospitals, timely participation in the peer evaluation processes and timely application of the quality checklist for health centers became items in the hospital's balanced score card, in which these elements became significantly weighted (with financial consequences). The district administration was nudged by the *Imihigo* contracts—those between the president of Rwanda and the mayors—that specified certain health-related performance indicators. The district health administration was therefore quickly aligned and funds were made available by the districts to carry out the monthly quantity verifications. Finally, the district PBF steering committees were put under a performance framework that rewarded timely and correct procedures. The minutes of committee meetings, along with the signed, consolidated district invoice, had to reach the central level before a set date (the 10th day of the 5th month). Although the financial reward to the district steering committees was not very high, this system of yardsticks, competition, and naming and shaming led to excellent adherence to the guidelines.

contracts, at the end of each quarter, one can judge and benchmark the performance of a district health department against that of others.

Usually, administration performance is measured once per quarter. In the majority of cases, the measuring is carried out by purchasing agency staff. Other arrangements can be suggested as well, as long as conflict-of-interest situations are avoided. The performance can be validated in the district PBF steering committees, which provide a good forum to discuss matters openly and guarantee some transparency. In practice, benchmarking and yardstick competition have had a significant influence on the performance of district

TABLE 8.1 Example of Performance Framework

No.	Performance measure	Data sources	Validation criteria	Weight
1	50 percent of HCs have been supervised at least once per quarter	Supervision report Travel request form approved and signed Travel form cosigned by the head of visited facilities	Supervision report exists and is readily available at the district health department. At least 50 percent of all HCs have been supervised during the past quarter, and these should not include those HCs that have been supervised in the quarter preceding the evaluated quarter. These supervisory visits are the formative visits and are not the same as the Quantity or Quality Audit visits. The reports should indicate the dates of visits and, at a minimum, summarize the findings and interventions of each visit. **If any criteria are not met: 0 points**	15
2	At least two monthly meetings with PB= HC in the district health department during the past quarter	Meeting minutes Participants list	Each of the two meeting reports must have the following: Date and time indicated Agenda available Signed participants list available Discussion on the contents of the past month's HC monthly reports using the printed monthly HC reports (from the HMIS database) Follow-up of recommendations and tasks from previous meeting Action points listed with tasks attributed **If any criteria are lacking: 0 points; 5 points per valid meeting according to the criteria**	10
3	At least one-half hour training on one specific topic, during the monthly HC staff meetings	Meeting minutes Participants list	In the meeting minutes, a description of the topic as follows: Objective of the training Short description of the session, referring to the available national protocol **If both criteria are not met: 0 points**	5
4	Monthly HC HMIS report entered in the HMIS database and report printed	Printed HC HMIS monthly cumulative report Data available in the HMIS database Monthly HC HMIS reports (original)	Printed monthly HC HMIS report is available and filed in a specific file. Original monthly HC HMIS reports are available and filed in the specific HC files at the district health department. All HC HMIS reports for all HCs in the district are available. **If one or more criteria are not met: 0 points**	5

(table continues on next page)

TABLE 8.1 *(continued)*

No.	Performance measure	Data sources	Validation criteria	Weight
5	Monthly activity calendar available	Activity calendar	Monthly activity plan is available and clearly describes planned activities with start and finish dates.	5
			Activity calendar for the current month is visible without difficulty on a wall of the district health department.	
			If one or both criteria are not met: 0 points	
6	Participation in quarterly district PBF steering committee meeting	District PBF steering committee meeting minutes	District PBF steering committee meeting has been held prior to the end of the fourth month.	20
		Participants list	Provision of secretariat to the district PBF steering committee has occurred, according to the set formats for such proceedings.	
			Eventual changes to the minutes of the previous meetings have been fully incorporated.	
			Presentation and discussion of the district PBF steering committee's last meeting minutes have occurred. Minutes have been sent out by email to all parties five calendar days prior to the meeting.	
			Discussion and eventual validation of three monthly PBF consolidated invoices (one per month per contracted HC) have occurred in the district PBF steering committee meeting.	
			Meeting has been held subject to the legal quorum defined in the district PBF steering committee agreement.	
			If one or more criteria are not met: 0 points	
7	Quarterly quality performance evaluation of all PBF HCs done	HC quality performance checklists completed	All HC quality performances for the past quarter have been evaluated before the end of the fourth month and evaluation has been completed prior to the district PBF steering committee meeting, using the designated quality checklists.	40
		Travel request forms signed and approved	The HC quality performance evaluation form (all items filled), including the recommendation sections, has been used correctly.	
			All HC performance evaluation forms have been correctly filed in a specific folder.	
			If one or more criteria are not met: 0 points	
			(Maximum 100 Points) Grand Total	

Source: World Bank data.

Note: HC = health center; HMIS = health management information system; No. = number; PBF = performance-based financing.

health department staff. The money attached to performance frameworks proves a good stimulus and facilitates the practical execution of the work. In addition, health administrators are frequently confronted with competing priorities such as attending training courses, where per diems can be earned. PBF performance frameworks help staff focus on the duties that are vital for PBF systems to function. At the same time, they offer good managerial tools for the district health directors to use in focusing and managing their staff.

8.4 How Much Money to Budget for PBF Performance Frameworks

Budget sufficiently for PBF performance frameworks. The exact amount will depend on the context. As a rule of thumb, think about the usual costs related to carrying out supervisory tasks and about the amount of additional income that would motivate district health staff to carry out the PBF work. The department staff may already have transportation available for supervision. However, there are always issues such as vehicle maintenance, lack of fuel money, or cars and motorbikes that are being used for other services. Often, district health staff members have competing priorities, because their income tends to be low and does not offer a living wage.

In many countries, there is ample opportunity to visit health facilities because of parallel vertical programs, each with its own budget and per diem structure. The money that can be earned through PBF will nudge district health staff to use existing resources more efficiently (see box 8.2).

BOX 8.2

A Second Scaling-up in Burundi: Applying Lessons Learned from Rwanda

Lessons learned in Rwanda during the scaling-up of PBF approaches to work through public financial management were applied in Burundi at the onset of the design of scaling-up PBF (in 2009–10).

In the Burundi approach, incentivizing the public health administration was applied immediately, from the district and province level to the central level (the Ministry of Health unit managing the PBF). The central level incentive scheme has generated much interest from various partners and has driven the policy dialog on civil service reform in the Ministry of Health. This experience is a good example of south-south learning and of application of best practices.

Incentivizing the public health administration, through output-based performance frameworks, is now an integral part of the PBF system-strengthening approach. It has been included in the best practice on how to scale up PBF through internal market mechanisms.

8.5 Links to Files and Tools

Short case studies and examples of performance frameworks can be accessed through this web link: http://www.worldbank.org/health/pbftoolkit/chapter08.

- Rwanda:
  - Rwanda district PBF steering committee
  - Rwanda sector PBF steering committee
  - Rwanda central PBF support unit (Cellule d'Appui a l'Approche Contractuelle, CAAC).
- Burundi:
  - Burundi central PBF technical support unit (CTN)
  - Burundi Provincial Verification and Validation Committee (CPVV)
  - Burundi provincial health office
  - Burundi district health office.
- Zambia:
  - Zambia District Health Management Team.
- Nigeria:
  - Nigeria Local Government Authority Primary Health Care Department.

Note

1. Health administrations differ among countries, such as prefectures in the Central African Republic; districts in Anglophone countries; provinces in Burundi; and departments in the Republic of Congo.

PART 2

DESIGN STRUCTURE AND ISSUES

CHAPTER 9

Investments to Help Start Health Facilities

MAIN MESSAGES

→ Health facilities respond faster to PBF when assisted by investments.
→ Investments are budgeted in investment units and are provided in cash.
→ The health facility management and community are told the amount of money available to them and are invited to set their own priorities and plan accordingly. A business plan is created by the health facility management and negotiated with the purchaser.

COVERED IN THIS CHAPTER

9.1 Introduction

Health facilities respond faster to performance-based financing (PBF) if there is room for targeted investments. In PBF, targeted investments can be provided through a negotiated business plan. Such investments should be provided in cash and hold the health facility accountable through a follow-up on their business plan.

9.2 The Investment Unit

The investment unit, also called a quality improvement unit, is a certain amount of money meant to assist the health facility in improving its service quality (Soeters 2013). Investment units are used for budgeting purposes by the purchaser. The purchaser can budget a certain sum for such activities and subsequently allocate "units," or sums of money, to finance certain activities carried out by health facilities. For example, such a unit can be set at US$1,000 or US$2,500. These investment units are provided in cash.

9.3 Why Investment Units Are Needed

Investment units are often necessary because many health facilities are in poor shape after years of disinvestment or outright negligence. In many places, years of turbulence or poor maintenance have led to a dilapidated infrastructure, broken or absent equipment or furniture, and lack of access to water or sanitation. Establishing some basic preconditions for providing quality health services is a major focus of any health improvement program, including PBF.

9.4 How Much Money Is Involved

The amount of money needed for such basic investments depends largely on the context. One size does not fit all. However, for illustration, for an average health facility with a catchment population of 10,000–15,000 in a low-income country, one could budget about US$5,000 per year. In this specific example, one could decide to work with investment units of US$1,000 (see box 9.1). This approach allows for targeting more (small unit) investments to the most destitute areas or to health facilities that are in need of more investments. Nevertheless, the required sums depend not only on what is necessary but also on what can be leveraged or coordinated from other sources. And apart from what is necessary and available through other sources, the investment units also depend on the actual budget available to the purchaser.

BOX 9.1

The Democratic Republic of Congo: Investment Units Make More Sense

The investment unit approach was first developed in the Democratic Republic of Congo after an earthquake in 2008 in the PBF intervention area. Several health facilities and staff houses were destroyed. The purchasing agency received an emergency grant from the government of the Netherlands. Instead of applying the traditional approach to contract an external agency to do the renovations, the purchasing agency requested the health facilities managers to propose renovations in their own business plans and to carry out the renovations themselves. Payments were made after the agreed-upon milestones were achieved and verified by an architect for quality. Six months later, all 37 health facilities and 6 staff houses, including those damaged in the earthquake, were renovated at a cost of about

US$220,000. About 30 percent of these contracts were for new construction.

The results were far above expectation, and a cost-effectiveness study was conducted in the same multisector project for the construction of standard six-class primary schools. The nongovernmental organization Cordaid had previously constructed four schools in the same area through an external agency at a cost of US$240,000. Based on earlier experience in the health facilities, the investment unit approach was then applied and 14 schools were constructed. The school management supervised the entire effort and also invested money from its own resources. The results showed a cost-effectiveness ratio of 3.2 (see table B9.1.1).

TABLE B9.1.1 Investment Unit Approach in the Democratic Republic of Congo, 2007–09

Unit	Cordaid Emergency Program November 2007–August 2009	Cordaid AAP-PBF September 2008–December 2009
Standard schools built	5	14
Investments	US$240,000	US$182,200
Unit cost	US$48,000	US$15,000
Improved cost effectiveness 2009/2008 = US$48,000/US$15,000 = 3.2		

Source: World Bank data.

Note: AAP = Agence d'Achat de Performance; PBF = performance-based financing.

9.5 How Investment Units Work

Investment units are negotiated through the business plans that are drawn up by the health facility and its community. They work through a decentralized priority setting by an autonomous health facility management.

Making health facilities and their communities responsible, and providing them with the autonomy to use the money for certain intended investment purposes, is a win-win situation. The health facility and its community win because they can work toward fixing their own problems, and the purchaser wins because the approach is a more efficient solution to building infrastructure. Investment units are provided in cash because this is a more efficient solution than attempting to micromanage reconstruction and deliver inputs to the health facility through central planning and input financing.

Providing cash and autonomy to health facility management will be a new development in many contexts. A certain degree of trial and error will certainly occur. The quantified quality checklist (see chapter 3) has proved to be very handy in this new situation. The health facility management can be guided through an initial planning process of how to invest a certain amount of money to upgrade its facility and how to respond best to the new quality standards. Setting quality standards is demanding, and choosing between competing priorities can be challenging. It is best to leave the priority setting to the health facility management itself. Health facility staff often knows best what is needed and what level of effort can be provided. This decentralized approach makes the health facility management and its community responsible for the upkeep of their health services and allows them to create local solutions to difficult problems (see box 9.2).

Health facilities know what drugs and medical consumables are out of stock and also possibly where to obtain such items of good quality and price locally. Equally, they will be aware of where to obtain minor equipment such as blood pressure gauges, weighing scales, and items necessary for a delivery kit. For repairing furniture or making new furniture and for repairing a leaking roof, a broken door, and so on, the health facility and its community might have ready cost-effective solutions. Making such choices in an open fashion, through a business plan, allows negotiation and agreement with the health facility management on these activities. The business plan is an important tool for the purchaser and the health facility alike and forms an integral part of the purchasing contract (for more details, see chapter 10).

BOX 9.2

Using Investment Units for Fast Improvements of Quality in a Nigerian PBF Project

In Nigeria, public health facilities suffered from years of disinvestment. Most of the public budget was spent on salaries, leaving barely any recurrent budget for drugs or other essentials. In three districts across three states, a PBF pilot was started. Health facilities opened a bank account, and a new public governance mechanism involving the local community was instituted. During training, the in-charge person of the health facility and the president of the health facility management were trained in the use of the business plan. The health facility management was allowed to budget up to US$3,000 for improvements and received up to two weeks to finalize the business plan and to negotiate it with the district health department and a representative of the purchasing agent. Within two weeks after agreeing on the business plan, the health facilities received this money in their bank accounts. All facilities purchased an initial stock of drugs and medical consumables to start a drug-revolving fund and spent the remainder of the money on minor repairs, equipment, furniture, and the like. Within a four-month period, the baseline quality in health facilities, as measured through a comprehensive quantified quality checklist, increased from 22 percent to 55 percent. Six months into the project, health facilities were provided the opportunity to plan again, through their business plans, for a second investment of US$3,000.[a]

a. For some of the results, see Nigeria National Primary Health Care Development Agency, PBF Portal, http://nphcda.thenewtechs.com.

Reference

Soeters, R., ed. 2013. *PBF in Action: Theory and Instruments—Course Guide, Performance-Based Financing.* The Hague: Cordaid-SINA. http://www.sina-health.com/?page_id=585.

CHAPTER 10

Improving Health Facility Management

MAIN MESSAGES

→ PBF must be accompanied by improvement in health facility management.

→ PBF introduces three important management-strengthening tools at the health facility level: (a) the business plan, (b) the individual performance evaluation, and (c) the indice tool.

→ PBF embraces advanced strategies to improve health facility results.

COVERED IN THIS CHAPTER

10.1 Introduction

Performance-based financing (PBF) contributes to and benefits from good health facility management. Already at the outset, PBF can improve health facility management considerably by using three basic management-strengthening tools and by exposing management to strategies that have worked to deliver good results elsewhere.

10.2 The Three Management-Strengthening Tools

Three PBF management strengthening tools:

1. Business plan
2. Individual performance evaluation
3. Indice tool

Three basic management-strengthening tools that greatly help advance management in PBF are (a) the PBF business plan, (b) the individual performance evaluation, and (c) the indice tool. These tools assist the health facility management in carrying out its planning processes, in managing individual staff performance, and in allocating performance bonuses. Two of the tools, the business plan and the individual performance evaluation, are discussed in this chapter. The third one, the indice tool, is discussed in chapter 4 (titled "Setting the Unit Price and Costing") of this toolkit, because it is of great importance in balancing the budget and in allocating performance bonuses.

Main Management Tool Number One: The PBF Business Plan

The business plan is a planning document created by the management of a health facility. It is negotiated with the purchaser and approved by the health facility management. The business plan describes the baseline situation for a given facility and indicates the results that can be expected. It also proposes clear strategies to achieve those goals. A business plan helps the purchaser engage in strategic purchasing (see chapter 4).

Most health facility staff members know their catchment population but are not used to planning and measuring activities according to actual targets. Even in situations in which targets are used for planning, a follow-up on the results is often rare. Moreover, when targets have a high visibility, such as the case with vaccination targets (Murray et al. 2003), overreporting is common. A business plan helps health facility staff members delineate where they want to go and assess where they find them-selves on the path to reaching certain goals.

Business plans are necessary because of the following:

- They help providers assess where they are and plan realistic targets (see box 10.1).
- They help clarify which resources the facility will invest in and which strategies the facility will apply.
- They allow the purchaser to control health facility performance better and to correct any deviations faster.

Business plans may have different formats (see various examples in the links to files in this chapter). One tested example is discussed below. But many other formats are possible.

Business Plan: An Example

A business plan could resemble the general outline found in table 10.1. In the "Content" column of table 10.1, a guiding question related to the target for a specific service and a formula for calculating the absolute target for that service (*in italics*) is provided. Following the general outline, we illustrate how a business plan works by discussing two sections in more detail—external consultations and institutional deliveries.

External consultations and institutional deliveries, sections 2 and 11, respectively, of table 10.1, are discussed in more detail below. These sections illustrate the types of issues that management must confront.

BOX 10.1

Business Plans Differ from Action Plans

Business plans are frequently mistaken for action plans. Although business plans resemble action plans, they differ in significant ways. First, business plans are an integral part of PBF purchase contracts and are negotiated carefully between the provider and the purchaser. A PBF contract is not valid without an approved busi-ness plan. Second, business plans contain realistic targets and fair descriptions of strategies to reach those targets. Because of these differences, PBF pioneers refer to such plans as business plans instead of action plans (Soeters 2013).

TABLE 10.1 The General Content of a Business Plan

No.	Section	Content
1	General information	• Administrative region • Population • Staff (qualified and support staff) • Eventual subcontracted facilities • Summary health facility statistics, such as those for select reproductive and child health services, outpatient services, and admission days
2	External consultations	• What is your monthly target population? *(Total population in your catchment area/12)* (The number of new curative consultations in this example is one per person per year.)
3	Referral of patients	• What is the monthly target for referral of seriously ill patients in your catchment area? *(Population/12 × 5%)* (The number of seriously ill patients in this example is 5%.)
4	Vitamin A distribution (children between 6 and 59 months) Preschool consultations (children between 12 and 59 months)	• What is the number of children between the age of 6 and 59 months who should receive each month a vitamin A capsule in your catchment area? *(Population × 18%/12 × 2 caps)* • What is the number of children each month who should finish six standard visits for preschool consultations between the age of 12 and 59 months? *(Population × 16%/12 × 6)*
5	Vaccinations	• Calculations related to five vaccination targets are required: • BCG • DPT3 • Measles • Fully immunized children • Fully immunized pregnant women (TT2+) *(The target group of children less than 1 year of age is [4.3%] of the population of the catchment area. The number of pregnancies in the catchment area is estimated at [4.8%].)*
6	Distribution of bed nets	• What is the monthly bed net distribution in your catchment area if the target is 100%? (The area of health population/5 years/12 months/1.5 people. One bed net has a life span of 5 years and is used by 1.5 persons on average [child with mother—couple].) • What was the bed net coverage rate in the previous quarter? *(Number of nets distributed during the past quarter/catchment area population/4 quarters/5 years/1.5 persons)*
7	Tuberculosis	• What are the monthly targets for TB detection *(population/100,000 × 150/12)* and the TB treatment *(population/100,000 × 150/12)* in your catchment area? (The incidence for AFB+ PTB in this example is assumed to be 150 new cases of AFB+ PTB per 100,000 population per year.)
8	New family using a latrine	• What is the monthly target for new families using latrines in your catchment area? *(Population/4.6 persons per household/12 months/3 years)* (The average household in this example has 4.6 persons and one latrine per household, and the average latrine lasts three years.)

TABLE 10.1 *(continued)*

No.	Section	Content
9	Family planning	Calculate the number of couples (women) who should use oral and injectable FP methods in your catchment area each month if 22.5% is the target. *(New + existing users = population × 25%/12 × 22.5% × 4)* (In this example, 22.5% of the population is women of childbearing age, while the unmet need is estimated at 25%. Only modern contraceptives are counted, and those are counted in three-month cycles. Modern contraceptives are injectable contraceptives, implants, IUDs, and OCPs.)[a]
10	Antenatal care	• What is the target for the number of new antenatal care consultations per month? *(Population × 4.8%/12)* • What is the target for the number of antenatal consultancies per month to achieve the target for pregnant women who visit during their pregnancy at least three times? *(Population × 4.8%/12 × 3)*
11	Delivery care and abortions	• What is the coverage for deliveries that took place in the health facility in the past quarter? *(Number of realized births during the past quarter/population × 4.8% x 3)* • What is the monthly target for institutional deliveries for your catchment area? *(Population × 4.8%/12 months)*
12	Human resource management	• What remuneration does the health facility pay to staff from different revenues (from government sources, own sources, and so on)?
13	Other resources	• Drugs and medical consumables • Medical equipment • Furniture and office supplies • Infrastructure
14	Financial planning	• Financial planning—forecasted quarterly income and expenses • Income-expense statement from the past quarter

Source: World Bank data.

Note: AFB+ = acid-fast bacillus positive; BCG = Bacillus Calmette-Guérin; DPT3 = diphtheria, pertussis, tetanus; FP = family planning; IUD = intrauterine device; No. = number; OCP = oral contraceptive; PTB = pulmonary tuberculosis; TB = tuberculosis; TT2+ = second to the sixth tetanus toxoid vaccination.

a. Implants and IUDs are paid separately and against a higher fee as their protection spans several years.

External Consultations

• What is the monthly target for outpatient department (OPD) consultations in your ward?

(Total population in the ward catchment area /12.)

• What are the problems concerning OPD consultations attending your health center?

Analyze the possible factors such as (a) purchasing power of the population to pay fees, (b) fee payment per act or fixed fees, (c) competition with other health facilities, (d) lack of medicines, (e) remote villages, (f) lack of qualified personnel, and (g) staff motivation. Are there any other problems?

- What strategies are proposed to solve those problems?

Consider (a) increasing qualified staff, (b) adding outreach strategies, (c) proposing new subcontracts with health posts and private clinics, (d) decreasing fees, (e) providing pricing for flat fees or per activity, (f) discussing with untrained practitioners how they will stop practicing, and (g) involving the local health authorities.

Institutional Deliveries

- What is the coverage of deliveries in the health facility in the past quarter?

(Number of realized births during the past quarter/population × 4.8% × 3.)

- What is the monthly target for institutional deliveries for your catchment area?

(Population × 4.8%/12 months.)

- What problems are encountered in your catchment area?

Analyze the following: (a) availability of qualified staff with permanent duty roster, (b) clean delivery room, (c) confidentially assured, (d) equipment (delivery kit, sterile delivery boxes, vacuum extractors, and sutures), (e) sterilization procedures (gloves, plastic apron, and disinfection), (f) conditions of hospitalization (space, ventilation, bed net), and (g) existence of partogram and correct use.

- What strategies do you propose in consideration of the above factors?

Examine the following: (a) increase qualified staff, (b) buy equipment, (c) change hygiene and sterilization procedures, (d) rehabilitate infrastructure, (e) train staff, and (e) open a new maternity ward.

- What problems concerning unsafe abortions are in your catchment area?
- Consider the following: (a) maternal deaths after illegal abortions, (b) cases of pregnancy after rape, and (c) lack of access to safe abortions.
- What strategies do you propose to solve the above problems?

Main Management Tool Number Two: The Individual Monthly Performance Evaluation

Individual staff performance is assessed monthly through a performance evaluation tool (table 10.2). The staff is assessed by its facility management. The individual performance bonus depends on the performance assessment.

Main PBF Management Tool Number Three: The Indice Tool

For more details on the indice tool and on its role in strengthening management, see chapter 4.

BOX 10.2

Developing the Individual Performance Evaluation Based on the Expressed Needs of Health Facility Management

Individual performance evaluations were developed during the scaling up of PBF in Rwanda in 2006–07. Health facility managers started experimenting with performance assessments to counter the impression that they were biased in favor of certain staff members. Many managers developed such procedures. A review of the national PBF approach during the second half of 2007 documented those practices and found them very useful as lessons learned. Subsequently, a working group developed a national tool that could be used for guidance by health facility managers. Managers were encouraged to adapt it to fit their own needs. A standardized nationwide tool was introduced in early 2008.

The performance evaluation tool is a grid that helps assess individual performance objectively. The example in table B10.1.1 has been applied successfully in Rwanda and Burundi. This tool is a good stimulus for individuals to give their full energy to the health facility's desired results.

The tool is applied once per month. Depending on the size of the facility, either the in-charge person (health center) or a committee (hospital) applies it. Assessing objectively the performance of the manager is a novel approach that is being piloted in Nigeria. In that pilot, verifiers from the purchasing agency assess the manager's performance once per quarter. They use a grid specifically designed for measuring and rewarding the degree to which the manager applies the various management tools (business plan, indice tool, and individual staff performance evaluations).

The individual performance evaluation is an integral part of the motivation contract that all health workers sign with their facility management (see chapter 11). This motivation contract contains the health worker's indice value (see chapter 4). The indice value is a certain share, expressed in a specific number of points according to professional ranking, to which the health worker is entitled from the total performance bonus budget for a certain month. For example, the in-charge person might have an indice value of 100, the second-in-charge person a value of 90, a nurse a value of 80, and a security guard or cleaner a value of 20. If the nurse were to score 75 percent on an individual performance evaluation, he or she would be entitled to 75 percent of 80 points, which is 60 points (see table 10.2).

TABLE 10.2 Example of Individual Performance Evaluation for Health Staff

No.	Criteria	25% Score	50% Score	100% Score	Max Score
1	**Professional awareness includes the following: (20 points)**				
	Timeliness	Arrived late frequently *(at least 4 times per month)*	Arrived late sometimes *(1 to 3 times per month)*	Arrived on time always	8
	Availability	Frequently absent from service without any clear motive *(at least 4 times per month)*	A few times absent from service without clear motive *(1 to 3 times per month)*	Never absent from service without known and valid motive	8
	Uniform	Did not wear a uniform during working hours *(even once per month)*	Neglected the uniform *(dirty, torn, or not ironed)*	Uniform always worn and proper *(washed, ironed, and not torn)*	4
2	**Team spirit includes the following: (30 points)**				
	Interpersonal relationships	Frequently in conflict with colleagues *(report by colleague filed with superior more than once per month)*	Sometimes in conflict with colleagues *(report by colleague filed with superior once)*	Never in conflict with colleagues	8
	Collaborative spirit	Frequently refused to assist colleagues when asked *(more than once per month)*	Sometimes refused to assist colleagues *(even once)*	Never refused to assist colleagues	8
	Dedication	Frequently left work unfinished without somebody taking over and used the argument that official working hours were ended *(more than 3 times per month)*	Sometimes left work unfinished without somebody taking over and used the argument that official working hours were ended *(1 to 3 times per month)*	Never left work unfinished without somebody taking over	8
	Initiative	Never did any additional work	Always awaited a command from higher up to carry out additional work	At least once did additional work without being asked by the supervisor	6

3 **Technical competency and flexibility during work: (40 points)**

Organization	Never had daily work schedule (assessed during internal work supervision)	Sometimes had a daily work schedule (at least once during internal supervision)	Always had a daily work schedule	10
Quality of work	Never adhered to specific work-related norms and standards (assessed during internal supervision)	Sometimes adhered to work-related norms and standards (found at least once during internal supervision)	Always adhered to specific work-related norms and standards	14
Quantity of work	Never finished daily work according to his or her daily work schedule (assessed during internal supervision)	Sometimes finished work according to his or her daily work schedule (found at least once during internal supervision)	Always finished work according to his or her daily work schedule	16

4 **Willingness and aptitude for personal development: (10 points)**

Takes into account advice and recommendations from previous internal and external supervisory visits	Never took care of such recommendations (concluded during internal and external supervisory visits)	Sometimes took care of such recommendations (if this happens once or more)	Always took into account recommendations of internal and external supervisory visits	10
			TOTAL POINTS	100

5 **Participation to results and the past monthly performance score**

Participation to results and the past month's performance score (quantity and quality) through presence during working days during the past month:

Note: We take into account **actual working days without taking into account any valid reasons for absence** such as vacation, leave, sickness, absence through disciplinary action, formal trainings, and so on. An exception to this rule is rest and recuperation days (allocated by the health facility management), which, when accorded, are considered official working days.

Number of official working days = (N)

Number of days actually worked = (n)

Percentage of days performed = (P)

(P) = (n/N) * 100

Result of the individual monthly performance evaluation = (Total of the scores for items 1 to 4) * P

Source: World Bank data.

Note: Max = maximum; No. = number.

10.3 Advanced Strategies for Improving Health Facility Results: Learning from Good Practices

In addition to application of the basic PBF management tools, a wide array of advanced strategies has been developed to improve results, both through demand-side and supply-side interventions. Advanced strategies have been developed by successful PBF health facilities in various countries and thus have been tested in various contexts.

It is useful to share such experiences to avoid reinventing the wheel. Examples of such advanced strategies are as follows:

- Supply-side strategies:
  → Increasing clinic opening times
  → Decreasing staff absenteeism
  → Enhancing staff attitudes
  → Increasing the number of qualified staff members
  → Enhancing infrastructure, equipment, and drugs
  → Increasing collaboration with community health workers
  → Increasing outreach
  → Subcontracting secondary facilities, including the private sector.
- Demand-side strategies:
  → Lowering fees for curative care
  → Lowering or abolishing fees for family planning
  → Offering a baby-welcome package to pregnant women
  → Paying traditional birth attendants a fee for bringing pregnant women to the health facility
  → Paying community health workers a fee for following up on tuberculosis patients
  → Enhancing quality in general
  → Enhancing staff attitudes.

Advanced strategies that have been proven to work in a particular situation can be shared with health facilities that are just beginning PBF. PBF involves new ways of working for the health staff. Sharing lessons learned in other contexts is often highly appreciated by health providers. Avoid inventing advanced strategies that already have been discovered by others (learn from those): invent original ones. Table 10.3 lists a range of advanced strategies.

Advanced strategies such as the ones listed in table 10.3 will serve the facility in improving its results. This improvement has been shown in practice. Many of the strategies are simply common sense, and some strategies are

TABLE 10.3 Some Advanced Strategies for PBF

No.	Service	Advanced strategy	To do's	Explanation
0	General management	Use PBF tools.	• PBF equals record keeping. Keep 100% of your records, and get paid 100% for your performance. • Record keeping should be done according to a PBF report standard, be complete and legible, and include a mobile phone number and household number. • Use the quality checklist to identify weak points in the performance. • Provide checklist items for each service (quantity and quality). • Train your staff and PBF committee in PBF. • Apply the monthly individual performance evaluation, and discuss it with the staff member. • Apply the indice tool each quarter, and discuss results with your staff. • Each month, select an employee of the month. • Each week, have general staff meetings and discuss performance. • Share performance results with your staff, including results from the indice tool and financial management decisions. • Each month, have at least one management team meeting. • Each month, have a meeting with the PBF facility committee. • Delegate to your senior management: do not micromanage. • Be fair to your staff. • Ensure good teamwork. • Do activities together outside work.	• Better use of PBF instruments leads to better results, and better results lead to more satisfaction among the staff and the community. • Better results lead to more income for health facility and staff bonuses. • Good management leads to a better motivated staff, which leads to a better performance. • Good teamwork will lead to better results and more satisfaction among staff. • Better teamwork and social relations between staff will lead to better performance. • Always learn from others who have been successful. • Actively seek management support for PBF black box tools[a] and data management.

(table continues on next page)

TABLE 10.3 *(continued)*

No.	Service	Advanced strategy	To do's	Explanation
			• Continuously emphasize the goal and the mission.	
			• As management, actively work on internal and external learning, use the manuals to teach your staff, and actively ask for certain trainings from the district PHC department and eventual partners.	
			• Actively seek support from other partners for your health services.	
			• Share your experiences during the monthly meetings at the local authority level with OICs and try to learn from others.	
			• Discuss performance data in weekly staff meetings and in monthly management meetings.	
			• Seek management training.	
1	New outpatient consultation	Have the district list all households in the community, and use the household number and the mobile phone number of clients to register them.	• Use household numbers and mobile phone numbers for all clients for all services.	• PBF will pay you for each such registration: if you do not do this, you will not be paid.
		Make available good quality drugs, and keep them in stock.	• Use tracer drug list.	• Use of cheap and effective generic drugs decreases cost to the patient. • Drugs are cheaper than in a local pharmacy and better quality. • Consistent availability of drugs leads to trust by the community.
		Lower the curative care consultation cost.	• Prescribe rationally (IMCI). • Subsidize from PBF (make the price cheaper than that of the local pharmacy). • Give multivitamins, mebendazole, iron, and folic acid free of charge. • Have a box of candies ready for young children (but tell them to brush their teeth).	• If you prescribe rationally, you prescribe fewer drugs, which saves money and will lead to cheaper and better health care. • The community will know you are interested in public health. • Gaining trust of young children is very important, and you can use the occasion to do IEC on dental hygiene.

#		Actions	Expected outcomes
	Increasing quality of care and reception attitudes of staff.	• Make drinking water available. • Provide a fan if you have electricity. • Provide seats for patients. • Have a ticket system. • Include a systematic IEC schedule; invite a qualified person from the community to talk about good food habits. • Provide a TV or a radio for patients.	• Patients will feel like clients. • Do not sell water: patients have walked from afar. • People will learn how to use outreach services.
2	New outpatient consultation for an indigent patient[b]	Decrease financial barrier to access to services by indigents. • Find ways for the indigent committee to exempt patients (and be reimbursed through PBF).	• The poorest of the poor will have access to free good-quality health care.
3	Minor surgery	Ensure good quality of procedures. • Provide good sterilization. • Have a professional attitude.	• Population will gain confidence in the health facility.
4	Arrival of referred patient at the cottage hospital	Refer effectively for emergencies. • Have the mobile phone numbers of the director and the deputy director of the GH ready. • Have the mobile phone number of the ambulance driver ready. • Have a referral form. • Subsidize the fuel for the ambulance. • Follow up with the GH doctor on each referral (call). • Follow up with the patient on the referral (use mobile number).	• Clients will know that your health facility will ensure continuity of care: if there is a problem during a delivery, they will quickly call an ambulance. • Patients will feel that they are taken very seriously and will pass on the message that this facility is high quality. • The doctor will understand that you are concerned about your patient and will take extra care with your patients.

(table continues on next page)

TABLE 10.3 *(continued)*

No.	Service	Advanced strategy	To do's	Explanation
5	Completely vaccinated child	Increase outreach and decrease missed opportunities.	• Use your staff. (You have plenty, and they should be out in the community. Encourage them to vaccinate the world.) • Create a list of all children under the age of 1 year in the community, and vaccinate them. Use household registration information • Ensure each child has a U-5 card. • Check the vaccination status of all young children who attend your clinic for any reason (or are just accompanying their mothers). • Use the other health posts in the vaccination: ensure subcontracting so that they can share in the PBF income. • Keep a sufficient stock of vaccines, and take action if the stock is low. • Calculate, on the basis of the number of children under 1 year, how much vaccine you will need for your ward to vaccinate 100%. • Find out the best time for mothers to bring their children for vaccinations (some mothers work in the fields in the morning): adapt your schedule accordingly. • Think of offering a cash reward to a mother if the child is fully vaccinated.	• You can reach 100% vaccination coverage. • You have sufficient staff: let them work.
6	Growth monitoring visit for a child	Increase growth monitoring for children under five years of age.	• Mobilize the community: use traditional leaders, religious leaders, and your PBF facility committee at all possible occasions to emphasize that each child under 5 needs to be monitored for growth monthly. • During a child's first 2 years, mebendazole should be given quarterly; after that, it should be given every 6 months. • Visit churches to find many children under 5. • Visit schools to find many children under 5.	• You can earn points for each child once per quarter from PBF. • You need to reach out to the community for such activities; people are busy and might not come if you don't actively invite and encourage them to come.

#	Activity	Objective	Actions	Notes
		Combine growth-monitoring activities with family planning as much as possible.	• Apart from weighing and measuring the child and providing mebendazole, ensure good quality IEC for personal hygiene and food preparation. • Offer a piece of candy or a biscuit for each growth-monitored child (and use IEC to emphasize importance of brushing teeth). • Always combine IEC for growth monitoring with IEC for family planning. • If women want a certain method, ensure that they can have access to it.	• Many women hesitate to use FP at the facility level because of stigma.
7	2–5 tetanus vaccinations of pregnant woman	Decrease missed opportunities.	• Systematically check TT status for all pregnant women. • Follow the immunization calendar for pregnant women: do not categorize as TT-1 each TT. • Ensure good planning for sufficient vaccine stock.	
8	Postnatal consultation	Increase PNC rate.	• Increase the number of women delivering in your facility. • Keep a close watch on all pregnant women under your care, and call them around their EDD (mobile outreach) to ensure that they deliver with you; if they did not, follow up to ensure they come for PNC. • Provide a gift for women who deliver in your facility and who come back for their PNC (you can combine the gift for those two occasions): provide the baby-welcome package (soap and, for example, second-hand baby clothing) during PNC.	• PNC is very important for the health of the mother (eventual infections, and so on) and for a check of the neonate.
9	First ANC consultation before fourth month of pregnancy	Get pregnant women to come as early as possible.	• Find out if you can give advice during weddings or such events. • Use ANC visits in general to emphasize that coming before the fourth month is important. • During each contact with the community, emphasize early ANC visits. • Offer a gift to a woman who comes early and completes all 4 ANC visits according to the calendar. • Provide free pregnancy tests.	• If they come before 4 months, you can do the 4 standard ANC visits. • If you propose this in the business plan, you can get financing for the tests kits. • You can propose conditional in-kind gifts (umbrellas, cloths, soap, and so on) in your business plans.

(table continues on next page)

TABLE 10.3 *(continued)*

No.	Service	Advanced strategy	To do's	Explanation
10	ANC standard visit (2–4)	Decrease missed opportunities, and get pregnant women in early for first ANC.	• See number 9 above.	• See number 9 above.
11	Second dose of sulfadoxine-pyrimethamine (SP) for pregnant women	Decrease missed opportunities.	• See number 9 above. • Ensure availability of SP. • Provide free SP.	• See number 9 above.
12	Institutional delivery	Increase institutional deliveries.	• Use IEC/BCC. • Improve quality at the health facility: have updated equipment and a relatively comfortable environment. • Be aware of the attitude of the staff: emphasize being kind to patients. • Continuously upgrade staff skills and systematically use partograms. • Actively seek internal (teach yourself and your colleagues) and external training on obstetrics and gynecology (through GH or SMOH or partners). • Do not charge for cleaning materials, gloves, and similar items. • Offer baby-welcome packages for women who deliver (and come for their PNC visit). • Offer free referrals in case of complications during deliveries (provide fuel for ambulance, organize the ambulance, and so on). • Mobilize the community and increase awareness using traditional and religious leaders. • Call the patient by telephone if EDD is near.	• A well-functioning emergency obstetric care center needs to gain the community's trust. • Word of mouth is important in the community: each successful delivery and happy mother will lead to many others. • Gain trust.

13	Family planning (modern FP methods)	Increase the FP coverage for those women who want child spacing.	• Ensure availability of condoms, pills, injections, implants, and IUDs. • Ensure confidentiality and respect, and do not be judgmental. Be kind and patient, and offer a free choice of products. • Offer the services for free (you receive subsidies to pay for the products). • Actively seek training for IUDs and implants. • Offer FP services each day of the week: be flexible and ready to offer advice at any moment. • Decrease missed opportunities by making information available at each IEC/BCC, each ANC visit, and each curative care consultation for any reason by a woman of child-bearing age. • IEC/BCC should be done by each clinical staff member. • Integrate FP with nutritional and outreach activities. • Explain and manage well the eventual secondary effects or side effects. • Use registers to remind clients of revisits (mobile phones). • Provide clients with their FP card registration numbers (leave main cards at the health facility, but give registration cards to clients).	• Many women want FP but do not know what it is or where to get it. • For many, FP is very expensive. • Investing in explaining the methods, advantages, and disadvantages will help you gain the trust of the community. • Of all women of child-bearing age (WCBA are 26% of the catchment population), 25% do not want more children or want to space their births.
14	FP: implants and IUDs	See number 13 above.	• See number 13 above.	• See number 13 above.

(table continues on next page)

TABLE 10.3 *(continued)*

No.	Service	Advanced strategy	To do's	Explanation
15	VCT/PMTCT/ PIT test	Increase VCT/ PMTCT/PIT testing.	• If you do not have VCT services, seek training and support to offer them. • For each pregnant woman, ensure PMTCT services are given. • Ensure the availability of products and equipment, and do not charge for such services. • Provide IEC/BCC. • Decrease missed opportunities and talk about VCT/PMTCT/PIT to all clients, especially for pregnant cases and STD cases. • Ensure confidentiality, and do not be judgmental. • Offer free condoms. • Put condoms in or near toilets and latrines so people can access them easily. • Have condoms ready in each consultation room. • Systematically offer HIV testing for partners of pregnant women.	• HIV is a serious issue, and you need to set a good example of health professionals who are there to help.
16	PMTCT: HIV+ mothers and children treated according to protocol	For all HIV+ mothers, offer ARV protocol and ensure delivery in the health facility.	• Ensure that you have the ability to treat HIV+ mothers who deliver in your facility according to protocol. • Ensure that when you do not have ARV services, you will refer HIV+ mothers to a PMTCT site. • Seek active support from partners to assist in increasing quality of services. • Find a strategy (such as calling on the phone) to ensure that all HIV+ mothers deliver in a health facility.	
17	STD treated	Offer syndromic treatment for all STDs.	• Ensure staff is trained in syndromic treatment for all STDs. • Ensure sufficient stock of such STD drugs. • Offer systematic HIV counseling and testing for couples.	• STDs and HIV are important public health problems.

18	New AFB+ PTB patient	Offer AFB testing in your laboratory, and seek active cases.	• Ensure that your laboratory offers TB services. • Seek active cases, and test for AFB.	• TB is an important public health problem.
19	PTB patient completed treatment and cured	Active DOTS	• Use your staff, and designate a TB focal point. • Use conditional cash reward and contracts with the PTB patient for adherence and cure.	• TB is an important public health problem.
20	ITN distributed	Increase bed net coverage in your community.	• Decrease missed opportunities. • Offer ITN to all pregnant women. • Ensure that you have a system to check whether households actually use bed nets. • Provide IEC/BCC. • Try to get donated bed nets; if not donated, then buy them yourself and offer bed nets for a subsidized rate.	• Include the subsidy for each bed net in your business plan.
21	New family using a latrine during the past month	Increase latrine availability and use in your community.	• Provide IEC/BCC. • Outreach can be combined with nutritional activities and vitamin A distribution and with FP activities. • Encourage a policy of one family, one latrine. • Ensure that you have a system that checks whether families are maintaining and using their latrines according to the guidelines. • Actively seek support from the district PHC department (advice and best practices).	• Not having a latrine is a serious health hazard.

Source: World Bank data.

Note: AFB = acid-fast bacilli; ANC = antenatal care; ARV = antiretroviral; BCC = behavior change communication; DOTS = directly observed therapy for the treatment of tuberculosis; EDD = expected delivery date; FP = family planning; GH = General Hospital; HIV = human immunodeficiency virus; IEC = information, education, and communication; IMCI = integrated management of childhood illness; ITN = insecticide-treated net; IUD = intrauterine device; No. = number; OIC = officer in charge; PBF = performance-based financing PHC = primary health care; PIT = provider-initiated testing for HIV; PMTCT = prevention of mother-to-child transmission of HIV; PNC = postnatal care; PTB = pulmonary tuberculosis; SMOH = state ministry of health (Nigeria); STD = sexually transmitted disease; TB = tuberculosis; TT = tetanus toxoid vaccination; U-5 = Under-5 VCT = voluntary counseling and testing for HIV; WCBA = women of childbearing age.

a. Black box tools are (a) the business plan, (b) the indice tool, and (c) the individual health worker performance evaluation.

b. Service number 2 has not yet been included in a pilot.

found in non-PBF facilities, too. However, health workers will be more likely to carry out such advanced strategies if, in addition to improving the results, using the strategies also improves their income. Here, PBF differs from traditional input-based approaches.

10.4 Links to Files and Tools

The following toolkit files can be accessed through this web link: http://www.worldbank.org/health/pbftoolkit/chapter10.

- Business plan for a Nigerian health center (2011)
- Business plan for a Nigerian district hospital (2011).

References

Murray, C. J., B. Shengelia, N. Gupta, S. Moussavi, A. Tando, and M. Thieren. 2003. "Validity of Reported Vaccination Coverage in 45 Countries." *The Lancet* 362 (9389): 1022–27.

Soeters, R. 2013. *PBF in Action: Theory and Instruments—Course Guide, Performance-Based Financing.* The Hague: Cordaid-SINA. http://www.sina-health.com/?page_id=585.

CHAPTER 11

Governance Issues and Structures

MAIN MESSAGES

→ Introducing separation of functions is a key governance element in PBF that poses major challenges.
→ Involving communities and nonstate actors in decision making at all levels strengthens good governance in PBF.
→ PBF contracts assist in clarifying the new rules of the game.

COVERED IN THIS CHAPTER

11.1 Introduction

All over the world, intense debates rage over "good governance" and what that term actually entails. The World Bank has adopted a definition of good governance that underscores the importance of (a) sound public sector management (efficiency, effectiveness, and economy); (b) accountability; (c) exchange and free flow of information (transparency); and (d) a legal framework that enhances development, justice, and respect for human rights and liberties. Other international agencies have echoed this definition by describing good governance as addressing four major components: (a) legitimacy (those who govern should have the consent of those governed), (b) accountability (ensuring transparency, being answerable for one's actions), (c) competence (effective policy making, implementation, and service delivery), and (d) respect for the law and protection of human rights (see ECOSOC 2006).

In performance-based financing (PBF), these notions of good governance have been translated into a number of clear practices. The separation of functions and the enhancing of transparency, voice, and accountability for results are key.

In other chapters of this toolkit, a number of individual governance structures are discussed in more detail. For the community and community client satisfaction surveys, see chapter 2. For the community health facility committee, see chapter 6. More on purchasing and fund holding can be learned in this chapter and chapter 12 (web-enabled application). Highlighted here is the separation of functions as one of the major governance challenges and, in particular, the purchaser-provider split. The chapter concludes with illustrations of how governance issues should be clearly defined in the various PBF contracts.

11.2 Separation of Functions: Fostering Transparency, Voice, and Accountability

In many walks of life, the principle of separation of functions is central to improving governance. Its purpose is to decrease conflict-of-interest situations (see chapter 2). In PBF too, it is best practice to strive for a full separation of functions between the chief players in the health care arena: the fund holder, the purchaser, the provider, the community, the community health facility committees, the local PBF steering committees, and the national PBF coordination mechanisms (figure 11.1). Separation of functions creates a clear division of labor between those players and contributes to

FIGURE 11.1 The Separation of Functions and Its Governance Issues

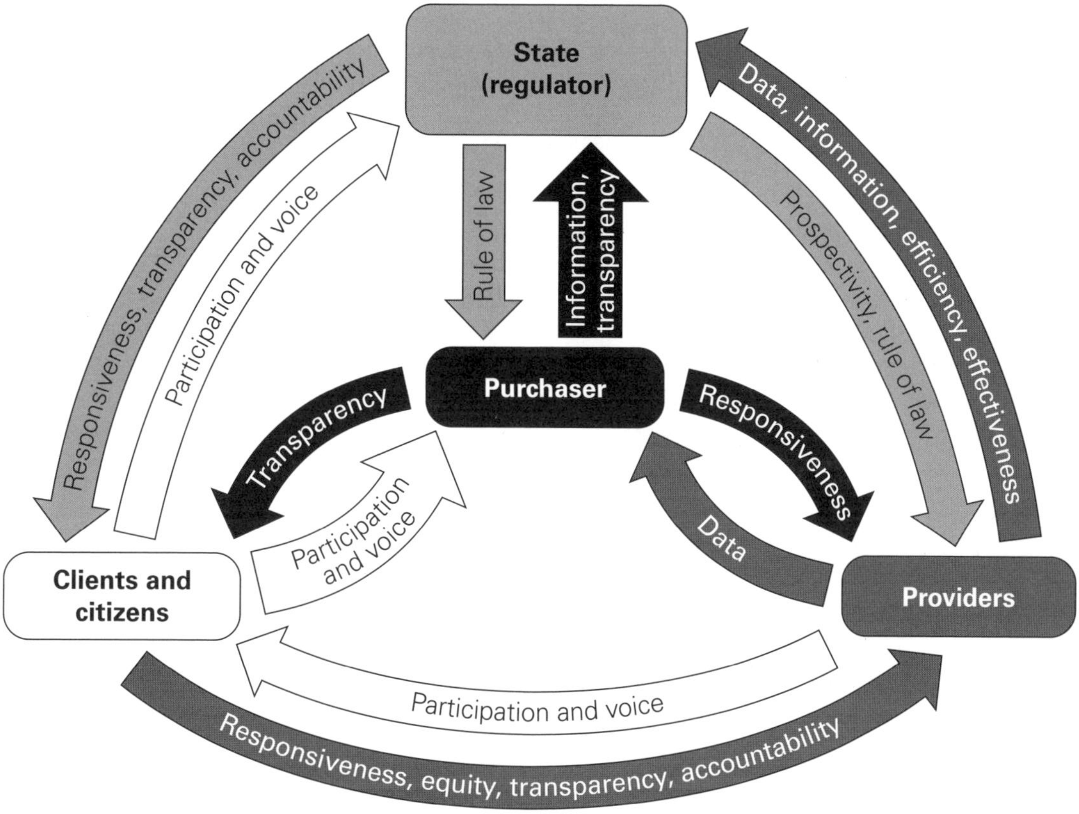

Source: Adapted, with permission, from Remme et al. 2012.

transparency in the sequence of executing PBF operations by doing the following:

- Starting accurate record keeping
- Linking pay-for-performance to accurate records
- Auditing the performance rigorously
- Involving nonstate actors at all levels in the health care system.

By linking nonstate actors in PBF to the measuring, reviewing, and improving of public health service delivery at all levels, government provides a strong voice to society in matters of public health care delivery (see box 11.1). Indeed, by setting up systems that reliably measure and reward performance, government greatly enhances the accountability and transparency of its public health system. In the separation of functions, different functions

BOX 11.1

Civil Society Is Convincing the Ministry of Health on Use of Community Client Satisfaction Surveys

In Rwanda in 2006, a new public purchaser system was introduced, largely based on lessons learned from three previous PBF pilot projects. The Ministry of Health initially was very reluctant to introduce community client satisfaction surveys, although their value had been proven in the pilot schemes managed by nongovernmental organizations. Decision makers were afraid that the reported results (which were excellent) would not be substantiated by community client satisfaction surveys. They feared this disparity would endanger their positions as civil servants. Nonstate actors involved in the scale-up of PBF in Rwanda lobbied with vigor to include the surveys in the national models. By the end of 2007, the results of the first community client satisfaction survey came out, and they did, in fact, show positive results (and demonstrated less than 5 percent phantom patients). The ministry was applauded for this success and subsequently embraced the method and included it in its national PBF approach.

are allocated to different health-system stakeholders. In PBF, the following functions are distinguished:

- Provision
- Regulation
- Purchasing
- Fund holding
- Community voice.

These various stakeholder functions are discussed in table 11.1.

In PBF's governance model, a clear focus on the distinct roles and functions of each of the stakeholders is married with a profound sense that PBF stakeholders depend on each other for producing results. This awareness of interdependency combined with proper checks and balances to avoid overlapping roles is being cultivated to diminish conflicts of interest.

In the past, in PBF's inception phase, some functions did overlap sometimes, such as purchasing and fund holding. Others, such as provision and regulation or purchasing and provision, however, should be separated from the start. In most current PBF designs, fund holding and purchasing are also immediately split and are carried out by different agencies. The more transparency and clear accountability for results that are included in the design, the better the PBF design. Transparency creates trust and gives access to credible data. Accountability for results stimulates people to improve their results.

TABLE 11.1 The Distinct Stakeholder Functions of PBF Key Players

Function	Explanation
Provision	In PBF, the providers are health facilities (and not the individual health workers). Health facilities are contracted. They can be public, quasi-public (faith based), or private for profit. Through subcontracting, a primary PBF contract holder can contract other health care facilities in its areas of responsibility.
	The provision is generally governed through three types of contracts: (a) the purchase contract between the purchaser and the provider, (b) the subcontract between the primary contract holder and a second health facility, and (c) the motivation contract between the health facility management and the individual health worker.
Regulation	The regulator is the MoH (at all levels, from central to local). The MoH organizes the financing, coordinates fund holders in its country, determines the type of services that should be present, costs out the services, and sets the norms and standards for the quality checklists. Coordination and capacity building are also organized through the MoH.
Purchasing	The purchasing role is undertaken on behalf of the MoH and its fund holders by a purchasing agency. This can be a private purchaser or a quasi-public one. (For more details on the various purchasing arrangements, see section 3 of this chapter.)
Fund holding	In PBF, fund holding is mostly coordinated by the ministry of finance and can involve a large number of additional fund holders. Virtual pooling of funds is often used to determine the overall budget and to set the various fees. Individual fund holders are then billed for their share of the performance invoice.
Community voice	The community voice is being solicited through different pathways: (a) community client satisfaction surveys, (b) community participation in health facility committees, (c) civil society involvement in the district steering committees, and (d) nonstate actor involvement in national-level coordination and capacity-building efforts. The purpose is to obtain the verdict of the community on the services provided and enable communities to influence public health care delivery.

Source: World Bank data.

Note: MoH = ministry of health; PBF = performance-based financing.

11.3 Governance Structures for PBF: Challenges and Types of Purchasers

An agenda for good governance of PBF pertains to all stakeholders: the purchaser, the provider, the fund holder, the community, the community health facility committee, the district PBF steering committee, and the national PBF coordination mechanisms. The governance principles and structures are translated into a number of concrete contracts that are supposed to enhance governance.

Several structural features of PBF contribute to good governance. A few examples follow:

- The separation of functions introduces a purchaser-provider split that enables pay for performance and improves verification of results (verification and transparency).

- Community oversight of health facility management leads to better management of public funds, and the separation of functions leads to a credible verification of results (verification, transparency, and community involvement).
- Separate fund holding enables credible financing (transparency).
- The district PBF steering committee creates a platform for greater civil society involvement in governance of public performance (community involvement and voice).
- The national PBF coordination mechanism ensures the involvement of development partners in improving the health system performance (multistakeholder approaches and transparency).

An example of such institutional arrangements is seen in figure 11.2. It represents the administrative structure of the Rwandese health center PBF approach (adapted from Brook and Smith 2001).

FIGURE 11.2 Health Center PBF Administrative Model

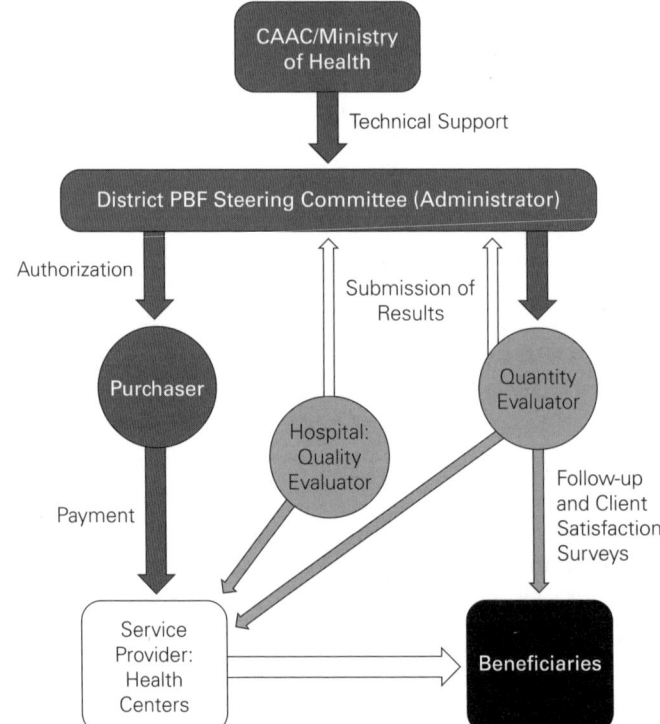

Source: Adapted from Brook and Smith 2001.

Note: CAAC = Cellule d'Appui a l'Approche Contractuelle (Performance-Based Financing Support Cell); PBF = performance-based financing.

Performance-Based Financing Toolkit

Governance Challenges

In table 11.2, a series of governance issues, governance structures, and characteristic interventions in PBF systems are listed. The table also lists the particular challenges that may be faced when such governance measures are implemented. Good governance is hard work.

> Well then, says I, what's the use you learning to do right when it's troublesome to do right and ain't no trouble to do wrong, and the wages is just the same?
>
> —Mark Twain, *Adventures of Huckleberry Finn*, 1884

Two Types of Purchaser Arrangements with Implications for Governance

In this section, we delve a bit deeper into one specific topic: the purchaser. More specifically, we point out the relationship between the separation of functions and the purchaser. We will discuss purchasing arrangements and the implications for the separation of functions.

In current PBF programs, we can find two predominant types of purchasing arrangements: (a) the private purchaser and (b) the quasi-public purchaser. In the private purchaser approach, a private agency carries out the role of the purchaser, while in the approach of the quasi-public purchaser, that function is embedded in government. In the field, the following purchasing arrangements have been observed:

- A private purchaser approach funded through bilateral funds
- A private purchaser approach funded through government sources
- A public purchaser approach funded through a mix of bilateral and government funds
- A quasi-public purchaser approach funded through a mix of bilateral and government funds.

The first arrangement is typical in PBF pilots (Meessen et al. 2006; Meessen, Kashala, and Musango 2007; Rusa et al. 2009; Soeters, Habineza, and Peerenboom 2006). A nongovernmental agency is engaged to do the purchasing, verification, and coaching. Fund holding rests typically with this nongovernmental agency (Soeters et al. 2011), although different variations exist, such as contracting a separate entity to do the fund holding, as is the case in the Cordaid Zambia PBF pilot (2011 to present).

In the second arrangement, a private purchaser is contracted by the government to carry out the purchasing, verification, and coaching activities. Fund holding will typically be in the hands of the ministry of finance. An example of this type of arrangement is the PBF pilot in Zimbabwe (2011 to present).

TABLE 11.2 Framework for Governance Issues and Structures

Governance structure	Governance issues[a]	PBF system	Implementation challenges
Community health facility committee	Accountability and voice	Local accountability: Community oversight of public funds; Community inputs in priority setting and strategies to enhance performance; Voice: Ability to influence	Finding the right balance between operational freedom for the health center and public oversight over public money; Avoiding capture of health center funds by community elite; Ensuring follow-up on health center committee minutes during quality check (part of quality score); Ensuring that the community health facility committee is involved in creating the business plan (requisite of business plan approval)
Community	Accountability and voice	Local accountability: Grassroots organizations used for community client satisfaction surveys; Voice: Ability to influence	Meeting the expense of community client satisfaction surveys; finding a balance between cost and its desired effects; Handling local NGOs' lack of experience with community client satisfaction survey methods (but experience can be built); Taking time to discuss findings at the health center at district and national levels; Convincing the government for the need of such surveys
Health facility and autonomous providers	Accountability and information on performance	Systematic performance audits of health facilities	Setting up rigorous performance audits at the health facilities for both quantity and quality performances; Separating functions and avoiding conflicts of interest
District PBF steering committee	Inclusive government, accountability, transparency and voice	Inclusive government: NGO participation in evaluating performance of publicly financed health institutions; Accountability: Accountability for performance (PBF data visible on the public front end of the PBF web-enabled application)[b]; Transparency: Ability to audit proceeds (accurate minutes of decision meetings and generalized access to performance data and invoices through a web-enabled application)[b]; Voice: Ability of nonstate actors to influence public health care delivery	Convincing stakeholders to create a district PBF steering committee with its own mandate; Getting technical assistance for the district PBF steering committee for agenda setting, preparing of content, and drafting of minutes; Getting district PBF steering committees to meet on time so as to not delay the approval of the health facility invoices; making the district health team responsible for the secretariat (and paying them based on the performance); Using a web-enabled application for data entry, invoicing, and public information sharing (see chapter 12 for how this is done); accessing data from any Internet connection; Using PBF data effectively for performance improvement needs continuous capacity building at all levels (health center, district, and national); Connecting with the Internet rapidly improving; data entry and accessibility in an Internet café at the district, province, or national levels

National level: Ministry of Health, national steering committee, extended team mechanism	Rule of law, inclusive government and voice, efficiency and effectiveness, transparency, accountability	**Rule of law:** Assurance that the new rules are followed	Creating effective institutional structures that coordinate well; reviewing progress systematically; taking action when necessary (the extended team mechanism to assist the government in ensuring that the new rules are followed; see chapter 14)
		Inclusive government and voice: Strong involvement of nonstate actors in verification, coaching, coordination, and capacity building tasks	Creating effective coordination mechanisms that co-opt nonstate actors to work with government to coordinate and steer the PBF approach (see "extended team mechanism" in chapter 14)
		Involvement of nonstate actors in oversight on and targeting of public and donor PBF money	Creating effective dashboards; having good-quality data analysis capability to analyze trends in service provision and expenditures
			Effectively lobbying decision makers, based on PBF data, for more funding and also balanced funding (health centers versus district hospitals versus national hospitals)
		Efficiency and effectiveness: Attempt to enhance coverage for good quality, cost-effective services	Effectively lobbying development partners to increase their support for PBF systems
			Implementing deeper reforms such as human resources for health reforms
		Transparency: Web-enabled application that offers easy access to information on results and payments	Involving nonstate actors at all levels of the PBF system:
			The community level for community-client satisfaction surveys
		Accountability: Public information on results, payments, and community client satisfaction surveys through website	The district level (district PBF steering committees) for decisions on pay for performance
			The national level in coordination bodies and technical working groups to refine the PBF approach based on lessons learned
			Convincing government on the advantage and importance of transparency versus the knee-jerk reaction of not sharing data
			Maintaining and continuously developing the web-enabled application and its website (hosting, subcommittees)

Source: World Bank data.

Note: NGO = nongovernmental organization; PBF = performance-based financing.

a. See Lewis (2006).

b. For example, see the Nigeria National Primary Health Care Development Agency, PBF Portal, https://nphcda.thenewtechs.com.

The third arrangement is a public purchaser approach. Here, the purchasing unit is located inside the ministry of health (MoH) and is staffed by civil servants with additional technical assistance financed through development partners. An example is the Rwandese PBF approach (2006 to present).

The fourth arrangement is a quasi-public purchaser approach. In this approach, an entity has been created that is separate from the MoH and that is staffed by a mix of civil servants and consultants or a contracted agency to fulfill the purchasing function. Examples of this approach are the Burundi PBF approach (2010 to present) and the Nigerian PBF approach (2011 to present). A further example is the Kyrgyz Republic PBF approach in which the purchasing unit is located in the National Health Insurance Fund. In table 11.3, further examples of both private purchaser and quasi-public purchaser approaches are given.

In opting for either approach, keep in mind the concept of separation of functions: How does the approach guarantee a separation of functions? How does it avoid conflict of interest situations? How does it promote good governance? Table 11.4 indicates some of the distinctions between the two approaches.

In general, a private purchaser approach is more desirable for getting a better separation of functions, although the quasi-public purchaser approach

TABLE 11.3 Examples of Private Purchaser and Quasi-Public Purchaser Approaches

Private purchaser PBF approach	Quasi-public purchaser PBF approach
Cambodia Pearang HNI pilot (1998)	Cambodia Takeo and Sotnikum New Deal (1999)
Rwanda Cyangugu Cordaid PBF pilot (2002–05)	Rwanda Butare HNI PBF pilot (2002–05)
Burundi Cordaid PBF pilot projects (2006–10)	Rwanda Ville de Kigali CTB PBF pilot (2005–06)
Democratic Republic of Congo South Kivu Cordaid PBF pilot (2006 to present)	Rwandese national PBF approaches (January 2006 to present)
Burundi SDC PBF pilot project (2008–10)	RDC European Union PS9FED (June 2006 to present)
Central African Republic Cordaid PBF pilot (2008 to present)	Burundi national PBF approach (April 2010 to present)
Cameroon Cordaid PBF pilot (2008 to present)	Zambia Katete district PBF pilot (2009 to present)
Indonesia Flores Cordaid PBF pilot (2008–11)	Benin PBF pilot (December 2011 to present)
Burundi HNI–TPO PBF pilot project (2008–10)	Nigeria PBF pre-pilots (December 2011 to present)
Zimbabwe Cordaid PBF pilot project (June 2011 to present)	Kyrgyz Republic PBF pilot (July 2013 to present)
Chad AEDES PBF pilot project October (2011 to present)	Burkina Faso PBF pilot (August/September 2013 to present)

Source: World Bank data.

Note: AEDES = European Agency for Development and Health; CTB = Coopération Technique Belge; HNI = Health Net International; HNI-TPO = Health Net International–Transcultural Psychosocial Organization; PBF = Performance-based financing; RDC = Republique Democratique du Congo; SDC = Swiss Agency for Development and Cooperation.

TABLE 11.4 Distinctions between the Private Purchaser and Quasi-Public Purchaser Approaches

Criteria	Private purchaser approach	Quasi-public purchaser approach
Acceptability for MoH	Difficult	High
Contracting	By choice of the best	By appointment
Flexibility for innovation	Likely	Difficult
Competition for contracts	Feasible	Difficult
Limited duration of contract (for example, 2 years)	Applicable	Once appointed, contract cancellation not easy
Potential of mixing roles, in particular with regulatory role	Less likely	More likely
Identity of fund holder	Different organization	Different organization
During start-up of PBF pilot	Highly recommendable	Difficult to organize
During scale-up of PBF	Politically less feasible	Politically more feasible

Source: World Bank data.

Note: MoH = ministry of health; PBF = performance-based financing.

is more attractive to many governments because of a greater sense of owner-ship. Sometimes, colleagues evoke the argument of "sustainability" or "cost" when expressing their interest in the quasi-public purchaser approach. However, the quasi-public purchaser approach is not necessarily cheaper than the private purchaser approach (Uwimpuhwe 2011). For more details, see chapter 14.

11.4 PBF Contracts: PBF at Scale, Internal Market, Contracts, and Governance

Contracts Embody Governance Rules

Contracts are used in PBF systems to clarify the new rules of the game. Even at the microlevel, contracts are important governance instruments. They embody the new roles of the health system stakeholders, the PBF services, and its fees, and they stipulate the rules for verifying and paying for perfor-mance. PBF works through an internal market mechanism created to pur-chase performance from a country's health system.

There are many types of contracts, ranging from health facilities contract-ing to deliver services to health workers signing motivation contracts that specify what is expected of them and make explicit the share they are enti-tled to from the performance bonus of the facility earnings. Or, some contracts require district PBF steering committee members to sign agreements that describe their new roles and responsibilities.

The number of contracts also vary considerably. For example, in the Rwandese PBF system three contracts are used for the health center PBF approach, two more for the community PBF approach, and an additional two for the hospital PBF approach. In Burundi, nine different contracts delineate the newly created institutional structures.

PBF contracting is frequently framed as a memorandum of understanding or a service agreement. This method is quite different from detailed legalistic frames found in many standard contracts used by development agencies. The chief purpose of internal contracts in PBF is to clarify the new "rules of the game" (North 1990). In fact, those contracts are frequently a summary of the PBF approach detailing in plain language the rights and obligations of each party.[1] In tables 11.5 and 11.6, the various types of contracts used in Rwanda and Burundi are described. To access the actual documents, see the links to files in this chapter.

TABLE 11.5 PBF Contracts Used in Rwanda

No.	Public purchaser or contract	Signatories
1	District PBF steering committee	The multilateral contract is between the district mayor and the district PBF parties (nine signatories including the Ministry of Local Administration, Ministry of Health; representatives of providers; and civil society).
2	Purchase contract for the health center	The contract is between the Ministry of Local Administration and the health center and is signed by the representative of the mayor (on behalf of the mayor) at the sector level (subdistrict) with the president of the health center management team (the board) (two signatories).
3	Motivation contract	The contract is signed by the health facility management team representative and the individual health worker (two signatories).
4	Purchase contract for the district hospital	The contract is signed by the minister of health, the hospital director, and the president of the governing board (three signatories).
5	Sector PBF steering committee	The contract is between the mayor and the sector PBF steering committee and is signed by the sector executive secretary (on behalf of the mayor) the in-charge person of the health center, the health center CHW cooperative supervisor, the president of the CHW cooperative, and a local community representative (five signatories).
6.	Purchase contract with the CHW cooperative	The contract is between the sector administration and the community health worker cooperative and is signed by the sector administration representative, the in-charge person of the health center, and the president of the CHW cooperative (three signatories).

Source: World Bank data.

Note: CHW = community health worker; No. = number; PBF = performance-based financing.

TABLE 11.6 PBF Contracts Used in Burundi

No.	Quasi-public purchaser or contract	Signatories
1	Contract between the ministry of health (MoH) and the Provincial Verification and Validation Committee (CPVV)	The contract is signed by representatives of the MoH and the CPVV (two signatories). The CPVV is a semi-autonomous body, created from the staff of the Provincial Health Office and contracted technicians.
2	Contract between the MoH and the provincial health office (PHO)	The contract is signed by representatives of the MoH and the PHO (two signatories). It lays down the rules related to the execution of the quality supervisory functions (of the health facilities) and a set of other performance measures as described in the performance framework for the PHO.
3	Contract between the MoH and the district health office (DHO)	The contract is signed by representatives of the MoH and the DHO (two signatories). It lays down the rules related to the execution of the quality supervisory functions (of the health facility) and a set of other performance measures as described in the performance framework for the DHO.
4	Purchase contract for the health center	The contract is signed by the CPVV representative, the in-charge person of the health center, and the president of the health center committee (three signatories).
5	Purchase contract for the district hospital	The contract is signed by the CPVV representative and the hospital director (two signatories).
6	Purchase contract for the tertiary hospital	The contract is signed by the MoH representative and the hospital director (two signatories).
7	Motivation contract	The contract is signed by the health facility management representative and the individual health worker (two signatories).
8	Contract between the CPVV and the GRO	The contract is between the CPVV and the GRO for the quarterly community client surveys. It is signed by representatives of the GRO and the CPVV (two signatories).
9	Contract between the central MoH department and the government	The contract is signed by the head of a central MoH department and the representative of the MoH in the government (Chef de Cabinet) (two signatories).

Source: World Bank data.

Note: GRO = grassroots organization; No. = number; PBF = performance-based financing.

Drawing up contracts needs care. Sometimes a copy of a contract from a country with a comparable PBF setup can be helpful, but adapt the language and details to fit a specific country's needs. Contracts are an important part of the PBF user manual (see chapter 15). Each stakeholder should be able to refer to the contracts when needed. Contracts are also an important part of PBF trainings, and a typical PBF training ends with a contract-signing ceremony. But most important, contracts give backbone to good governance.

PBF at Scale: Market, Contracting, and Governance

PBF at scale works through a regulated internal market mechanism. Internal markets or quasi-markets were introduced in health care in the 1990s in countries such as New Zealand and the United Kingdom. Those countries intended to introduce some market forces into the rigid national health system–type public health systems (Enthoven 1991; Grand 2003; Walsh 1995). Regulated markets as a policy model were further elaborated in European countries like the Netherlands.

The terms *internal market* or *quasi-market* are appropriate to describe how PBF works at scale. It does so through introducing an internal market for the purchase of performance. PBF approaches introduce a purchaser-provider split in which different functions are allocated transparently to different bodies. Price signals are introduced in rigid public health systems, and social entrepreneurship of health facility managers and providers is stimulated. Even in rural settings in low-income countries where there are often very few competing providers for public health, PBF facilities that offer better services might draw clients from the catchment population of facilities that offer lower-quality services. Even in such settings, it has become clear that PBF stimulates "voting with the feet" and "money following the patient."

In the context of PBF internal market developments, the terms *contracting in* and *contracting out* are used. Contracting in was first used to describe the contracting experience in Cambodia in the late 1990s (Bhushan et al. 2007; Loevinsohn and Harding 2005). The term referred to nonstate actors who were contracted in to assist the government to improve health service delivery. Contracting in was adopted to contrast with contracting out, which meant that health service delivery was allocated by contract to nonstate actors. In both approaches, of course, public money is being used.

One could argue that PBF originated in Cambodia through a contracting-in experience (Soeters and Griffiths 2003). Nonstate actors set up methods that assisted the Cambodian government's public health system to improve its performance (Meessen et al. 2006; Meessen, Soucat, and Sekabaraga 2011).

Conceptually, PBF projects are close to contracting-in methods. This insight is important because it has design implications for the role of technical assistance in PBF systems (see also chapter 14).

Many governments are not used to working with nongovernmental organizations (NGOs). Governments often resist working with NGOs, especially when the NGO sector is large such as in complex emergencies. However, governments need to realize the consequences of the health system strengthening activities through PBF. Nonstate actors are not only essential for a good separation of functions, but also important in assisting the government to improve the performance of its health system.

11.5 Links to Files and Tools

The following toolkit files can be accessed through this web link:
http://www.worldbank.org/health/pbftoolkit/chapter11.

- Rwanda:
  - District PBF steering committee contract
  - Purchase contract for the health center
  - Motivation contract
  - Purchase contract for the district hospital
  - Sector PBF steering committee
  - Purchase contract with the community health worker (CHW) cooperative.
- Burundi:
  - Contract between the Ministry of Health (MoH) and the Provincial Verification and Validation Committee (CPVV)
  - Contract between the MoH and the provincial health office (PHO)
  - Contract between the MoH and the district health office (DHO)
  - Purchase contract for the health center
  - Purchase contract for the district hospital
  - Purchase contract for the tertiary hospital
  - Motivation contract
  - Contract between the CPVV and the grassroots organization (GRO)
  - Contract between the central MoH department and the government.

Note

1. Contacting a lawyer for advice on the way to introduce these contracts is your choice. However, because these contracts are internal agreements and because plain language is used, an uninitiated lawyer might object to the form and the content.

References

Bhushan, I., E. Bloom, D. Clingingsmith, R. Hong, E. King, M. Kremer, B. Loevin-sohn, and B. Schwartz. 2007. "Contracting for Health: Evidence from Cambodia." Weatherhead School of Management, Case Western Reserve University, Cleveland, OH. http://faculty.weatherhead.case.edu/clingingsmith/cambodia 13JUN07.pdf.

Brook, P., and S. Smith, eds. 2001. *Contracting for Public Services: Output-Based Aid and Its Applications*. Washington, DC: World Bank.

ECOSOC (United Nations Economic and Social Council). 2006. "Definition of Basic Concepts and Terminologies in Governance and Public Administration."

E/C.16/2006/4, Committee on Experts on Public Administration, ECOSOC, New York. http://unpan1.un.org/intradoc/groups/public/documents/un/unpan022332.pdf.

Enthoven, A. C. 1991. "Internal Market Reform of the British National Health Service." *Health Affairs* 10 (3): 60–70.

Grand, J. L. 2003. *Motivation, Agency, and Public Policy*. London: Oxford University Press.

Lewis, M. 2006. "Governance and Corruption in Public Health Care Systems." Center for Global Development Working Paper 78, World Bank, Washington, DC.

Loevinsohn, B., and A. Harding. 2005. "Buying Results? Contracting for Health Service Delivery in Developing Countries." *The Lancet* 366 (9486): 676–81.

Meessen, B., J.-P. Kashala, and L. Musango. 2007. "Output-based Payment to Boost Staff Productivity in Public Health Centres: Contracting in Kabutare District, Rwanda." *Bulletin of the World Health Organization* 85 (2): 108–15.

Meessen, B., L. Musango, J. P. Kashala, and J. Lemlin. 2006. "Reviewing Institutions of Rural Health Centres: The Performance Initiative in Butare, Rwanda." *Tropical Medicine and International Health* 11 (8): 1303–17.

Meessen, B., A. Soucat, and C. Sekabaraga. 2011. "Performance-Based Financing: Just a Donor Fad or a Catalyst Towards Comprehensive Health-Care Reform?" *Bulletin of the World Health Organization* 89 (2): 153–56.

North, D. C. 1990. *Institutions, Institutional Change, and Economic Performance*. Cambridge, UK: Cambridge University Press.

Remme, M., P. B. Peerenboom, P.-M. Douzima, D. M. Batubenga, M. I. Inoussa, and J. van de Weerd. 2012. "Le Financement basé sur la Performance et la Bonne Gouvernance: Leçons apprises in République Centrafricaine." PBF CoP Working Paper Series WP8, African Performance-Based Financing Community of Practice, World Bank, Washington, DC. http://www.hha-online.org/hso/system/files/wp8fbpenrca.pdf.

Rusa, L., W. Janssen, S. van Bastelaere, D. Porignon, J. de Dieu Ngirabega, and W. Vandenbulcke. 2009. "Performance-Based Financing for Better Quality of Services in Rwandan Health Centres: 3-Year Experience." *Tropical Medicine and International Health* 14 (7): 830–37.

Soeters, R., and F. Griffiths. 2003. "Improving Government Health Services through Contract Management: A Case from Cambodia." *Health Policy and Planning* 18 (1): 74–83.

Soeters, R., C. Habineza, and P. B. Peerenboom. 2006. "Performance-Based Financing and Changing the District Health System: Experience from Rwanda." *Bulletin of the World Health Organization* 84 (11): 884–89.

Soeters, R., P. B. Peerenboom, P. Mushagalusa, and C. Kimanuka. 2011. "Performance-Based Financing Experiment Improved Health Care in the Democratic Republic of Congo." *Health Affairs* 30 (8): 1518–27.

Uwimpuhwe, S. 2011. "Cost Analysis of the Performance-Based Financing Scheme in Rwanda." School of Public Health, National University of Rwanda, Kigali.

Walsh, K. 1995. *Public Services and Market Mechanisms. Competition, Contracting, and the New Public Management*. London: Macmillan Press.

CHAPTER 12

Data Gathering and Dissemination

MAIN MESSAGES

→ Linking data to money and accountability and implementing an auditing process force positive changes in the way data are managed.

→ The PBF web-enabled application is the backbone of any mature PBF administrative system.

→ PBF web-enabled applications link service delivery and invoicing and enable good governance (accountability for results and transparency).

COVERED IN THIS CHAPTER

12.1 Introduction: Data Gathering and Usage Are Crucial to PBF

Data gathering and usage are a central part of performance-based financing (PBF) systems. If well applied, PBF leads to better quality data and better availability of data at all levels—from the smallest health center to the health ministry. Linking data to payment changes the way data are managed. Web-based information technology solutions have been developed and form the backbone of PBF administrative systems. At the same time, better-quality data and more data-driven systems require enhancing data analysis capabilities at all levels. In this chapter, we discuss how to achieve these requirements.

12.2 How Data Collection for PBF Is Different

PBF leads to better data and better usage of data. PBF payment systems require and stimulate more effective data management and data availability at all levels. PBF drives better usage of data precisely because the data are linked to payments. In practice, 100 percent data availability is being achieved because health facilities or agencies must report data or forfeit performance incentive payments. In addition, data quality is also enhanced because data must be checked at health facility, district, and national levels before any payment is disbursed. If data are not available at any of these three levels, payment cannot proceed. These specific procedures for paying for performance ensure that providers deliver data that are complete and available at all levels of the system.

Linking data to payments and to accountability and auditing data changes the way data are managed. Data become the equivalent of earnings. And both earnings and data are audited at all levels: community, health center, district, and national. For PBF, if the quantity and quality of services produced determine how much money is earned—and both are under heavy scrutiny at all levels—the importance of data collection increases substantially from "data collection as usual."

Data are scrutinized at health facility, local (district/varies per country), and national levels. At the health facility level, data are tallied from the registers. At the district level, quantity and quality data are verified and approved. At the national level, a consolidated payment order is produced and quantity and quality data for the entire country are compiled. At all three levels, relative performance is analyzed (for the type of analysis used in such exercises, see chapter 13).

The Differences

In general, PBF data systems differ from routine health management information systems (HMISs):

- For PBF, a limited data set is collected.
- In PBF, there is rigorous data verification of all data at the source and the data are triangulated at various levels.
- In PBF, all data are tied to an automated invoicing and payment module.

The PBF administrative system is primarily set up to provide solutions for invoicing and payment for performance. But a welcome side effect of having data tied to payment is that the system also leads to valuable performance information.

Limited Data Set Collected

In PBF systems, a more limited set of data is tracked. In a typical PBF system, about 20 services are purchased at each level (health center and district hospital) and lead to a total of about 40 services. The data are collected monthly and are not disaggregated for personal information such as name, age, gender, and address. Personal information remains in the registers at the health facilities, and only summary quantity data are entered in the database. In addition to the quantitative data, summary quality data are entered (consolidated scores, but not the full set) for about 15 services. This approach is done once every three months. In terms of workload, it reduces monthly data elements, which in a typical MHIS are many and, as an example, totaled about 10,000 in the pre-2012 Rwandese HMIS.

Data Rigorously Verified at the Source

PBF data verification is rigorous and is double-checked against routine data at the source. At the health facility level, specially designated primary data collection tools (registers and individual patient cards) are used. Each month, all services purchased are verified at the source. These data are double-checked against similar data of the HMIS. The PBF data quality verification process can result in improvements to HMIS data reliability too (see chapter 2).

Data Tied to Automatic Invoicing and Payment Module for PBF

Invoicing and payment are core functions of PBF data management systems. Such functions are usually not included in an ordinary HMIS. PBF quantity data and quality data are entered in the web-enabled application. Once per quarter, a consolidated district invoice is printed from the system and presented to the district steering committee for approval. After the invoice goes through validation procedures and receives approval at the higher level, a payment order is printed. This payment order is approved and sent to the fund holder(s). A flexible PBF system can manage different purchasers and fund holders. It can easily be adapted to fit contextual needs.

12.3 How PBF Web-Enabled Application Works

Two Components

Web-based information technology for PBF generally consists of two components: (a) a database that is accessible through the Internet (web-enabled) at all times and (b) a public website through which PBF tools and results are actively shared.

Web-Enabled Database

The web-enabled database is the information technology solution for scaled-up PBF systems that at one time used spreadsheets or off-line databases for data management. This database system enables users to enter PBF performance data, maintain PBF system parameters (such as which data elements are purchased and at what tariffs), calculate PBF payments, and print payment orders. The system also links to other analysis tools such as Microsoft Excel or geographic information software to enable district- and national-level staff to analyze service performance.

The data management and validation system, which includes the web-enabled database, currently forms the administrative backbone of two scaled-up PBF systems (Rwanda and Burundi). Interest in using this solution is rapidly growing in PBF systems in Benin, Burkina Faso, Cameroon, Congo-Brazzaville, Chad, the Democratic Republic of Congo, Lesotho, Nigeria, Senegal, and Zambia, among others.

This solution has many advantages:

- Issues with unreliable virus-prone personal computers in areas lacking routine maintenance and technical expertise for information technology hardware and software are circumvented; any functioning Internet access will suffice.
- A platform for a multidirectional information exchange is provided; all participants at all levels have access to the same information.
- The need for all paper-based health facility invoices to be sent to the central level is avoided; only consolidated district invoices are sent.
- A repository is provided for very reliable health information that can be used to monitor and evaluate health sector performance data over time and to verify each service has been accounted for and paid for.

- Efficient and reliable invoicing and strategic purchasing are facilitated.
- Virtual pooling of all funds for PBF is possible; up to 10 different fund holders are managed through the Rwandese and Burundi scaled-up systems.

The overall majority of countries have opted to use software that is freeware or shareware and can be adapted by programmers. An advantage of using freeware or shareware is that no licensing fees must be paid. A mix of free software (PHP) and open source software (Joomla, WordPress, MySQL, and PostgreSQL) is applied. MySQL and PostgreSQL are popular open source databases,[1] Joomla and WordPress are free open source content management systems,[2] and PHP is a widely used programming language that was originally designed for web development to produce dynamic web pages but is now used predominantly for server-side scripting.[3]

These information and communication technology (ICT) solutions are the backbone of PBF systems. Without them, obtaining timely, accurate, and complete datasets for use in paying providers on time and for enabling good governance (accountability for results and transparency; see chapter 11) would be difficult.

The Public Website

The public website contains news, pictures, a calendar of PBF-related events, and information on the PBF facility's performance and earnings (hence the "public front end").

There are also opportunities to build on existing data collection systems to develop a hybrid PBF solution. This type of solution can have the advantages of reducing duplication of data entry through a parallel PBF data capture system and enhancing the use of HMIS data generally. In this case, the data are gathered through the routine HMIS system and passed to the PBF system for analysis, validation, and invoice processing. New web-based platforms for HMIS, such as the District Health Information Software 2 (DHIS 2), have application program interfaces that enable data to be exchanged in real time with other systems.

Data Analysis: Capacity Building Required

Data-driven systems require a higher level of data analysis capability. Focusing more on data in PBF exposes the fact that data analysis capabilities can be rather weak at many levels of the health systems. The best techniques for data analysis and the different strategies to enhance such capabilities are discussed further in chapter 13.

12.4 How to Arrive at a Functional Web-Enabled Application

General Considerations

To establish a functional PBF web-enabled application, seek assistance from a consultant, but be very clear about the application requirements. In addition, define how you wish to train the end users and discuss maintenance and security. Take the following steps:

- Define your PBF system requirements (data flows, type of data to be collected, payment methods, fund holders, system users, and so on).
- Get technical ICT support from a systems developer or programmer to do the following:
  - → Match your requirements to existing PBF applications, and decide whether you will need to develop software or can adapt an existing system.
  - → Configure the system to local requirements.
  - → Develop custom reports.
- Train the end users.
- Plan for maintenance, security, and continuous development.

Find a Consultant for Software Development

Experience with PBF web-enabled application is fairly recent, and therefore limited, albeit growing. In each country, a local information technology programmer is trained to maintain and further develop the web-enabled application, so expertise is increasing. An off-the-shelf product, which can be adapted by any programmer with some experience in MySQL and PHP, is available. In the links to files in this chapter, you will find the generic terms of reference for such an information technology consultant.

Train the End Users

End users will need training in using this web-enabled application. Training should target district-level administrative and health authorities, technical assistants, and ministry of health staff working at the national level. Training is frequently started by reviewing the general level of computer literacy in a given situation: the basics of Internet use, security issues related to accounts and passwords, and information about working on public computers. Two-to-three day training programs seem to be appropriate. District staff can use real performance data to practice data entry. Trainings like this were given in Rwanda for its 2006 performance data and in Burundi during the first six months of its 2010 performance data.

In addition, training a local PHP (software) technician in script, website management through Joomla or WordPress, and maintenance of the database (including its back-up procedures) is helpful.

Plan for Maintenance, Security, and Continuous Development

The database can be located on a server in the capital of the country or based in the cloud overseas. Using a server within the country has various advantages: it enhances the sense of ownership, and, frequently, the access speed is better. However, the server can be located anywhere, especially if access is through a satellite connection. Around-the-clock guaranteed server function, data back-up possibilities, and professional storage (power back-up and climate control) are essential.

In searching for a suitable server in the capital, select an experienced information technology technician who knows about installing and maintaining servers. Analyze two or three Internet service providers. Choose the most reliable one. Purchase the server(s), write a contract with the Internet service provider of your choice, and install the software on the server. Then you are ready to begin.

An example of a contract with an Internet service provider can be found in the links to files in this chapter.

Finally, set up a website editorial committee and a database management committee. The editorial committee manages quality control and oversight of information published on the website and also manages access to the registered portion. The database management committee oversees database security and access, back-up related issues, ongoing development of the web application, and issues related to the ability to analyze performance data. Examples of terms of reference for a website editorial committee and database management committee can be found in the links to files in this chapter. For information on the PBF data centers of Rwanda and Burundi, see boxes 12.1 and 12.2, respectively.

BOX 12.1

Rwanda and Its PBF Data Center

The Rwandese PBF approach for health centers at the national level and for those at the community level relies on a web-enabled database as the backbone of the PBF administrative system. The centralized system uses one set of unit fees for the quantity indicators, which are set at the national level. Composite measures from the quantified quality checklist are also entered in this database.

(box continues on next page)

Fourteen measures are related to the services in the quality checklist. Each composite measure contains multiple subcomposite measures and many data elements. The paper-based information on all subcomposite measures and data elements remains at the decentralized level and is not entered in the database. Its purpose is to enable targeted managerial action at a decentralized level. The idea was that this decentralized approach would allow changing the underlying quality criteria and data elements regularly (putting the quality performance barrier incrementally higher), without having to change the software and its interface each year.

The interface creates consolidated quarterly invoices (consolidating the quantity data with the quality measure) for the minimum package of health services and human immunodeficiency virus (HIV) services. It also contains a menu of graphs, which compare trend lines among indicators.

Screenshot B12.1.1 shows the monthly invoice for the minimum package of services of one health center. These data correspond to the verified paper invoice, which is retained in the district administrative office, with a validated copy left in the health center. The quantities can be verified in the registers, and thus the clients can be traced to their communities by third-party counterverification agents.

SCREENSHOT B12.1.1 Monthly Invoice, Rwanda

REPUBLIQUE DU RWANDA

PROVINCE DU NORD
DISTRICT DE GICUMBI

FACTURE MENSUELLE PROVISOIRE PMA

FORMATION SANITAIRE : CS MANYAGIRO   PERIODE : Juillet 2010

No	Indicateur	Quantité	Validation	Tarif Unitaire	Montant FRW
1	CPC : Nouveaux cas	1,283	1,283	45	57,735
2	CPN: Nombre de femmes enceintes ayant reçu la MII lors de leur première visite	5	5	180	900
3	CPN : Femmes avec 4 visites	7	7	1,500	10,500
4	CPN : VAT 2 - 5	34	34	225	7,650
5	CPoN: Nombre de nouveaux cas en consultation postnatale endéans 10 jours après l'accouchement	0	0	2,000	0
6	PF : Nouvelle utilisatrice	88	88	900	79,200
7	PF : Utilisatrice en fin du mois	1,227	1,227	90	110,430
8	Vaccination : Enfant complètement Vacciné	57	57	450	25,650
9	Accouchement assisté au CS	35	28	3,750	105,000
10	Accouchement : référence d'urgence pour accouchement	0	0	3,750	0
11	References pour malnutrition severe	0	0	1,800	0
12	Références d'urgence	20	20	900	18,000

Montant total = 415,065

Arrêté la présente Facture Mensuelle Provisoire PMA de la Formation Sanitaire de CS Manyagiro pour le mois de Juillet 2010 à la somme de (**415,065 FRW**); quatre cent quinze mille soixante-cinq **Francs Rwandais.**

Source: Rwanda, Ministry of Health, Performance-Based Financing database.

BOX 12.2

Burundi and Its PBF Data Center

The Burundi web-enabled application has been designed to enable decentralized strategic purchasing of essential health services. There are several differences between the Rwandese and the Burundi applications.

First, the Burundi application allows specific budgets to be set for provinces and thereby is able to work toward horizontal equity (getting more money to destitute areas).

Second, in Burundi, the provincial semiautonomous purchasing body can allocate more output budget to more destitute health facilities. This is also meant to enhance horizontal equity by categorizing all health facilities under contract in categories from 0 percent to 40 percent of the budget. Each category has a 10 percent unit fee difference with the following category.

Third, the Burundi system provides the ability to do strategic purchasing and to remain within a given output budget. The provincial purchaser can, using cloud computing, set fees prospectively (each quarter if necessary; adding one-page amendments to the principal purchase contract is an option) and thereby manage its output budget, which is capped for one year.

The ability to monitor budget balance is enhanced by interactive graphic displays, which show in minute detail the level of disbursement against available budget. Levers on high-volume services can be applied to titrate expenditure patterns upward, or adjust them downward. The purpose of this function is to enable the provincial purchaser to direct its Pigouvian subsidies to those services that are lagging.

Screenshot B12.2.1 shows the first quarter report for a province of the national PBF system (which started in April 2010). The province's

SCREENSHOT B12.2.1 Quarterly Report

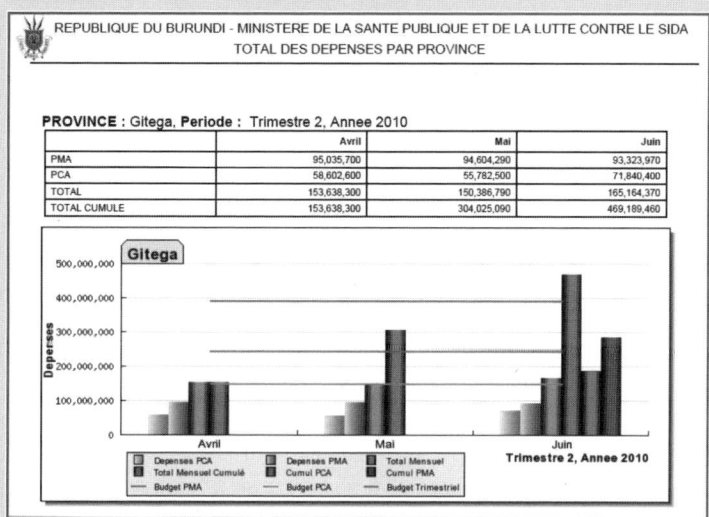

Source: Burundi Performance-Based Financing database.　　　*(box continues on next page)*

actual expenses for the minimum package of activities (PMA), its complementary package of activities (PCA), and its quarterly budget are shown. The data show slight overspending, which can be corrected easily by slightly adjusting one or two levers.

12.5 Links to Files and Tools

The following toolkit files can be accessed through this web link: http://www.worldbank.org/health/pbftoolkit/chapter12.

- Sample terms of reference for a PHP programmer
- Sample contract with an Internet service provider
- Terms of reference for a website editorial committee
- Terms of reference for a database management committee.

Notes

1. MySQL, http://www.mysql.com/products/enterprise/database/, and PostgreSQL, http://www.postgresql.org.
2. Joomla, http://www.joomla.org/, and WordPress, http://wordpress.org.
3. PHP, http://en.wikipedia.org/wiki/PHP.

CHAPTER 13

Data Analysis and Learning

MAIN MESSAGES

➜ The key analytical methods in PBF are analyzing an increase from base-line, analyzing trends over time, analyzing coverage, and performing benchmarking.

➜ Data analysis capabilities are urgently needed at all levels.

COVERED IN THIS CHAPTER

13.1 Introduction

Much can be learned from performance-based financing (PBF) data. Data analysis and learning are essential parts of PBF systems. Comparing performance trends, looking at the percentages of population coverage obtained, and benchmarking are the three most important analytical methods.

Comparing performance may leave stakeholders with a sense of urgency about those that underperform. Comparing performance and rewarding performance are linked in PBF, which is definitely an asset.

Given the rapid international developments around data management, stakeholders at all levels need to boost their capabilities for analyzing data. Data analysis capabilities can be strengthened through automated dashboards, but also through familiarization with Microsoft Excel PivotTable analysis. This chapter discusses how to perform capacity building.

13.2 Comparison of Performance

Data analysis and learning are essential in PBF. A clearer focus on results can change and improve systems considerably. Focusing on outputs and quality spurs actions that are different from those that occur when concentrating only on inputs. Focusing on results rapidly reveals how much can actually be achieved by even relatively small amounts of additional financing. When systems focus on results, they tend to become more efficient and effective while also casting light on what may still be needed to reach the desired levels of performance.

As there are many ways to Rome, there are also many ways to produce results. Therefore, comparing different methods for reaching results and comparing the relative cost-effectiveness of one approach to another is important (Maynard 2012).

The most commonly used data analysis methods in PBF are (a) analyzing an increase from baseline, (b) analyzing trends over time, (c) analyzing coverage, and (d) performing benchmarking.

Analyzing an Increase from Baseline and Trends Over Time

Analyzing an increase from a baseline typically uses line graphs with a monthly breakdown. The longer the time frame, the more meaningful the line graph becomes. A trend line can be created that provides the slope for this line graph—the trend line provides the middle- to long-term-expected performance. Such a trend line can be used for forecasting, and it becomes more reliable when the data series are longer. See box 13.1 later in this chapter.

Analyzing Coverage

Analyzing coverage is derived from calculating the percentage population covered of a certain PBF service and works as follows. Each PBF service has a saturated target. For example, a common target for the number of curative

care consultations per person is one per year. And the target for fully vaccinated children is the total number of children under one year of age. The
coverage for curative care is 50 percent when there is 0.5 consultation per
person per year (as the target in this example), and the coverage for fully vaccinated children is 75 percent if 75 percent of the children under the age of
one have been fully immunized (see also chapter 4).

In table 13.1, the coverage for institutional deliveries in 23 Rwandese districts over a 24-month period is shown. Those deliveries occurred in health
centers; the deliveries in hospitals were omitted in this table. The average
coverage for deliveries was 23.8 percent in January 2006 and 38.2 percent in
December 2007. This change represents a 60 percent increase from baseline

TABLE 13.1 Analyzing Coverage for PBF Services in Rwanda, 2006–07

District	Deliveries target, 2006	Deliveries, January 2006	Coverage, January 2006	Deliveries target, 2007	Deliveries, December 2007	Coverage, December 2007	Change in 24 months (%)
Nyarugenge	10,796	49	0.05	11,077	82	0.09	63.1
Gasabo	14,601	238	0.20	14,981	336	0.27	37.6
Gisagara	11,941	319	0.32	12,252	321	0.31	1.9
Rusizi	15,122	373	0.30	15,515	411	0.32	7.4
Gicumbi	16,387	317	0.23	16,813	452	0.32	39.0
Nyanza	10,260	191	0.22	10,526	294	0.34	50.0
Nyaruguru	10,546	153	0.17	10,820	316	0.35	101.3
Rubavu	13,332	210	0.19	13,679	411	0.36	90.8
Gatsibo	12,913	135	0.13	13,249	409	0.37	195.3
Nyamasheke	14,807	357	0.29	15,192	470	0.37	28.3
Ngororero	12,858	274	0.26	13,192	413	0.38	46.9
Kickiro	9,467	207	0.26	9,713	309	0.38	45.5
Rulindo	11,447	307	0.32	11,744	385	0.39	22.2
Ruhango	11,199	353	0.38	11,490	383	0.40	5.8
Burera	14,612	465	0.38	14,992	517	0.41	8.4
Huye	12,093	180	0.18	12,407	432	0.42	133.9
Rutsiro	12,043	230	0.23	12,356	437	0.42	85.2
Ngoma	10,711	107	0.12	10,989	302	0.43	257.1
Gakenke	14,671	180	0.15	15,052	540	0.43	192.4
Bugesera	12,153	349	0.34	12,469	455	0.44	27.1
Kayonza	9,554	140	0.18	9,802	368	0.45	156.2
Muhanga	13,084	423	0.39	13,425	550	0.49	26.7
Rwamagana	10,045	92	0.11	10,300	624	0.73	561.1
Total/Average	**284,642**	**5,649**	**0.2382**	**292,043**	**9,307**	**0.3824**	**60.6**

Source: Rwanda, Ministry of Health, Performance-Based Financing database.

and a 14.4 percentage point increase in coverage. As the table shows, there is a large variation in coverage among districts. In general, about 80 percent of deliveries need to take place in a health center, and 20 percent need to take place in a hospital. Rwamagana district is close to the 80 percent target.

In box 13.1, the average number of deliveries is presented in a line graph with its trend line. In table 13.1, the average increase hides large differences in performance in the individual districts. The overall majority of the districts are comparable. All are rural and predominantly agricultural. Furthermore, the geography is hilly, and the population is dense. All districts are poor, and the poverty is fairly homogeneous. The health delivery networks in the districts are comparable.

BOX 13.1

Forecasting Institutional Deliveries in Rwandese PBF

Rwanda started with PBF on January 1, 2006, in 23 districts. In figure B13.1.1, the number of institutional deliveries each month in all health centers in these 23 districts is depicted. The graph shows 36 months of data with 100 percent data availability. (All monthly records from all health centers during those 36 months were available. This availability is quite common in PBF systems. See chapter 12.) The trend line predicts with reasonable accuracy that each month the number of deliveries increases by 188.

FIGURE B13.1.1 Total Number of Deliveries in Health Centers in 23 PBF Districts in Rwanda, 2006–08

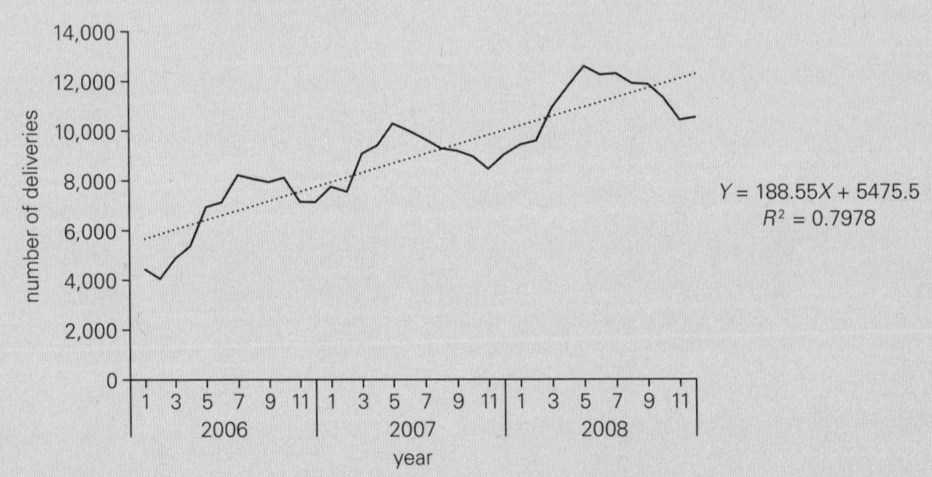

$Y = 188.55X + 5475.5$
$R^2 = 0.7978$

Source: Rwanda, Ministry of Health, Performance-Based Financing database.

Two Technical Caveats

Because the average performance across those 23 districts hides large underlying differences, it draws attention to two experience-based technical caveats in PBF. The first caveat is financial risk forecasting: the smaller the area forecasted, the harder it becomes to be reliable. This result is due to the unpredictability of growth. And this unpredictability is why larger populations are preferred for such risk forecasting.

The second caveat is related to paying for percentage point coverage increases. (This issue is discussed in more detail in chapter 1.) Table 13.1 shows that setting performance goals accurately and predicting future performance would be very difficult. It will be even more difficult for individual facilities (as opposed to districts) to set goals accurately, because the variability and the unpredictability of future growth and performance are pronounced for health facilities (see figure 13.1). As figure 13.1 illustrates, certain facilities started with very high coverage but then declined. A wrong catchment population is the most likely cause of any coverage higher than 100 percent. Such situations are not uncommon. Therefore, in PBF a fee-for-service system is used as a basis for rewarding performance (see chapter 1).

Performing Benchmarking

What can be the underlying cause for the very large discrepancies in district performance or health facility performance for institutional deliveries in Rwanda in 2006–08? Exploring this question is important. To get at causes

FIGURE 13.1 Coverage for Deliveries in Five Health Centers in Rwanda, 2006–08

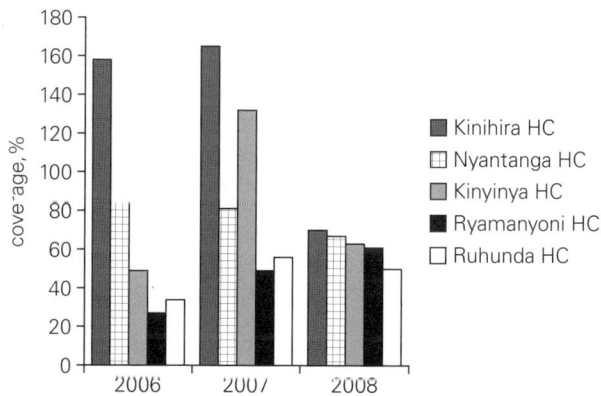

Source: Rwanda, Ministry of Health, Performance-Based Financing database.
Note: HC = health center.

BOX 13.2

Proxy Indicators for Overall Performance and Efficiency

Arguably, the best proxy indicator for overall performance is total earnings. The total reflects the earnings from the entire package of PBF services. A very good proxy indicator for efficiency is total earnings divided by the number of qualified staff members.

You can have a quick overview on what the performance and the efficiency are of which facility, which district, or which province or state, meaning that by looking at money, or total earnings, you can compare health facilities among each other and see the high and low achievers, compare districts among each other and see the high and low achievers, and so on (see figure B13.2.1). And this works best when you adjust the earnings to the catchment area population.

FIGURE B13.2.1 Example of Earnings as Proxy Indicator for Performance and Efficiency

	Earnings Q1–Q2 (US$)
HC 1	6,000
HC 4	5,000
HC 3	4,000
HC 2	3,000

Note: HC = health center, Q = quarter.
Source: World Bank data.

and to learn how the best performing districts and health facilities reached their level of performance, we use benchmarking.

Benchmarking is comparing individual performance (of a health facility or an agency) against the best performance of a group. For example, compare a district health center against the best performing health facility in the whole area on certain metrics such as family planning, institutional deliveries, or fully vaccinated children.

In addition, quality and income can be compared through PBF. Income through PBF happens to be a high-level proxy for total performance (see box 13.2). But beware: if quantity performance between different settings is compared, it would be best to normalize the data (adjust the values measured on different scales to a notionally common scale) to get a meaningful comparison (see box 13.3).

Of the analytical methods discussed here, the most important method appears to be performance benchmarking because of the following:

- Performance benchmarking compares relative values in a situation where the normative values are unknown (effectiveness and efficiency). Comparing relative values will show the best possible result, and such results will drive continuous improvements.

Benchmarking Performance in Nigeria PBF

In the Nigeria State Health Investment Project (NSHIP), a PBF field test was started in December 2011 in a select district in each of the three project states (Adamawa, Nasarawa, and Ondo). For a comparison of relative performances among those three very different districts, the quantity data were normalized for populations of 100,000. This normalization was done by adjusting the actual quantity obtained to a population of 100,000. Over seven months, large differences became obvious. One of the three states was clearly underperforming compared to the other two (figure B13.3.1).

FIGURE B13.3.1 PBF Performance in Select Districts in Nigeria, December 2011–June 2012

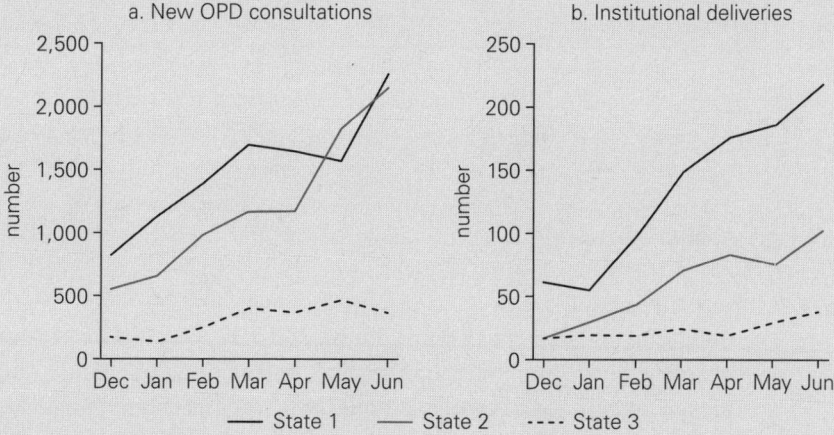

Source: Nigeria Performance-Based Financing portal, http://nphcda.thenewtechs.com.

Note: OPD = outpatient department; PBF = performance-based financing. Data are normalized for populations of 100,000. In both panels, data lines are not identified by district.

- Performance benchmarking allows analysis and discussion of the various strategies that have led to better or worse results. Good strategies can subsequently be adopted by others who want to get similar results (for advanced strategies, see chapter 10).

In figure 13.2, the y-axis shows the number of deliveries each month, and the x-axis shows various months. Nyaruguru district had 13 health centers, of which Cyahinda health center performed best over a 30-month period. Nyamyumba health center performed worst. The average performance is the

FIGURE 13.2 Benchmarking Individual Health Facility Performance for Institutional Deliveries in Nyaruguru District, Rwanda, January 2006–June 2008

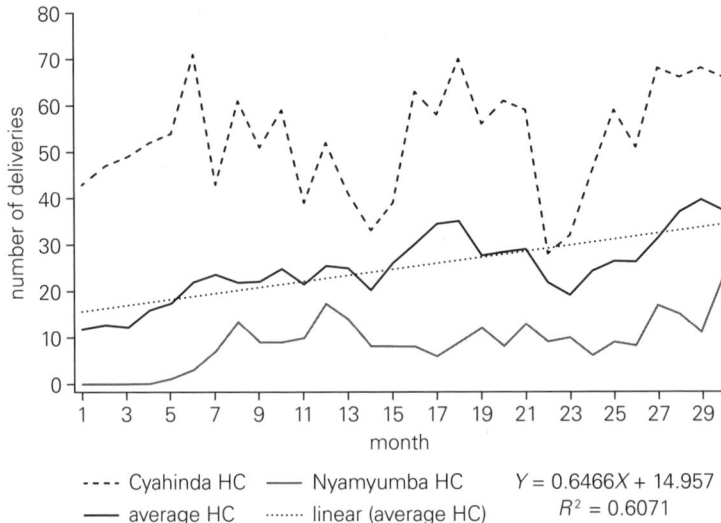

Source: Rwanda, Ministry of Health, Performance-Based Financing database.

Note: HC = health center.

middle line. Using those types of analysis is very useful for managers. For example, Nyamyumba has consistently been an underachiever (although it picked up in the last months). Similarly, it looks like something happened in months 14 and 21–22 in Cyahinda health center. In month 14, the performance increased dramatically, whereas in month 21, the performance suddenly declined sharply. On average, the number of deliveries increased by 0.65 per health facility per month over 30 months. The large variation is reflected by the R^2 value of 0.6.

Figure 13.3 reflects the situation in Gicumbi, another Rwandese district. Rushaki health center had the highest overall performance, and Muko health center had the lowest. Both health centers show a peak between months 3 and 4, which then decreases. This peak was due to PBF without verification. Health centers were told to submit their monthly reports as of January 2006, before any PBF system had been designed. The system was designed between January and April, and in Gicumbi district, the first trainings started in May. The first verification, for the May performance, was carried out in June. In fact, between January and April, there was a

FIGURE 13.3 Benchmarking Individual Health Facility Performance for Institutional Deliveries in Gicumbi District, Rwanda, January 2006–June 2008

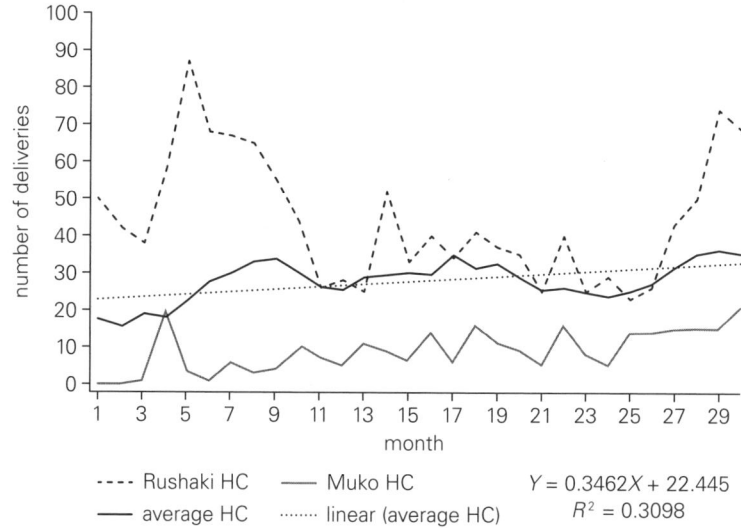

Source: Rwanda, Ministry of Health, Performance-Based Financing database.

Note: HC = health center.

PBF system without verification, which resulted in overreporting. This example demonstrates again how crucial verification is for PBF systems (see also chapter 2). In Gicumbi district, the counterverification (community client satisfaction surveys) started in January 2007 (month 13 in figure 13.3). At that time, less than 5 percent of phantom patients[1] were found. In the Rushaki health center, a very competent in-charge person of the health center left in month 15, and the health center took a long time to return to the same high level of performance as before the departure. In PBF systems as elsewhere, good management is very important for a good level of performance.

Thematic mapping is another powerful method of comparing performance. Thematic maps use geographic information system software to map results. See map 13.1, which uses color coding to show the level of coverage for new consultations at Rwandese health centers in 2007—the darker the color, the higher the coverage. Seven districts without color have no data. These seven districts were control districts in the Rwandan impact evaluation, and had no PBF intervention until April 2008.

MAP 13.1 Coverage for New Consultations, Rwandese Health Centers, 2007

New Curative Consultations per Capita per Year

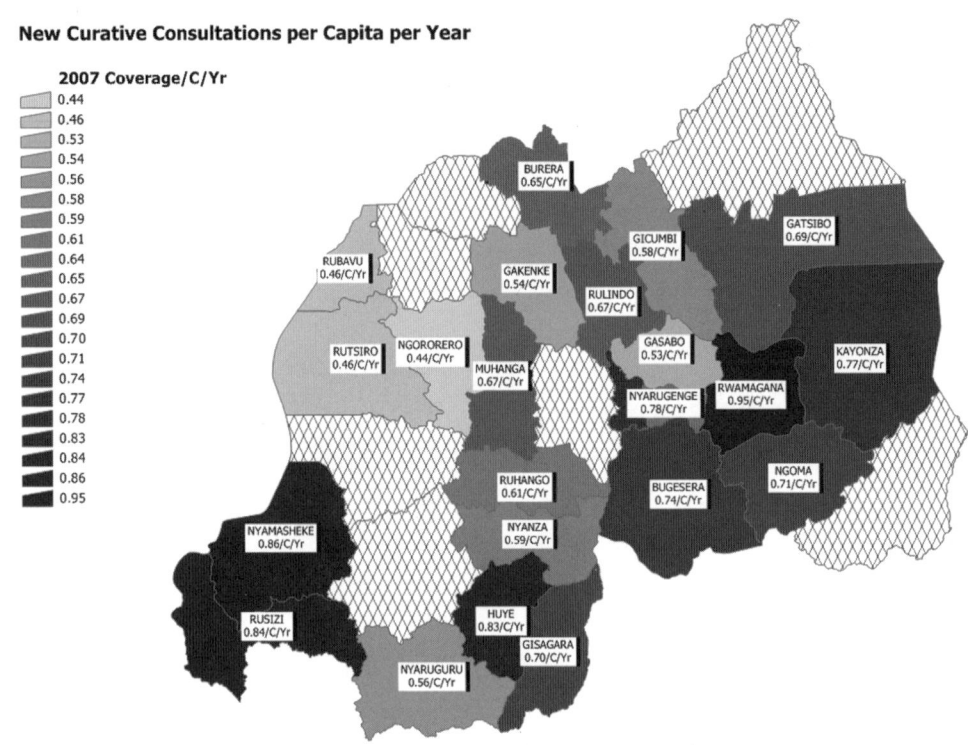

Source: Rwanda, Ministry of Health, Performance-Based Financing database.

Note: Coverage/C/Yr = coverage per capita per year.

13.3 Strategies to Boost Data Analysis Capabilities

Given the importance of solid, reliable data management, stakeholders at all levels in PBF need to strengthen their data analysis capabilities. In many health care systems, general data analysis capabilities are lacking among many staff members, even though such capabilities are crucial for analyzing and improving performance.

Data analysis capabilities are not fully developed because previously, many systems were not driven by results. Data were collected routinely without too many consequences if they were incomplete or faulty. Inaccurate data are the scourge of many routine reporting systems in low- and middle-income countries (Murray et al. 2003). Because of a renewed focus on results and the concomitant need for data analysis capabilities, the gaps in data analysis capabilities have become blatant.

Each level in the health system has different data analysis needs that require distinct capabilities to analyze. At the health center and community level, analysts need to know actual and desirable coverage of services, because those data are necessary for planning and for drawing up a business plan. At this level, obtaining accurate coverage estimates is always a problem. One confounding factor at this level is the often-problematic demarcation of a health center's formal catchment area. Although the issue is challenging, agreement on some formal demarcation for catchment areas is important.

At the district level, figures for the actual coverage for all health centers, the trends over time, and the benchmarking of performance are important. Here, relative performance and strategies to reach a higher level of performance are discussed. At the national level, the various types of coverage are important as is the benchmarking of districts for their relative performance. Higher-level benchmarking can inform strategies to assist lower-performing districts to increase their achievements. Districts may lag because of a wide array of reasons, ranging from a lack of district health leadership to geographical challenges and difficult terrain. Trends over time of indicators can be used to inform financial risk forecasting models that are necessary to set the fees.

Some tools may help. Automated dashboards, for instance, track key performance indicators and are automatically updated to show the most recent results available. They enable key indicators to be followed with a minimum amount of effort and provide a quick overview of how the system is performing in relation to those key indicators. Figure 13.4 provides an example of such a dashboard element. In Burundi, managers can follow disbursements and determine whether or not they are overspending. As figure 13.4 shows, by January 15, 2011, 77 percent of the 2010 PBF budget was spent.

A Microsoft Excel PivotTable analysis allows managers to customize an analysis through tables or graphs of any of the performance indicators present in their database. The tool is versatile, but managers need specific, more advanced training to create and analyze these data. Because of the relative difficulty of the method, refresher trainings might also be necessary.

FIGURE 13.4 A Dashboard Element for Burundi PBF

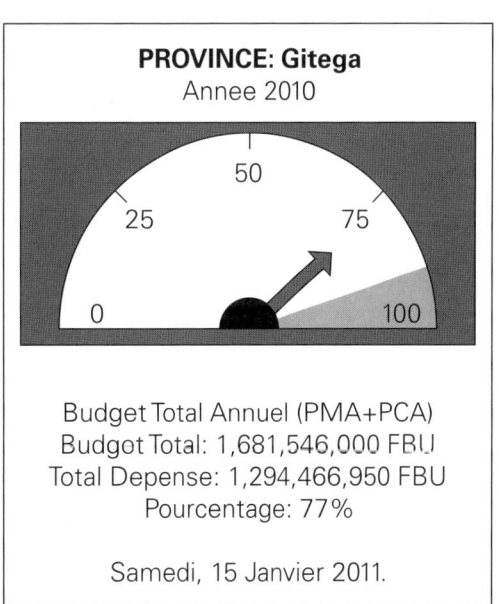

Source: Burundi Performance-Based Financing database.

Note: FBU = Burundi Franc; PCA = package of complementary activities; PMA = package of minimum activities.

13.4 Links to Files and Tools

The following toolkit files can be accessed through this web link:
http://www.worldbank.org/health/pbftoolkit/chapter13.

- Training reports for two Microsoft Excel PivotTable trainings showing methodology and content

Note

1. Phantom patients are those who are claimed to have been served by the health center and are recorded in its register so as to claim the service fee. But then, after a community client satisfaction survey has been carried out, the patients cannot be traced in the community or can be traced but claim not to have received that service. Hence, the term *phantom patient*.

References

Maynard, A. 2012. "The Powers and Pitfalls of Payment for Performance." *Health Economics* 21 (1): 3–12.

Murray, C. J., B. Shengelia, N. Gupta, S. Moussavi, A. Tandon, and M. Thieren. 2003. "Validity of Reported Vaccination Coverage in 45 Countries." *The Lancet* 362 (9389): 1022–27.

CHAPTER 14

PBF Technical Assistance and Training

MAIN MESSAGES

→ PBF requires targeted technical assistance and regular training.
→ Technical assistance is very important, especially for PBF functions such as good governance and independent verification.
→ Civil society involvement is essential and enhances good governance.
→ The promotion of South–South technical assistance is vital because such assistance more rapidly creates local ownership for PBF.

COVERED IN THIS CHAPTER

14.1 Introduction

Performance-based finance (PBF) requires intense technical assistance. External expertise is often necessary for different functions, but the type of assistance varies over time, while the intensity of assistance declines. The technical assistance functions can be manifold. They span the entire technical field of PBF. Nonstate actors figure prominently in governance for PBF and have distinct importance, for instance, in the separation of functions. Certain roles should not be executed by the government. Coordination of technical assistance for PBF is mostly organized through the extended team mechanism. Significant emphasis is put on capacity building of local technicians and researchers, and increasingly technical assistance is provided South–South (cooperation or the sharing of technology and knowledge between developing countries). This exchange enhances ownership.

14.2 Types of Technical Assistance Necessary for PBF

In most settings, PBF requires initial intensive technical assistance. For many countries, PBF involves novel ways of financing health services and of strengthening the health system. It introduces financing of health services based on outputs, a method that is conditional on the quality of those services, instead of financing based on inputs, and a method that most countries tended to use before PBF. In addition, PBF insists on considerable autonomy at the health facility level and involves cash management that frequently was absent prior to PBF. PBF strengthens the health system because it increases the quantity and quality of health services while boosting the transparency and accountability of the health system through institutionalizing civil society roles in the governance of PBF. All those shifts constitute major transitions, in which some technical assistance may be welcome.

Functions, for which external support may be needed, especially at the outset, include the following:

- Counterverification
- Coordination
- Financing
- Database development and maintenance
- Capacity building of stakeholders
- Participation in governance
- Training (which is treated later in this chapter).

Capacity building is especially important for the following:

- Implementation
- Research
- Data analysis
- Monitoring of quality
- Essential regulatory functions (revenue generation, budgeting, and costing, and so on).

In addition, frequently there is an overarching need for an external body (external to the government, or ring fenced to ensure relative impartiality) to assist the government in the separation of functions such as purchasing, verification, and regulation. Without such an external body, often there is not sufficient separation of functions.

The specific desiderata for technical assistance depend on the local situation. Table 14.1 lists a number of potential areas for technical assistance,

TABLE 14.1 Technical Assistance Areas in PBF

PBF element	Technical assistance areas	Type: Duration, intensity, and personnel
PBF assessment	<ul><li>Public-private mix</li><li>Health worker coping strategies</li><li>Quality issues</li><li>PBF package</li><li>HMIS assessment</li><li>Budget estimate</li><li>Feasibility and willingness</li></ul>	<ul><li>2–4 weeks</li><li>Senior PBF expert</li></ul>
PBF pilot (in 1–2 districts)	If no in-country experience with PBF <ul><li>Contracted out to agency</li><li>Agency contracted in</li></ul>	<ul><li>1–2 years</li><li>Agency with PBF expertise</li></ul>
Setting of fees	<ul><li>Assessment of baselines from different sources, mostly from health facility level</li><li>Costing out of services</li></ul>	<ul><li>2 weeks</li><li>Senior PBF expert with public health expertise</li></ul>
Web-enabled application (creation, maintenance, development)	<ul><li>Adaptation of off-the-shelf software</li><li>Training of local IT programmers in maintenance</li><li>Training and backstopping of end users</li><li>Maintenance and development</li></ul>	<ul><li>30–40 days in year 1</li><li>About 12 days per year in years 2–4</li><li>PHP software programmer</li><li>TA involvement with local counterparts on maintenance and continuous development of the database and website</li></ul>
PBF tools (registers, services, contracts, checklists, manuals, and so on)	<ul><li>Standardizing of registers and data collection tools for use with PBF</li><li>Contracts</li><li>Quality checklist</li><li>Performance framework for the health administration</li><li>MPA/CPA</li><li>Manual</li></ul>	<ul><li>1–2 months (depending on process)</li></ul>

(table continues on next page)

TABLE 14.1 *(continued)*

PBF element	Technical assistance areas	Type: Duration, intensity, and personnel
Training (early CB, snowball training during rollout)	• Initial intense training of key decision makers and implementers • Training of trainers • Training manual • Snowball training and supervision	• Early CB: 2-week intense training • TOT: 2–4 weeks • Manual: 2 weeks • Snowball training and supervision: 4–6 weeks
Separation of functions	• Purchasing • Verification • Community-client satisfaction surveys	• Contracted to a purchasing agent (ideal separation of functions) or agency contracted in to support purchasing through a quasi-public-purchaser approach • Involvement of grassroots organizations • Entire duration of PBF
Capacity building (research, data analysis)	• Research • Monitoring • Data analysis	• TA needs vary • Intensity typically high • Needs typically high • Ongoing and incremental
Quality monitoring	• Field testing of quality checklist • CB of district health staff[a] • Ongoing development • Counterverification of quality scores at health centers and hospitals	• Initial field testing: 2 weeks • Intensity of TA dependent on intervention size • Once per quarter
Budget follow-up, strategic purchasing	• Budgeting • Incorporation of multiple fund holders through virtual pooling • Adaptation of costing based on results obtained • Adaptation of fees in case of budget surplus, overspending, insufficient results, and so on	• At least one full-time position during PBF until sufficient capacity created at the national level
Policy dialogue with Ministry of Finance, development partners	• Advice and technical support • Lobbying of national and international partners	• Ongoing during PBF project • Intensity dependent on support needed
Advocacy, communication	• Advice and technical support • Lobbying of national and international partners	• Ongoing during PBF project • Intensity dependent on support needed

Source: World Bank data.

Note: CB = capacity building; CPA = complementary package of activities; HMIS = health management information system; IT = information technology; MPA = minimum package of activities; PBF = performance-based financing; PHP = Hypertext Preprocessor; TA = technical assistance; TOT = training of trainers.

a. The quality checklist is applied through the district health staff. The counterverification of the results is done by double-checking a random sample of reported (and paid-for) results. The counterverification uses technical assistance, central-level Ministry of Health staff, or a third party.

based on a variety of experiences over the past decade. Successful PBF projects and scaled-up PBF systems have used technical assistance in these areas to differing extents.

The type and volume of technical assistance vary over time. By and large, the need for external assistance declines in the course of the program once local capacity and expertise is being built. Eventually, local technicians take over various functions (see figure 14.1).

The costs for technical assistance depend on the size and type of the intervention. As a rule of thumb, it can consume 20–30 percent of the total project costs. Technical assistance is an area of ongoing learning. A study of PBF in Rwanda costed staff time, agency overheads and involvement in coordination, capacity building, and monitoring and verification activities (Uwimpuhwe 2011) (see box 14.1). It demonstrated that in Rwanda, international (Northern) technical assistance decreased and national technical assistance increased over a four-year period (2006–09), which demonstrated capacity transfer. At the same time, Rwandese technical assistance experts became international (South–South) technical assistants in other developing countries.

Remember that the time frame for technical assistance covers the *entire* duration of the PBF scaling-up process and beyond. Experience has taught us that elements of technical assistance, especially those related to the separation of functions, and elements linked to good governance cannot be phased out without weakening the entire PBF design. Similarly, civil society

FIGURE 14.1 Technical Assistance Requirements Varied Over Time in Rwanda

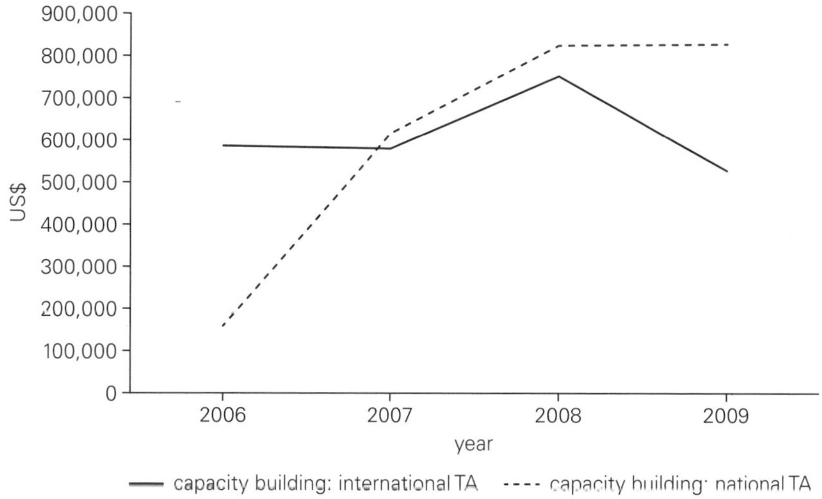

Source: Uwimpuhwe 2011.

Note: TA = technical assistance.

Calculating the Costs of PBF Technical Assistance in Rwanda

Knowledge of technical assistance costs for PBF is limited. Technical assistance costs, which actually are investment costs, are a large part of the overhead costs of PBF. Such investment and operating costs of well-designed and well-performing nongovernmental organization–managed PBF projects have a range of US$0.30–US$0.40 per capita per year (Soeters et al. 2011; Toonen et al. 2009). In very challenging physical environments (for example, South Sudan), the costs may be higher.

An extensive study on the costs of scaling up the PBF approaches in Rwanda found that over a four-year period (2006–09), the average overhead costs (both investment and operating costs) were 23.5 percent and were estimated at US$0.28 per capita per year (16.8 percent of total budget) in the fourth year (Uwimpuhwe 2011). Table B14.1.1 presents information drawn from that study.

The proportion was much higher in the first years of PBF implementation, especially in 2006 when 28.5 percent of the total budget was spent on overhead costs. So, in 2009, the cost to push US$1.00 through PBF was US$0.21. Or in different terms, of each dollar spent through PBF in 2009, US$0.17 was used to make the system work. Significant economies of scale exist, and increasing the output budget would bring down the costs significantly.

To put the costs in perspective, it is useful to compare them to costs in another health financing arrangement in Rwanda. The PBF overhead costs are about the same as those for the first risk pool of the Rwandese community-based health insurance scheme. The costs of running a health mutual organization in each Rwandese health center to collect US$1.77 per person per year carried about the same percentage transaction cost. PBF overhead costs in Rwanda were between US$0.14 and US$0.34 per capita per year.

TABLE B14.1.1 Overhead Costs as a Percentage of Total Costs

Year	Output payments (US$)	Overhead cost (US$)	Total (US$)	Overhead cost (%)
2006	3,181,425	1,269,135	4,450,560	28.5
2007	5,997,471	2,137,560	8,135,031	26.3
2008	8,313,465	3,253,925	11,567,390	28.1
2009	13,178,941	2,744,185	15,923,125	16.8
Total	**30,671,302**	**9,404,805**	**40,076,107**	**23.5**

Source: Based on Uwimpuhwe 2011.

involvement cannot be phased out because civil society has been institutionalized in the PBF setup and constitutes a structural component of good governance for PBF. Those functions cannot be taken over by government.

Technical assistance functions in which the ministry of health can take the lead are those that do not jeopardize the separation of PBF functions or diminish civil society's engagement in governance. After establishment of the initial PBF system, ongoing capacity building continues to be needed, for instance, in the domain of data management, data analysis, and research capabilities. Technical assistance remains important in those areas.

14.3 The Extended Team Mechanism

Implementing and sustaining a PBF health reform program, especially during the scale-up, is arduous. We will analyze some implementation challenges and focus on one key prerequisite for good implementation—good information and coordination.

We examine the case of the scale-up of PBF in Rwanda in 2006, analyzing how the coordination and communication were handled and how different fund holders and technical agents were mobilized. This latter aspect of the scale-up seems crucial (see box 14.2). The Ministry of Health would not have been able to exercise its leadership nor effectively run the program had it not received the technical assistance to do so.

BOX 14.2

The Predictors of Success in the Rwandese PBF

Hogwood and Gunn's (1984) Perfect Implementation Model lists 10 preconditions for the successful implementation of a top-down policy (Hogwood and Gunn 1984):

1. Circumstances external to the implementing agency do not impose crippling constraints.
2. Adequate time and sufficient resources are made available to the program.
3. The required combination of resources is actually available.
4. The policy to be implemented is based on a valid theory of cause and effect.
5. The relationship between cause and effect is direct, and there are few, if any, intervening links.
6. The dependency relationship is minimal.
7. There is understanding of and agreement on objectives.
8. Tasks are fully specified in correct sequence.
9. There is perfect communication and coordination.
10. Those in authority can demand and obtain perfect compliance.

This Perfect Implementation Model can be used to assess a proposed policy in the likelihood that it gets implemented. It can also be used after the fact to assess what went wrong or what might explain any current situation. This model was used retrospectively to assess the Rwandese national scale-up of PBF in 2006–09. A very mixed picture emerged of conditions that predicted failure and conditions that predicted success.

The positive factors were in the majority, and three of the five negative factors were balanced by some positive features. It was remarkable that (a) resources were abundant, including the proper mix of resources (resources for output payments and resources for technical assistance), and (b) tasks were fully specified in correct sequence—perfect communication and coordination existed, and those in authority could demand and obtain perfect compliance. Although there were weak points, hallmarks of successful implementation were (a) available resources, including the proper mix of resources; (b) strong leadership from the Ministry of Health, especially from the second half of 2007 onward; and (c) good communication and coordination.

Rwandese Case: Two Consecutive Teams—Technical Working Group Followed by Extended Team Mechanism

In Rwanda, two types of formal groups and meeting grounds were steering the development of the PBF system. The first was the technical working group, and the second, introduced in April 2007, was the extended team mechanism.

- Technical working group meetings were national-level meetings on policy and strategy. They constituted a forum for the Rwandese Ministry of Health (MoH) in which technical assistants and heads of agencies could discuss broad details of the PBF approach. The meetings involved approving tools, manuals, and so on. The group was presided over by the PBF coordinator of the MoH and received secretarial support through a technical agency
- Extended team meetings were national-level meetings that assembled technicians and built an implementation-oriented coordination mechanism. The meetings involved technical assistants from three MoH departments and eight development partners who were mostly working in a number of specific districts. The meetings were chaired by an MoH technician with secretarial support through a technical agency.

In the first phase—design—18 intensive, well-documented technical working group meetings were held between February and August 2006. Then, the working group met six more times up to April 2007. After April, the working group meetings stopped. The extended team meetings began in April 2007, amounting to 23 sessions until July 2009. In short, an implementation-oriented coordination team took over from the technical working group.

The Extended Team Mechanism as a System-Strengthening Instrument

The Rwandese extended team was meant to coordinate the provision of technical assistance to the decentralized district PBF steering committees. It was also intended to bridge the gap between policy and implementation. Staff members from three MoH departments and eight development agencies were assembled, totaling more than 40 technical assistants. Meetings were scheduled from 9 a.m. to 1 p.m. on the last Thursday of the month, and the agenda was carefully prepared. Minutes were distributed quickly and, after approval, were posted on the documentation section of the PBF website.

The extended team became the focus of most capacity building activities. The team was targeted to grow into master trainers in PBF and in advanced trainers in data analysis. All of those efforts were supported by team-building activities.

What were the main strategies used to build this extended team that turned it into such an effective system-strengthening tool? Four important features of this process are as follows:

- Mapping stakeholders to assess who is interested
- Mobilizing support from the government and key development partners
- Using a bottom-up approach to obtain buy-in
- Setting agendas, documenting meetings, and running the program.

Mapping Stakeholders to Assess Who Is Interested

The extended team mapped stakeholders for their experience with PBF and their areas of interest. The team listed organizations that were already paying for performance (MoH, Management Sciences for Health [MSH], and the Belgian Development Agency) and agencies that had been managing the PBF pilot programs but had stopped paying for performance (International aid agencies Cordaid and Health Net International–Transcultural Psychosocial Organization [HNI-TPO]). The names of technical staff members from those agencies were noted. Because MSH purchased human immunodeficiency virus (HIV) preventive and curative services performance from about 100 health facilities that were supported by five U.S. government collaborating agencies, those agencies were also mapped. The MoH contacted the U.S. government collaborating agencies to nominate technical staff members to become their PBF technicians.

Mobilizing Support from the Government and Key Development Partners

The extended team contacted the United States Agency for International Development (USAID) and informed the agency of the purpose of coordination. The Belgian embassy in Rwanda was also mobilized to participate. USAID convened a meeting between the MoH and the U.S. government collaborating agencies. The USAID health officer requested that the heads of the collaborating agencies provide PBF support to the MoH. One strategy to boost involvement of the collaborating agencies consisted of parceling out 100 purchase contracts among the five agencies, thereby effectively tying them into the system. The collaborating agencies would have to take the national system seriously. This acceptance was to their own interest: they would otherwise not be able to endorse the veracity of the HIV performance data that they had paid for so far. In fact, the HIV/AIDS (acquired immune deficiency syndrome) treatment and care agencies were urged to take an interest in the general health services, because the general quality measures were affecting the HIV payments. Any disturbances in the non-HIV services would undermine the credibility of the HIV measures, too. All of those services were measured through the same mechanism—the same local administration verifier and the same hospital supervisory team.

With this procedure, the U.S. government–funded HIV/AIDS technical agencies had been effectively co-opted into taking an integral interest in the entire health system.

Using a Bottom-Up Approach to Obtain Buy-In

A bottom-up approach was used to determine the actual scope of work of the new coordination mechanism. The idea was to create a horizontal coordination mechanism in which stakeholder participation would arise more from a sense of common purpose and common objectives and less from a sense of command and control.

The first two meetings of the extended team were a few days apart. In the initial meeting, the participants separated into small groups to draft a list of tasks that (a) the extended team ought to perform (its scope of work) and (b) the individual members of the team, the so-called district PBF focal points, would have to carry out. The small groups presented their work in a plenary session, and common elements were compiled. This effort led to a first draft of the scope of work of the extended team and a draft terms of reference for the PBF focal points. In the second meeting, the documents were submitted, discussed, amended, finalized, and adopted. District PBF focal points were mapped to specific districts, mostly coinciding with the geographical interest area of each technician's organization. Technicians who were full-time PBF specialists were given multiple districts to support; other technicians were assigned to one district only. The extended team was created.

In the links to files of this chapter, find the agenda for the first extended team meeting, the terms of reference for the extended team, and the terms of reference for the district PBF focal point.

Setting Agendas, Documenting Meetings, and Running the Program

Careful agenda setting, accurate minutes keeping, and fast dissemination of documentation were the hallmarks of both the technical working group and the extended team meetings. For the remainder of their activities, their modus operandi was different. Members of the extended team were troubleshooting in dysfunctional district PBF steering committees. They were called in to deal with accountability mechanisms for the district hospital peer-evaluation mechanisms. They helped to address counterverification mechanisms for the quality measures in the health centers and led the review of the various PBF tools in the last quarter of each year. The team members also worked extensively as trainers for PBF.

Representatives of the MoH chaired both groups. The extended team meetings allowed for easy operation of the PBF system by the MoH.

The Rwandese case is a good example of what may be required to optimize technical assistance in a given situation.

14.4 Capacity Building, Training, and Working South–South

PBF always emphasizes using local technicians and researchers. Ultimately, local experts are best positioned to help transform their health systems and carry those systems through the many necessary transitions. PBF systems are new and need evidence-based adaptations to local circumstances. Local experts can easily become the champions who will help manage and change the system with messages of *couleur locale* (local color) rather than with messages from abroad. Local experts possess fine-tuned knowledge of how to communicate most effectively the various transformations required. In short, technical assistance from as close to a local setting as possible is preferred for PBF. There is a rapidly growing number of southern technicians who are closer to the many local realities and closer to the local know-how at the health facility level. Training such key technicians should be taken on from the beginning.

Training of Trainers

When starting PBF, disseminate and make understood the new rules to all frontline health workers in all health centers and hospitals, the district administrative and health staff, and the political leaders in the country. Scaling up PBF through an entire country demands a well-planned, thorough training strategy. This section and the next recommend how to do so.

A key component of the scaling-up strategy of PBF is the development of a pool of persons capable of the following:

- Transferring PBF knowledge and skills to others through technical assistance, training, supervision, and coaching
- Supporting the various partners who are assisting the health sector in the country as it transforms financing into PBF.

The basic idea is to train trainers who will subsequently (a) execute the training of the health center management and the district health staff, (b) remain the resource persons for the staff during the start-up and the implementation phases, and (c) become the de facto PBF specialists for the country. Data use, analysis and interpretation, dissemination of good practices, and a different and more effective way of working will come to the fore after PBF is introduced. Permanent education is needed for ongoing capacity building to do PBF better.

The national-level trainers and technical assistants will assist the MoH in building PBF capacity through technical assistance, training, management, and evaluation skills at the central, district, health facility, and community levels. The trainers and assistants will demonstrate a high level of knowledge about PBF tools and how and when to use them. They will also understand the roles of the various PBF actors and the process of data management.

The extended team is the natural source for such training of trainers. Available human resources for PBF have been identified in various organizations. Focus on their capacity development. Often, a substantial number of the nation's high-capacity individuals have been contracted by bilateral agencies that fund vertical programs. For example, the group of HIV/AIDS implementers in Sub-Saharan Africa and similar agencies form a natural pool from which to select staff members for capacity building. We assume that you have already identified these agencies and invited them to join your extended team.

Finding a Master Trainer

PBF is a paradigm shift. For trainers to really grasp the depth of PBF programming, to learn from each other, and to become enthusiastic proponents, they need to be guided through a learning process.

A very good master trainer is needed to do this teaching. Such processes take about two weeks of full-time engagement of the trainers, about one week of preparatory work before the training of trainers, and one to two weeks after training to compile the training manual. This process of about five weeks also requires time to supervise the actual trainings. The master trainer, who is unlikely to know much about PBF, will need very close and full-time technical support by the senior PBF specialist.

Training Development Process

This particular capacity-building strategy aims to develop a cadre of trainers at all levels with a solid understanding of PBF principles, tools, and processes. In some cases, trainees show the interest and aptitude to become master trainers themselves, and they should receive additional coaching that will enable them to develop or adapt training curricula to meet the needs of a particular level of the health system. The PBF training of trainer programs use principles of adult education and experiential learning to maximize active participation and capacity transfer. The strategy chosen for this training of trainers is to let future trainers devise the training curriculum. By having future trainers devise the curriculum, they will learn PBF, confront the level of their competence, and grow in the subject matter. They will accomplish those tasks while discussing their learning with more experienced PBF practitioners. By actually teaching the various PBF modules, trainers will be brought up to speed with all the technicalities of PBF approaches. They will become active PBF practitioners and a valuable resource for ongoing PBF development in their country.

On average, this process involves one week of intense training in adult learning techniques and a second week of creating the training modules with the trainers, using methods and principles learned in the previous week. The training modules are presented to the group, whereby the group comments on and finalizes the modules. Then, all draft materials are compiled in a training manual. See the Rwanda PBF training manual in the links to files in this chapter.

The PBF trainer development adopted in Rwanda and Burundi consists of a series of sequential and iterative steps that follow the experiential learning cycle (see figure 14.2).

FIGURE 14.2 Trainer Development Cycle

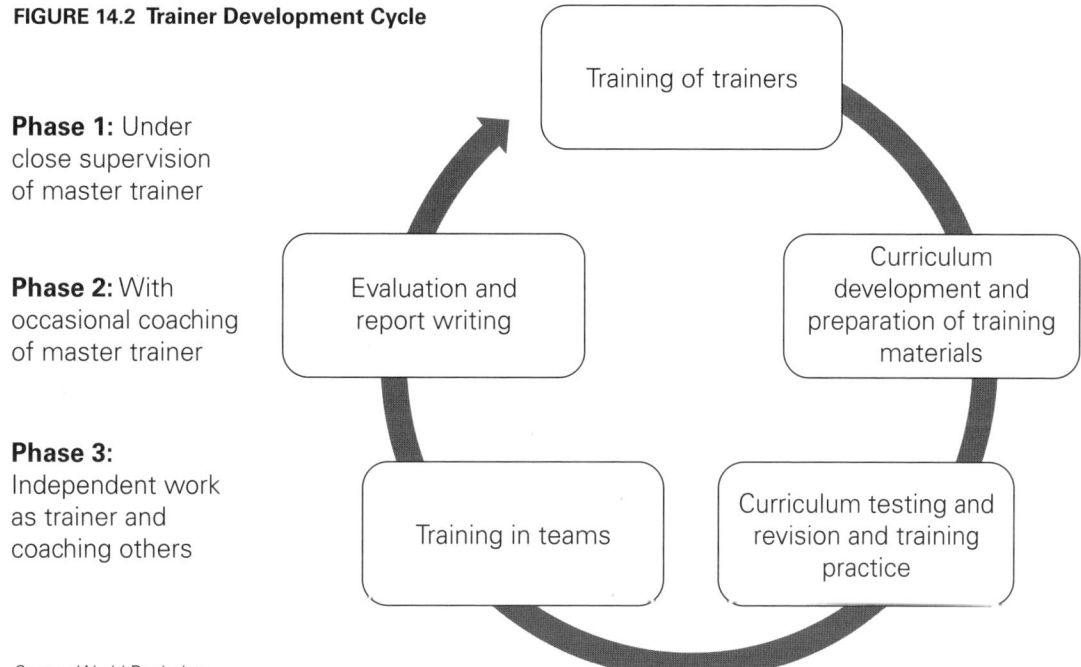

Phase 1: Under close supervision of master trainer

Phase 2: With occasional coaching of master trainer

Phase 3: Independent work as trainer and coaching others

Source: World Bank data.

At the national level, the steps are as follows:

1. Selection of target group (at national level by identification of national trainers)
2. Mid-level training of trainers (TOT), including a module on how to develop training curricula
3. Curriculum development and training design in PBF for identified target groups at different levels by trainers having completed the TOT with coaching by the master trainer
4. Co-training practice with the master trainer to test curriculum and practice training skills with daily self-assessment and feedback
5. Curriculum redesign and modification based on testing
6. Co-training of target groups in teams of three to four national-level PBF trainers with coaching by the master trainer to practice training skills with daily self-assessments and feedback
7. Co-training in teams of two to three national-level PBF trainers independent of the master trainer (repeated several times to scale up PBF and reinforce learning)
8. Identification of national team members who have achieved the level of master trainer.

At the provincial and district levels, the steps are as follows:

1. Selection of target group (sector and health center level)
2. Preparation of the training
3. Co-training in teams of three to four people with coaching from master trainers (repeated several times to scale up PBF and reinforce learning).

Terms of Reference for Master Trainer

Sample terms of reference for a master trainer can be found in the links to files in this chapter.

Example of Training Manuals

Two examples of training manuals can be found in the links to files in this chapter. Although the manuals are in French, the layout and content will be more or less understandable. The manuals have been created in such a fashion that the individual sessions can be extracted from the Adobe file and used as stand-alone modules.

Start planning for the actual trainings well in advance. Printing the PBF user manuals and finalizing and printing the PBF training manuals might take quite some time. In low- and middle-income countries, delays in preparing the training materials need to be factored in to the process: they are bottlenecks.

Training for Rollout

How do you plan and execute training for all health staff in an entire country? From our experience, it is very challenging work. But it is doable. And it is extremely rewarding if you are successful. This training is hands-on: get involved.

The basic strategy is incremental training: begin small, and build upward. You will have already identified and trained your trainers. You will have finalized your PBF manual. You will have done your training of trainers. And you will have finalized your PBF training manual.

Typically, you will have two types of target groups for trainings: (a) the health center management (the health center in-charge person and the president of the health center management committee) and (b) the district PBF steering committee members, the quantity verifiers, and the quality verifiers.

- *Health center management.* Four days of training is typical. About 30–40 participants (less is better) and 2–3 PBF trainers per training session are needed. The idea is for the health center management to explain the PBF system to their health center staff. The training ends with a ceremony in which the purchase contracts are signed. This approach nicely formalizes the end of training and the start of the new PBF system. The PBF trainers should be those who are mapped to that particular district and who will provide hands-on support during the implementation of PBF.
- *District PBF steering committee.* Three to four days of training is typical. About 30–40 participants (less is better) and 2–3 PBF trainers per training session are needed. The training ends with the signing of the multilateral contract and, hence, formalizes the district PBF steering committee. The multilateral contract is signed by the head of the district administration (commissioner or mayor) and by various parties, including the district health director and civil society.

Planning for Further Training

The planning for the larger-scale training is done during the closing days of the TOT. Plans are drawn up, allocating various districts to various agencies and technical assistants. Here, the importance of the extended team arises; the various agencies in this team have a combined operational capacity that far surpasses the capacity of any of them individually.

Planning and executing one high-quality, decentralized four-day training for 40 field staff members is not easy. Now, imagine organizing such training for 500 health centers and 40 district hospitals and their management committees: that effort involves training 1,000 people in all parts of the country in groups of 30–40. At the least, you will have to organize 25–30 four-day trainings throughout the country. In addition, those trainings will have to be done within a reasonable time because the PBF system must start functioning by a set date. Assuming that you have 30 districts in a given country, then you will have to organize a further 20–30 trainings for the district PBF steering committees.

Your task is to organize 50–60 high-quality, three- to four-day trainings for a total of about 1,500–2,000 people within about eight weeks. This objective

14.5 Links to Files and Tools

Terms of reference and other documents for a PBF technical expert (field work) can be accessed through this web link: http://www.worldbank.org /health/pbftoolkit/chapter14.

- Terms of reference for a PBF technical expert (national-level work)
- Examples of terms of reference for a PBF technical assistance agency
  - Burundi
  - Cameroon
  - Lesotho
  - Nigeria
  - Zimbabwe.
- Agenda for the first Rwandese extended team meeting
- Terms of reference for the Rwandese extended team
- Terms of reference for the district PBF focal point
- Minutes of the Rwandese extended team meetings (2007–09)
- Rwanda PBF training manual for health centers and hospitals
- Rwanda PBF training manual for community PBF
- Schedule of the Rwandese 2008 health center and district hospital trainings (nationwide scaling-up)
- Schedule of the Rwandese 2009 Community PBF trainings here (nationwide scaling-up)
- Schedule of the Burundi 2009/2010 PBF trainings (nationwide scaling-up)
- Terms of reference for a master trainer.

would be difficult enough if it were just a financial issue—an estimated US$6,000 per training that totals US$300,000–US$360,000 is needed. But that is not the full story. It is physically impossible for one agency to organize all the trainings and to carry out simultaneous training sessions in all parts of the country. Therefore, you need to request heads of agencies to chip in, not so much for funding (although requesting them to fund this would be a demonstration of their commitment) as for expertise in organization and logistics. They need to help with informing districts and the health facilities; organizing the training sites; and handling all the detailed work of logistics, accommodations, and so on.

We have applied this methodology successfully in the trainings for scaling up PBF in two countries. Trained during the scale-up in the first country, two very competent trainers became the master trainers in the second country. The latter is an excellent example of South–South capacity transfer.

References

Hogwood, B., and L. Gunn, eds. 1984. *Policy Analysis for the Real World.* Oxford: Oxford University Press.

Soeters, R., P. B. Peerenboom, P. Mushagalusa, and C. Kimanuka. 2011. "Performance-Based Financing Experiment Improved Health Care in the Democratic Republic of Congo." *Health Affairs* 30 (8): 1518–27.

Toonen, J., A. Cananvan, P. Vergeer, and R. Elovainio. 2009. *Performance-Based Financing for Health: Lessons from Sub-Saharan Africa.* Amsterdam: Royal Tropical Institute (KIT).

Uwimpuhwe, S. 2011. "Cost Analysis of the Performance-Based Financing Scheme in Rwanda." School of Public Health, National University of Rwanda, Kigali.

Designing and Updating a PBF Manual

MAIN MESSAGES

→ A PBF project needs a concise manual, written in plain language.
→ The PBF manual is primarily meant for frontline health workers and their managers.
→ Tools and checklists described in the manual need to be tested and updated regularly.

COVERED IN THIS CHAPTER

15.1 Introduction

A performance-based financing (PBF) project needs a manual. At a minimum, the manual should contain the following:

- Description of the institutional arrangements, such as the separation of functions
- Roles of the different actors
- Monitoring and verification mechanisms
- List of PBF services
- Contracts
- Checklists.

The manual should be written in plain language because it is meant for frontline health workers and their managers. Creating ownership by developing the manual in close collaboration with the PBF counterparts is very important. Regular revision of the manual is advisable; once per year is recommended.

15.2 Contents of a PBF Manual

A PBF project needs a well-organized and concisely written manual, because PBF is a new and different way of doing business. The various rules need to be spelled out clearly to avoid any ambiguities. Especially when practices diverge from current procedures, it is important to introduce these changes very clearly. One can demonstrate, for instance, how health services will be documented and in which registers, how money will be managed, and how performance of individual health workers will be assessed and rewarded.

In practice, the three most important changes from usual procedures to which implementers refer are (a) the level of detail and accuracy related to routine data recording; (b) the fact that services are paid for and, hence, staff members are evaluated and paid on the basis of their performance; and (c) the high level of quality required, which is measured regularly. Most of the new rules pertain to aspects of these changes and are described in detail in the various contracts that come with PBF.

A PBF manual has certain standard features. It contains a description of the PBF approach and its main principles. For instance, the manual describes the separation of functions as a governance requirement and illustrates what this means for the roles and responsibilities of all PBF actors. It describes the monitoring and verification mechanisms and the possible sanctions related to fraud. It details the PBF services, the unit fees, and the registers with their various column headers. The manual also contains the contracts and the performance checklists for the health facilities and the health administration.

Given this content, the user manual is vital. It sets out all the new stipulations. Examples of user manuals from Rwanda and Burundi are provided in the links to files in this chapter. These user manuals were created for the national scale-up of PBF in these countries (see box 15.1). Those were large

---

The Rwandese and Burundi PBF User Manuals

Rwanda

The first user manual in Rwanda was created in haste: the government had started purchasing performance as of January 1, 2006, before a national model had been designed. The manual was created after the February 2006 national workshop in which the new health center PBF approach had been designed. It was used from March 2006 onward in the training of district staff.

During the second half of 2007, the user manual was revised. All tools were reviewed and incrementally modified on the basis of lessons learned. A training manual was created, on the basis of this user manual, to introduce the revised national PBF approach in all 23 districts using PBF and, from April 1, 2008, in the eight control districts, which had completed the impact evaluation and joined the PBF approach.

The PBF manual was very elaborate; the working group felt a need to lay out all rules in a very clear and unambiguous manner and to be much more precise and specific in various matters. For example, the annex provided instructions for the district PBF steering committee meetings. In addition, a ministerial instruction was issued with very detailed directions related to agenda content and form, meeting process and content, and documentation.

The hospital PBF approach was finalized in July 2006, after a working group had finalized the approach between March and June 2006. A formal user manual was not created; the focus was on the quantified quality checklist and balanced scorecard. This tool was also revised in the second half of 2007, and a user manual was created, too.

The community PBF approach was revised during the final quarter of 2008. A user manual was created and, based on this manual, a training manual was developed.

Burundi

The Burundi PBF user manual was created with technical assistance from the World Bank and experts drawn in from Rwanda. A long, deliberative process followed. Such national PBF manuals are typically subject to incremental change each year. In this chapter, we provide a template that can be used to develop a PBF user manual. The Burundi PBF manual was developed from such a template.

The Rwandese and Burundi manuals describe the national PBF approaches. A crucial lesson learned is to pay due attention to process, process documentation, coordination, and communication. In the real world, such processes are frequently rushed, with insufficient consultation of all involved stakeholders, which might create trouble later. Ensure a clear and transparent process.

operations. But even for a pilot project, standard practice is to develop a user manual.

A PBF user manual contains the collection of all tools used in the PBF scheme. The following is an example of a table of contents:

- Introduction
- Background of and rationale for PBF
- Description of the institutional setup (separation of functions; roles and responsibilities)
- Listing and description of the PBF indicators and their data collection tools (listing of registers in annex)
- Description of the quantified quality checklist (tool in annex)
- Description of the verification process
- Description of the counterverification process
- Description of the contractual relationships (contracts in annex)
- Description of the business plan
- Description of the indice tool
- Description of the community client satisfaction surveys
- Description of the coordination mechanisms
- Description of the role of technical assistance and civil society
- Description of the web-enabled database
- Annexes: all contracts, checks lists, column headers of the registers used, and so on
- Date of the manual.

The links to files in this chapter provide a template, which can be adapted to context. The template is not complete, but it contains some sections that are illustrative and meant to provide a head start. For instance, five contracts are in this template. They demonstrate how contracts permeate the entire health system and include the public health administration at various levels.

Keep the manual as short and concise as possible. If the document is too long, too difficult to understand, or too bureaucratic, then health workers and their managers might be confused or intimidated, which would defeat the purpose.

15.3 Regular Revision of the Tools

Creating ownership through close collaboration with counterparts is important. The many tools and instruments need careful discussion and adaptation to the local context. Avoid taking a manual from another context and merely copying and pasting the contents. Essential tools such as PBF registers and patient files may differ significantly between contexts, and more important, the quality checklists may need fine-tuning to local norms, local realities, and local infrastructure. For example, the Rwandese health center quality checklist could not be transferred to the Zambian context but had to be adapted thoroughly to serve any purpose in Zambia because, among other differences, Zambian health centers were much smaller and had a much smaller staff.

If starting a pilot in a country that lacks experience with PBF projects, be proactive. Propose to test a certain approach, using a particular manual, with the explicit understanding that the manual will most likely be revised in a year or so. Certain elements of the manual, such as the quality checklist, may need field testing and adaptation. Create sufficient room to make these revisions.

In any new context, the various tools will need to be tested:

- *Quantity verification procedures.* Note the time taken because you will need to train staff to follow these procedures; you need to ensure that registers and column headers are standardized, to assist in thinking through the best schedules for the entity that has been tasked with this activity, and so on. You, as a health planner, would typically be involved in this stage.
- *Quantified quality checklist.* The checklist must be tested. Note the time taken because you will need to train staff to follow these procedures; you need to assist in thinking through the best schedules for the entity that has been tasked with this activity, which includes an important element of monitoring the intraobserver and interobserver reliability, and so on. There are differences between the health centers and the hospitals

15.4 Links to Files and Tools

The following files can be accessed through this web link:
http://www.worldbank.org/health/pbftoolkit/chapter15

- Rwandese health center PBF user manual (2008)
- Rwandese District Hospital PBF user manual (2009)
- Rwandese community health worker PBF user manual (2009)
- Burundi PBF user manual (2010)
- Nigerian PBF user manual (2011)
- Generic template for a PBF user manual.

that influence decisions. Here too, you, as the health planner, would be involved.

Regular revision of the manual is wise. Stakeholders must have the chance to review to what extent the system works and to adapt the approach where needed. It is essential to regularly update the quality checklist to incorporate lessons learned and to introduce new criteria with new developments. Manual revisions are best done once per year. Stay dynamic in improving the quality of the system.

CHAPTER 16

Pilot Testing PBF

MAIN MESSAGES

➜ Carry out a small-scale pilot before attempting PBF at scale in a country without PBF experience.

➜ A small-scale pilot is less threatening to decision makers and creates local capacity to implement PBF.

➜ Adapt the approach to the local context.

COVERED IN THIS CHAPTER

16.1 Introduction

Before attempting performance-based financing (PBF) on a larger scale in a country without PBF experience, carry out a small-scale pilot. A pilot is less threatening to decision makers and creates local capacity to implement PBF. Before conducting a PBF pilot, inform stakeholders about the approach and assess the context. It is important to adapt the approach—that is, budget, services, checklists, technical assistance, and general institutional arrangements—to the local setting. A well-designed and well-implemented PBF pilot will generate interest among decision makers because it will be seen as a homegrown program.

A checklist for implementers is provided at the end of this chapter. It lists in chronological order the steps to be completed when starting a PBF pilot.

16.2 Why Do a PBF Pilot?

A pilot[1] is desirable because PBF involves some profound health-system changes. Considerable resistance to such large transformations can occur, especially if the country has no experience with the substance of PBF or the way to implement it. A country that lacks experience with PBF means that it lacks local experts who can design and scale up the approach, advocate for PBF, or explain the benefits of the reform. Starting PBF in a small area has many advantages. Necessary changes can be introduced while building local experience and know-how. Starting small makes a lot of sense.

The following changes tend to be the most visible or contentious in introducing PBF:

- The change toward autonomy and cash management in health facilities
- The change toward health facilities purchasing inputs directly (as opposed to receiving inputs from the central level)
- The separation of functions
- The involvement of civil society in governance
- The dominant focus on results and the increased need to analyze the results.

Some changes generate more friction than others. Over the past decade, the separation of functions has caused the most resistance. In addition, some contexts do not allow health workers to benefit from PBF income while other contexts have stirred debates about cash management by health facilities.

Resistance to change occurs predominantly at the central level. The decentralized levels of health systems—the health facility staff members, their managers, and the district-level health officers—in general appreciate the changes that PBF proposes. However, for a system that is habitually planned, financed, and managed from above through central-input financing, PBF transformations such as increasing health facility autonomy may be perceived as a loss of control over resources by central planners. Hence, their resistance to such change can be fierce.

A pilot offers the opportunity to experiment with the larger changes without jeopardizing the whole system. You can propose that decision makers try the desired changes in only a tiny part of the health system, an approach that is less threatening. Hiring an external agency or consultants as implementers automatically introduces a separation of functions, if the consultants or the agency will be put in charge of the contracting, verification, and counterverification. Visiting successful demonstration sites with decision makers is a very practical way to see PBF in action.

If PBF pilots are well designed and well implemented, tangible improvements in both quality and volume of care plus mounting staff enthusiasm can often be shown in a very short period of time. Dramatic improvements, especially in situations with lower baselines for quality and volume of services, can help to convince decision makers to attempt to scale up PBF.

16.3 How to Start a PBF Pilot: Gather Information and Assess the Context

Starting a PBF pilot requires in-depth understanding of the health system, its performance, the existing incentives, the constraints, and the opportunities. Here, we assume a context in which there is little or no experience with PBF.

First, assess the context before designing the PBF program. Each context is unique. Simply copying and pasting a PBF approach from one country to another is asking for trouble. In addition to assessing the context, do the following:

- Gather intelligence.
- Assess demand- and supply-side constraints to service delivery.
- Identify PBF champions and windows of opportunity.
- Assess the degrees of autonomy of health facilities.
- Assess the existing degree of management of user fees.
- Assess the market for drugs.
- Assess the human resources for health.
- Consider the wider health reforms necessary for PBF to work better, and inform the stakeholders (see section 16.5 of this chapter).

Gather Intelligence

Collect and analyze specific information related to the specific context of the pilot. Often, such information is dispersed and of poor quality. Therefore, do field work and carry out targeted studies to obtain the relevant PBF information. The importance of gathering this information is threefold. First, essential health intelligence is needed to make the case for PBF, which will include a comparison of these data with international benchmarks, country-specific Millennium Development Goals, and peer countries. Second, baselines for financial risk forecasting are needed. And third, become familiar with the country's experience with other results-based financing programs (for example, voucher schemes and conditional in-cash or in-kind transfer programs) or existing PBF schemes.

For a PBF assessment, gather more detailed information on the following:

- The level of autonomy of health facilities—whether they have bank accounts; how they manage their cash flows, if any; and whether they have decision rights related to their income (from clients' out-of-pocket payments, drug sales, and so on)
- The cash income and expenditure of the health centers and first-level referral hospitals
- Whether clients are charged for services (formally or informally) and whether free health services exist for certain groups (for example, pregnant women and children under five years of age)
- The staffing patterns of health facilities, including the staff members' take-home salaries
- The way the health workers are paid and employed (through a basic salary with allowances, through employment by the health facility with a possible bonus system, and so on)
- The way the health facility is financed (salaries and inputs, output financing, out-of-pocket payments by clients, or a mix of these)
- The type of salaries health workers would need to earn to make a difference in their socioeconomic status, which would be important for a health facility in-charge person in order to attract qualified staff
- The organization of the drug supply (a Bamako-type revolving drug fund, central medical stores, and so on), and the way it functions in practice
- The additional financial resources that would be necessary, in addition to the budget implied by the assessment of the earnings gap, to make a difference in the health facility's capacity to deliver good quality health services.

Most of the above information can be obtained through interviews with key informants (ministry of health technicians, donor technical agency staff members, multilateral agency technical staff members, district-level health managers, and health facility staff members). A stakeholder analysis can be useful to explore a complex health system in which many actors have diverging opinions on a proposal such as introducing PBF. It is crucial to visit health facilities—both health centers and first-level referral hospitals—and study the district-level administrative arrangements that are related to planning, supervision, capacity building, and potential roles in the supply of drugs and vaccines. In some instances, in Rwanda for example, the district administration is responsible for those functions, while the Ministry of Health manages the district hospitals. In Burundi, the Ministry of Health is nominally in charge of both public health and hospital services.[2]

To obtain practical information and impressions on the issue of autonomy, out-of-pocket payments, income and expenses, drugs, and human resources, visit health facilities. If you lack PBF experience, this is one of the steps where a public health expert with PBF experience would be very helpful. Although valuable documentation on such systems can always be obtained, field visits are mandatory to assess the district health system in practice. Field visits are expensive and time consuming, and results obtained are sometimes confusing. A visit to a health facility can benefit from the use of structured interview guides. The information obtained on field visits needs to be double checked at various levels. This can be done during a formal debriefing with field practitioners and health managers.

Collecting such a large amount of health information can be tedious, especially when further research on some aspects of the health system such as human resources or the pharmaceutical sector is desired. Balance the search for information with other time constraints. Here again, it is better to be approximately right than precisely wrong after exhaustive efforts to look at all the details.

Intelligence Gathering: Example of Assessing the Necessary Output Budget

Intelligence gathering is especially important in determining the output budget. Elaborate studies can be commissioned to gain more knowledge on the exact incentive environment and all the multifarious motives of health workers. But that knowledge may become an obstacle for serious action (see also chapter 4).

It is important to note that the output budget used by PBF is not meant solely for paying the variable bonuses for health workers. The output budget ought to help bridge the earnings gap by providing the approximate amount of money—to be paid through performance bonuses necessary for improving quantity and quality performance. The output budget is meant to achieve this adjustment through a mix of interventions (accountability, transparency, targeted demand-driven technical assistance, much enhanced monitoring arrangements, adequate cash resources for nonbonus recurrent expenditures, much enhanced performance-based earnings of health workers, and so on). For details, see chapter 4.

Assess Demand- and Supply-Side Constraints to Service Delivery

For each context you will work in, it is crucial to have a clear idea of the demand- and supply-side constraints to health service use and delivery.

Demand-side barriers can be as follows:

- Geographical
- Financial
- Cultural (see box 16.1)
- A combination (Ensor and Cooper 2004).

Supply-side constraints relate to the following:

- Inefficiencies
- Low quality of service in health facilities
- Absence of services.

BOX 16.1

The Ghost in the Tree

A remarkable story from Cambodia explains the potential force of supply-side solutions to demand-side problems. According to established anthropological knowledge, Khmer women would not give birth in a health facility. They believed that ancestral spirits would not allow deliveries to take place far from the house where the deceased grandparents had lived. And indeed, two years (1999–2000) into the contracting program, the institutional delivery rate remained at a dismal 2–3 percent irrespective of the subsidies. However, the health facility's subsidy for each delivery was increased about every six months to ever higher levels.

Then in 2001, in a Khmer health center, one doctor achieved 50 percent institutional delivery coverage in his community. This achievement was spectacular. When asked how he did this, he said that during the Pol Pot regime, the health center location had been a killing field and that people believed that bad spirits lived in the trees around the health center. This belief stopped women from agreeing to stay at the health center through the night. The doctor was unhappy to lose the PBF subsidies. After consulting with local authorities, he cut down the trees. From that moment on, women started to come to the health center to give birth. Based on his success, chiefs in the surrounding health centers took similar measures such as chasing spirits or paying demand-side incentives to beneficiaries.

Interventions on both the supply and the demand sides can have a powerful influence on use of essential health services. Much of the increase in use is through suppliers influencing the demand side, such as the following:

- Qualitative improvements will lead to a higher demand.
- Much improved attitudes of staff versus their clients will lead to a higher demand.
- Through the systematic proposal of preventative services, lost opportunities for family planning, voluntary counseling and testing, or vaccinations will be minimized.
- Health facility managers frequently use demand-side incentives to attract clients, such as in the case of certain health facilities in Rwanda that offer baby-welcome packages. The package consists of a piece of soap, a cloth, and some baby clothes that the mother will receive when delivering at the health facility.

More specific demand-side interventions could relate to the following:

- Obligatory community based–health insurance schemes (as in the case of Rwanda) decrease significantly the financial barriers to access to services and protect largely against catastrophic health expenditures.
- Health equity funds, in the case of high out-of-pocket expenditures, could be an important tool to protect the poorest of the poor (Annear 2010; Hardeman et al. 2004).

Most of the time, low use of health services has complex origins, often involving supply-side issues as well as demand-side issues. This complexity becomes obvious in cases such as one involving a conditional cash transfer program for pregnant women to deliver in health facilities. In Ghana, experts discovered that women incur considerable costs to deliver in a health facility, although nominally, deliveries are free of charge. It is convenient to think that cultural barriers were mostly to blame for the low use of delivery room services. Yet the reality was different. When the value of the items that women had to bring for their delivery, the objects that were taken from them by the staff and not returned, and the cost of travel and other expenses were totaled, women needed US$25 per delivery. This amount completely outstripped the budget available for the conditional cash transfer program (an estimated US$11 per delivery). This example suggests that focusing only on the demand side is improper when there are obvious supply-side problems. For demand-side interventions to maximize their effect, health systems need reasonably well-functioning delivery systems. Well-designed interventions on both the supply side and the demand side should work synchronously.

Tackling the supply side through incentives for quantity and quality of health services means frequently dealing with seemingly intangible quality issues. Those issues include the reception of patients and a phenomenon called the "performance gap" or the "know–do gap"—the gap between what providers know and what they do. This gap is well documented. Providers do less than what they know should be done (Gertler and Vermeersch 2012). In any case, assess what exists for incentivizing supply- or demand-side activities.

Identify PBF Champions and Windows of Opportunity

When conducting a pilot of complex health reforms such as the introduction of PBF, the following well-known phenomena are worth considering:

- Champions or change agents (Walt 1994)
- Window of opportunity (Kingdon 1995)
- Path dependency (Gómez 2011).

Champions or change agents are vital to introduce and sustain an attitude of change toward PBF. The most powerful change agents are national staff members, senior technicians, and high-level ministry of health officials. When entering a new context without any experience in PBF, identify any such champions. A minister, a deputy minister or permanent secretary, directors of policy and planning, or other high-level technical staff members at the ministry of health may be potential champions and should be lobbied. Sometimes, lobbying other ministries, such as the ministry of finance, can be a strategic approach, too. Combining the support of these parties with a successful PBF pilot may be a particularly effective way to gain broad-based buy-in from the government for PBF (Loevinsohn 2008, 21).

Window of opportunity refers to a certain opening through which the existing system is more prone to change. This can be, for example, the appointment of a new minister who makes innovation a policy or who is favorable to PBF. The Millennium Development Goals, when first championed, offered such a window of opportunity for health reformers. But such windows can, alas, be closed.

Finally, *path dependency* refers to the particular history of a country that has shaped its health institutions and, to some extent, determines how people respond. For instance, a strong socialist background with central command and control—such as health systems built according to the type of classic national health system organization—could be very resistant to the introduction of PBF[3] because of the perceived imbalance in civil servant remuneration and the perception that health facilities ought not to manage a cash budget. An example of path dependency is the difficulty experienced by the Obama administration with introducing national health insurance in the United States. Different stakeholders thought they would lose out because of the reforms and therefore opposed any of the changes.

Assess the Degree of Autonomy of Health Facilities

PBF for health services is premised on the autonomy of health facilities, and PBF projects will not be successful without sufficient autonomy in those facilities. In the ideal situation, such autonomy would consist of (a) autonomous human resource management (hire and fire), (b) autonomous procurement of supplies on a competitive and well-regulated market, and (c) autonomous management of assets (both fixed and liquid). In the world of dysfunctional health systems in poor countries, the reality is far from this ideal situation.

Autonomy is required to improve the quantity and quality of health services through PBF. The health facility manager needs freedom (and sufficient funds) to manage resources to increase the quantity and quality of health services.

One cannot quickly or easily deal with human resource issues such as hiring and firing, with a rigid and dysfunctional central medical procurement and supply system, or even with the perception that the health staff cannot manage cash. However, each one of those three points is worth studying in depth and pointing out in early discussions with government counterparts, too.

For autonomy, there are immediate prerequisites such as bank accounts and enough decision rights on spending and on hiring additional staff, if necessary. Decision rights are important for establishing PBF, but they will require deeper reforms such as civil service reforms (like in the case of Rwanda). See also chapter 6.

Assess the Existing Degree of Management of User Fees

Managers need cash to fix infrastructure, to purchase and maintain equipment, to procure drugs and medical consumables, to hire additional staff, and to pay performance bonuses. In many countries, frontline health managers receive no direct government cash contributions to pay for the aforementioned items that are necessary for providing quality health services.

User fees can be an important source of cash at the health facility level. In an assessment of a health facility, the level of income and expenditure is always analyzed. Some systems attempt to work without formal cash flows. In other systems, cash collected is sent upward into the system to be used for general budgeting. In such systems, coping strategies that will appear include retaining cash income and modifying health information system data to fit the reported cash. Allowing health facilities to earn income through user fees is also an effective technique to formalize informal payments.

In situations of selective free health care, cash-starved systems with underpaid staff members, a lack of budgeting for recurrent costs, and Bamako-type revolving drug funds, health staff will use coping mechanisms such as under-the-table payments and drug pilferage. However, in situations with some form of revolving drug fund, where there is a price signal for drugs and, therefore, a value to a service, adding PBF can be a good fit.

User fees can be a lever through which the health facility manager can balance the budget. Ideally, those fees ought to be negotiated with the local community and approved by the ministry of health. In situations of selective free health care declarations that are nonnegotiable, the shortfall needs to be financed through PBF funding and, consequently, the PBF budget needs to be larger. Unfortunately, an absence of a direct price signal makes the introduction of a health insurance unlikely.

However, those PBF systems need additional safe guards, such as health equity funds (Annear 2010; Hardeman et al. 2004), to protect the poorest of the poor.

Assess the Market for Drugs

Analyzing the drug procurement and supply system at the health facility level is an important part of any initial PBF assessment.

Drugs and medical consumables make up a sizeable proportion of the costs at the health facility level.[4] How those are financed will determine not only the size of this portion but also the way the drugs are managed and dispensed by the health facility.

In an ideal world, central procurement and timely and complete supply through a pull system—a system based on customer demand—ought to work. In the real world, such systems lead too often to a delayed and incomplete supply, corruption, and mismanagement of stock and waste (Soeters et al. 2011).

PBF systems offer the opportunity for health facilities to decentralize drug procurement. Integrated budget management (managing funds from different sources in an integrated manner as opposed to a vertical manner) allows the health facility manager to access drugs with certified suppliers at a good price. The medical stores can be suppliers if they provide quality drugs at reasonable cost and at the time required.

The regulator, that is, the ministry of health can be incentivized to carry out its regulatory role related to the certified suppliers and to regularly apply the quantified quality checklist that is integral to PBF systems. Such quality checklists have an important effect on the performance measure (that is, the performance payments). The checklists typically include an exhaustive section on pharmaceuticals management and availability as well as process and content measures of quality of care (for example, the adherence to well-established clinical treatment algorithms).

Client perceptions of quality of care, including drug availability, are routinely sought through community client satisfaction surveys. Survey results can be quantified and included in the performance payments, such as in Burundi.

Assess the Human Resources for Health

Analyzing human resources during the initial assessment is important. Background documents to the health work force are useful. More important, however, go into the field and assess the human resource situation first-hand in a good selection of health facilities. Basic information relates to the following:

- Function and title of staff, civil servant versus contract worker, and numbers
- Remuneration, in terms of base salary and take-home salary (taxes, allowances, bonuses), and whether salaries are paid regularly
- Information on cost of living for the health staff members
- Any private practice in the vicinity of the health facility (and average income of the health staff involved)
- Ratio of qualified staff linked to population in the catchment area (could be a staff shortage mainly in rural areas and an abundance of staff in urban settings, which makes the health facilities very difficult to assess)
- Open discussion with key informants, which can be through a focus group, on job satisfaction, remuneration, the issues staff members face in delivering quality health services, and so on[5]
- Use of available contingent valuation studies (studies that describe the wage levels) (Serneels et al. 2006).

16.4 How to Start a PBF Pilot: Adapt the Approach to the Local Context

Each context is different. Adapting the PBF approach to the local circumstances is important. Even minor differences can call for adapting the approach.

Some contexts such as the following are more favorable to PBF than others:

- Contexts with a Bamako-type revolving drug fund with good community participation or with some existing cash management because of user charges managed at the facility level
- Contexts with cash budgets provided by government or financing partners
- Situations where a large part of the workforce are contract workers (managed by the facility and financed through health facility income)
- Settings with relatively low salaries and relatively significant performance bonuses.

Some specific examples in which the PBF approach was adapted to meet context-specific challenges include the following:

- Benin: a health insurance program for the poorest was linked to financing through PBF (providing services to the poorest is financed by a higher fee through PBF).
- Burundi: a selective free health care program for vulnerable groups was linked to financing through PBF (providing curative services to children under five and pregnant women are financed by a higher fee through PBF).
- Nigeria (see box 16.2): management benchmarking was introduced to strengthen human resource management and to put pressure on health facility managers to manage available resources better.
- Zambia: a separate district PBF steering committee was not acceptable; hence it was subsumed as a subcommittee in the existing district health management team structure.
- Zimbabwe: no performance bonuses were allowed.

Adaptations may affect the budget, the services provided, checklists, technical assistance needs, and general institutional arrangements. For budgets, see chapter 4 of this toolkit; for services, see chapters 1 and 3; for checklists, see chapters 3 and 8; and for general institutional arrangements, see chapter 11.

BOX 16.2
Adapting the PBF Approach: The Case of Nigeria

Nigeria started PBF with three prepilot districts in three states (Adamawa, Nasarawa, and Ondo) in December 2011. The Nigerian PBF approach purchases a basic and a complementary package of services in rural areas in mostly public facilities with a single faith-based institution among the 35 contracted facilities. The situation analysis showed a combination of extremely low productivity (as low as 0.1 patient per qualified nurse per day), very poor quality of services, and overstaffing (predominantly among nonqualified staff, but also with qualified staff). Medical staff was paid relatively well (as compared to the Sub-Saharan Africa average). The population was clearly not using public services, but instead was using the private sector (pharmacies) to purchase drugs over the counter. Public facilities were out of stock for drugs or nurses ran informal revolving drug funds with a very high cost to the population.

The PBF approach was adapted by introducing (a) a formal revolving drug fund (with generic drugs and a focus on rational prescribing), (b) incentives aiming at preventive services and quality, (c) benchmarking of health facility managers with a specific instrument (focus on application of business plans, individual performance evaluations, and indice tool), and (d) a rigorous benchmarking of district and facility performance across the PBF states. The output budget, although set relatively high at US$2.70 per capita per year, was meaningless to health facility staff members who had become accustomed to working very little. Therefore, in addition to PBF, a management benchmarking and strengthening program had to be introduced for better managing available resources (money and staff). Nonperforming health facility managers were replaced. The Nigerian PBF approach emphasizes the systemic nature of PBF: apart from introducing health facility autonomy, coaching of health facility managers and strengthened supervision, more profound human resources for health reforms are needed to tackle Nigeria's public health problems.

16.5 Pilots: Stakeholder Information, Knowledge Sharing, and Training

PBF usually generates considerable interest from government and development partners. Frequently, ministry of health technicians and donor technical agency specialists already agree that business as usual in the health sector does not lead to the desired results. Yet the desirability of PBF as an alternative strategy is often put under the microscope as well. PBF may appear to be a lot of work or complicated. Officials may argue that PBF efforts would disrupt other planned activities. Some may be convinced that PBF would not work in poor countries. Those and other misconceptions underscore the need to inform the stakeholders upfront. There are various ways to communicate with decision makers: organize a workshop or PBF courses, direct

BOX 16.3

Scaling Up PBF: The Case of Sierra Leone

Just as with any golden rules, exceptions exist such as in the case of Sierra Leone. The country scaled up a public PBF purchaser approach during 2011 without any PBF experience. The Sierra Leoneans, however, did receive implementation support from an experienced PBF expert, and the scaling-up benefited from a uniquely high degree of political support and leadership from the Ministry of Health. Nonetheless, Sierra Leone's approach lacks several design features that are common in other successfully scaled-up systems. For instance, its separation of functions is weak. The system lacks civil society involvement at any level of governance. It offers no technical assistance for the technical support functions. The system does not have a web-enabled application with a public front

end. It has no third-party counterverification mechanism. In addition, the PBF budget (to pay for performance) is very low. A study visit by a Sierra Leone delegation to Burundi highlighted the absence of those features, and the delegation expressed its desire to include those elements in the Sierra Leone design soon. The Sierra Leone case shows that countries can attempt to implement PBF without a range of essential design elements. However, the absence of some of those elements will lead to a less successful result later. Without any rigorous evaluation of the Sierra Leone scaling-up, it will be difficult to draw lessons regarding the effectiveness of this approach and to compare the approach to other PBF approaches or non-PBF interventions.

bilateral meetings with decision makers, or stimulate exchange visits or study tours.[6] Further ways to access and exchange information are through reading, inviting consultants, or joining the growing number of web-based communities of practice, such as the African PBF community of practice.

Conference for Sharing Information and Pilot Experience

Sharing experiences from pilots at conferences can be very useful, but like for any conference, careful preparation is everything. The following are several examples of conferences in which results-based financing (RBF) approaches were presented with links to the agendas and to the Microsoft PowerPoint presentations. One example—Kigali in January 2006—is meant to show the in-country experience with three different PBF pilot programs and to present the set up of the national PBF-design workshop in February 2006. The other examples are conferences and workshops held in Abuja, Jaipur, Bujumbura, and Washington, D.C. The March 2009 Bujumbura workshop can be seen as an information-sharing and consensus-building workshop that set the stage for the emergence of a national PBF model. The Jaipur, Abuja, and Washington, D.C., conferences were meant for information sharing.

Kigali, January 2006

PBF pilot programs had been introduced in Rwanda since 2002. By the end of December 2005, Rwanda had three PBF pilot projects: two by the non-governmental organizations (NGOs) Cordaid and Health Net International–Transcultural Psychosocial Organization (HNI-TPO) (a Dutch aid agency) and one by the Belgian Technical Cooperation. By the end of 2005, approximately 40 percent of the service delivery network of Rwanda was covered by PBF schemes. The government of Rwanda had included PBF in its national health strategic plan 2005–09 and decided that PBF ought to start January 1, 2006.

The government started paying for performance in January 2006 before any clear picture had emerged of how this national PBF model ought to look.[7] The government had issued instructions to health centers requesting them to report on services rendered, which the government would pay for. However, there was no clear idea how the institutional arrangements ought to be set up. Nor was it clear what services should be bought and for how much. Also, three sometimes very conflicting PBF approaches with different institutional set-ups existed along with a disagreement among main PBF actors on how the national model ought to look. At the same time, many development partners knew nothing about PBF approaches. The workshop met for two days in Kigali, and it became a prelude to the February 2006 design workshop. An additional level of complexity was added because the United States Agency for International Development, through its President's Emergency Plan for AIDS Relief, wanted to purchase human immunodeficiency virus (HIV) services using PBF, an issue that was not appreciated by all PBF partners, many of whom were afraid that HIV funds would skew the PBF system (Rusa and Fritsche 2007; Rwanda, Ministry of Health 2008).

Bujumbura, March 2009

PBF pilot programs were introduced in Burundi from 2006 onward. Cordaid, HNI-TPO, and the Swiss Development Cooperation managed those pilot programs. Cordaid's program was the largest. PBF actors and Burundi Ministry of Health officials made numerous visits to neighboring Rwanda to learn how the Rwandese had scaled up PBF. Discussions started in Burundi for scaling up its approach, too. Design differences existed among the Burundi PBF pilot programs, but not to the extent of Rwanda. There was a fair amount of agreement between NGO and PBF actors on the type of PBF approach needed to be scaled up nationwide.

The government had different ideas. The Ministry of Health, backed by two of its multilateral partners, envisioned a set up like that in Rwanda, where the government played an important role in the purchasing and verification and the approval and payment processes. A team of consultants negotiated a compromise between the two positions. During the March 2009 workshop, this compromise solution was presented, discussed, and agreed upon. The compromise consisted of creating a semiautonomous body at the province level—the Provincial Verification and Validation Committee (CPVV)—that would consist of a mix of public servants and contracted staff members.[8] During the workshop, experiences from Rwanda were also presented to illustrate some of the challenges for the scaling-up process.

Jaipur, January 2010

Although India has made important economic gains over the past years, basic health services have failed to keep up. Health indicators such as maternal mortality and infant and child mortality are worse than they should be. The uptake of basic preventive services such as vaccinations and antenatal care is much lower than that of neighboring countries. In addition, health worker absenteeism, compounded by an important discrepancy between what health workers know and what they do, affect the quality and accessibility of care for the majority of the Indian population (Pritchett 2009). Health services in the public health sector in India are financed through input financing and managed through central planning. Although an important public health service delivery network is available, up to two-thirds of public health workers are estimated to be absent from their posts, and 84 percent of all curative care visits are accessed through the private sector. A workshop was organized in Jaipur in January 2010, with a select number of states, to present the international experience on supply-side RBF (examples from Brazil, Haiti, Rwanda, and the United States were presented) and to showcase the Indian experience with RBF, too (MSG Strategic Consulting 2009).

Abuja, January 2010

Nigeria houses about one-fifth of the African population. Recent studies of the Nigerian health care system paint a dire picture.[9] In these reports, the diagnosis made and the advice offered are as follows: (a) introduce output focus or notion/incentive mechanisms for health facilities, through a performance-based remuneration; (b) increase health facility autonomy; (c) fix the drug procurement and supply system; (d) improve supervision of these health facilities; and (e) secure more budget for health from the state and local government authorities. The Abuja workshop was planned to present the Nigerian federal- and state-level decision makers with various RBF approaches: conditional cash transfer programs, performance-based contracting, and performance-based financing. The result of this conference has led to a decision to try a comprehensive RBF program in three states, which, structurally, will be a PBF program.

Workshops for Sharing Regional- and Global-Level Information and Experience

Bujumbura, February 2010

The February 2010 Bujumbura workshop was meant to assemble PBF practitioners from Africa's Great Lakes region and those involved in these PBF programs to present and discuss PBF-related issues and to launch the African PBF community of practice. Preparations were under way for the start of the Burundian nationwide scale-up of PBF on April 1, 2010. But for most participants, this was still quite a challenging endeavor.

Washington, D.C., Global Health Council, June 2010

The June 2010 Global Health Council meeting included a panel on PBF. Presenters were from agencies deeply involved in PBF programming. The panel was composed of an international European NGO, a U.S. private voluntary agency, a European academic institution, and the World Bank.

16.6 Checklist for Implementers

When starting PBF in a new context, you must consider many factors. As a help in moving forward, we have created a checklist for a systematic approach to introducing PBF in your context (table 16.1).

TABLE 16.1 Checklist for PBF Implementers

Phase	No.	Step	Description and toolkit chapter
1. Setting the stage	1	Gather intelligence. Look at coverage of key services, and identify areas with low coverage.	Get information on coverage rates from reliable sources (DHS, MICS). See chapters 4 and 16.
2. Assessment of the current situation	2	Assess demand- and supply-side constraints.	Are the bottlenecks to service delivery mostly on the supply side or on the demand side? Are the people not coming because of distance, cultural factors, or financial barriers, or is it more an issue of poor quality, poor staff attitude, lack of drugs, clinic opening hours, and so on? Frequently, it is a mix of factors. See chapter 16.
	3	Identify PBF champions, and train them.	Seek out champions. You need these influential people who can push for things to happen. See chapter 16.
	4	Assess the degree of autonomy of health facilities.	Health facilities need degrees of freedom for PBF to work as designed. Freedoms include the right to hire and fire, to spend funds, and to share some of the gains. See chapters 6 and 16.

(table continues on next page)

TABLE 16.1 *(continued)*

Phase	No.	Step	Description and toolkit chapter
	5	Assess existing cash management.	What revenue sources are available for the health facilities? (And how much?) How does the health facility currently manage cash resources (if any)? What is the state of the banking sector in rural areas? How do funds flow within the government? See chapters 4 and 16.
	6	Assess the market for drugs.	Where are the drugs coming from? Is there a reliable supply from the central level? Are there other potential sources for drugs? See chapter 16.
	7	Assess the human resources for health.	How many and what type of health workers are available? Where are they located? How much do they earn? See chapters 4 and 16.
	8	Assess the HMIS.	What registers are available at the health facilities? How are they kept? What is the exact layout of these registers? See chapters 2, 12, and 16.
	9	Assess the private sector.	How will the private sector be involved? Which private providers will be involved? Consider part of the initial assessment of the delivery network and the public-private mix. See chapter 16.
	10	Identify institutions and NGOs that can carry out verification activities.	Consider the institutional setup; the separation of functions; and the eventual agencies or institutions that could do contract management and verification functions. See chapter 11.
	11	Examine governance at the health facility level, and consider governance for PBF in general.	Look at local accountability mechanisms: Is the community involved? When introducing autonomy, think of local checks and balances. Think of district-level governance mechanisms, too. See chapter 11.
	12	Keep in mind wider health reforms, and inform the stakeholder.	More profound health reforms are necessary to make PBF function better. PBF is a clothes hanger for other reforms such as human resources for health reforms, reforms in the way drugs are procured, and eventually reforms in health insurance arrangements. See chapters 16 and 17.
3. Design	13	Plan for a small-scale pilot.	Always start with a small-scale pilot; even one district will do. See chapter 16.
	14	Identify the different types of technical assistance required.	TA will likely be needed for implementation of the PBF pilot. There also may be a need for technical support to health facilities to strengthen their management. See chapters 14 and 16.
	15	Assess the available budget.	Sufficient money is needed to do PBF. See chapter 4.
	16	Create bank accounts for each health facility, and establish cash management procedures.	Plan for one bank account per health facility and also an income and an expense register. See chapter 7.
	17	Define the services, and create the service packages.	Get agreement on services to purchase. If there is no in-country experience on what to purchase, then propose a list. See chapter 1.

TABLE 16.1 *(continued)*

Phase	No.	Step	Description and toolkit chapter
	18	Weight the individual services.	Each service has a relative value as compared to the other services. See chapter 4.
	19	Perform financial risk forecasting.	Set the prices, and calculate the geographic equity adjustments. See chapter 4.
	20	Create the quality checklists for health centers and hospitals, and test the checklists.	These quantified quality checklists can be borrowed from other contexts and adjusted to fit local realities. Test them first. See chapter 3.
	21	Create the performance frameworks for the health administration.	Performance frameworks are needed for the health administration, and sometimes for other institutions also. See chapter 8.
	22	Create the web-enabled application.	A web-enabled application forms the backbone of a PBF system. It typically has a public interface and is important for good governance. See chapters 11, 12, and 13.
	23	Create the business plan.	Create a business plan template, which can be borrowed from other contexts. See chapter 10.
	24	Create the indice tool.	Create an indice tool: a paper-based one for health centers and an electronic one for hospitals. Borrow from other contexts as needed. See chapter 7.
	25	Create the contracts.	Design the contracts. Borrow from other contexts as needed. See chapter 11.
	26	Write a PBF user manual.	Draft a PBF user manual, meant for use by health workers, managers, district health staff members, and technical assistants. See chapter 15.
	27	Plan for training.	Depending on the scale of the training, it can be a challenging exercise. Plan well ahead for the training capacity, the training manual, and logistic and administrative issues. See chapter 14.
4. Implementation	28	Train health staff community and health administration, and sign contracts.	Good-quality training is essential. The various contracts are signed at the end of the trainings. See chapter 14.
	29	Negotiate the business plans, and pay the investment units.	Business plans are explained during the trainings, and health managers have a certain amount of time to create their business plans. The business plans will be negotiated. Investment units will have to be paid, too. See chapters 9 and 10.
	30	Carry out coaching.	Coaching health facility managers in enhancing performance of their health facility is crucial, especially in the early days of PBF. See chapters 10 (mainly), 12, 13, and 14.
	31	Perform the quantity verification.	Monthly verification of the quantity, in the health facilities, is especially important in the first 6 to 12 months of the PBF scheme. See chapters 1 and 2.

(table continues on next page)

TABLE 16.1 *(continued)*

Phase	No.	Step	Description and toolkit chapter
	32	Perform the quality verification.	Verification once per quarter for the quality of services must be carried out. Also think about piloting of a counterverification of the quality measure and mechanisms and the way to institutionalize these. See chapters 2 and 3.
	33	Carry out the district PBF steering committee meeting.	Once per quarter, the district PBF steering committee, which includes local authorities, the ministry of health, TA, and civil society, meets to discuss and vet the PBF results. This is important for governance. See chapter 11.
	34	Transfer funds to health facilities.	The first time that money is deposited in the health facility bank accounts is a reason to celebrate. Test the accounts by sending a small amount of money first, or you would have found out already because of the investment units that you had sent. See chapter 4.
	35	Plan for publicity and for showing early results to decision makers (field trips).	Especially when baselines are unsatisfactory, early results can be quite impressive. Within the first six months, some clear frontrunner health facilities will appear. Bring in the decision makers for a field visit, and showcase the results. See chapter 16.

Source: World Bank data.

Note: DHS = Demographic and Health Surveys; HMIS = health management information system; MICS = Multiple Indicator Cluster Surveys; NGO = nongovernmental organization; No. = number; PBF = performance-based financing; TA = technical assistance.

16.7 Links to Files and Tools

The following files can be accessed through this web link: http://www.worldbank.org/health/pbftoolkit/chapter16.

- Structured interview to guide discussions with health facility staff
- Instruments to conduct a stakeholder analysis
- Three Rwandese PBF pilot projects
- Rwanda February 2006 workshop agenda, report, and linked files
- Burundi March 2009 workshop content, including the consensus declaration
- Abuja January 2010 conference agenda, methodology, and presentations
- Jaipur January 2010 RBF conference
- Bujumbura February 2010 workshop, http://performancebased financing.wordpress.com/
- Washington, D.C., Global Health Council June 2010 panel presentations.

Notes

1. In some countries such as Zambia, a PBF pilot consists of a pilot covering more than half the country's health system. Such pilots were mostly preceded by a so-called PBF prepilot in one or two districts. The purpose of such prepilots, or field tests, was the same: to introduce the concept on a small scale and to gain experience before attempting a larger intervention.

2. In Burundi, 40 percent of hospitals are managed by faith-based organizations.

3. Sometimes the reverse could happen in such situations. Some actors become so frustrated that they are ready for change.

4. According to studies using the indice tool, drugs and medical consumables make up approximately 15–25 percent of the costs at this level.

5. It is crucial to review which proportion of PBF subsidies should be paid in performance bonuses to create a situation where the staff is satisfied. However, the idea is not to then impose the findings but to simply have an average that guides the costing. This costing is not an exact science, and such information needs to be double checked at various levels.

6. Bilateral meetings for explanations of PBF to ministers and director generals are very effective, and those sessions usually take place before a conference.

7. In fact, there was an important period not well known by many: the Butare and Cyangugu Provinces were identified as the two pilot provinces for the Ministry of Finance. Having two pilots required harmonization between the two schemes (at least for relative prices). This coordination was a major step toward a national model.

8. In the compromise solution, the idea was that the CPVV would be a body gathering different stakeholders, including civil society and local government. Enough checks and balances would exist while acknowledging the concern of the government to keep some control.

9. See Das Gupta, Gauri, and Khemani (2003); McKinsey and Company (2009); and World Bank (2008).

References

Annear, P. 2010. "A Comprehensive Review of the Literature on Health Equity Funds in Cambodia 2001–2010 and Annotated Bibliography." Health Policy and Health Finance Knowledge Hub Working Paper No. 9, Nossel Institute for Global Health, University of Melbourne, Melbourne.

Das Gupta, M., V. Gauri, and S. Khemani. 2003. "Decentralized Delivery of Primary Health Services in Nigeria: Survey Evidence from the States of Lagos and Kogi." African Region Human Development Working Paper Series No. 70, World Bank, Washington, DC.

Ensor, T., and S. Cooper. 2004. "Overcoming Barriers to Health Service Access: Influencing the Demand Side." *Health Policy and Planning* 19 (2): 69–79.

Gertler, P., and C. Vermeersch. 2012. "Using Performance Incentives to Improve Health Outcomes." Policy Research Working Paper 6100, World Bank, Washington, DC.

Gómez, E. 2011. "An Alternative Approach to Evaluating, Measuring, and Comparing Domestic and International Health Institutions: Insights from Social Science Theories." *Health Policy* 101 (3): 209–19.

Hardeman, W., W. Van Damme, M. Van Pelt, I. Por, H. Kimvan, and B. Meessen. 2004. "Access to Health Care for All? User Fees Plus a Health Equity Fund in Sotnikum, Cambodia." *Health Policy and Planning* 19 (1): 22–32.

Kingdon, J. 1995. *Agendas, Alternatives and Public Policies.* New York: Longman.

Loevinsohn, B. 2008. *Performance-Based Contracting for Health Services in Developing Countries: A Toolkit.* Health, Nutrition, and Population Series. Washington, DC: World Bank.

McKinsey and Company. 2009. "Scaling Up Primary Health Care in Nigeria, Initial Findings." Discussion document, McKinsey and Company, Washington, DC.

MSG Strategic Consulting. 2009. "Results-Based Financing in Public Health Sector in India." Draft report for the World Bank. MSG Strategic Consulting, Delhi.

Pritchett, L. 2009. "Is India a Flailing State? Detours on the Four Lane Highway to Modernization." HKS Working Paper No. RWO09-013, Harvard Kennedy School of Government, Harvard University, Cambridge, MA.

Rusa, L., and G. Fritsche. 2007. "Rwanda: Performance-Based Financing in Health." In *Emerging Good Practice in Managing for Development Results: Sourcebook,* 2nd edition, 105–16. Washington, DC: World Bank.

Rwanda, Ministry of Health. 2008. "Annual Report 2007: Performance-Based Financing in the Rwandan Health Sector." CAAC/Ministry of Health, Kigali.

Serneels, P., M. Lindelow, J. G. Montalvo, and A. Barr. 2006. "For Public Service or Money: Understanding Geographical Imbalances in the Health Workforce." *Health Policy and Planning* 22 (3): 128–38.

Soeters, R., P. B. Peerenboom, P. Mushagalusa, and C. Kimanuka. 2011. "Performance-Based Financing Experiment Improved Health Care in the Democratic Republic of Congo." *Health Affairs* 30 (8): 1518–27.

Walt, G. 1994. *Health Policy: An Introduction to Process and Power.* London: Zed Books.

World Bank. 2008. "Nigeria, Improving Primary Health Care Delivery: Evidence from Four States." Report No. 44041–NG, World Bank, Washington, DC.

PART 3

EVIDENCE OF PBF SCHEMES

CHAPTER 17

Evaluations of PBF and Frequently Asked Questions

MAIN MESSAGES

→ PBF in LMIC is relatively new and so are serious evaluations of well-designed and well-implemented programs.

→ Be aware of simple analogies between PBF programs in LMIC and OECD countries, because contexts differ more than they resemble each other.

→ "Evidence" for PBF is built gradually in many ways. So far, in practice there is a wide variety of programs and designs.

→ Policy makers in LMIC should be selective in copying lessons learned from PBF schemes in OECD countries.

COVERED IN THIS CHAPTER

17.1 Introduction

Performance-based financing (PBF) in lower- and middle-income countries (LMIC) is relatively new. Only recently, people have started to engage in serious evaluations of well-designed and well-implemented programs. Although PBF evaluations in LMIC are still in a developmental stage, there are a number of similarities and differences between PBF programs in LMIC and Organisation for Economic Co-operation and Development (OECD) countries. OECD countries have extensive knowledge on pay-for-performance schemes and health reforms, which can be used to inform PBF reforms in LMIC. Although similarities exist between PBF programs in LMIC and OECD countries, remember that contexts differ significantly. In fact, the differences between these contexts are greater than the similarities. Policy makers in LMIC should, therefore, be selective in copying lessons from OECD countries.

Despite the scarcity of well-evaluated, well-designed, and well-implemented PBF programs in LMIC, there are practical signs that such programs show promising results. Research evidence shows that functional design and solid implementation of PBF programs are prerequisites for attaining useful evaluation results.

In the chapter's discussion about building research evidence, a range of programs that exist in practice and offer incentives to health facilities is covered. There are programs on the supply side and on the demand side. On the supply side, various results-based financing (RBF) programs are highlighted. Because PBF is a very specific type of RBF—distinguishable from other RBF approaches (Musgrove 2011)—PBF programs will be denoted as "PBF." Demand-side incentive schemes, which offer incentives to clients for certain health actions, are not discussed here. For a comprehensive review on demand-side incentives, see Fiszbein and Schady (2009).

17.2 Building Research Evidence for PBF Is a Work in Progress

Building a solid evaluation practice for PBF programs in LMIC is a work in progress. Currently, the results of PBF on health outputs and outcomes are still inconclusive (Miller and Babiarz 2013). A lack of research during the pioneering years and the subsequent weak research designs that did not take into account a counterfactual are partly to blame. Well-designed PBF programs in LMIC are generally complex to research because of their comprehensive and systemic nature (Meessen et al. 2012). Moreover, many existing PBF programs differ significantly in design. This variation makes it hazardous to apply results too quickly from a particular program evaluation to another context. Besides evaluation of the quantity and quality of outputs, other dimensions of PBF warrant serious research because well-designed PBF programs in LMIC are real health reforms that may change various dimensions and various levels of a health system all at once (Meessen, Soucat, and Sekabaraga 2011). Examples are as follows:

- Changes at the health facility level can simultaneously affect the availability of resources to deliver services and the motivation of health workers. In addition, there can be an increase in the autonomy of the health facility and a demand for better health facility management. Also, a change in the pattern of service delivery can occur with more preventive services offered against better quality. Public health facilities will function more like cooperatives with staff behaving more like shareholders. Private facilities can become better regulated and will offer more preventive services while being held accountable for delivering quality services. The community near the health facility will formally engage in providing oversight over finances and strategies. Community client satisfaction surveys will lead to knowledge about community perceptions on the quality and availability of services.
- Changes at the district level include a strengthening of the public health administration in supervisory, coordination, and regulatory roles. The public health administration will be nudged through an incentive scheme to deliver results while its performance is being benchmarked. In parallel, the creation of a governing board for PBF that includes community representation alongside that of government institutions will enhance transparency and accountability. Such changes lead to improved and more inclusive governance and a strengthened public health administration.
- Changes brought about by the PBF purchasing arrangements involve a separation of functions among the purchaser, the public and private providers, the regulator, and the community. Accountability mechanisms can thereby change profoundly.
- Changes at the national level include a refocusing of the ministry of health (MoH) on its stewardship role, a promotion of intense collaboration with development partners, a shift of additional financing to cost-effective curative and preventive services, a change in planning mechanisms, and a shift of focus to results and to an intensified use of data for performance management.

In building of solid evidence for PBF, two lines of reasoning apply. First, to be meaningful, research efforts should focus on well-designed and well-implemented PBF programs. Second, research efforts should not be confined to rigorous randomized trials, but should include quantitative research techniques and complement these with good qualitative research. Broadening the methodological scope is pertinent to capturing the wide range of systemic changes brought about by well-designed PBF schemes (Alexander and Hearld 2012; Meessen et al. 2012).

The following topics are discussed in the next section:

- How evidence on PBF in LMIC varies
- How the evidence on PBF in OECD countries compares
- How to deal with the problem of overall weak evaluation designs
- How to deal with the fact that rigorous impact evaluations are often difficult in practice
- Why PBF programs are difficult to research.

How Evidence on PBF in LMIC Varies

The combined evidence on PBF in LMIC has been inconclusive according to Witter et al. (2012) in a Cochrane review from 2012. However, their evidence for this statement was drawn from evaluations of PBF programs that greatly varied in design and implementation characteristics.

Witter et al. (2012) applied one rigorous assessment framework to evaluation studies as divergent as program evaluations of various—and different—country programs of a nongovernmental organization (Toonen et al. 2009) to a quasi-experimental randomized controlled trial of a nationwide scale-up (Basinga et al. 2011). Moreover, both the type of evaluation methodology and the type of PBF intervention studied varied significantly.

The Witter et al. (2012) review concluded—perhaps a little too categorically—that there was a lack of rigorous evidence for PBF in LMIC. The report correctly pointed out, however, that more comprehensive research was needed. Importantly, the report underscored that the effect of PBF depended on design and implementation.

Although there is indeed a paucity of good-quality research data, two recent well-designed randomized controlled trials of PBF programs in LMIC settings showed opposing evaluation results. Although one evaluation—of a well-designed PBF intervention in Rwanda—pointed at significant results, the other evaluation—of a poorly designed PBF intervention in Uganda—demonstrated no results. We tentatively conclude that good design and implementation of PBF are preconditions for getting positive evaluation results. When embarking on a rigorous evaluation, make sure the PBF program to be evaluated is properly designed and implemented carefully too.

The following well-designed impact evaluations are discussed in more detail. Both evaluations are randomized controlled trials of PBF programs, one in Rwanda and the other in Uganda.[1]

The Rwandese Impact Evaluation Showed Significant Results

The Rwandese impact evaluation showed good results for quantity and quality of services as compared to a control (Basinga et al. 2011; de Walque et al. 2013; Gertler and Vermeersch 2012). Not only did the quantity and quality of services increase significantly, but also a significant effect occurred on the size and weight of children under five years of age living in the catchment areas of PBF facilities (Gertler and Vermeersch 2012). The impact evaluation was built into a nationwide scaling-up of PBF from 2006 to 2008. This impact evaluation is unique in that health facilities in the control district received exactly the same amount of cash as those in the treatment districts. By providing the same amount of cash to both treatment and control sites, researchers could isolate the incentive effect from the effect of increasing resources alone. The study is cited as being exemplary because this rigorous approach has not even been seen in OECD countries (OECD 2010).

Well-designed PBF pilot projects from 2002 to 2005 preceded the Rwandese scaling-up and showed positive results (Meessen et al. 2006; Meessen, Kashala, and Musango 2007; Rusa et al. 2009a; Soeters, Habineza, and Peerenboom 2006; Soeters, Musango, and Meessen 2005). In fact, it was these results that convinced the government to embark on the scale up of PBF in the country (Logie, Rowson, and Ndagije 2008; Meessen, Soucat, and Sekabaraga 2011; Rusa and Fritsche 2007; Rusa et al. 2009b; Sekabaraga, Diop, and Soucat 2011).

Despite the study's positive effect on policy makers, there were critics as well. They criticized the evaluations for having a before-and-after design, for not having a control group, for having been carried out by PBF advocates, and for suffering from publication bias (Elridge and Palmer 2009; Ireland, Paul, and Dujardin 2011; Kalk, Paul, and Grabosch 2010; Oxman and Fretheim 2009; Witter et al. 2012).

In South Kivu, the Democratic Republic of Congo, a well-designed PBF project showed positive results compared to areas that received traditional program support (Soeters et al. 2011). The study had a before-and-after design. With regard to design, this project was similar to the scaled-up approach in Rwanda.

The Ugandan Impact Evaluation Showed No Results

In Uganda, an impact evaluation was carried out on a performance-based contracting project from 2003 to 2006 (Lundberg, Marek, and Okwero

2007; Morgan 2010; Ssengooba, McPake, and Palmer 2012). This evaluation showed no difference between districts with PBF and the control districts. In relation to the program design and implementation, the researchers concluded as follows:

> What emerges . . . is that the main reasons for the failure . . . were unrealistic design of the intervention, ill-considered adaptations made hastily as the inadequacies of the design revealed themselves, and poor anticipation of the responses of institutions and individuals both inside and outside the change process. Key factors were the under financing of the initiative, the underestimation of the technical and institutional capacity requirements for successful implementation, the overloading of the implementation team with additional research activities and the failure to consider important actors who influence outcomes but are not directly included in the change process. (Ssengooba, McPake, and Palmer 2012, 382)

In Short

Although there is a plethora of PBF program designs in LMIC settings, there is a scarcity of rigorous evaluations. However, two randomized controlled trials of PBF in LMIC settings show contradictory evaluation results. One evaluation of a well-designed PBF intervention in Rwanda showed significant results, while the other evaluation of a poorly designed PBF intervention in Uganda showed no results. The way in which PBF programs are designed and implemented appears to be crucial for getting positive evaluation results. This is further discussed below.

How the Evidence on PBF in OECD Countries Compares

The evidence for PBF deriving from evaluations in OECD countries is very mixed. Initially, there was a similar lack of evaluations as in LMIC. However, the research on PBF program evaluations in OECD countries grew very rapidly over the past decades. In broad terms, two categories of research exist: studies related to PBF (often called "pay-for-performance") programs in which provider payments are closely tied to quality of care and studies in which provider payments are not associated with quality of care.

To date, paying providers for improving the quality of care has mixed results in OECD countries. However, data are emerging that indicate the importance of design and implementation for achieving results. Paying providers for service outputs does lead to a higher service provision. An incomplete description of the various contexts in which this occurs prohibits easy application of such information elsewhere.[2]

Provider Payment Mechanisms Tied to Quality of Care

The first category of research is related to provider payment mechanisms that are tied to quality of care, that is, PBF programs. PBF programs in OECD countries have been evaluated frequently, and the number of evaluations is still increasing (Van Herck et al. 2010). Unfortunately, many of these types of evaluations either (a) measure difference between before and after or (b) provide monitoring or process information. Such evaluations do not provide convincing evidence to direct policy (Gertler et al. 2011). In addition, a focus on effectiveness alone will not answer the question about the *relative cost-effectiveness* (Maynard 2012).

A systematic review (up to July 2009) of 128 evaluation studies of PBF programs in OECD countries produced a large body of evidence concerning clinical effectiveness and equity (Van Herck et al. 2010). Less evidence was found for the effect on coordination, continuity, patient-centeredness, and cost-effectiveness. In addition, the extent of the effect varied according to design choices and the context in which the program was introduced. In this review, only nine of 128 studies used a randomized design. The review highlighted the relationship between evaluation findings and PBF design choices and context. The following tips were recommended to obtain better results (Van Herck et al. 2010):

- Select and define PBF targets according to baseline room for improvement.
- Use process and intermediary outcome indicators as target measures.
- Involve stakeholders, and communicate program information thoroughly and directly.
- Implement a uniform PBF design across payers.
- Focus on both quality improvement and achievement.
- Distribute incentives to individuals and at the team level.

Mixed evaluation results (Petersen et al. 2006; Rosenthal and Frank 2006; Rosenthal et al. 2007) might be the product of suboptimally designed PBF programs (Werner et al. 2011). In a study of 126 Premier, Inc., hospitals in the United States, it was found that in hospitals that faced less competition and in those that were better financed the extent of the effect was larger with a larger incentive. So for design purposes, tailor incentives to the context: offer higher incentives in settings where the predicted effect is smaller (Werner et al. 2011).

Provider Payment Mechanisms Not Tied to Quality of Care

A second, quite substantial body of research is related to provider payment mechanisms that are not tied to quality of care, that is, those mechanisms that describe the relationship between the way the provider is paid and the amount (quantity, length, frequency, or type) of services that are rendered. A recent Cochrane review examined the effectiveness of financial incentives on provider behavior (Flodgren et al. 2011). In this study of provider payment mechanisms in high-income countries, financial incentives were grouped in five categories:

- Payment for work during a specified time period
- Payment for each service, episode, or visit
- Payment for provision of care for a patient or specific population
- Payment for provision of a prespecified level or of a change in activity or quality of care
- Mixed methods.

Payment for work during a specified period (salary) was generally not effective. All other incentive mechanisms showed positive effects, while mixed methods showed mixed results.

Financial incentives were generally effective for the following:

- Improving processes of care
- Improving referrals and admissions
- Improving prescribing costs outcomes.

Financial incentives were generally ineffective for the following:

- Improving compliance with guidelines outcomes.

The review states: "For a majority of studies, the comparison intervention was not clearly stated, compromising a reader's ability to understand the context within which the study was conducted and therefore how it might translate to another setting" (Flodgren et al. 2011, 11).

In Short

Paying providers on the basis of outputs leads to a higher volume of services rendered. Sharper documentation of the context in which such provider payment mechanisms are evaluated is important for using evaluation findings in other settings.

How to Deal With the Problem of Overall Weak Evaluation Designs

Weak evaluation designs combined with a general lack of evaluations in LMIC lead to a lack of strong evidence on PBF program effectiveness. Program evaluations are generally of two types: monitoring and evaluation (see box 17.1).

BOX 17.1

Very Positive Trends in PBF Programs: The Case of Family Planning Services in Rwanda

In Rwanda, PBF was scaled up in 2006, after a pilot period. Family planning (FP) was among the services that were purchased through PBF. Three of the 24 services purchased were related to FP: a new user of modern FP methods, an existing user of modern FP methods, and an HIV (human immunodeficiency virus) client put on modern FP methods. The 2005 Demographic and Health Surveys (DHS) found the uptake, of all methods combined, to be 10 percent. During the monitoring of the PBF results from 2006 to 2008, a very quick and rapid increase in these services was noted (see figure B17.1.1). A mini-DHS in 2007 found that FP use had increased to 27 percent.

Although the figures for the 23 PBF districts showed large variation in absolute and relative achievements for FP services, PBF proponents were quite impressed by the average increase and expected to see this reflected in the impact evaluation. This was not the case. The impact evaluation showed no statistical difference between the PBF districts and the control district (Basinga et al. 2011). The same type of average increase in FP service uptake had occurred throughout the entire country in a similar fashion. So if PBF was not the cause of the increase in FP services, then what was?

FIGURE B17.1.1 Average Number of Clients Using Modern FP Methods in a PBF Health Facility, 2006–08

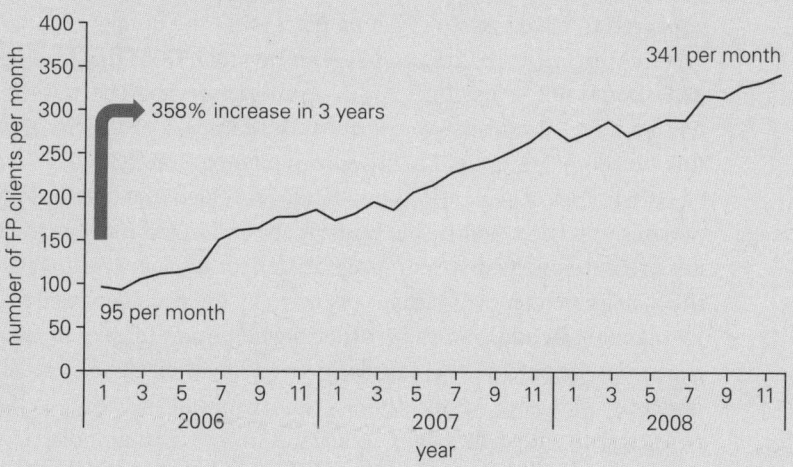

Source: World Bank based on Rwanda Performance-Based Financing database.

Note: FP = family planning; PBF = performance-based financing.

Evaluations can be divided into three types (Gertler et al. 2011; Imas and Rist 2009):

- Monitoring
  - → The monitoring of results tracks inputs, outputs, and results of a project or program.
- Evaluations
  - → Descriptive questions are used to assess what is taking place and what are the organizational processes and to describe the processes through stakeholder interviews.
  - → Normative questions are used to analyze what is actually taking place, compare this against what is supposed to take place, and assess whether the targets are accomplished.
  - → Cause and effect questions are used to examine outcomes. These also try to assess what difference the intervention makes to outcomes. Impact evaluations fall in this category.

The story on family planning in Rwanda in box 17.1 demonstrates that reliance on monitoring information from PBF districts alone might have led to a conclusion that PBF was the cause of this strong increase. However, the impact evaluation showed no difference between the increases of the contraceptive prevalence rate in the treatment and the control districts. PBF appeared to have had no effect on increasing the uptake of family planning services during its scaling-up phase in Rwanda. Does this finding mean that PBF should not be used for family planning services (because it apparently had no effect according to the Rwandese impact evaluation)? And should this "wisdom" be applied to other contexts? Not really.

Other types of evaluations might have revealed that at that time, in-charge persons of health facilities in both treatment and control districts were under pressure by the district mayors to deliver family planning results. While the district mayors were under pressure by the president to deliver on family planning in addition to 80 other development targets across all sectors, the in-charge persons were under pressure by their district mayor to deliver on family planning. Many stories circulate about in-charge persons in control districts who called their colleagues in the treatment districts and asked about the tools they were using to measure performance and to direct performance to individual health workers. The nonconditional cash payments received each quarter by the control facilities were therefore also conditioned on reaching performance results.[3] Qualitative research using focus group discussions would have informed the impact evaluation results and would have provided more contextual information on why some methods worked, while others, seemingly, did not. For this reason, there are a large number of rigorous impact evaluations financed through the Health Results Innovation Trust fund; by 2013, there were 15 such impact evaluations, and their number is growing. These impact evaluations will add significantly to the body of evidence on such approaches through a mix of different evaluations: alongside quantitative methods, there are also qualitative methods, process evaluations, and so on.

In Short

Using mixed methods, that is, a mix of quantitative techniques (for example, impact evaluations) and qualitative techniques (for example, focus group discussions) would have explained why there was no difference in Rwanda between the treatment and control groups for family planning services (Tashakkori and Teddlie 2003).

How to Deal with the Fact That Rigorous Impact Evaluations Are Often Difficult in Practice

Rigorous impact evaluations are difficult to carry out. Significant technical and financial resources are required. In a recent book, Gertler et al. (2011) describe impact evaluations in more detail. The impact evaluation toolkit, which the World Bank has recently published, provides useful tips and tools.[4]

Why PBF Programs Are Difficult Research

PBF programs are systemic interventions (de Savigny and Adam 2009; von Bertalanffy 1969). Their systemic reform character necessitates applying a wide range of monitoring and evaluation techniques that use a mix of quantitative and qualitative methods (Alexander and Hearld 2012; Meessen et al. 2012). In systematic interventions, many variables operate at the same time. They work together in reaching a range of desirable effects, and many of these variables are not easy to research.

Intervention actions may also interfere with each other. Consider, for example, the Rwandese family planning case discussed above. The influence of the performance agreements of the president on the behavior of the in-charge persons of health facilities in control districts during the impact evaluation was not foreseen. So is it correct to conclude—on the basis of lack of effect of PBF on family planning services in Rwanda during 2006–08—that this result will be the same in other countries? No. In fact, quite a number of other evaluations indicate that PBF does have an effect on family planning services.

17.3 PBF Programs in LMIC and OECD Countries Have Both Differences and Similarities

Although PBF programs in LMIC differ from those in OECD countries in important ways, there are also similarities. Evaluation results, however, cannot be extrapolated from OECD to LMIC countries. The following sections discuss how LMIC and OECD programs differ, how they are similar, and what LMIC can learn from OECD country approaches to PBF.

Differences Between PBF Programs in LMIC and OECD Countries

PBF programs in LMIC and OECD countries differ in the following respects:

- Coverage for essential health services
- Baseline quality of services
- Health worker coping strategies
- Size of output budget
- Type of PBF program
- Institutional arrangements.

Coverage for Essential Health Services

Essential health services have much poorer coverage in low-income countries compared to OECD countries. In a low-income country, a person visits a health provider on average once in two years, but in OECD countries, a person visits a doctor on average 6.5 times per year (OECD 2011). A further example is institutional deliveries. In Sub-Saharan Africa, 40 percent of the women deliver with a qualified provider, while in OECD countries the rate is close to 100 percent. So while there is underconsumption of health services in low-income countries, there is overconsumption in OECD countries. This is one of the main reasons that PBF programs in LMIC incentivize service provision (OECD 2010). Stimulating service provision for preventive services—a key element of PBF approaches in LMIC—is also a common feature of many health programs in OECD countries (Xingzhu and O'Dougherty 2004).

Baseline Quality of Services

The quality of health services in LMIC is very low compared to OECD countries. LMIC face both poor coverage and low quality of health services (Berendes et al. 2011; Das 2011). Quality of care is considered a challenge in OECD countries, too (IOM 2001; Kohn, Corrigan, and Donaldson 2000). However, the worst health institution in any OECD country would probably still score better than most best health facilities in LMIC.

Quality baselines differ, and the problems facing LMIC health facilities are different. For instance, LMIC health facilities often lack basic equipment, struggle with deficient infrastructure, have problems with water and sanitation, and lack basic products to ensure adequate hygiene. All such basic inputs are commonly available in OECD country health facilities.

Consequently, the quality problems that confront LMIC and OECD health systems are in different categories and are difficult to compare, a phenomenon known as the "category problem" (Ryle 1949). Therefore, PBF programs in LMIC use different measures as compared to those in OECD countries. These unique instruments incentivize different dimensions of quality (Donabedian 2005). For instance, the dimensions in LMIC emphasize the structural aspects of quality and those elements of patient-provider interactions that can be captured in various documents.

Health Worker Coping Strategies

In addition to poor coverage and quality problems, LMIC must deal with health workers who have low salaries and compensate with coping mechanisms to pay for daily living expenses. Health worker coping strategies in LMIC are sizable and pervasive, and they are a type and form that is uncommon in OECD countries. Coping mechanisms such as absenteeism, moonlighting, double-practice, acceptance of informal payments or gifts, and drug pilfering pervade LMIC health systems (Van Lerberghe et al. 2002). This situation is different from OECD countries where health workers do not face such challenges to their most basic needs. Many theories support the observation that insufficient pay to meet basic needs leads to less work effort—from Maslow's (1943) pyramid of needs to Akerlof's (1982) wage fairness theory and Herzberg's (1968) motivation-hygiene theory.

Size of Output Budget

With respect to percentage, the size of the PBF output budget is large compared to similar programs in OECD countries. Correcting the need for health worker coping strategies requires a relatively large PBF budget. Whereas in OECD countries a pay-for-performance program could be equivalent to a maximum of 5 percent of additional financing (OECD 2010),[5] in LMIC this could be closer to 30–40 percent. PBF programs in LMIC attempt to finance a large gap composed of significant health worker bonuses and a considerable sum to procure basic equipment and missing drugs, repair basic sanitation, and so on. The size of the incentives is known to be positively correlated with results (Miller and Babiarz 2013).

Type of PBF Program

PBF programs in LMIC differ from those in OECD countries in basic aims. First, delivering more cash into health facilities to pay health worker bonuses and to finance infrastructure, equipment, and drugs is a core aim of PBF systems in LMIC.[6] In contrast, OECD countries have a different aim. Pay-for-performance programs in OECD countries are focused on quality and have cost-containment objectives (Maynard 2012). Second, in OECD countries a wide variety of PBF approaches are found under the title "Pay for Performance," or P4P, schemes. By contrast, PBF programs in LMIC are primarily comparable to one another: they increase the volume of services (through a fee-for-service mechanism) and the quality (through a balanced scorecard with the level of quality affecting on the payment). Meanwhile, PBF programs in OECD countries increase the quality (through different means) while hoping that this will lead to cost containment and savings in the mid-term.[7]

In Short

PBF programs differ significantly between LMIC and OECD countries. Such differences render evaluation results drawn from OECD country PBF programs not directly applicable to LMIC.

Similarities

Besides significant differences between PBF programs in LMIC and OECD countries, there are also a number of similarities. Such similarities are particularly clear if an analogy is drawn between PBF programs in LMIC and provider payment mechanisms and health reforms in OECD countries. The following elements of OECD health systems have parallels to PBF programs in LMIC.

Fee-for-Service

Paying providers a fee-for-service leads to more services. Paying providers a fee for each service clearly leads to an increase in those services (Averill et al. 2010; Chaix-Couturier et al. 2000; Flodgren et al. 2011; Jegers et al. 2002; Langenbrunner, Cashin, and O'Dougherty 2009). This phenomenon is also described in LMIC (Lagarde and Palmer 2008). In other words, output-based payments (such as fee-for-service, case-based payments, and diagnosis-related groups) have the potential to increase service provision. This is similar to PBF systems in LMIC in which providers are paid a fee-for-service conditional on quality (Basinga et al. 2011; de Walque et al. 2013; Gertler and Vermeersch 2012).

Purchaser-Provider Split

A purchaser-provider split in OECD countries and former Soviet republics is similar to PBF separation of functions in LMIC. The purchaser pays providers a fee-for-service. A purchaser-provider split creates a market for health services whereby the purchaser is split from the provider (Langenbrunner, Cashin, and O'Dougherty 2009). Such purchaser-provider splits have been a cornerstone of health reforms in OECD countries and former Soviet republics (Busse et al. 2005). Similarly, PBF health reforms introduce a separation of functions by splitting the purchasing of services from the provision and regulation of services (see chapter 2) (Bertone and Meessen 2010).

Health Reforms and Market Reforms

PBF health reforms are similar to internal market or quasi-market reforms in OECD country health systems. PBF health reforms introduce market forces in centrally managed LMIC health systems (Meessen, Soucat, and Sekabaraga 2011). Such reforms are similar to those introduced in the United Kingdom and New Zealand under the New Public Management thinking (Le Grand 2003; Le Grand and Bartlett 1993). A better distribution of health care while improving efficiency was a stated goal of internal market reforms (Busse et al. 2005; Enthoven 1991). Just like in OECD countries, PBF health reforms in LMIC attempt to enhance allocation efficiency—by channeling existing resources from the macrolevel to the lower levels of the health care pyramid—and to improve technical efficiency at the health facility level.

Strategic Purchasing

Purchasing of well-defined basic and complementary health packages through PBF in LMIC is conceptually similar to strategic purchasing in OECD countries. Purchasing a service requires the service to be defined, a fee to be attached to it, and the service package to be made explicit. Whereas passive purchasing refers to just paying the bill that providers send, strategic purchasing refers to actively determining what to buy, from whom, and for how much (WHO 2000). PBF systems in LMIC define clearly the type of services and the amount to be paid for each service. Also, such PBF systems allow the purchasing process (how much is purchased from whom) to be monitored and enable purchasers to change the service fee regularly based on budget realities or strategic choices.

Path Dependency

Path dependency, a well-known phenomenon in health reforms in OECD countries, also applies to PBF reforms in LMIC. Path dependency means that what has been done in the past will determine what will likely be done in the future. How health services have been organized, financed, and delivered in the past determine to a very large degree the preference of that country's health system (Walt 1994). This phenomenon, which is well known in the OECD country health reform literature (Busse et al. 2005; Figueras, Robinson, and Jakubowski 2005), explains why in some countries PBF health reforms catch on easily and in others the reforms seem to fail or have difficulties catching on. In addition to such preferences for a certain way of doing things, some powerful stakeholders have entrenched interests, and it is very difficult to go against their interest (for instance, Obama care). In fact, path dependency is the reason that it is important to introduce such PBF reforms through a well-designed and well-implemented pilot first, before attempting to scale up PBF (see chapter 16). A PBF pilot allows local advocates to stand up, to learn PBF, to adapt it to their context, and to show results to policy makers. Influencing path dependency is a key aspect of PBF reforms.

In Short

Although there are significant differences between LMIC and OECD country PBF systems, there are also similarities. These similarities are in internal market reforms, path dependency, purchaser-provider splits, strategic purchasing, and the influence of fee-for-service on provider behavior. Policy makers in LMIC countries should take into account such similarities when designing their PBF systems.

What LMIC Can Learn from OECD Countries

OECD country PBF systems can inform PBF systems in LMIC in two areas. These areas are noncommunicable diseases and verification based on health information systems.

LMIC face an increasing burden of noncommunicable diseases and, in some instances, a double burden of infectious diseases and a developing burden of noncommunicable diseases (WHO 2011). Because treatment options for cardiovascular conditions are limited (due to the cost of medical technology), the focus will be on prevention. Including noncommunicable disease–related measures in PBF, on both the quantity and the quality aspects, could benefit LMIC systems. The "how-to" could be gleaned from more advanced systems such as the United Kingdom's Quality and Outcomes Framework, in which a few years of experimentation has led to valuable experience in this domain.

The second area in which LMIC can learn from OECD countries involves information and communication technology (ICT) solutions. Advanced PBF systems in LMIC use web-enabled data systems and increasingly also incorporate mobile phone use in administration and verification activities. These systems link paper-based administration at the health facility level to Internet-based data management at the district and national levels. As LMIC health care administration moves from a paper-based data system to an electronic-based one, more opportunities will exist to use modern ICT to the benefit of PBF systems.

17.4 PBF Programs Need Appropriate Design and Implementation to Be Successful

Appropriate design and implementation are vital for obtaining good results in PBF programs. As discussed, evaluation results of PBF programs in LMIC and OECD countries show that in both LMIC and OECD country settings, better-designed and better-implemented PBF programs show better results (see box 17.2).

Based on years of trial and error, PBF programs evolved to certain design and implementation characteristics. In table 17.1, these characteristics are shown with an explanation of their importance for health system performance. The chapter in this toolkit in which this characteristic is explained in detail is referenced for further information.

Most PBF programs exhibit a mix of the characteristics listed in table 17.1. In addition, PBF programs are continuously evolving on the basis of lessons learned, which is why design and implementation characteristics are expected to evolve too. Even if PBF programs do not fully meet all characteristics in table 17.1, they can still show results. Table 17.2 provides examples of what type of effects can be expected when aspects of these design and implementation characteristics are changed.

BOX 17.2

Different Ways to Enhance Health System Performance

There are many ways of improving health system performance in LMIC countries, and there is no easy solution for achieving results. PBF programs that blend various successful approaches into one have shown promising results. Such PBF programs rely on both observational and incentive effects; that is, such programs use a mix of causal pathways. In addition, such programs also introduce and rely on larger reforms such as health facility autonomy and human resources reforms and interventions that affect demand-side barriers to access to care by the population.

TABLE 17.1 Design and Implementation Characteristics Linked to Improved Results

Characteristic	Detailed information	Toolkit chapter
Well-balanced benefit package at all levels	A minimum of 15–25 services exist at each level: health center/community level and first-level referral hospital.	Chapter 1
Rigorous results verification	A mix of ex ante verification and ex post verification occurs.	Chapter 2
Separation of functions	Separation of functions among regulator, provider, and purchaser serves to improve accountability and credibility of results.	Chapter 2
Use of community client satisfaction surveys to gather information from clients on use and to gather their opinions	Feedback is gained on use of services and opinion of the population	Chapter 2
Use of a quantified quality checklist (balanced score card) with the result tied to payments	A comprehensive mix of measures on structure and process gives a balanced view on quality. The quality checklist is applied by the district or provincial health administration (regulatory function). Other results include observational and supervisory effects and improvement of technical efficiency.	Chapter 3
Use of a fee-for-service provider payment mechanism	Using a fee-for-service mechanism is evidence based. It makes measuring outputs easier and links efforts directly to rewards.	Chapter 4
Strategic purchasing with a focus on underprovided and underutilized preventive services	Fees are open at the microlevel (health facility), which leads to money following the effort, and budgets are closed at the macrolevel, which leads to cost containment. Fees are adapted as a function of results (what is desired) and available budget (use of lever services—high-volume services such as curative services—to stay within budget at the macrolevel). ICT solutions allow individual health facility fees to be managed on a quarterly basis.	Chapter 4
Individual fees and total earnings that are significant and paid regularly	Income from PBF and other sources needs to be sufficient to (a) pay staff a significant monthly bonus income and to hire additional staff if necessary and (b) pay for nonsalary recurrent cost items.	Chapter 4
Most money to the most cost-effective services	Two-thirds of the money goes to the community or health center level and one-third to the first-level referral hospital. Improvement of allocation efficiency (reprogramming existing money to the frontlines) occurs.	Chapter 4

TABLE 17.1 *(continued)*

Characteristic	Detailed information	Toolkit chapter
Equity	Various equity instruments exist: (a) delivering more money to destitute areas (ring-fenced global budget), (b) delivering more budget to destitute health facilities (higher fees), and (c) providing higher fees for services consumed by indigents.	Chapter 5
Autonomy	Health facilities' decision rights include procuring their drugs and other inputs, having their own bank accounts, and deciding on their income. Hiring and firing of staff would be ideal.	Chapter 6
Health facility management committee	The committee enhances local decision rights of health facilities combined with making the local population part of the oversight and governance mechanisms.	Chapter 6
Payments and financial management	A quarterly payment cycle can still be combined with a monthly bonus payment to staff. The indice tool aids in managing all-cash income in a holistic fashion and managing bonus payments.	Chapter 7
Performance frameworks for the regulator	Health administration at the district and provincial levels and sometimes at the national level is made responsible for tasks that are under its control.	Chapter 8
Quality improvement units and investment units	Negotiated through the business plan, the quality improvement and investment units provide means for a health facility to upgrade its quality.	Chapter 9
Health facility management instruments	Instruments include the business plan, indice tool, and individual monthly performance evaluation.	Chapters 7 (indice tool) and 10 (business plan and individual performance evaluation)
Coaching and technical assistance	Usually occurring with the purchasing agent, coaching and technical assistance are vital.	Chapter 14
District PBF steering committee	The committee furnishes governance at the decentralized level, links health system performance to the health administration, and provides a platform for government and the local community to discuss health system performance.	Chapter 11
Web-enabled application with public front end	The application provides access to data at all levels, enables strategic purchasing, and enhances public accountability for performance.	Chapters 11, 12, and 13
Coordination	Coordination occurs between technical assistance and the government to support and enhance system performance.	Chapter 14
Capacity building	System strengthening occurs at health facility, district, and national levels.	Chapter 14

Source: World Bank data.

Note: ICT = information and communications technology; PBF = performance-based financing.

TABLE 17.2 Possible Effects of Weak Design and Implementation

Advised design and implementation	Actual design and implementation	Possible effects of weak design and implementation
Well-balanced benefit package at all levels	Less than 15 services in a benefit package; only one level covered	Focus on certain services to the detriment of others; lesser linkage between health center and hospital levels
Rigorous results verification	Ex ante verification not well executed and no ex post verification	Increase in phantom patients; lack of trust in results
Separation of functions	Separation of functions not well executed; regulator and purchaser too close to provider	Decrease of trust in reported results; decrease in sustainability because of lesser funding (both internal and donor fundings)
Use of community client satisfaction surveys to gather information from clients on use and to gather their opinions	Community client satisfaction surveys not done	Lack of trust in results; increase in phantom patients; no feedback on perception of clients on services rendered
Use of a quantified quality checklist (balanced score card) with the result tied to payments	Simple quality measures consisting of single indicators or no quality measure used instead of a comprehensive quantified quality checklist	Increase of quantity combined with a lesser increase of quality, no increase in quality, or even a decrease in quality
Use of a fee-for-service provider payment mechanism	Percentage point coverage increase of select services purchased instead of a fee-for-service	Narrow focus on certain services; problems with catchment population (denominator); unreliable baselines; penalties for high achievers; conflicts in assessing performance; long payment cycles
Strategic purchasing with a focus on underprovided and underutilized preventive services	Fees fixed for a prolonged period of time; no ability to analyze expenditures because of lack of appropriate ICT tools; focus on reimbursements for curative care	No ability to renegotiate fees in case forecasts were mistaken; no ability to follow budget expenditure; focus on reimbursing curative care that leads to the underprovision of preventive services
Individual fees and total earnings that are significant and paid regularly	Income from PBF and other sources insufficient to (a) pay staff a significant monthly bonus income and hire additional staff if necessary and (b) pay for nonsalary recurrent cost items	Small bonus payments insufficient to remedy staff coping mechanisms; insufficient funds for the purchase of drugs, medical consumables, equipment, and minor repairs, leading to lesser quantity and quality production
Most money to the most cost-effective services	Most money to hospital services	Financing of less cost-effective services (hospital) to the detriment of more cost-effective services
Equity	Equity instruments not used	Facilities in hard-to-reach areas will struggle to attract qualified staff and therefore to offer quality services; in case of user charges, higher barriers to access to services for indigents than for the less poor
Autonomy	Very limited or no autonomy or money managed by higher levels of administration (none own bank account); no gain share (no bonuses paid); and so on	Drugs frequently out of stock; staff less motivated; lesser innovations

TABLE 17.2 *(continued)*

Advised design and implementation	Actual design and implementation	Possible effects of weak design and implementation
Health facility management committee	No specific health facility management committee or no involvement in local governance of the health facility	Lesser sense of ownership of community; fewer checks and balances
Payments and financial management	A six-month or annual payment cycle used; no indice tool used	Lesser link between individual performance and overall achievement results; conflicts related to bonus payments; fragmented management of income
Performance frameworks for the regulator	No performance frameworks for the health administration	Quantified quality checklist not timely carried out by health administration; data not complete, leading to difficulties in paying for performance of the health facilities; less supervision and training or coaching from the district and provincial health administration
Quality improvement units and investment units	No quality improvement units and investment units used	No improving of aspects of structural quality such as lack of equipment; certain minor infrastructural repairs to be slower or not done due to financial constraints
Health facility management instruments	No business plan, no indice tool, and no individual monthly performance evaluation used	No ability for the purchaser to negotiate certain targets; more difficult to intercept moral hazard of the provider; difficulties managing cash income in a holistic manner; difficulties in distributing performance bonuses; staff conflicts
Coaching and technical assistance	No coaching of health facility management provided; no or very limited technical assistance provided to the health facilities and district health administration	At the health facility level, less performance because of less advanced strategies; at the district level, less capacity development related to analyzing performance and less ability to support enhancing performance of health facilities
District PBF steering committee	No district PBF steering committee	Less ownership of government of the PBF system; no leveraging of health administrative capacity; less input from the local community in governance of public health system
Web-enabled application with public front end	Fixed database or Microsoft Excel–based management tool	No public access to data or financial information; much less availability of data for action
Coordination	Poor coordination or no coordination between government and technical assistance agencies	Less availability of technical assistance; more fragmentation of health system than could be the case; less support of development partners than could be the case
Capacity building	Very little or no capacity building	Less quality and quantity performance results than could be the case

Source: World Bank data.

Note: PBF = performance-based financing.

17.5 Frequently Asked Questions

PBF is new to many governments and amounts to a different way of doing business. Reaching results through output financing is different from financing through inputs (salaries, equipment, training, and so on). Questions that are frequently asked in the transition to PBF, and their answers, are provided in table 17.3.

TABLE 17.3 Frequently Asked Questions and Corresponding Answers

	Question	Answer
1	Are PBF and other incentive-based approaches effective?	PBF leads to more and better quality health services if it is well designed and well implemented. When PBF is not well designed or well implemented, it may lead to a lesser (or no) effect or to wrong results, such as the overproduction of certain services and the underproduction of others. More evidence is needed to document PBF effects, and such research is increasingly being carried out. See chapter 17.
2	Even if PBF is effective, is it really cost-effective? Could the same or better results be more easily achieved by using the additional money in other ways (like raising health workers' salaries or providing better supplies)?	Well-designed research in Rwanda indicates that PBF leads to more and better quality health services as compared to just providing more money. This research also shows that children living near PBF facilities have a better nutritional status than children living near non-PBF health facilities. The PBF effect is so strong that it affects child health status. For the same amount of payment, the intervention group delivered higher results. See chapter 17. More research is needed about the cost-effectiveness of PBF as compared to other system-strengthening approaches. A large amount of research on this subject is being planned.
3	Can PBF actually make inequality worse because richer areas capture most of the money?	This could indeed be a real danger if the PBF is not well designed, which is why PBF pays higher fees to health facilities that are in more destitute areas: health facilities located in the worst areas will be paid the highest fees for their services and receive relatively more income through PBF. These facilities can then recruit more staff. See chapter 5.
4	Does PBF lead to gaming of the system by (a) outright fraud and cheating, (b) reducing of quality of care so as to maximize volumes, and (c) providers' focusing on the easiest services and the easiest-to-reach populations?	Gaming is a real danger in PBF: (a) Rigorous verification and counterverification are done to certify the quantity and quality of services. In well-designed PBF, less than 5 percent of clients cannot be traced back in the community. (b) PBF payments are conditional based on the quality of services. Making fee-for-service payments conditional on quality leads to an increase in the quality of these services at the same time as the volume increases. (c) PBF closely monitors the size of the fees and the relative value of each fee as compared to the other. PBF also rigorously monitors the amount and type of services that are produced. Such monitoring would intercept the underproduction of certain services. Moreover, providers in the most destitute areas are paid the highest fees for their services, and there is increasing experimentation with paying higher fees for indigents. See chapters 2, 3, 4, and 5.

TABLE 17.3 *(continued)*

	Question	Answer
5	Does PBF destroy intrinsic motivation, so that health workers work only when given incentives, which results in reduced professionalism?	Research on this subject is mostly from OECD countries and resulting arguments are ambiguous and cannot be directly applied to LMIC. PBF uses a systemic approach that not only works with relatively high incentives (because take-home salaries are very low), but also provides autonomy on the use of funds and strong management support. Research from Rwanda shows that health providers did much better under PBF. Providers under PBF stayed more within their area of expertise than did those that were not under PBF; PBF providers were more professional. Most health workers and their managers prefer PBF to previous systems. See chapter 17.
6	Does PBF distort health systems so that nonincentivized services deteriorate?	Nonincentivized services could deteriorate, which is a real danger if PBF is not well designed or implemented. Thus, PBF purchases a balanced package of services at all levels of the health system. PBF also strengthens the role of the district health administration to ensure that monitoring and quality supervision are carried out regularly. These tactics help avoid such health system distortions. See chapters 1 and 4.
7	Is PBF just a way of privatizing health services?	PBF introduces market forces in rigid public health systems by creating an internal market. This is not the same as privatizing health services, and in the case of public health facilities, ownership remains with the government. However, health facilities and their communities are given more autonomy (and much more money) to better manage their health services. Health workers are made stakeholders in their own facilities, which is quite similar to the idea of a cooperative. In addition, private not-for-profit or for-profit facilities are also targeted by PBF (because PBF attempts to cover the entire health network and not just the public system). See chapter 6.
8	Is PBF just another way of introducing or perpetuating user fees?	On the contrary, PBF pays providers significant fees to enable these providers to offer more services of better quality. If the fees are high enough (when the PBF budget is high enough), then PBF can also subsidize partly or fully the out-of-pocket expenses of patients. In the latter case, user fees could be decreased or abolished. Unfortunately, public budgets are insufficient to finance all health care costs. See chapter 4.
9	Is PBF just a modest reform that perpetuates the ineffective, inefficient, and inequitable systems currently in place?	PBF involves significant reforms, which is why PBF is often difficult to implement. PBF calls for major reforms exactly because many health systems are ineffective, inefficient, and inequitable. For PBF to work well, significant reforms are required in (a) autonomy, (b) human resources management, (c) drug and medical consumables supply, and (d) financial barriers to access to services. Currently, two country health systems (Rwanda and Burundi) showcase the effects of such successful reforms. See chapter 17.
10	How can PBF create any positive effect before the human resources, physical infrastructure, and supplies of the health facilities are strengthened?	These factors are indeed important, which is why PBF works (a) on increasing autonomy, including hiring and firing practices, and (b) with investment units so that health facilities can start fixing infrastructure, procure missing equipment, and purchase supplies quickly. Greatly increased income through PBF enables health facilities to hire additional staff, too. See chapters 6 and 9.

(table continues on next page)

TABLE 17.3 *(continued)*

	Question	Answer
11	PBF comprises many facets, so which one is key? Maybe the incentives are not the most important part?	PBF is a complex multifaceted approach that acknowledges the systemic nature of health systems. Incentives are an important part of the PBF approach, but so are autonomy and much enhanced monitoring, verification, and technical support. Local context and design and implementation features determine the relative contribution of each facet. See chapters 4 and 16.
12	Is it true that PBF works only in situations where there is already good governance and a well-functioning civil service?	PBF might not be necessary in cases where there is good governance and a well-functioning civil service. However, PBF has proven to work very well in cases where there is a lack of good governance or an absence of a functioning civil service. In such settings, PBF can be an excellent tool to strengthen good governance and to help civil service function even better. See chapter 11.
13	Does PBF require so much technical assistance that it is unsustainable and creates dependency on foreigners?	Well-designed and well-implemented PBF needs technical assistance. However, PBF also needs an independent agency to perform verification for results and to carry out community client satisfaction surveys. Obtaining good-quality, reliable data has a cost. Without good-quality data, you cannot pay for performance. Most, if not all, technical assistance can be organized in the country. For a short time initially, actors outside the country might be needed if in-country technical capacity has not yet been built. However, PBF creates many new technicians rapidly. In Africa, a PBF community of practice actively nurtures South-South technical assistance. Technical assistance costs for PBF are not different from other well-designed development programs. See chapter 14.
14	Is PBF unethical because it gives providers an incentive to promote family planning and limits the choice of couples?	Well-designed PBF ensures that a well-balanced package of services is purchased and not just family planning services (although family planning is very important). Currently, many women and men do not have access to family planning services, although they may have expressed their need for such services. Many providers do not provide quality family planning services because they do not earn money from it, they do not have time to provide such services because of coping strategies, or they do not have family planning products in their pharmacies. Ensuring that clients are offered a balanced package of reproductive health services is important for PBF. Thus, PBF uses a rigorous quantified quality checklist each quarter to check whether, for instance, the norms and standards related to family planning services remain as high as possible. Mother and child health services, including family planning services, are important for PBF (and the community), and further guidance on family planning can be obtained from a paper on this topic (Eichler et al. 2010). See chapters 1 and 3.
15	Was the improvement seen in Rwanda largely a result of the introduction of health insurance and not PBF?	In Rwanda, health insurance reimbursed providers for the provision of curative care services while PBF financed providers for the provision of preventive services. A well-designed impact evaluation documented significant differences in quantity and quality of services in PBF facilities. Both PBF facilities and non-PBF facilities had exactly the same health insurance for their population and received exactly the same amount of money to finance health services. So it is unlikely that health insurance was the only reason for Rwanda's health system improvements. However, health insurance was important because it decreased financial barriers to access to services, enabling more patients to use services,

TABLE 17.3 *(continued)*

Question	Answer
	including preventive services. PBF ensured that the much increased demand for services was met with an enhanced supply of services against a higher quality. A further reason for the improvements were concomitant human resources for health reforms, which led to a much better distribution of health workers and a redistribution of health workers from the capital to rural areas.

Source: World Bank data.

Note: LMIC = lower- and middle-income countries; OECD = Organisation for Economic Co-operation and Development; PBF = performance-based financing.

Notes

1. Two other well-designed PBF program evaluations showed good results: one in the Philippines (Peabody et al. 2011) and one in Indonesia (Olken, Onishi, and Wong 2012). However, because of very different contexts (Sub-Saharan Africa versus the Philippines and Indonesia) and PBF design characteristics—in the Philippines, Peabody et al. (2011) measured and rewarded doctors' knowledge and practice using vignettes, and in Indonesia, Olken, Onishi, and Wong (2012) rewarded villages if the health providers performed better—these are not discussed.

2. Every case is different from the other in terms of contexts and institutional arrangements. Pay-for-performance programs in OECD are introduced in settings where there is already a lot of output-based payment.

3. In fact, the impact evaluation of PBF in the health sector was hurt by another PBF scheme (in the control districts), inspired by the PBF scheme in the treatment districts.

4. The web-accessible impact evaluation toolkit contains a host of instruments and tools to plan, design, and implement an impact evaluation: http://go.worldbank.org/IT69C5OGL0.

5. But most of their revenue is already linked to outputs such as diagnosis-related groups, fee-for-service, and so on.

6. But there is also a large heterogeneity among PBF programs in LMIC, such as in Haiti, Pakistan, and so on.

7. There is one large exemption to this general tendency: in the United Kingdom's Quality and Outcomes Framework, one of the initial goals was to significantly increase a general practitioner's income.

References and Other Sources

Akerlof, G. 1982. "Labor Contracts as Partial Gift Exchange." *Quarterly Journal of Economics* 97: 543–69.

Alexander, J. A., and L. R. Hearld. 2012. "Methods and Metrics Challenges of Delivery-System Research." *Implementation Science* 7: 15.

Averill, R. F., N. I. Goldfield, J. C. Vertrees, E. C McCollough, R. L. Fuller, and J. Eisejhandler. 2010. "Achieving Cost Control, Care Coordination, and Quality Improvement through Incremental Payment System Reform." *Journal of Ambulatory Care Management* 33 (1): 2–23.

Basinga, P., P. Gertler, A. Binagwaho, A. Soucat, J. Sturdy, and C. Vermeersch. 2011. "Effect on Maternal and Child Health Services in Rwanda of Payment to Primary Health-Care Providers for Performance: An Impact Evaluation." *Lancet* 377 (9775): 1421–28.

Berendes, S., P. Heywood, S. Oliver, and P. Garner. 2011. "Quality of Private and Public Ambulatory Health Care in Low and Middle Income Countries: Systematic Review of Comparative Studies." *PLoS Medicine* 8 (4): e1000433.

Bertone, M. P., and B. Meessen. 2010. "Splitting Functions in a Local Health System: Early Lessons from Bubanza and Ngozi Projects in Burundi." Report, Cordaid, The Hague.

Busse, R., J. Figueras, R. Robinson, and E. Jakubowski. 2005. "Strategic Purchasing to Improve Health Systems Performance: Key Issues and International Trends." *HealthcarePapers* 8 (Special issue): 62–76.

Chaix-Couturier, C., I. Durand-Zaleski, D. Jolly, and P. Durieux. 2000. "Effects of Financial Incentives on Medical Practice: Results from a Systematic Review of the Literature and Methodological Issues." *International Journal for Quality in Health Care* 12 (2): 133–42.

Das, J. 2011. "The Quality of Medical Care in Low-Income Countries: From Providers to Markets." *PLoS Medicine* 8 (4): e1000432.

de Savigny, D., and T. Adam. 2009. *Systems Thinking for Health Systems Strengthening*. Geneva: World Health Organization.

de Walque, D., P. J. Gertler, S. Bautista-Arredondo, A. Kwan, C. Vermeersch, J. de Dieu Bizimana, A. Bingawaho, and J. Condo. 2013. "Using Provider Performance Incentives to Increase HIV Testing and Counseling Services in Rwanda." Policy Research Working Paper 6364, World Bank, Washington, DC.

Donabedian, A. 2005. "Evaluating the Quality of Medical Care." *Milbank Quarterly* 83 (4): 691–729.

Eichler, R., B. Seligman, A. Beith, and J. Wright. 2010. "Performance-Based Incentives: Ensuring Voluntarism in Family Planning Initiatives." Bethesda, MD: Health Systems 20/20 project, Abt Associates Inc. http://www.healthsystems 2020.org/content/resource/detail/2686/.

Elridge, C., and N. Palmer. 2009. "Performance-Based Payment: Some Reflections on the Discourse, Evidence, and Unanswered Questions." *Health Policy and Planning* 24 (3): 160–66.

Enthoven, A. C. 1991. "Internal Market Reform of the British National Health Service." *Health Affairs* 10 (3): 60–70.

Figueras, J., R. Robinson, and E. Jakubowski, eds. 2005. *Purchasing to Improve Health Systems Performance*. European Observatory on Health Systems and Policies Series. New York: World Health Organization on behalf of European Observatory on Health Systems and Policies.

Fiszbein, A., and N. Schady. 2009. "Conditional Cash Transfers: Reducing Present and Future Poverty." Policy Research Report, World Bank, Washington, DC.

Flodgren, G., M. Eccles, S. Shepperd, A. Scott, E. Parmelli, and F. R. Beyer. 2011. "An Overview of Reviews Evaluating the Effectiveness of Financial Incentives in Changing Healthcare Professional Behaviours and Patient Outcomes." *Cochrane Database of Systematic Reviews* (7).

Gertler, P., S. Martinez, P. Premand, L. B. Rawlings, and C. M. J. Vermeersch. 2011. *Impact Evaluation in Practice.* Washington, DC: World Bank.

Gertler, P., and C. Vermeersch. 2012. "Using Performance Incentives to Improve Health Outcomes." Policy Research Working Paper WPS6100, World Bank, Washington, DC.

Herzberg, F. 1968. "One More Time: How Do You Motivate Employees?" *Harvard Business Review* 46 (1): 53–62.

Imas, L. G. M., and R. C. Rist. 2009. *The Road to Results: Designing and Conducting Effective Development Evaluations.* Washington, DC: World Bank.

IOM (Institute of Medicine), ed. 2001. *Crossing the Quality Chasm: A New Health System for the 21st Century.* Washington, DC: National Academy Press.

Ireland, M., E. Paul, and B. Dujardin. 2011. "Can Performance-Based Financing Be Used to Reform Health Systems in Developing Countries?" *Bulletin of the World Health Organization* 89 (9): 695–98.

Jegers, M., K. Kesteloot, D. De Graeve, and W. Gilles. 2002. "A Typology for Provider Payment Systems in Health Care." *Health Policy* 60 (3): 255–73.

Kalk, A., F. A. Paul, and E. Grabosch. 2010. "'Paying for Performance' in Rwanda: Does It Pay Off?." *Tropical Medicine and International Health* 15 (2): 182–90.

Kohn, L. T., J. M. Corrigan, and M. S. Donaldson, eds. 2000. *To Err Is Human: Building a Safer Health System.* Washington, DC: Institute of Medicine.

Lagarde, M., and N. Palmer. 2008. "The Impact of User Fees on Health Service Utilization in Low- and Middle-Income Countries: How Strong Is the Evidence?" *Bulletin of the World Health Organization* 86 (11): 839–48.

Langenbrunner, J. C., C. Cashin, and S. O'Dougherty, eds. 2009. *Designing and Implementing Health Care Provider Payment Systems: How-to Manuals.* Washington, DC: World Bank and U.S. Agency for International Development.

Le Grand, J. 2003. *Motivation, Agency, and Public Policy.* London: Oxford University Press.

Le Grand, J., and W. Bartlett, eds. 1993. *Quasi-Markets and Social Policy.* London: Macmillan.

Logie, D., M. Rowson, and F. Ndagije. 2008. "Innovations in Rwanda's Health System: Looking to the Future." *The Lancet* 372 (9634): 256–61.

Lundberg, M., T. Marek, and P. Okwero. 2007. "Contracting Health Services in Uganda." Unpublished report, World Bank, Washington, DC.

Maslow, A. H. 1943. "A Theory of Human Motivation." *Psychological Review* 5 (4): 370–96.

Maynard, A. 2012. "The Powers and Pitfalls of Payment for Performance." *Health Economics* 21 (1): 3–12.

Meessen, B., J. P. Kashala, and L. Musango. 2007. "Output-Based Payment to Boost Staff Productivity in Public Health Centers: Contracting in Kabutare District, Rwanda." *Bulletin of the World Health Organization* 85 (2): 108–15.

Meessen, B., L. Musango, J. P. Kashala, and J. Lemlin. 2006. "Reviewing Institutions of Rural Health Centres: The Performance Initiative in Butare, Rwanda." *Tropical Medicine and International Health* 11 (8): 1303–17.

Meessen, B., A. Soucat, and C. Sekabaraga. 2011. "Performance-Based Financing: Just a Donor Fad or a Catalyst Towards Comprehensive Health Care Reform?" *Bulletin of the World Health Organization* 89 (2): 153–56.

Meessen, B., G. van Heteren, R. Soeters, G. Fritsche, and W. van Damme. 2012. "Time for Innovative Dialogue on Health Systems Research." *Bulletin of the World Health Organization* 90 (10): 715–715A.

Miller, G., and K. S. Babiarz. 2013. "Pay-for-Performance Incentives in Low- and Middle-Income Country Health Programs." NBER Working Paper 18932, National Bureau of Economic Research, Cambridge, MA.

Morgan, L. 2010. "Some Days Are Better than Others: Lessons Learned from Uganda's First Results-Based Financing Pilot." World Bank, Washington, DC. http://www.rbfhealth.org/news/item/296/some-days-are-better-others-lessons -learned-uganda%E2%80%99s-first-results-based-financing-pil //rbfhealth.org.

Musgrove, P. 2011. "Financial and Other Rewards for Good Performance or Results: A Guided Tour of Concepts and Terms and a Glossary of RBF." World Bank, Washington, DC. http://www.rbfhealth.org/library/doc/381/financial-and -other-rewards-good-performance-or-results-guided-tour-concepts-and-ter.

OECD (Organisation for Economic Co-operation and Development). 2010. *Value for Money in Health Spending.* OECD Health Policy Studies. Paris: OECD.

———. 2011. *Health at a Glance: OECD Indicators.* Paris: OECD. http://www.oecd .org/health/health-systems/49105858.pdf.

Olken, B. A., J. Onishi, and S. Wong. 2012. "Should AID Reward Performance? Evidence from a Field Experiment on Health and Education in Indonesia." NBER Working Paper 17892, National Bureau of Economic Research, Cambridge, MA.

Oxman, A. D., and A. Fretheim. 2009. "Can Paying for Results Help to Achieve the Millennium Development Goals? Overview of the Effectiveness of Results-Based Financing." *Journal of Evidence-Based Medicine* 2 (2): 70–83.

Peabody, J., R. Shimkhada, S. Quimbo, J. Florentino, M. Bacate, C. E. McCulloch, and O. Solon. 2011. "Financial Incentives and Measurement Improved Physicians' Quality of Care in the Philippines." *Health Affairs* 30 (4): 773–81.

Petersen, L., D. LeChauncy, L. Woodard, T. Urech, C. Daw, and S. Sookanan. 2006. "Does Pay-for-Performance Improve the Quality of Health Care?" *Annals of Internal Medicine* 145 (4): 265–72.

Rosenthal, M., and R. Frank. 2006. "What Is the Empirical Basis for Paying for Quality in Health Care?." *Medical Care Research and Review* 63 (2): 135–57.

Rosenthal, M. B., B. E. Landon, K. Howitt, H. R. Song, and A. M. Epstein. 2007. "Climbing Up the Pay-for-Performance Learning Curve: Where Are the Early Adopters Now?" *Health Affairs* 26 (6): 1674–82.

Rusa, L., and G. Fritsche. 2007. "Rwanda: Performance-Based Financing In Health." In *Emerging Good Practice in Managing for Development Results: Sourcebook,* 2nd ed., 105–16. Washington, DC: World Bank.

Rusa, L., W. Janssen, S. van Bastelaere, D. Porignon, J. de Dieu Ngirabega, and W. Vandenbulcke. 2009a. "Performance-Based Financing for Better Quality of Services in Rwandan Health Centers: 3-year Experience." *Tropical Medicine and International Health* 14 (7): 830–37.

Rusa, L., M. Schneidman, G. Fritsche, and L. Musango. 2009b. "Rwanda: Performance-Based Financing in the Public Sector." In *Performance Incentives for Global Health: Potentials and Pitfalls,* edited by R. Eichler, R. Levine, and Performance-Based Incentives Working Group, 189–214. Washington, DC: Center for Global Development.

Ryle, G. 1949. *The Concept of Mind.* Middlesex: Penguin Books.

Sekabaraga, C., F. Diop, and A. Soucat. 2011. "Can Innovative Health Financing Policies Increase Access to MDG-Related Services? Evidence from Rwanda." *Health Policy and Planning* 26 (supp 2): 52–62.

Soeters, R., C. Habineza, and P. B. Peerenboom. 2006. "Performance-Based Financing and Changing the District Health System: Experience from Rwanda." *Bulletin of the World Health Organization* 84 (11): 884–89.

Soeters, R., L. Musango, and B. Meessen. 2005. "Comparison of Two Output Based Schemes in Butare and Cyangugu Provinces in Rwanda." Report, Global Partnership on Output-Based Aid, Washington, DC, and Ministry of Health, Rwanda, Kigali.

Soeters, R., P.-B. Peerenboom, P. Mushagalusa, and C. Kimanuka. 2011. "Performance-Based Health Financing Experiment Improved Health Care in the Democratic Republic of Congo." *Health Affairs* 30 (8): 1518–27.

Ssengooba, F., B. McPake, and N. Palmer. 2012. "Why Performance-Based Contracting Failed in Uganda—An 'Open-Box' Evaluation of a Complex Health System Intervention." *Social Science & Medicine* 75 (2): 377–83.

Tashakkori, A., and C. Teddlie. 2003. *Handbook of Mixed Methods in Social and Behavioural Research.* Thousand Oaks, CA: Sage.

Toonen, J., A. Canavan, P. Vergeer, and R. Elovainio. 2009. *Performance-Based Financing for Health: Lessons from Sub-Saharan Africa.* Amsterdam: Royal Tropical Institute (KIT).

Van Herck, P., D. De Smedt, L. Annemans, R. Remmen, M. B. Rosenthal, and W. Sermeus. 2010. "Systematic Review: Effects, Design Choices, and Context of Pay-for-Performance in Health Care." *BMC Health Services Research* 10: 247.

Van Lerberghe, W., C. Conceicao, W. Van Damme, and P. Ferrinho. 2002. "When Staff Is Underpaid: Dealing with the Individual Coping Strategies of Health Personnel." *Bulletin of the World Health Organization* 80 (7): 581–84.

von Bertalanffly, L. 1969. *General System Theory: Foundations, Development, Applications.* New York: George Braziller.

Walt, G. 1994. *Health Policy: An Introduction to Process and Power.* London: Zed Books.

Werner, R. M., J. T. Kolstad, E. A. Stuart, and D. Polsky. 2011. "The Effect of Pay-for-Performance in Hospitals: Lessons For Quality Improvement." *Health Affairs* 30 (4): 690–98.

WHO (World Health Organization). 2000. *The World Health Report 2000: Health Systems—Improving Performance.* Geneva: WHO.

———. 2011. Global Status Report on Noncommunicable Diseases 2010. Geneva: WHO.

Witter, S., A. Fretheim, F. L. Kessy, and A. K. Lindahl. 2012. "Paying for Performance to Improve the Delivery of Health Interventions in Low- and Middle-Income Countries (Review)." *The Cochrane Database of Systematic Reviews* (2).

Xingzhu, L., and S. O'Dougherty. 2004. "Purchasing Priority Public Health Services." HNP Discussion Paper, Washington, DC, World Bank.

INDEX

Boxes, figures, maps, notes, and tables are indicated by b, f, m, n, *and* t *following the page numbers.*

gap in health care use between
poorest and richest, 114–15, 114*f*
health care issue, 114–16, 309*t*
innovative approach to enhancing,
116–17, 118*t*
measuring and monitoring, 113,
130–34
OECD countries' clinical
effectiveness and, 293
policy informed by equity
analysis, 134
pro-poor schemes, 113, 117–30. *See
also* pro-poor schemes
recommended resources, 135–36
European Agency for Development and
Health (AEDES), 155*b*
evaluations, 287–316
design and implementation
requirements for success, 303–4*t*,
303–7, 303*b*
difficulty of research, 297
impact evaluations, 291–92
LMIC vs. OECD countries, 288,
292–94, 298–303
overview, 288
provider payment mechanisms not
tied to quality of care, 293–94
provider payment mechanisms tied
to quality of care, 293
research evidence, development of,
288–97
weak evaluation designs, 294–97,
306–7*t*
ex ante verification
of quality of services, 74*b*
of quantity of services, 45–46
ex post verification
of quality of services, 74*b*
of quantity of services, 46–47
extended team approach, 245–49
buy-in, obtaining through bottom-up
approach, 248
documenting meetings, 248–49
mapping stakeholders to assess
interest, 247
mobilizing support from government
and key development partners,
247–48

running the program, 248–49
setting agendas, 248–49
external consultations, in business plan,
185–86

F

family planning, 22, 295*b*, 296, 297
fee-for-service, 87, 88, 94, 123*b*, 128,
231, 300
field visits, 54*b*, 266, 267
Figueras, J., 108
financement basé sur la performance, 12*n*5
financial management. *See* health facility
financial management
financing gap, 90, 91
first-level referral hospitals
how to select services, 27*t*
quality checklists, 75, 82–83, 82*b*
quality frameworks, 60–61
staff performance payments, 92
visiting, 266
forecasting, 228, 230*b*, 231, 231*f*
fragile states, 9
francophone Africa, 12*n*5
fraud, 53, 55*n*1, 55*n*3, 308*t*
free health services, 91, 110*n*3, 127, 127*b*,
129–30, 266, 272
freeware, 221
frequently asked questions, 308, 308–11*t*

G

GAVI Alliance, 38
geographic information software, 220
geographic targeting, 121–24
Gertler, P., 297
Ghana
bonus and salaries of health workers
in, 91–92
costs of institutional deliveries
in, 269
Global Fund, 38
Global Health Council (Washington,
D.C., June 2010), 279
governance issues and structure, 201–16.
See also health facility autonomy
challenges, 207
community involvement, 206, 206*f*.
See also community involvement

International Development Association, 6
investments in health facility startups,
175–79
how much money is involved,
176–77, 177b
investment units, 176
for fast quality
improvements, 179b
how they work, 178
overview, 176
invoicing
PBF special requirements for, 219–21
sample monthly invoice, 224b
isolation bonuses, 121–24

J
Jaipur workshop (January 2010), 278
Jakubowski, E., 108

K
Kigali workshop (January 2006), 276, 277
Kyrgyz Republic
birth deliveries in, 19
bonuses and salaries of health
workers in, 92
carrot-and-carrot approach in, 61
quality checklists in
adoption of Rwanda checklist,
69, 82
rayon (first-level referral)
hospital, 69, 75, 82–83, 82b
quasi-public purchaser approach in,
210, 210t

L
Lao PDR, health equity funds in, 128
lessons learned
advanced strategies for improving
health facility results, 190, 191–99t
data analysis providing. See data
analysis
LMIC learning from OECD
countries, 302–3
Rwanda lessons applied in
Burundi, 171b
leveraging, 94–96
Liberia, performance-based contracting
in, 21b

local health authorities, quality reviews
by, 58–59
lower- and middle-income countries
(LMIC), 10, 288–92
compared to OECD countries,
292–302
learning from OECD countries,
302–3
weak evaluation designs in, 294–97

M
management. See health facility
management
management by results, 89
Mandatory Health Insurance Fund
(MHIF, Kyrgyz Republic), 83
manuals. See training; user manuals
Maslow's pyramid of needs, 91, 299
Maternal Mortality Ratio (MMR), 19
Mayo-Ine Health Center (Nigeria), 5b
MDGs (Millennium Development Goals),
119, 266, 270
means testing, 120
MEASURE DHS Statcompiler, 119
Medicare fraud, 55n3
Mexico's PROGRESA (now called
Oportunidades) program, 124
Microsoft tools used, 79, 108, 156,
220, 237
Millennium Development Goals (MDGs),
119, 266, 270
minimum package of health services,
costing of, 96–108
ministry of health
governance role of, 209t, 210, 267
mobilizing support from government
and key development partners,
247–48
quality checklists and drug
availability, 273
refocusing of role of, 289
technical assistance for, 245, 246. See
also technical assistance
MMR (Maternal Mortality Ratio), 19
modified Delphi technique, use of, 31–38,
32b, 33–34t, 36b, 37t, 75
Multiple Indicator Cluster Surveys, 96
Musgrove, P., 6

N

National Health Insurance Fund (Kyrgyz
Republic), 210
NCDs (noncommunicable diseases),
119, 302
negotiable fees, 87, 94, 110n2
New Zealand, regulated internal market
in, 214
NGOs. *See* nongovernmental
organizations
Nigeria
benchmarking performance in, 233*b*
carrot-and-carrot approach in, 61
decentralized decision making in,
151–52*b*
indice tool in, 156–64. *See also*
indice tool
investment units to improve PBF
project quality in, 179*b*
LGA Results-Based Financing (RBF)
Steering Committee in, 151–52*b*
local context challenges in, 274, 275*b*
Mayo-Ine Health Center, 5*b*
minimum package of health services,
costing of, 96–108, 98–99*t*, 110*n*4
mix of financing approaches used for
State Health Investment Program
in, 7–9
quantified quality checklist, 70,
70*b*, 71*t*
quasi-public purchaser approach in,
210, 210*t*
State Health Investment Project in,
151–52*b*, 233*b*
workshop on pilot program in, 278
noncommunicable diseases (NCDs),
119, 302
nongovernmental organizations (NGOs)
carrot-and-carrot approach
preferred by, 61
community client satisfaction
survey, role in, 47
contracting-in, use of, 12*n*4, 214
fund holder health center, quality
tool, 76, 80
payment for patient successful
completion of treatment program
by, 129

PBC, use of, 21*b*
PBF, use of, 4
strategic purchasing by, 108
vouchers, use of, 129–30
nonincentivized services, 40

O

OECD countries, evidence from, 288,
292–94
compared to LMIC countries
baseline quality of services,
298–99
essential health services, 298
fee-for-service, 300
health reforms and market
reforms, 301
health worker coping
strategies, 299
output budget, 299
path dependency, 301–2
purchaser-provider split, 301
similarities, 300–302
strategic purchasing, 301
type of PBF program, 300
open source software, 221
output-based aid (OBA), 8*t*
output budgets. *See* budgeting

P

path dependency, 270–71, 301–2
pay for performance (P4P), 9*t*, 20*b*, 167,
168*b*, 292, 300, 311*n*2
PBC (performance-based contracting),
4, 7, 8*t*, 9
PBF. *See* performance-based financing
PBI (performance-based incentives), 8*t*
peer reviews, 58, 79–80, 248
PEPFAR (U.S. President's Emergency
Plan for AIDS Relief), 30*b*, 38, 277
Perfect Implementation Model
(Hogwood & Gunn), 245*b*
performance-based contracting (PBC),
4, 7, 8*t*, 9
performance-based financing (PBF)
bonus systems. *See* bonuses for
health workers
buying services in, 18–19. *See also*
services, purchasing of

the poor. *See* pro-poor schemes
poverty cards, use of, 136*n*4
poverty mapping, 136*n*2
preventive care purchasing
    compared to curative care, 109*b*
    PBF focus on, 146
    underprovided and need to
        stimulate, 19, 147
primary health care, PBF use in, 4
private purchaser approach, 207–8,
    210–11*t*
privatization, 309*t*
program-for-results, 9*t*
PROGRESA (Mexico), 124
pro-poor schemes, 113, 117–30
    balanced scorecard, used to achieve
        equity of services to the poor,
        124–26, 125*f*
    concentration index, use as equity
        measure, 124–26, 125*f*, 131–32, 132*f*
    conditional financial in-kind
        incentives for community health
        workers, 118–19, 128–29
    demand-side financial or in-kind
        incentives for patients, 129–30
    design elements in, 2*b*, 117–19, 118*t*
    paying more to reach poor than
        nonpoor, 118, 120–26
    subsidizing user fees, 118, 126–28
    underused services, selection of, 118,
        119–20
provider recognition program (PRP), 9*t*
Provincial Verification and Validation
    Committee (CPVV), 49*b*, 54*b*,
    278, 283*n*8
proxy indicators for overall performance
    and efficiency, 232*b*
proxy means testing, 120
public purchaser approach, 207,
    210, 212*t*
purchaser-provider split, 301
purchasing of services. *See* services,
    purchasing of; unit price and costing

Q

quality measurement and verification,
    57–83
    access to quality health services, 2*b*
    average quality scenario, 67

carrot-and-carrot vs. carrot-and-
    stick approach, 60–69, 63–68*t*
diversification of quality stimulation,
    60–69
frameworks for health center and
    first-level hospitals, 60–61
links to files and tools, 83
overview, 58–60
paying for quality through PBF tools,
    22, 69–72
quantified quality checklists, 59,
    69–71, 70*b*, 71*t*, 72–75. *See also*
    checklists
    drug availability, 273
    examples of, 75–83
    revision on regular basis, 261
    testing of, 261–62
separation from quantity
    verification, 44–45
quantity of services, 22–23, 29–31
    health workers' influence on, 24*b*
    verification of, 43–55. *See also*
        verification of quantity of services
quarterly reports
    indice tool's statement of quarterly
        financial activities, 156–58, 157*t*
    sample, in web-enabled
        application, 225*b*
quasi-public purchaser approach, 207,
    210–11, 210–11*t*, 213*t*

R

RBF. *See* results-based financing
RBF Impact Evaluation Toolkit (World
    Bank), 134, 297
realistic PBF services, 25
registers as cornerstone of PBF, 50–51
remoteness and isolation bonuses, 121–24
reproductive health services, 130, 295*b*.
    See also antenatal care and institutional
    deliveries; family planning
results-based financing (RBF), 6–10
    diagram of, 7*f*
    equity measure included in, 124
    explained, 9*t*
    incentives for, 7*f*
    supply side, 288
    types of awards, 7*f*
revolving funds. *See* drug supply

Robinson, R., 108
rural services, 93*b*, 121–24. *See also* pro-
  poor schemes
Rwanda
  benchmarking performance for
    institutional deliveries in, 232–35,
    234–35*f*
  bonus and salaries of health workers
    in, 92, 93*b*
  budget of health facilities in, 84*n2*
  calculating costs of technical
    assistance in, 244*b*
  carrot-and-carrot approach in, 61
  carrot-and-stick approach in, 61, 78
  civil service reforms in, 143
  community client satisfaction
    surveys in, 48–49*b*
  contract health employees in, 143
  contracts used in, 212, 212*t*
  counterverification mechanism
    in, 54*b*
  coverage analysis for PBF services
    in, 229–30, 229*t*
  extended team approach in, 246–49
  family planning services in, 295*b*,
    296, 297
  forecasting institutional deliveries
    in, 230, 230*b*, 231*f*
  health facility administration in, 206,
    206*f*, 267
  health facility autonomy in, 141
  human resource management in
    health facilities in, 93*b*
  impact evaluation in, 290, 291
  individual performance evaluations
    in, 187*b*
  lessons learned from, 30*b*, 171*b*
  modified Delphi technique, use in,
    32*b*, 36*b*
  PBF data center in, 223–24*b*
  PBF development in, 4, 5, 223–24*b*
  PBF user manual in, 259*b*
  peer evaluation mechanism in, 79–80
  performance frameworks in, 166–
    67, 168*b*
  predictors of success in, 245*b*, 310*t*
  public purchaser approach in,
    210, 212*t*
  quality checklists in
    annual review and modification,
      72, 261
    disagreements over, 71
    district hospital, 75, 77–78
    health center, 75, 76
    Kyrgyz Republic adoption of,
      69, 82
    performance frameworks
      and, 167
    unannounced visits vs. official
      visits to hospitals and, 54*b*
    Zambia adoption of, 73, 81, 261
  reproductive health services and in-
    kind payments in, 130
  services included in, 29
  technical assistance requirements in,
    243, 243*f*, 244*b*, 246–49
  thematic mapping for institutional
    deliveries in, 235, 236*m*
  trainer development in, 251
  web-enabled database in, 220
  workshops on pilot projects in,
    276–79

S

salary of health workers, 91–92, 93*b*, 266
scaling-up processes, 71–72, 108, 147*n1*,
  171*b*, 245, 276*b*, 295*b*
segregation of duties. *See* separation of
  functions
Senegal, pay for performance in, 20*b*
separation of functions
  governance issues and structure,
    202–5, 203*f*, 205*t*
  nonstate actors and, 240, 241
  research needed on, 289
  verification of quantity of services,
    44–45, 51–52, 52*f*
service protocol reference guide,
  45–46
services, purchasing of, 17–41
  advance payment from purchasing
    agencies, 59
  compatibility between services
    and routine information system,
    22–23, 22*t*
  cost-effective services, 18

links to files and tools, 54
operational challenges, 47–52
purchasing agency handling, 44,
  47, 55n2
reliable registers, 50–51
role in PBF, 44
sample sizes, 47–50, 48–49b
separation from quality verification,
  44–45
separation of functions in, 51–52, 52f
systems of, 44–45
testing of procedures, 261
training of verifiers, 45
transitional issues, 53–54
voice, 145–46, 145b, 202–5
volume purchasing, 18–19
vouchers, 9t, 129–30

W

Washington, D.C., Global Health Council
  (June 2010), 279
web-enabled database, 217, 220–21
  consultant for software
    development, 222
  general considerations, 222
  how to create, 222–26
  maintenance, security, and
    continuous development, 223–26
  training end users, 222–23
windows of opportunity, 270–71
Witter, S. A., 290
workshops for sharing information and
  pilot experience, 276–78

World Bank
  definition of good governance, 202
  Health Equity and Financial
    Protection country datasheets, 119
  HealthStats database, 119
  RBF Impact Evaluation Toolkit,
    134, 297
*World Development Report 1993:
  Investing in Health,* 18
World Health Report (2010), 115

Z

Zambia
  carrot-and-carrot approach in, 84n1
  carrot-and-stick approach in, 61
  fund holding by separate entity in, 207
  local context challenges in, 274
  PBF use for primary health care in, 4
  quality checklists in
    adoption of Rwanda checklist,
      73, 81, 261
    health center, 75, 81–82
  reproductive health services and in-
    kind payments in, 130
  scope of pilot project in, 283n1
Zimbabwe
  carrot-and-carrot approach in, 61
  local context challenges in, 274
  private purchaser approach funded
    through ministry of finance in,
    207, 210t
  remoteness bonuses for providers to
    the poor in, 121